Life and the Law in the Era of Data-Driven Agency

Life and the Law in the Era of Data-Driven Agency

Edited by

Mireille Hildebrandt

Research Professor of Interfacing Law and Technology, Vrije Universiteit Brussel, Belgium; Full Professor of Smart Environments, Data Protection and the Rule of Law, Radboud University Nijmegen, the Netherlands

Kieron O'Hara

Associate Professor in Electronics and Computer Science, University of Southampton, UK

Cheltenham, UK • Northampton, MA, USA

© The Editors and Contributors Severally 2020

Cover image: © Karen LaMonte. Photo credit: Martin Polak

All rights reserved. No part of this publication may be reproduced, stored in a retrieval system or transmitted in any form or by any means, electronic, mechanical or photocopying, recording, or otherwise without the prior permission of the publisher.

Published by
Edward Elgar Publishing Limited
The Lypiatts
15 Lansdown Road
Cheltenham
Glos GL50 2JA
UK

Edward Elgar Publishing, Inc.
William Pratt House
9 Dewey Court
Northampton
Massachusetts 01060
USA

A catalogue record for this book
is available from the British Library

Library of Congress Control Number: 2019951884

This book is available electronically in the **Elgar**online
Law subject collection
DOI 10.4337/9781788972000

ISBN 978 1 78897 199 7 (cased)
ISBN 978 1 78897 200 0 (eBook)

Typeset by Servis Filmsetting Ltd, Stockport, Cheshire
Printed and bound by CPI Group (UK) Ltd, Croydon CR0 4YY

Contents

Contributors		vii
Preface		xii
1.	Introduction: Life and the law in the era of data-driven agency *Mireille Hildebrandt and Kieron O'Hara*	1
2.	Between the editors *Kieron O'Hara and Mireille Hildebrandt*	16

PART I

3.	Data-driven agency and knowledge *Paul Dumouchel*	45
4.	The emergent limbic media system *Julie E. Cohen*	60
5.	Smart technologies and our sense of self: Going beyond epistemic counter-profiling *Sylvie Delacroix and Michael Veale*	80
6.	Rethinking transparency for the Internet of Things *m.c. schraefel, Richard Gomer, Enrico Gerding and Carsten Maple*	100
7.	From the digital to a post-digital era? *Charles Ess*	117

PART II

8.	Do digital technologies put democracy in jeopardy? *Gerard de Vries*	135
9.	In defence of 'Toma': Algorithmic enhancement of a sense of justice *David Stevens*	156

10.	The conservative reaction to data-driven agency *Kieron O'Hara and Mark Garnett*	175
11.	Artificial intelligence, affordances and fundamental rights *Christoph B. Graber*	194
12.	Throttling machine learning *Paul Ohm*	214
13.	In the hall of masks: Contrasting modes of personification *Niels van Dijk*	230

RESPONSE

14.	Life and the law in the era of machine agency *Mireille Hildebrandt*	253

Index 265

Contributors

Julie E. Cohen is the Mark Claster Mamolen Professor of Law and Technology at the Georgetown University Law Center. She teaches and writes about surveillance, privacy and data protection, intellectual property, information platforms, and the ways that networked information and communication technologies are reshaping legal institutions. She is the author of *Configuring the Networked Self: Law, Code and the Play of Everyday Practice* (Yale University Press, 2012), which won the 2013 Association of Internet Researchers Book Award and was shortlisted for the Surveillance & Society Journal's 2013 Book Prize; *Between Truth and Power: The Legal Constructions of Informational Capitalism* (Oxford University Press, 2019); and numerous journal articles and book chapters.

Gerard de Vries is Emeritus Professor of Philosophy of Science at the University of Amsterdam, a visiting fellow of Wolfson College, Cambridge, and a former member of the Scientific Council for Government Policy (WRR), the think-tank for long-term policy issues of the Dutch government in The Hague. His previous work is chiefly concerned with the social, political and ethical aspects of contemporary science and technology. He has published widely on philosophy of science, political philosophy, and science and technology studies. His latest book, *Bruno Latour*, is published by Polity Press, Cambridge, 2016. The French translation is published by La Découverte, Paris, 2018.

Sylvie Delacroix is Professor in Law and Ethics at the University of Birmingham. She focuses on the intersection between law and ethics, with a particular interest in Machine Ethics and the role of habit within moral decisions (*Habitual Ethics?* Bloomsbury, 2020). Her research focuses on the design of computer systems meant for morally-loaded contexts. She is also considering the potential inherent in 'bottom-up' Data Trusts as a mechanism to address power imbalances between data-subjects and data-controllers. Her work has notably been funded by the Wellcome Trust, the NHS and the Leverhulme Trust, from whom she received the Leverhulme Prize. She is a commissioner on the Public Policy Commission on the use of algorithms in the justice system (Law Society of England and Wales). She is also a Fellow of the Alan Turing Institute.

Paul Dumouchel is Full Professor of Philosophy at the Graduate School of Core Ethics and Frontier Sciences at Ritsumeikan University in Kyoto, Japan. Together with Luisa Damiano he wrote *Living with Robots* where they show that as roboticists become adept at programming artificial empathy into their creations, they are abandoning the conventional conception of human emotions as discrete, private, internal experiences. Rather, they are reconceiving emotions as a continuum between two actors who coordinate their affective behaviour in real time. See www.hup.harvard.edu/catalog.php?isbn=9780674971738 and www.researchgate.net/profile/Paul_Dumouchel.

Charles Ess is Professor of Media Studies, Department of Media and Communication, University of Oslo, Norway. He works across the intersections of philosophy, computing, applied ethics, comparative philosophy and religious studies, and media studies, with emphases on research ethics, digital religion, virtue ethics, and social robots. Ess has published extensively on ethical pluralism, culturally-variable ethical norms and communicative preferences in cross-cultural approaches to information and computing ethics, and their applications to everyday digital media technologies; the 3rd edition of his *Digital Media Ethics* will be published in early 2020. His current work focuses on the meta-theoretical and meta-disciplinary complementarities between ethics and the social sciences, and their implications for applied ethics in ICT design and implementation, including social robots and AI. He serves as an advisor to numerous research projects on social robotics, research ethics, and as a co-chair of the Association of Internet Researchers (AoIR) Ethics Working Group 3.0.

Mark Garnett is a Senior Lecturer in the Department of Politics, Philosophy and Religion at Lancaster University. His research is chiefly concerned with UK Politics post-1945, with particular reference to the relationship between ideas and practice, conservatism and the UK Conservative Party, British foreign policy, and the influence of think tanks. He was the authorised biographer of William Whitelaw, the biographer of Sir Keith Joseph, and has written and edited many books about UK politics. See www.lancaster.ac.uk/ppr/about-us/people/mark-garnett.

Enrico Gerding is an Associate Professor in Electronics and Computer Science at the University of Southampton. His research field is artificial intelligence and multi-agent systems with a particular focus on automated negotiation, auctions and game theory, and applications including privacy, the smart grid, and transportation systems. See www.ecs.soton.ac.uk/people/eg.

Richard Gomer is an Interaction Design practitioner and a Research Fellow in the Web and Internet Science group at the University of Southampton. His main research interests lie in designing systems that support meaningful human control and agency, and reframing design praxis to treat thoughtfulness and even outright rejection as worthwhile design goals. See www.richardgomer.uk.

Christoph B. Graber is Professor of Law, studied law at the Universities of Bern and St. Gallen, received his admission to the bar in Switzerland, a Ph.D. from the European University Institute (Florence) and his Habilitation from the University of Bern. He holds the Chair for Legal Sociology with particular focus on Media Law at the University of Zurich, Faculty of Law. He is currently Faculty Associate at The Berkman Klein Center for Internet and Society at Harvard University. He teaches in the fields of legal sociology and theory, cyberspace and media law, intellectual property and art law. His main research interests relate to analysing issues of normativity on the internet in relation to technology, intellectual property and freedom of expression and information from a law and society perspective.

Mireille Hildebrandt is a Research Professor on 'Interfacing Law and Technology' at Vrije Universiteit Brussels (VUB), appointed by the VUB Research Council, and co-director of the research group of Law, Science, Technology and Society studies (LSTS) at the Faculty of Law and Criminology of VUB. She also holds the part-time Chair of Smart Environments, Data Protection and the Rule of Law at the Science Faculty, at the Institute for Computing and Information Sciences (iCIS) at Radboud University Nijmegen. In 2018 she was awarded an ERC Advanced Grant for her project on 'Counting as a Human Being in the era of Computational Law' (2019–24). See www.cohubicol.com.

Carsten Maple is Professor of Cyber Systems Engineering and Director of Cyber-Security Research at WMG, University of Warwick. He leads the GCHQ-EPSRC Academic Centre of Excellence in Cyber Security Research and has particular interest in multidisciplinary approaches to privacy and trust in cyber-physical systems. See https://warwick.ac.uk/fac/sci/wmg/people/profile/?wmgid=1102.

Kieron O'Hara is an Associate Professor in Electronics and Computer Science at the University of Southampton, where he researches into digital modernity, privacy, openness and trust, with a particular focus on the World Wide Web. He also works on the philosophy of conservatism, and is the author of *Conservatism* (Reaktion Books, 2011). His latest book is *The Theory and Practice of Social Machines* (Springer, 2019, with Nigel

Shadbolt, David De Roure and Wendy Hall). He is a Director of the Web Science Institute, and is a Visiting Professor in Law at the University of Winchester. He is one of the leads on the UKAN network of anonymisation professionals, and co-author of the Anonymisation Decision-Making Framework. See www.ecs.soton.ac.uk/people/kmoh.

Paul Ohm is a Professor of Law and the Associate Dean for Academic Affairs at the Georgetown University Law Center in Washington, DC. He specializes in information privacy, computer crime law, intellectual property and criminal procedure. He teaches courses in all of these topics and more and he serves as a faculty director for both the Center on Privacy and Technology and Institute on Technology, Law, and Policy at Georgetown. In his work, Professor Ohm tries to build new interdisciplinary bridges between law and computer science. Much of his scholarship focuses on how evolving technology disrupts individual privacy.

m.c. schraefel is Professor of Computer Science and Human Performance in the Electronics and Computer Science School University of Southampton, Fellow of the British Computer Society, a Chartered Engineer and Alumna Research Chair, Royal Academy of Engineering. mc founded and directs the wellthLab (wellthlab.soton.ac.uk) to use the engineering, science and design of human-systems interaction to help #makeNormalBetter. http://users.ecs.soton.ac.uk/mc/.

David Stevens is an Associate Professor in Political Philosophy, Faculty of Social Sciences at the University of Nottingham. He is interested in a variety of questions within the broad field of normative political philosophy/theory. In particular, this includes questions about social justice, certain aspects of rational choice theory, and other areas of applied ethics (such as education, information technology, and environmentalism). An overarching theme of his work has been the proper place of religion within politics and society. See www.nottingham.ac.uk/politics/people/david.stevens.

Niels van Dijk is a Lecturer in Legal Philosophy at the law faculty of the Vrije Universiteit (VUB) at the Centre for Contextual Research in Law (CORE), and at the Université catholique de Louvain (UCL, Saint-Louis), both in Brussels. He is also a post-doctoral researcher at the VUB Research Group for Law Science Technology and Society (LSTS), and director of the Brussels Laboratory for Privacy and Data Protection Impact Assessments (d.pia.lab). Niels van Dijk has been a researcher in several national and European interdisciplinary research projects (FP7, H2020). His research focuses mainly on the challenges digital technologies pose to practices of law, especially in the fields of privacy, data protection and intellectual rights, including perspectives from legal theory, science and technology studies (STS) and ethnography of legal institutions. Niels van Dijk holds a PhD degree in law by the VUB, and LLM and MA degrees in law and philosophy by the University of Amsterdam. He has been a (visiting) researcher at the digital security department of Radboud University Nijmegen and the law department of the London School of Economics. Personal websites: https://lsts.research.vub.be/en/niels-van-dijk-0/, www.researchgate.net/profile/Niels_Dijk.

Michael Veale is Lecturer in Digital Rights and Regulation in the Faculty of Laws at University College London and Digital Charter Fellow at the Alan Turing Institute. His research sits at the intersections of emerging digital technologies, Internet and data law, technology policy and human–computer interaction. Michael has authored and co-authored reports for a range of organizations, including the Law Society of England and Wales on Algorithms in the Justice System, the Royal Society and British Academy on the future of data governance, the United Nations on AI and public services, and the Commonwealth Secretariat on electoral cybersecurity. He has worked with a range of government departments and regulators in various capacities around issues of emerging technologies, law and society, including in the UK and the Netherlands. He holds a PhD from UCL, an MSc from Maastricht University and a BSc from the London School of Economics. Michael is a member of the Advisory Council of the Open Rights Group. He tweets at @mikarv.

Preface

In 2015, after a long period of study acquainting herself with the detail of machine learning, artificial intelligence and the transformation of agency through the analysis of data, one of us (Mireille) published her book *Smart Technologies and the End(s) of Law* (hereafter *The End(s)*). This also followed Mireille's participation in the Onli*fe* Initiative, an EU initiative spearheaded by Nicole Dewandre and Luciano Floridi, which explored a number of key technological transformations, including the blurring of previously clear distinctions between 'reality' and 'virtuality', 'human' and 'machine', and 'natural' and 'artificial', in a world where information was no longer scarce but abundant. These transformations have modified our relations to ourselves, to each other, and to the social world in general. In particular, the public sphere – hardly an unproblematic concept at the best of times – is now a far more complex, and potentially dangerous, place than it was throughout the twentieth century. Notions of privacy, identity, autonomy, non-discrimination, due process and the presumption of innocence are altered, subtly or not so subtly, with the result that we need to be vigilant to ensure that law remains an instrument of justice.

The End(s) struck a chord with a number of commentators and thinkers, and was critically discussed in a number of forums; it also formed the kernel of a successful bid with the European Research Council, resulting in an ERC Advanced Grant for Mireille, to engage a cross-disciplinary research team on the subject of computational law.[1] Given the range of views on the topic of smart technologies and data-driven agency, and the range of disciplines over which the debate sprawls, one danger is that relevant viewpoints or arguments are not brought into contact with each other, especially in the siloed academic world, where lawyers talk to lawyers, technologists to technologists, philosophers to philosophers, and so on. Mireille therefore instigated deliberately interdisciplinary discussions, debates and critiques, which have resulted in a dedicated special issue,[2] as well as the follow-up volume that now sits in your hand or on your e-reader screen, containing chapters by a representative and deliberately diverse group of experts on topics raised in the original work.

Kieron and Mireille had already worked together on a previous edited volume, in the series of Digital Enlightenment Yearbooks on *The Value of Personal Data*.³ This, despite, or more likely because of, our different disciplinary backgrounds and political outlooks, was a pleasure for us both, and so Kieron was very happy, not to say flattered, to be asked to join Mireille as co-editor. As a team, we hoped to solicit and attract high-quality chapters from as diverse a set of perspectives as possible. Kieron focused on his own areas of computer science, Web science, politics and analytic philosophy, Mireille on her specialisms of law and philosophy of technology.

All the authors were asked to give their ideas on some aspect of data-driven agency using *The End(s)* as a jumping-off point, to ensure the thematic unity of this volume. The resulting collection is (we believe) a significant contribution to the debate about the transformation of agency, and demonstrates the range of expertise that is required for us to produce acceptable social, political and legal responses. Naturally, the chapters collectively come to no conclusion. Even the editors disagree about several issues, some of which are laid out for the reader in chapter 2. But understanding the position of one's interlocutor is half the battle for a civilised politics, and is sadly rare enough nowadays.

The project has been a joy upon which to work. For that, we have to thank firstly the splendid set of authors who were kind enough to devote time and effort to produce and polish their chapters, and cooperative enough to do it to the deadlines we set. We are also indebted to Amber Watts of Edward Elgar, our constructive and sympathetic editor who piloted us through the publication process. And last but not least, our gratitude to Aniek Den Teuling, at the time master student of computer science, for spending part of her research internship at the computer science department of Radboud University on copy-editing the chapters and preparing the content of chapters 1 and 14.

Finally, one of the most distinctive features of *The End(s)* as a physical object was its intriguing cover, an image of Karin LaMonte's sculpture 'Dress 3', which portrays in cast-glass a sumptuous garment defined by the form of the woman who is wearing it – but the woman herself is missing. Only the contours of the dress remain, as mute testimony to its absent wearer.⁴ We are pleased and privileged that the cover of this companion volume *Life and the Law* is graced by another of LaMonte's sculptures, 'Lark-Mirror (Hysteria)'. Here, we confront a mirror that retains the fading image of a girl or young woman, somehow leaving an uncanny impression. Once more, the sculpture, by some unspecified miracle, preserves the memory of one not present. We look into the mirror and see, not ourselves, but the record of a fleeting moment from another time, another place. The mirror reveals a little, but not all; the sleeping beauty cannot disappear from memory while the mirror exists. Neither can she be fully known. Does the mirror reveal or mislead? Is it a lark-mirror or the tempting hysteria of our data-driven agency?[5] The essays in this book ask the same question about another representational technology.

Kieron O'Hara and Mireille Hildebrandt

NOTES

1. 'Counting as a human being in the era of computational law' (COHUBICOL), see www.cohubicol.com.
2. Book Forum *in Critical Analysis of Law*, Vol 4 No 1 (2017), containing reviews by Roger Brownsword, Ryan Calo, Julie E. Cohen, Ian Kerr, Charles Raab and a reply by Mireille Hildebrandt, see https://cal.library.utoronto.ca/index.php/cal/issue/view/1869.
3. Hildebrandt, M. K. O'Hara, and M. Waidner (eds.). 2013. *The Value of Personal Data. Digital Enlightenment Yearbook 2013*. Amsterdam: IOS Press.
4. On this work see the 'Between the covers' in *The End(s)*, pp. xv–xvi in the paperback version.
5. The 'lark mirror' has been described as: 'a small mirror used to attract and trap small birds attracted to shiny things. In several languages (French, Italian, etc.) the saying "mirror for larks" is used to refer metaphorically to an apparently attractive offer that is really just trying to attract gullible people', see Rob Rushing on *The Phrase Finder*, www.phrases.org.uk/bulletin_board/59/messages/167.html.

1. Introduction: Life and the law in the era of data-driven agency

Mireille Hildebrandt and Kieron O'Hara[1]

WHAT'S NEXT?

This volume targets the issue of how data-driven agency affects everyday life and everyday law, highlighting potential transformations of human agency and the emergence of new types of human-machine hybrid intelligence. Human agency will be considered as depending – in part – on the affordances of our technological environment, meaning that insofar as modern law assumes a specific type of human agency, we cannot take for granted that this assumption will survive the era of data-driven information and communication infrastructures. This invites a reflection on 'the political' in the realm of algorithmic systems that act on the feedback they gain from their sensors and/or other data input. Are we moving towards a driverless democracy that overcomes old school notions such as sovereignty, or will a driverless democracy result in a clueless form of *un*government? Shall we lose track of the values and institutions that we need to preserve if we wish to survive the scaling of personalized manipulation in the realm of public debate? And what if a driverless law arrives to overdetermine the choice architecture of our machinic environments?

THE END(S)

Data-Driven Agency

In her monograph, *Smart Technologies and the End(s) of Law. Novel Entanglements between Law and Technology* (which will be referred to as *The End(s)* throughout this volume), Hildebrandt develops a theoretical framework to understand what data-driven agency means for law and the Rule of Law. She defines agency broadly as the ability to observe an environment and to act upon it based on such observation. Data-driven agency is a type of agency where observations are limited to digital data and actions are informed by the computational processing of such data. This brings any deterministic data-driven decision-system under the concept of data-driven agency, for instance an application that determines when to start the central heating based on a decline in temperature, or one that determines social security benefits based on input of relevant data and the specified decision tree. Next to deterministic systems, which are in principle predictable, we now have systems that apply machine learning (ML), meaning that the system updates its own operational rules based on the feedback it receives. The thermostat tries to guess whether you are home, what time you will arrive, and which temperatures you prefer based on your past behaviours. The social security system may include an early warning system that flags people whose behaviours correlate with fraud, autonomously requiring them to provide additional information or autonomously instigating more detailed monitoring (and, potentially, autonomously deciding on punitive or other sanctions).

Issues of Privacy, Non-Discrimination and the Presumption of Innocence

Clearly both types of data-driven agency have their promise and drawbacks. *The End(s)* investigates how the surge of agential applications in our 'everyday' lifeworld reconfigures issues of privacy, non-discrimination, due process and the presumption of innocence, while remaining largely invisible, and hard to test and contest. These systems cross borders into what we thought was our private life and refine business and government abilities to apply fine-grained, mathematically-based discriminations. They determine who will be monitored more closely and allow human decision-makers to hide behind novel modulations of 'computer says no'. The aim of Hildebrandt's theoretical framework is to provide conceptual instruments to assess the implications of both deterministic and the more unpredictable data-driven applications, in relation to a more in-depth understanding of the grammar that informs law and the Rule of Law. She argues that this grammar cannot be taken for granted and will have to be reinvented in part, to ensure that individual human persons and groups can develop the capability to speak law to power, notably to the power generated by data-driven agents.

Theorizing the Implications of Data-Driven Agency

We believe that nothing is as practical as good theory. We witness an upsurge of initiatives around fair, accountable and transparent machine learning (FAT ML), the fake news challenge (FNC), and artificial intelligence now (AINOW), as well as concerns about singularity or recursively-improving artificial intelligence (RIAI) leading to artificial superintelligence (ASI). Simultaneously, we see growing fears for a progressive erosion of privacy, non-discrimination, freedom of speech and freedom of information. To ensure the effectiveness and continuity of such initiatives in the long run it is crucial that scholarship is developed that faces and explores the assumptions that inform data-driven computing systems, detecting how and to what extent they undermine the familiar assumptions of previous information and communication infrastructures (ICIs) such as script, typescript, analogue telephone and telegraph and mass media. *The End(s)* has generated fruitful debate with a wide range of interlocutors, raising a number of pivotal questions. Reviews have been published (Diver 2018, McGee 2016, Keenan 2016, Jewell 2016, Van der Sloot 2015), including a special issue of *Critical Analysis of Law* featuring five reviews by leading thinkers in the domain, with Hildebrandt's reply.[2] However, the questions raised by *The End(s)* deserve further and deeper responses, developed into more precise arguments, not constrained by the format of a review. We have therefore invited a multi-disciplinary range of authors to contribute considered responses, developing their own positions on the core issues raised by *The End(s)*.

Pertinent Explorations of Core Themes of *The End(s)*

This edited volume can be read independently of *The End(s)*. It contains a wealth of new ideas on the interrelated topics explored in *The End(s)*. It targets two main research domains investigated by Hildebrandt, both of which concern the dramatic changes initiated by practices around data-driven innovation that have resulted in what has been called an onli*fe* world (Floridi 2014).[3] The first domain involves the shape of this new world and the ways in which it will, or may, affect human agency within it. Second, this book looks into the kind of politics this world does and does not afford and considers the challenges it contains to law and the Rule of Law.

This introductory overview by the editors is followed by a debate between the editors, and it ends with a response by Hildebrandt. In between the reader will find two parts: one on 'human agency in a data-driven environment' and one on 'the political and the law'.

PART I. HUMAN AGENCY IN A DATA-DRIVEN ENVIRONMENT

With regard to the rise of an onli*fe* world, we note that smart technologies are not yet mature; we see hype next to impressive substance. Much of the potential of smart technologies, for good or ill, is premised on a view of an integrated set of AI methods running over linked data, yet reality is (currently) far more fragmented and the results less rosy than some would have it. In fact, two of the founding fathers of machine learning emphasize the limited capacities of reinforcement learning, and deep learning (DL) (Brooks 2017, Le Vine 2017), warning against unrealistic expectations. However, we cannot rest our civil protections on the hopes that the technology will not deliver. Instead, we need to face the fact that many decision-making systems are based on a belief in the salience of ML and DL, with far reaching implications for those depending on them ('if machines define a situation as real, it is real in its consequences').[4]

Philosopher of robotics Paul Dumouchel considers the epistemology of big data, focusing in particular on two aspects which impact on its political and legal effects. Firstly, machine learning is a 'black box' process, where explaining why or how a particular output was reached is non-trivial – even designers of machine learning systems cannot explain a decision because there is no propositional content to their internal workings. Dumouchel marks the implications of the belief that data and correlations are all we need, warning against the rise of a new reductionism in the slipstream of a new 'Unity of Science' project, where all science becomes data science. The idea that causality does not matter and research on data is equivalent to empirical research, however, seems more prominent in the social domain than in the natural sciences. Dumouchel recounts that in the natural sciences data is often collected for a specific purpose, whereas the social domain tends to work with the data-exhaust produced as a side-effect of commercial applications or government services. This seems to make the social domain even more vulnerable to unfounded beliefs in the 'truth' of big data inferences. Secondly, when machine learning is embedded into real-world decision-making, it alters the world it models. For instance, smart signage on a motorway does not just describe traffic flow – it affects the flow itself, creating feedback loops that may be hard to predict, and which may result in the production of self-fulfilling prophecies. Dumouchel highlights the fact that in many applications of data science knowing and doing are conflated, and this is where human agency is at stake, as these systems act upon the behaviours they observe. This confirms a dire need to reflect on the potential repercussions of questionable beliefs in supposedly objective, neutral and omniscient algorithms.

Legal scholar Julie Cohen takes on Dumouchel's epistemological challenges, and their consequences for human agency. In parallel with Hildebrandt's notion of a 'digital unconscious', Cohen explores the metaphor of the human limbic system, a set of brain functions associated with emotion, motivation, learning and memory. Her analysis builds on a rich account of how online platforms manage to subliminally influence the behaviour of their users by way of algorithmic systems that optimise for more behavioural data, more user engagement and thus for a kind of participatory consumer surveillance. Given these developments, the issue of the human response and adaptation to smart technologies is further explored, in particular, the contrast between the propositional, surface level of human and social reasoning, and the lower level, non-propositional, non-declarative depth of so-called deep learning. Cohen uses contrasting notions such as cognitive/precognitive and conscious/subconscious to explore the distinction between the big data 'limbic' constructs and the idea that technology would lead to human freedom, and that 'knowledge is power'. In her new book, *Between Truth and Power. The Legal Constructions of Informational Capitalism* (forthcoming 2019), she further elaborates on the affordances of this new limbic system, with keen attention to the economic incentive structure that drives their exploitation. This implies that restricting one's analysis to individual agency will not do, and meaningful consent must be considered from the perspective of what the digital unconscious affords.

Computer scientist and human-computer interaction researcher mc schraefel and her co-authors aim to turn meaningless into meaningful consent by way of 'seamful' interaction design. They discuss the interface issues between humans and the machines that surreptitiously adjust their new onlife world. This frame, tellingly dubbed the Internet of Things (IoT), in many ways resembles Cohen's limbic system and Hildebrandt's digital unconscious. schraefel et al. provide important insights on how to rethink human capabilities in an environment that thrives on subliminal influencing. They notably consider the role of human machine interaction (HMI) and user experience (UX) design, to argue for the importance of making unexpected usage of data apparent to data subjects using implicit signals at the point of contact between human and machine. Given the notion of what they call 'apparency', humans could at least be alerted to the use of their data, and use whatever legal (data protection) powers they may have to demand to see what goes on in the black box. Apparency, in this sense, must precede transparency if machines are to be accountable. This seems to bridge Hildebrandt's focal interest in Gibson's concept of affordances with Norman's understanding of affordances, the latter being core to intuitive design. schraefel et al. note that apparency will create an onlife world that is not seamless (as IoT aficionados would have it) but seamful (Chalmers and Galani 2004), thus developing technical articulations of Cohen's (2012) semantic discontinuity. A seamful environment will provide both semantic transparency (about what one consents to) and pragmatic transparency (about the actual consequences of clicking the consent button). This connects with Dumouchel's emphasis on the new connection between knowing and doing on the side of the limbic system; algorithmic systems built on big data do not merely know or predict us, but act on this knowledge by e.g. pre-empting us. Apparency and pragmatic transparency, finally, are meant to integrate actionable transparency on the side of the user, who wishes to prevent or even pre-empt their IoT environments from making incorrect, unfair or otherwise undesirable decisions. This connects the need for apparency and transparency with the need for controllability and accountability, thus closing the loop that should inform the design of our new onli*fe* world.

The main concern of **legal philosopher Sylvie Delacroix** and **policy scientist Michael Veale** is neither privacy or autonomy, but 'a fundamental commitment to equality' that aims to protect human agency against manipulability on the basis of invisible profiling and targeting (which subjects human agency to differential treatment based on statistical inferences). Instead of focusing on the fairness or correctness of algorithmic decisions, they target the implications of profiling for human agency and its relationship with the 'double contingency' that is inherent in human intercourse. They analyse Hildebrandt's suggestion of 'counter-profiling' to see how this may afford new ways to nourish and protect our 'double contingency' and the agency it enables. To explain how this relates to their commitment to equality they explore the example of 'social cruelty', notably that of genocide, which implies a fundamental intent to treat a specific group of people as unequal and not worthy of respect. The authors explain how this eradicates the capability of constructing one's own identity in the process of interacting with others. Their position is that the invisible, profile-based optimization of current data-driven environments entails a similar 'social cruelty', as it defines people based on their inferred characteristics, increasingly forcing them to behave as their dynamic profiles assume they will behave. They mark the use of affective computing, based on emotion-recognition, which enables precisely the kind of subliminal influencing that Julie Cohen refers to in the second chapter. To counter such 'social cruelty' the authors develop some ideas for passive and active interventions. They reject the attempt to reduce transparency requirements to a mere rectification of epistemic imbalances, referring to the 'transparency fallacy' as a mistaken attempt to put the burden of informed consent on the shoulders of individual agency. In fact, they seem to agree with Dumouchel and schraefel et al. on the integration of knowing and behaving that is core to smart systems, arguing that rebalancing cannot be restricted to 'mere' knowledge symmetry, requiring what schraefel et al. call pragmatic (actionable) transparency, next to semantic transparency. In terms of passive interventions, in alignment with the previous chapter, Delacroix and Veale emphasize the need to turn the seamlessness of smart environments inside out, creating triggers for users to resist the way they are targeted, notably by showing them how others may 'read' and 'target' them. In terms of active interventions they develop two very interesting ideas to counter the 'social cruelty' of being defined by smart environments: surprises and appropriation. This is a rich contribution to the discourse, way beyond attempts to counter overdetermination by means of 'propositional, surface level of human and social reasoning', instead countering 'the lower level, non-propositional, non-declarative depth of so-called deep learning' (Cohen's limbic system) by way of intuitive counterings.

Philosopher of technology Charles Ess follows Hildebrandt's lead to explore the intriguing possibility of a 'post-digital world', invoking virtue ethics to explore a world in which the very medium of law itself is evolving in the face of technological change. Dubbing this world 'post-digital', Ess refers to a stance that neither embraces nor rejects the digital, instead taking seriously the novel affordances it creates for our embodied, analogue existence. This raises interesting questions about the relationship between law, ethics and the political, and the extent to which virtue ethics could contribute to new types of interaction between humans and their predictive environments. Ess makes two further points, first, warning against a determinist understanding of the relationship between media and its users, and, second, providing a convincing argument of the relevance of virtue ethics in what he calls a post-digital era. The first point addresses readers versed in old school media theory, that could misread Hildebrandt's concept of affordances and her stress on the impact of smart technologies on both human agency and the Rule of Law. Though *The End(s)* does not endorse a determinist position, being rooted in a postphenomenological philosophy of technology, those not familiar with the empirical turn in philosophy of technology may misread its core claim: whether a technology is determinist or not is an empirical question and depends on whether it induces or forces, inhibits or precludes behaviour. The second point addresses both developers and users of digital technologies as moral agents, inviting them to develop the practical wisdom (*phronēsis*) that should inform the design of technologies that contribute to human flourishing and enable others to develop their practical wisdom. This is a compelling argument because practical wisdom is a key concept in some strands of legal theory, notably for those that believe 'that the life of the law is not logic but experience' (Holmes 1997, pragmatism), noting that judgement is not equivalent to calculation (Ricoeur 2003, hermeneutics), meaning that discretion is inherent in legal decision-making but should not be understood as arbitrary subjectivist decisionism (Dworkin 1982, hermeneutics).

PART II. THE POLITICAL AND THE LAW

The second set of issues considered in this book revolves around the political[5] and the law. Big data and machine learning, together with other sociotechnical practices such as social networking and personalization, have produced a series of effects, such as fake news, filter bubbles, chaotic pluralism and a dramatic reduction in private space. Some believe these effects have actually invigorated our democracy, whereas others find them somewhat disconcerting to say the least. These are not arcane issues: we saw the debate played out as national psychodrama in 2016, when Donald Trump used Twitter and the expertise of an advisor from the Breitbart news site to rout mainstream (and not-so-mainstream) Republicans to gain the nomination, and then to outflank the Democratic candidate who showcased her great experience and traditional political virtues. Away from the campaign trail, the political is also implicated as decision-making is being distributed away from traditional representative institutions – but to whom? Though some power is devolving to individuals whose opinion can more easily be consulted, there is a great deal of power in the machines that set the parameters for interaction and discussion.

Philosopher Gerard de Vries examines the threats posed by digital technologies for both democracy and the Rule of Law, raising the question of whether the weaponizing of these technologies merely changes the way democracy operates or invokes an existential crisis for both. De Vries faces this question by asking how digital technologies generate new vulnerabilities for democracy, tested against two conceptions of democracy. One, the minimalist, defines democracy merely in terms of voting, but offers little protection against manipulation of the constituency either before or after the vote takes place. De Vries argues, instead, for a relational understanding of democracy, focused on the public interest, as argued by Dewey and Latour, with historical roots in Montesquieu's *On the Spirit of the Laws*. This entails keen attention to the web of relationships between citizens, businesses, government agencies and other institutions, highlighting the need for hard work to keep the network of interacting actors stable and in place. In the final part of his chapter, De Vries demonstrates how this relational understanding of democracy better explains the threats of digital technologies to both its *nature* (institution of government by way of popular vote) and its *principle* (care of the public interest). The automation of fake news that is enabled by digital technologies is hidden from public scrutiny, which endangers the assumptions of free and informed general elections, thus threatening the *nature* of democracy. Big data and AI, in the meantime, threaten the *principle* of democracy, as they do not merely manipulate existing political preferences but frame and subliminally constitute publics, replacing the difficult process of negotiating the public interest with algorithmic shortcuts.

Political philosopher David Stevens takes a daring stand by developing a sophisticated argument in favour of governments' efforts to induce 'attitudes and beliefs in citizens regarding a sense of social justice and cooperation' via artificial agents such as the personal assistant (Toma) that features in the narrative opening of *The End(s)*. Whereas many readers frame Toma's interferences as a corruption of human autonomy and dignity, Stevens comes out with a justification for a specific type of subliminal influencing that boils down to a specific type of nudging, described as 'structuring the background against which individuals can be led to make better (more optimal) choices, given their desires'. He notes that Toma 'frames' choices, and 'primes' its human master, and builds a sustained argument under what conditions this could actually be justified. The main condition is that such surreptitious nudging by the digital limbic system concerns a type of behaviour that does not depend on reasonable agreement, e.g. behaviour that should be enforced irrespective of whether people find such enforcement acceptable. This concerns, notably, deliberate harming of others, so – according to Stevens – the state should be applauded for influencing people's moral beliefs or sense of justice in the direction of rejecting deliberate harming of others. Basically, Stevens follows Rawls' distinction between an individual's choosing their own version of what they consider the good life, and an individual's sense of social or public justice. He argues that whereas the state is not allowed to manipulate a person's preferences for the good life, it is allowed to interfere – even subliminally – in the formation of a person's sense of justice, as long as absence of such a sense of justice would be unacceptable. Though Stevens admits that it would be great if children were primed for justice as a matter of course through education and upbringing, to the extent that this fails, the state would be justified in employing what Hildebrandt calls the digital unconscious to nudge citizens into developing a sense of social and public justice.

Next, ***computer scientist Kieron O'Hara*** and ***political scientist, historian and biographer Mark Garnett*** take another daring stand by defending a conservative philosophy that prizes familiarity and problematizes change, instead of clinging to the liberal paradigms that seem to underline human autonomy. To begin with, O'Hara and Garnett reject right-wing appropriations of conservative thought, instead building on Burke, Tocqueville and Oakeshott. For them, conservatism is a sceptical philosophy that problematizes the rationalist underpinnings of social engineering (think smart cities and IoT, and the pre-emptive nudgings of Julie Cohen's limbic system). Simultaneously, they emphasize the need to preserve and sustain tested institutions that protect against the volatility of innovative disruption and against untenable assumptions about a free-floating human autonomy combined with naïve notions of human perfection. Interestingly, O'Hara and Garnett are suspicious of the idea that human behaviour is predictable as long as we have access to big data, and wary of attempts to use emotion-recognition as a way to subvert first order preferences. They value organic, mostly given relationships rather than egalitarian, 'designed' and seamless interaction, based on an inquiry into the 'mystical state' heralded by Burke, the disintermediated community (multitude) detected by Tocqueville, and the agonistic pluralism put forward by Oakeshott. The latter speaks of the *individual manqué*, who submits to the lure of communal pressure instead of following their own line of action. This accords with the idea of the state as a civil association (*societas*) of independent individuals, rather than the state as a monolithic entity (*universitas*) that imposes itself on the *individuals manqués* that are the target of its public management. It is interesting to note that the conservative Oakeshott seems to beat liberals at their own game, foregrounding the individual as an independent agent that should not be treated as a manipulable pawn, whether by their government or powerful social networks (or does this mean that Oakeshott was really a liberal in disguise?). The authors suggest that this particular strand of sceptical conservatism may have more clout in protecting the values of contextual integrity and individual agency than the utilitarian vision of an atomistic liberalism.

Legal scholar Christoph Graber looks at the composition of rights in the onli*fe* world. Graber rejects the view of lawyers who tend to take the technology as a given black box, and the perspectives of scholars of science, technology and society (STS) who tend to view the law as a closed book. Instead, building on Luhmann's and Teubner's systems theory and Gibson's concept of affordance, Graber investigates how law and technology development may interact to further the public interest. He employs the concept of affordance to refer to the enabling and constraining implications of a technology, staying close to Gibson's original notion. He then adds Ihde's notion of the multistability of a technology, arguing that technologies have multistable affordances, a notion developed by Pfaffenberger to indicate that a particular technology will have multiple affordances that depend on how the technology has been interpreted. This leads Graber to an interesting employment of Pfaffenberger's 'technological drama theory', which enables him to confront the design constituency that develops a technology and thus creates its multiple affordances with the impact constituency that constructs various interpretations of the technology, depending on what it affords. This way Graber can sort out the actors in the drama (those create the technology, those who interpret and those who redesign it), the processes (of creation, interpretation, redesign and reconstitution) and the politics involved (dominant mythos on the intended use, a counter mythos based on actual, alternative uses, thus creating a counterartefact that results from the negotiations between the design constituency and the impact constituency). What makes this chapter so very interesting is the application of this frame of reference to the AI narrative, the role of big tech platforms and the need for counter-narratives and activism to reconstitute AI in ways that afford a proper engagement with the public interest.

Legal scholar Paul Ohm introduces two metrics to ensure that machine learning systems are sufficiently civilized to enter the domain of human intercourse. The first metric requires that for an ML system to replace a human decision-maker it should demonstrate far better performance than the human, instead of mere equivalence. The second metric requires that the training data of an ML system should be less than complete, to prevent availability of behavioural data at a scale that enables overdetermination. These metrics both aim to throttle ML systems, in order to tame their performance in line with human expectations and human empowerment, to reintroduce seamfulness. This chapter is refreshing if only because it moves from diagnosis to solutions, while rejecting the mantra that speed, completeness and automation of data-driven decision-making will by itself solve the problems they create. The idea of throttle mechanisms goes beyond the usual calls for transparency, accountability and interpretability, providing for direct hands-on criteria to intervene in the process of developing and adopting ML systems. Such intervention includes prevention, in the sense of shrinking back from investing in systems that do not clearly demonstrate added value for those subject to their decision-making. It also includes intervention that slows down the blind progress of machineries that may hold promise while simultaneously involving huge societal costs. Building on his previous work on 'Desirable Inefficiency', Ohm and Frankle (2018) explains how these metrics would serve as tools to slow down the inexorable march of disruptive innovation, giving us time to turn away from untested implications while taking the time to develop ML systems that actually do good work without externalizing potential costs to others.

Legal philosopher Niels van Dijk has been triggered by the European Parliament (EP)'s recommendation to consider attributing electronic personhood to specific types of AI systems. In the last chapter of this volume, he discusses and juxtaposes a range of different 'persons', thus hoping to clarify to what extent e-persons could make sense. He distinguishes (1) juristic persons (legal subjects other than 'natural persons') as fictions with effect, (2) public persons (notably Hobbes' state), as unifying a multitude, (3) average persons (based on the mean of an aggregate population), as statistical realities, (4) profile persons (inferred from a training set), as machine-generated group portraits, and (5) digital persons (targeting of a particular person based on inferences gained from aggregate data, or software agents), as dividual data portraits and smart agents. Having presented the context, history and background of different types of persons, Van Dijk pins down overlaps, similarities and differences. He notably discusses the composition, what is represented and what is afforded to whom. His final point is that introducing a new (juristic) person does not necessarily imply a new ontological entity with a claim to semi- or pseudo-human personhood; rather it is a pragmatic invention meant to produce specific legal effects in order to solve practical problems. Besides, the public person that initiated the discussion (the EP), should be reminded that the introduction of novel legal subjects will have myriad implications within the legal system – that should be considered before making such a move.

AN INVITATION TO OPEN THE BLACK BOX

A set of scholars such as these will naturally provoke debate, disagreement and contestation. This is, of course, the point of this book. Yet, while there are distinct viewpoints on offer, there is also surprising (and at the same time cheering) convergence on a number of key points. Most notably, the authors are as one in resisting technophilic myths of omniscience and omnipotence. They also all focus on existing social practices, institutions or ideals (different ones in each case), and consider data-driven agency not in the abstract but in the context of the particular. Seamlessness, the great ideal of technologists, outlaws interruption and contingency; but society as we know it *is* discontinuous, *is* haphazard. If it is to remain plural, then surely it must remain untidy and scruffy. And so many of our authors, like Cohen, schraefel and O'Hara and Garnett, think about reintroducing or protecting the seams, even unsightly ones; others, like Stevens and Ohm, want to make sure the power of the technology enhances something inherently desirable at a higher level than its merely local effect. Put another way, the public interest, which features in many of the chapters, is not a parameter to be optimised within systems, but a commons whose manipulation must be open to debate and control.

In his *Dialogues Concerning Natural Religion*, David Hume (2018 (1779)) expressed the problem of evil – if God is omniscient, omnipotent and infinitely good, then how is there evil in the world? This argument seems to reappear in Silicon Valley solutionism: if we are omniscient (we have all the data), and omnipotent (we have totally effective computing power and control of an increasingly virtualized world), how can bad things happen? Answer: they mustn't, the technology should ensure happiness. But happiness can only be ensured if the technology itself is allowed to define and determine it.

The US *Declaration of Independence* promised life, liberty and the pursuit of happiness. Data-driven agency goes further – according to the solutionists it promises happiness itself. But achieving that may have severe effects on liberty, as Aldous Huxley argued almost a century ago. The French *Declaration of the Rights of Man and of the Citizen* and its subsequent revolutionary uptake promised freedom, equality and community, and data-driven agency may be as severe on these ideals, as e.g. Oscar Gandy (2010) and Frank Pasquale (2015) have argued more recently. Of the two editors, O'Hara is more enthusiastic about the American vision, Hildebrandt about the French (and we will explore our differences in more detail in the next chapter), but we are equally concerned about the potential for social harm. All our authors are clear that data-driven agency may present opportunities to enhance, through its affordances, human flourishing. Most of us, however, warn against expecting too much and elaborate in salient detail how data-driven agency presents a framing problem that surreptitiously reconfigures our choice architectures. We hope that the reader will come to appreciate the many loopholes and pitfalls that face whoever promises that we can eat our cake and have it all: life, liberty, equality, community and happiness.

NOTES

1. With credits to Aniek van den Teuling for helping to prepare this and the final chapter; her 'reading' of the chapters of this volume further clarified what makes this a salient volume.
2. Brownsword (2017), Calo (2017), Cohen (2017), Kerr (2017), Raab (2017), Hildebrandt (2017).
3. Further developed in *The End(s)*, notably in Part 1.
4. This is a modulation of the Thomas Theorem: 'If men define a situation as real, it is real in its consequences', see *The End(s)* at 26.
5. On the difference between 'the political' and 'politics' see Mouffe (2005). 'The political' refers to the dimension of ineradicable antagonism that is inherent in human society, whereas 'politics' refers to concrete attempts to institutionalize ways to cope with such antagonism.

REFERENCES

Brooks, R. 2017. 'Machine Learning Explained', MIT RETHINK, *Robots, AI, and Other Stuff* (blog), 28 August, <http://rodneybrooks.com/forai-machine-learning-explained/>

Brownsword, R. 2017. 'Disruptive Agents and Our Onlife World: Should We Be Concerned?' *Critical Analysis of Law* 4 (1), 61–71

Calo, R. 2017. 'Technology, Law, and Affordance: A Review of Smart Technologies and the End(s) of Law'. *Critical Analysis of Law* 4 (1), 72–7

Chalmers, M. and A. Galani. 2004. 'Seamful Interweaving: Heterogeneity in the Theory and Design of Interactive Systems'. In *Proceedings of the 5th Conference on Designing Interactive Systems: Processes, Practices, Methods, and Techniques*, 243–52. DIS'04. New York, NY: ACM, <https://doi.org/10.1145/1013115.1013149>

Cohen, J. E. 2012. *Configuring the Networked Self: Law, Code, and the Play of Everyday Practice*. New Haven, CT: Yale University Press

Cohen, J. E. 2017. 'Affording Fundamental Rights: A Provocation Inspired by Mireille Hildebrandt'. *Critical Analysis of Law* 4 (1), 78–90

Cohen, J. E. 2019. *Between Truth and Power. The Legal Constructions of Informational Capitalism.* Oxford: Oxford University Press

Diver, Laurence. 2018. 'Law as a User: Design, Affordance, and the Technological Mediation of Norms'. *SCRIPTed* 15 (1) 4–41, <https://doi.org/10.2966/scrip.150118.4>

Dworkin, Ronald. 1982. 'Law as Interpretation'. *Texas Law Review* 60 (2), 527–50

Floridi, L. 2014. *The Onlife Manifesto. Being Human in a Hyperconnected Era.* Dordrecht: Springer

Gandy, Oscar H. 2010. 'Engaging Rational Discrimination: Exploring Reasons for Placing Regulatory Constraints on Decision Support Systems'. *Ethics and Information Technology* 12 (1), 29–42, <https://doi.org/10.1007/s10676-009-9198-6>

Hildebrandt, M. 2017. 'Law as an Affordance: The Devil is in the Vanishing Point(s)'. *Critical Analysis of Law* 4 (1), 116–28

Holmes, Oliver Wendell. 1997. 'The Path of the Law'. *Harvard Law Review* 110, 991–1009

Hume, David. 2018 (1779). *Dialogues Concerning Natural Religion.* Greenwood, WI: Suzeteo

Jewell, M. 2016. 'Book Review Smart Technologies and the End(s) of Law'. *SCRIPTed* 13, 215–18

Keenan, Bernard. 2016. 'Mireille Hildebrandt, Smart Technologies and the End(s) of Law, Cheltenham: Edward Elgar'. *The Modern Law Review* 79 (4), 733–8, <https://doi.org/10.1111/1468-2230.12209>

Kerr, Ian. 2017. 'The Devil is in the Defaults'. *Critical Analysis of Law* 4 (1), 91–103

Le Vine, S. 2017. 'Artificial Intelligence Pioneer Says we Need to Start Over', *Axios*, 15 September, <https://www.axios.com/ai-pioneer-advocates-starting-over-2485537027.html>

McGee, K. 2016. 'On Legal Replicants'. *Jurimetrics* 56, 305–18

Mouffe, C. 2005. *On the Political.* Abingdon: Routledge

Ohm, Paul and Jonathan Frankle. 2018. 'Desirable Inefficiency'. *Florida Law Review* 70, 777–838

Pasquale, Frank. 2015. *The Black Box Society: The Secret Algorithms That Control Money and Information*. Cambridge, MA: Harvard University Press

Raab, Charles D. 2017. 'Hildebrandt's Onlife World: Public Goods, Design and Politics'. *Critical Analysis of Law* 4 (1), 104–15

Ricoeur, Paul. 2003. *The Just*. Translated by David Pellauer. Chicago, IL: University of Chicago Press

Van der Sloot, B. 2015. 'Book Review Smart Technologies and the End(s) of Law' *European Data Protection Law Review* 1, 157–9

2. Between the editors
Kieron O'Hara (KOH) and Mireille Hildebrandt (MH)

INTRODUCTION

This chapter contains a crossing of swords and thoughts between the editors, who come from different disciplinary backgrounds and different philosophical traditions, but nevertheless occupy much common ground. The conversation is too short to enable the cutting edge of Occam's razor (pun intended), but refers to other work with more extensive argumentation. We agree on a great deal. In particular, we share a precautionary approach that requires proactive consideration of how one's experimental business models or progressive politics may impact others. However, as the reader will see, at that point we part company! The ensuing dialogue has been illuminating for us, and hopefully will whet the reader's appetite for the excellent chapters that follow.

THE ONLIFE WORLD

KOH: The Place of Privacy in Digital Modernity

There are lots of myths about technology, but since those myths are often held dear by policy-makers and inspirational for technologists, it behoves us to take them seriously. In particular, I think that the myths of modernity can help explain why privacy was taken relatively seriously in the final quarter of the twentieth century, but is now seen rather as the embarrassing uncle at a wedding. We have to invite him, but we'll make sure he doesn't give a speech.

Privacy did not loom large in pre-modern thought. Let's concentrate on three aspects of privacy – the ability to associate without interference, the ability to make decisions without interference and the records made of one's past. In the pre-modern world, association was often imposed rather than chosen. In decision-making, practice and tradition were important, and a justification for doing something was often that 'this is what we have always done', not 'this is what I want to do'. Archives were often based on memory or arbitrary records; what was recorded depended on who was doing the recording (cf. Krogness 2011 for a detailed example).

Hence, in the pre-modern world, there was little need for a privacy framework. Instead of privacy, the individual had (arbitrary, inconsistent and unprotected) obscurity, with no entitlement to concealment or a private space, but equally the reach of the state and other authorities was relatively feeble and partial. The result was a world in which individuals were not always legible to the state or to authorities, in the sense of Scott (1998).

The key value espoused in the modernity myth is individuality, as opposed to pre-modern values of hierarchy and social roles. The Enlightenment brought us new sources of authority grounded in human capacities, particularly reason; individuals became more important as political entities; liberty became an ideal; and self-interest, happiness and human nature became part of the political psychologists' toolkit (O'Hara 2010).

Individuality expressed itself through autonomous choice. Democratic processes developed, and free markets were newly theorized. Arranged marriages were superseded by romantic love. The social contract is based upon choice, which is the foundation for any contractual arrangement. In the conditions of modernity, the world presents itself to the individual, who then makes choices from the range it offers.

Where individuality is expressed through choice, privacy is central. Authentic choices require autonomous individuals; romantic relationships require intimacy; Locke identified a translation away from common dominion towards private ownership as vital for a free and prosperous society. Privacy is essential for autonomy, intimacy and private property, and is therefore baked into the ideals of modernity, which helps explain the admittedly gradual move through the twentieth century toward the provision of a principled legal, regulatory and rights-based privacy framework.

The moderns are toying with a new myth, a variant on the old which I call digital modernity (O'Hara 2018). Individuality remains its chief value, but its means of expression is different. Instead of a world presented to an individual to select the aspects he or she prefers, in digital modernity data is used to personalize the world around the individual's preferences.

Digital modernity consists, we might say, of a shift in tense. The pre-modern world was *eternal*, traditions and institutions conceived as changeless (even though they weren't). Analogue modernity put the emphasis on the *present*: current preferences are paramount, so that, as Henry Ford said, history is bunk. Digital modernity, on the other hand, brings us systems which can 'read' the state of a digital avatar, and provides the goods that the individual *would* have chosen if he or she possessed total knowledge about choices and future happiness; tense shifts again, to the *subjunctive*.

In this subjunctive world, association is mediated by recommender systems; apps are now routinely used to suggest people to date, marry, go to bed with, befriend, employ, or suck up to because they will be valuable for our careers. Decision-making is anticipated, and the choices individuals would make are made apparent to them. The curated archives characteristic of modernity are increasingly being superseded by large-scale, open, searchable information spaces, whose data is increasingly straightforward to discover and link to data from other sources.

With digital modernity, privacy not only loses its pivotal position, it becomes a hindrance. The provision of personalized services is only possible to the extent that the individual is transparent to the provider. In the subjunctive world, privacy is not only not a route to the expression of individuality – it stands in its way.

MH: From Digital Modernity to an Onli*fe* World

As O'Hara points out, privacy is connected with the idea of individual autonomy. However, other than O'Hara implies, autonomy should not be reduced to individual choice, as utilitarian policy-makers would have it. In point of fact, I would argue that framing our autonomy as such, invites both nudge theory and machine learning to come up with clever choice architectures that diminish our agency instead of enhancing it – whether in the service of a benevolent administration that wishes to coax us into its image of a 'good' citizen, or in the service of a benign service provider that claims to help us by offering what best suits our inferred preferences. As should be clear by now, benevolence and benign intent are not enough. We need the Rule of Law and a vigilant democracy to ensure that the choice architectures we face are not meant to manipulate us by playing on our first order preferences (Frankfurt 1971). We have come to a point where the digital modernity that O'Hara describes moves from the separate spheres of offline and online to an integrated onli*fe* world that thrives on behavioural data, meant to pre-empt our intent before we become aware of it.

My analysis in *The End(s)* has been focused on developing a vocabulary that circumvents the myths that have been created around big data, artificial intelligence (AI) and e.g. the Internet of Things (IoT). Instead, I have proposed to think in terms of a *distributed big data space*, a subliminal data-driven *digital unconscious* and a new type of *mindless distributed agency* that feeds on what O'Hara ingeniously frames as the *tense of the subjunctive*. This refers to the subliminal operations of microtargeting in advertising, price discrimination, recommender systems, search and political influencing, but also to those of the cloud-driven architectures of the Internet of Things that connect our vacuum cleaner robot with its service provider, the black box of our smart car with the insurance company and a plethora of wearables with data brokers and the health care industry (directly or indirectly).

Other than O'Hara I do not believe that microtargeting as used by commercial platforms is meant to provide us with personalized services. The current economic incentives force platforms to compete in manipulating our inferred preferences to increase market share in economic and political markets, by making us click on ads or memes that further their clout. Our personal preferences are nurtured, rerouted, multiplied, produced and eradicated in a high dimensional information ecosphere that is not merely about smart homes (fridges) or clothes (say, socks), but about the linkability of IoT output with inferences gained from social networks, search engines and data brokers. This enables a novel (by now familiar) type of 'newsfeed' (from search engine indexing to YouTube ranking and Twitter threading), that incentivizes fake news whenever this provides a competitive advantage, in turn creating both market failures and a fragmented democratic discourse.

The *subjunctive tense* that rules our environment enables pre-emption, though whether it does cannot be tested, precisely because whatever was pre-empted did not occur. In terms of *The End(s)*, this *subjunctive tense* connects with the double mutual anticipation that characterizes human interaction. Being a human person means that I am forever – intuitively – anticipating how others anticipate me, noting that 'I' and 'me' seem to refer to the same person, but the 'I' actually does the referring and the 'me' is its object. This curious way of interacting, which is constitutive of the human subject as a reflective animal, depends on the grammatical first person that enables us to face the world from the inside out (consciousness) and to simultaneously face our self from the outside in (self-consciousness).

Awareness of the self is thus based on awareness of others, both individual and institutional others, whom we recognize as similar types of subjects, forever anticipating how they are anticipated. That is where I speak of *mutual double anticipation*. Dennett (2009) has framed double anticipation in terms of our taking the intentional stance, assuming that others have good reason to act as they do, and in *The End(s)* I have suggested that the onli*f*e world requires that we take a modulated intentional stance towards environments that turn on*life* in the particular sense of forever anticipating us. To restore our capabilities, we need to anticipate that anticipation, facing the mindless distributed agency of our data-driven environment.

In point of fact, to develop our autonomy (which is not given), it becomes pivotal to intuitively grasp how we are being anticipated by what mindless agency. We need to be able to answer questions such as: 'what if I were to share my location data or my energy usage data or my eating habits with whom, how will it affect the reconfiguration of the choices I am presented with?' We thus need to re-engage the *subjunctive tense* from our own, first person, perspective.

LEGAL PROTECTION BY DESIGN

MH: From Text-Driven to Data- and Code-Driven Legal Protection?

In *The End(s)* I develop the concept of 'legal protection by design' (LPbD) (p. 214):

> The argument is that without LPbD we face the end of law as we know it, though – paradoxically – engaging with LPbD will inevitably end the hegemony of modern law as we know it. There is no way back, we can only move forward. However, we have different options; either law turns into administration or techno-regulation, or it re-asserts its 'regime of veridiction' in novel ways.

In chapter 8, where I trace the technological embodiment of law, demonstrating that there is no such thing as technologically neutral law, I extensively argue that modern law as we know it is text-driven (without as yet using that term). In many ways the concept of 'text-driven law' is more interesting than that of data- or code-driven law. The latter refer to various types of 'legal tech', whether based on machine learning or e.g. blockchain.[1] Such 'legal tech' is so obviously different from the prevailing legal paradigm that naming them is the least of our worries. However, to come to terms with 'legal tech' we must first come to terms with the implicit assumptions and undertheorized affordances of 'traditional' modern law.

Above, O'Hara observes that previous ICIs basically afforded people opacity, as it were 'by accident':

> Hence, in the pre-modern world, there was little need for a privacy framework. Instead of privacy, the individual had (arbitrary, inconsistent and unprotected) obscurity, with no entitlement to concealment or a private space, but equally the reach of the state or other authorities was relatively feeble and partial.

By coining modern positive law as text-driven law, I argue that O'Hara's modern world had little need for LPbD. Instead of being protected by LPbD, the modern subject enjoyed (arbitrary, inconsistent and unprotected) obscurity based on the fact that stone walls, the inaccessibility of the brain and other physical barriers offer good enough protection against invasive behaviours, next to the text-driven legal protection offered by modern positive law. However, once law has to operate in an environment that is saturated with pre-emptive tech, capable of capturing and inferring what goes on behind stone walls, inside the brain and within social relationships, text-driven protection may no longer suffice. We may have to embed the legal normativity of human rights into the architecture of the novel information and communication infrastructure (ICI) to achieve the practical effectiveness of legal protection in the era of data-driven 'anywares'.

The End(s) explains that LPbD should not be confused with techno-regulation, as this is contingent upon a regulatory paradigm, based on a behaviourist, external perspective on law-as-regulation. With the advent of 'legal tech', notably code-driven versions of 'compliance by design' (e.g. smart regulation based on blockchain technologies (Wright and De Filippi 2015)), some proponents explicitly refer to such 'tech' as enabling human behaviour to be 'legal by design' (LbD) (Lippe, Katz, and Jackson 2015). This enables me to mark the difference between LPbD and LbD and the urgent need to consider the difference while rethinking their relationship.

LbD is what Brownsword (2016) calls 'technological management'. As an instrument to achieve policy goals, it may be far more efficient and in the short term possibly also more effective than law. This is due to (1) the fact that the legislator is not involved, so things can move faster and (2) legal safeguards will not necessarily be considered when designing LbD, so again things can move fast without taking into account all kinds of public goods and individual rights and freedoms. According to Brownsword, LbD is not law, because it is no longer possible to disobey the rules that are imposed. Though we have a duty to obey the law, such duty only makes sense if we are able to ignore its imperatives. If not, we are under a rule of discipline or administration.

LPbD, on the other hand, ensures (*The End(s)*, p. 218):

> that the technological normativity that regulates our lives: first, is compatible with enacted law, or even initiated by the democratic legislator; second, can be resisted; and third, may be contested in a court of law. This is what differentiates LPbD from techno-regulation. .... The 'resistability' requirement rules out deterministic environments, and the contestability requirement rules out invisible regulation.

This raises two types of questions. The first concerns who will decide, based on what values and what wisdom, when we can safely rely on LbD (better framed as compliance by design, as it is unclear in what sense this is law), and how such LbD solutions can be embedded in a broader framework of LPbD. The second type of question concerns when we require what kind of LPbD. *The End(s)* is not a handbook or a catalogue of practical policy solutions, but I hope that it raises these questions in a way that gives direction to the answers.

KOH: Whose Norms? Which ICI?

The distinction raised between LbD and LPbD is crucial, and I'm grateful to Hildebrandt for bringing it out. It draws attention to a particular mindset that focuses on ends rather than means – the same mindset that valorizes the use of data in policy (not that it shouldn't be used, but there are other things to do than measure the outcomes), and looks to utilitarian calculation of consequences. It's a common enough position: 'we want people to behave in accordance with norm X, so why not make it impossible for people not to behave in accordance with X?' One reason is that doing what you have to is very different from following a norm, and what Brownsword calls 'technological management' is more likely to result in atrophied norms than wonderful behaviour. 'Legal by design' is a truly scary concept (unless it means 'anything goes', which is awful in a different way).

Hildebrandt's statement of LPbD, quoted by herself, is unobjectionable from this point of view, with resistance and legal contest written in. Will this work? What form should it take, if it is to be feasible?

I tend toward a sceptical view of life. So vast and complex is the totality of our interactions that the effects of innovations are for all practical purposes unknowable. So connected are we that a small change here will create all sorts of unintended ripples over there. A.O. Hirschmann (1991) laughed at conservative thinkers complaining that innovation will have the opposite effect from that intended, or if not, will fail to produce any change at all, or, if it does produce the intended effect, will produce lots of less desirable changes as well. These can't all be true, he correctly said, but they are all possible, and most importantly policy-makers cannot rule any of them out. This insight doesn't prevent innovation, but it strongly suggests that the risk of innovation is lowest when the current state is lowest in value. In other words, if it ain't broke, don't fix it (see my final contribution to this chapter for more).

This impacts on LPbD (and LbD for that matter) at the invocation of design. Designing is what is hardest to do, particularly in open and global environments at scale. We design a system to facilitate conversation and free speech, and we end up with fake news and Russian Twitter bots drowning out more desirable discourse.

But why is design necessary? Let's revisit Hildebrandt's three characteristics of LPbD. First, the tech needs to be compatible with enacted law. Yes of course, and if it is not compatible, the job of the state is to prosecute, rather as the European Courts are increasingly doing to the tech giants. Let us gloss over the possibility of the democratic legislator initiating anything technological, a terrible-sounding prospect. Second, the tech can be resisted. In other words, the environment is not deterministic, so I can do something other than the nerds intended. Excellent.

Third, most importantly, I can test the technology's norms in court. But what measure do I test them against? If I am allowed to show that I am harmed in my own terms, which might, for example, include a violation of what Nissenbaum (2010), in a great conservative text, called contextual integrity (a concept which applies more widely than privacy, of course), then we start to see how a digital common law might grow up, which requires no design beyond a consideration of what people feel is harmful and more importantly no specification (or anticipation) of the norms that should be embedded in the information and communication infrastructure (ICI) from a European Commissioner or an 'Ethics Tsar' or some other grey panjandrum in a suit.

We would then have a chance at least of preserving the valuable applications of technology while cracking down on the pernicious ones. It may be that this is the sort of structure that Hildebrandt is thinking of, but it seems to me that the key thing here is transparency rather than design. Let someone else embed the values in the tech, but make sure they are accountable for the evils that they do.

DATA, KNOWLEDGE AND INFORMATION

KOH: Bullshit 2.0

There is an oft-cited hierarchy of representative structures, represented as a pyramid with data at the bottom (uninterpreted symbols), information above it (interpreted data), knowledge above that (actionable information) and wisdom at the top (practical reason, Aristotle's *phronesis*). This is nearer PowerPoint than philosophy, but it has been influential. It is missing a layer, however: something which has many names, of which the pithiest is *bullshit*.

Perhaps surprisingly, bullshit has been the topic of some philosophical analysis. Frankfurt (2005) discussed it in the context of everyday life, where he characterized it as discourse that was purporting falsely to be an attempt to tell the truth. The difference between lying and bullshit, for Frankfurt, is that the liar is attempting not to tell the truth, to tell a falsehood, whereas the bullshitter doesn't really care whether what he says is true or false. He says what he feels it is appropriate, and valuable for his purposes, to say.

Bullshit is spread consciously almost everywhere, where it helps fertilize all sorts of interactions. It is produced to achieve a particular goal – an utterance or ritual of some kind is needed, and the bullshitter provides it, whether or not it corresponds to reality. Chat-up lines, corporate mission statements, advertisements, political speeches, the writhing around of footballers in mock pain following a tackle – all these are familiar types of bullshit. The 45th President of the United States is an artist in the medium.

The problem for data-driven agency is that so much data is also bullshit. We fill in forms which purport to mean something, about our work patterns, or our birthday, or about our satisfaction with a website, and we fill in whatever will make the pop-up go away or preserves our privacy. That's fine, it's a ritual, until others interpret this as a statement about what work we have done, or when we were born, or whether we enjoyed the online experience.

Performance data are inherently bullshit, since to understand a performance management system is to be incentivized to game it. Academics publish all sorts of guff because we are paid to publish. There is even a literature on the least publishable unit, i.e. the quantum of information that will make up a respectable academic paper (Broad 1981). Privacy policies are a species of bullshit because although they are contracts, they are designed to be unread.

Bullshit can also be produced unconsciously, where the properties of data – what we might call its social life – are not appreciated or understood. Data does not just magically appear as a faithful reflection of reality, sitting in an abstract, Platonic heaven. It is crafted, built, created, argued about, paid for, compromised over, resisted and economized on. As with sausages, its fans should probably avoid watching it being made.

What about big data – how much of that is big bullshit? It's a pressing question, because much of what gets done is done via the analysis of lots of it. It is often held by policy-makers and commentators as sacrosanct because machine learning merely shows us the significant correlations, N = all (as Mayer-Schönberger and Cukier [2013] put it), and all the bullshit will come out in the wash. I wonder how good their washing powder might be.

MH: The Missing Link in Humbug 2.0 is Agency (572)

In 2005, in his booklet on human bullshit, Harry Frankfurt (the same Frankfurt who treated the world to the distinction between first and second order preferences in 1971), saliently wrote:

> The realms of advertising and of public relations, and the nowadays closely related realm of politics, are replete with instances of bullshit so unmitigated that they can serve among the most indisputable and classic paradigms of the concept. And in these realms there are exquisitely sophisticated craftsmen who with the help of advanced and demanding techniques of market research, of public opinion polling, of psychological testing, and so forth dedicate themselves tirelessly to getting every word and image they produce exactly right.

Digital data is a trace of, an imprint from or a representation of something 'out there' in the 'real world'. Raw data is an oxymoron, there is no such thing (Gitelman 2013). Digital data is the result of hard work, just think of the need for hardware devices capable of capturing behavioural data online or offline, via e.g. cookies or other online tracking software, sensors and RFID systems, or smart energy meters; human experts that label and curate data; data scientists who develop feature spaces and other ways of sorting and qualifying data as one type rather than another.

Data – to be productive – assumes active gathering and curation, or capture as Agre (1994) coined it. This is always based on background knowledge, a context and a purpose. Whether data is information actually depends on the knowledge background that enables a human or machine agent to sort and curate it (Marcus 2018). The same applies to defining a machine-readable task that tells a machine learning system what 'counts as success'. This, in turn, is closely related to the choice of a performance metric that specifies even more precisely which variables determines the accuracy of the system's output (against what 'ground truth'?) (Mitchell 1997).

What is information for me may be noise for you; what is noise today may be information tomorrow. Knowledge refers to what an agent knows about the world, it is a complex web of interrelated assumptions, presumptions, experience, reasonings and institutionalized 'ways of seeing things'. I will avoid the term truth as it has religious overtones. Knowledge and information determine how we navigate the world (Brooks 2018), whether in the physical sense of not bumping into a wall, a tree or car, or in the institutional sense of not gaining access to education, employment, or in the sense of not understanding the language or habits of our fellows and thereby standing on their toes or rubbing their hair the wrong way.

Surviving and flourishing depends on having adequate knowledge and that includes recognizing relevant information when it becomes available.

This goes for individual agents but also for institutions. Wisdom is about not merely *knowing* to do the right thing, but actually doing it and learning from the consequences. There is no pyramid. Everything counts simultaneously, though that does not mean it is all the same.

The missing link here is agency. Data can be stored and manipulated but to become information and to build knowledge we need to figure out who is/are the agent(s). There is no information or knowledge that is not agent-dependent. Just like there is no agent that is not environment-dependent. That is what both knowledge and information are about: the survival and the flourishing of an agent, and of agents that share a particular environment.

AFFORDANCES

MH: Situating Agency

The linkages between data, knowledge and information are dependent on the agents that process the data, work with the knowledge and share or hide information. Gibson's (1986) concept of an 'affordance' is the vanishing point of *The End(s)* (Hildebrandt 2017, Calo 2017, Diver 2018). One of the most salient descriptions of the crucial importance of the idea of 'affordances' for the law has recently been written under the heading of 'Law as a User: Design, Affordance, and the Technological Mediation of Norms' by Laurence Diver. Though I am wary of the use of 'user', I will follow his line of argument, also in relation to LPbD (above) and the previous theme on 'knowledge, data and information'.

Diver traces the provenance of the term 'affordance' to psychology, human-computer interaction (HCI), and science and technology studies (STS). My own use of the term, however, derives from a salient concurrence with insights from philosophy of technology, notably those of one of its founding fathers, Don Ihde (1993, 1990). Both Ihde's postphenomenological work and Gibson's understanding of 'affordances' frame perception and action as simultaneously agent- and environment-dependent. More specifically, Ihde shows how technologies mediate both human perception and action, which highlights the importance of tracing the 'affordances' of technologies in terms of what they enable and how they constrain. Affordances are not, however, properties inherent in a technology per se, but relational 'properties' that are inherently agent-dependent.

Diver observes that theories on affordance and law basically do two things. First, they 'explain how the technologies which embody law have affected its development', e.g. understanding law as an affordance of, say, the printing press. Second, they may depict 'law as an affordance per se', which Diver interprets as law having specific affordances for those under its jurisdiction. In recent work (Hildebrandt 2017), I have embraced both positions: law has certain affordances, which are in part constituted by the affordances of the technologies that embody law (e.g. the ICI of the printing press). I agree with Bertolotti and Magnani (2016) that institutions, just like physical objects, have specific affordances for the human agents that interact with them. As these affordances are core to the constitution of society it is crucial to figure out how they are enabled or constrained by the prevailing ICI.

Though Diver seems to reject the second use of affordance, because Gibson highlighted affordances as part of a material or physical environment, it may actually fit well with Diver's proposal to frame the relationship between law and its embodiment in terms of law as a user of such embodiment. Though the ICI that grounds the law is much more than an instrument in the neutralist sense (where subject and instrument are separate and independent things), we could see both the printing press and upcoming data- and code-driven architectures as instruments in the relational and pluralist sense that I advocate in chapter 8 of *The End(s)*.

If we acknowledge that instruments co-constitute their users (Dewey 1916), we can accept that text-driven law is an affordance of the printing press, while also accepting that printed text is its instrument. This – as Diver hopes – enables 'law as a user' to formulate specific requirements for the ICI that must be seen as its instrument. From that perspective, LPbD would focus on the affordances that should be designed into this instrument, whether it is text-, data- or code-driven.

KOH: . . . But Are All the Agents That Matter Present at the Table?

The nexus that Hildebrandt reveals between agency, technology and the law is important, and valuable in curbing the hegemonic tendencies of both legal and technological thinkers. The law is constrained/facilitated in part by the technology and agents of the day, technology ditto by agents and law, and agents ditto by law and technology. We can't really understand any of these without the others. But can we turn this essentially descriptive schema into something that is going to help us (or, perhaps more accurately, help *me* understand where LPbD is going to go)?

Hildebrandt objects to the term 'user' – I agree. 'Participant' is far more polite, and I would venture to suggest more accurate too (Shadbolt et al. 2019). But who are the participants, the afforders and affordees?

I'm driven here by Edmund Burke's critique of social contract theory, and one of the attractions of Hildebrandt's mention of affordance is that it reveals to us the absurdities of the social contract. A contract is a type of legal arrangement that assumes a whole set of pre-existing practices, including promising, forgiving, shaming, compensating and cooperating, and also assumes the existence of a legitimate authority (the state) which will ultimately guarantee the contract. Contract relies on a whole set of affordances from society, its practices and its institutions, and surely on pain of fatal circularity can't simultaneously act as guarantor for all those things.

Be that as it may, Burke's critique focuses on the institutions and allegiances whose affordances are vital for refining the agent's world and its limits. To that end, Burke rejected the transactional social contract: 'the state ought not to be considered as nothing better than a partnership agreement in a trade of pepper and coffee, calico or tobacco, or some other such low concern, to be taken up for a little temporary interest, and to be dissolved by the fancy of the parties'. Rather, society

> is a partnership in all science; a partnership in all art; a partnership in every virtue, and in all perfection. As the ends of such a partnership cannot be obtained in many generations, it becomes a partnership not only between those who are living, but between those who are living, those who are dead, and those who are to be born. (1968, 194–5, and cf. Scruton 2017a, 44–53)

This vision of a thread through history is eloquently descriptive of the needs of those protected and nurtured by the law; we respect our forebears, and we wish to make a future for our children, in a society that we expect to change but that we would find legible to us far into the future. We might borrow Hegel's term *Sittlichkeit* to describe what we mean, a moral and social order that persists through time and generations. And because of the timescales involved, institutions are the only things in which our trust can be reposed to maintain that order.

So when we talk of affordances, are we extending the range of reference generously into the past and the future? Or are we speaking only of the interactions that take place in some vague interval we dub the present? It's not clear yet that we are being expansive enough – we must preserve some semblance of the law as a textual matter, even as we think about how to incorporate code (and I certainly agree with Hildebrandt that that is a vital task). We must do this, just as the law has preserved elements of its spoken antecedents, with physical courtrooms, *habeas corpus*, oral testimony, and in many cultures the adversarial trial, while slowly accepting the affordances of written (and then printed) elements, and letting them be accreted over its time-honoured (to use an apposite phrase) practices.

Hildebrandt approvingly cites work that 'frame[s] perception and action as simultaneously agent- and environment-dependent'. I don't disagree, but do those agents include the dead and the unborn? Does the environment include its history? And can we determine effectively enough the 'affordances that should be designed into' the ICI of LPbD, or should we take a step back and let the common law do its work of discovering those affordances unaided?

THE DIGITAL UNCONSCIOUS

KOH: Meaning and Power

In 2014 there was a flurry of indignation around an experiment using social media data. Academics from Cornell in cooperation with Facebook 'manipulated the emotions' of 689,003 social networkers, adjusting their newsfeeds so that expressions of emotions or sentiment were filtered. Result: those who received more negative stories were more likely to write a negative story themselves, and those blessed with happy news responded with unconfined joy. Or rather, the number of positive words they used increased by 0.06 per cent relative to a control. The authors proudly announced, 'the results show emotional contagion'. The intrusion, they claimed, was minimal and proportional. The contagion was pretty minimal too (O'Hara 2015).

Such events seem to demonstrate our powerlessness – mere data points to be pushed around in the ongoing quest to remove the last vestiges of unpredictability from the world. But more, I think, is going on than that. The experiment seemed to conflate the people and the data – the researchers tracked the vocabulary of users' posts, which seems a relatively remote proxy for emotional state. Did they prove more than that the vocabulary we use is conditioned by the vocabulary of others? That is hardly news. But maybe no-one cares about such fine distinctions nowadays. Indeed, one could be forgiven for wondering whether the real value to Facebook of the experiment was the boost to its share price (which rose 8 per cent over the next month), by feeding the myth of its omnipotence.

All coordination systems need feedback about the states of the things they are coordinating, and any system that is dealing with people – be it a government, social network or big data cruncher – needs to find out what those in its charge are doing. But people are disorganized, complex and have their own agendas, producing, in Kant's phrase, 'the crooked timber of humanity [from which] no straight thing can ever be made'. So, recalling Scott once more, governments and big data need to render us legible to them, so they can read what we do (1998). This means straightening that timber, cramming our infinitely variable behaviour into the insensitive but tractable confines of categories and concepts. If a few beams crack, then no problem – Leviathan doesn't mind the odd splinter.

Indeed, if behavioural psychology backed up by loads of data can show that certain correlations occur under laboratory conditions, the temptation for paternalistic policy-makers is to reproduce the laboratory conditions in the world. So whereas the purpose of government might, once, have been to make me happier, so much easier if its aim was to get me to publish more positive words. This has two advantages. We know how to do it. And it is verifiable. 'Did you make the people happier?' 'Sure we did – look at all the positive words they posted. They are 2.3 per cent happier. Vote for me!'

But legibility is asymmetric. We are legible to the algorithms, but the algorithms are not legible to us. Algorithms are a classic technocratic way of avoiding politics, threatening a blander world. Maybe that's a good thing – but we should be debating it. Where to start? Transparency about the algorithms being used? Transparency is no good unless we have some compensating agency and can do something about what is revealed. Increase awareness that the data is only one of a plurality of indicators of human potential? Or do we need a playful class of politicians, scientists, financiers, businessmen, entrepreneurs and artists enjoying the act of creation and putting content before the public, taking a risk and not simply doing what the algorithms say.

MH: Digital Unconscious and Human Agency

Human autonomy is not absolute or independent as rational choice theory assumes, but neither is it predictably irrational as nudge theory and behavioural economics would have us believe. This is precisely why microtargeting is so disruptive; it works – but not as professed by those who stand to gain from others' belief in its magic.

In *The End(s)* I proposed thinking in terms of a *distributed big data space* that nourishes data-driven infrastructures and applications, turning into a *digital unconscious* that continuously reconfigures our choice architecture. The best way to understand this is to think of AB testing, which enables websites to continuously update their interface (and computational back-end system), based on surreptitiously gained feedback from their visitors. Note that while interfaces may seem user-friendly contraptions meant 'to improve the user experience', for all practical purposes they are meant to increase click behaviours to enlarge advertising revenues. Interfaces hide as much as they facilitate, or maybe more (Kittler 1997). As research seems to confirm, this induces a preference for more extreme and less nuanced content, which in turn generates confusion and fragmentation of public discourse, affording a tactics of 'paralyze and polarize' (Tufekci 2018) rather than gaining control over individual minds. This is largely a matter of bots (online software scripts) that interfere in public debate by means of automated scripts, collaborating in the form of botnets (coordinated bots operating across platforms and devices) to disrupt public discourse (Howard, Woolley, and Calo 2018).

Microtargeting suggests that individual persons can be targeted in a surgical manner, eliciting the kind of behaviour that is wished for. Here O'Hara paints the bigger picture:

> if behavioural psychology backed up by loads of data can show that certain correlations occur under laboratory conditions, the temptation for paternalistic policy-makers is to reproduce the laboratory conditions in the world. So, whereas the purpose of government might, once, have been to make me happier, so much easier if its aim was to get me to publish more positive words.

Whereas microtargeting may have surgical effects in theory, and even in a laboratory, its accuracy in real life depends on reductive metrics. These 'fantastic' metrics serve as proxies for real life effects, which are, however, far more complex and far less predictable than nudge theory's alignment with machine learning suggests.

This does not stop the new digital unconscious from affecting human agency. It does so in two ways. First, though it may not actually operate with the surgical precision that is claimed for it, political parties, journalists and tech platforms may believe it does and base numerous decisions on this belief. This goes for decisions on spending (investing huge parts of their budgets to enabling or using microtargeting), decisions on what kind of content to write and disseminate (tweet-like messages, single-issue targeting, prioritizing of negative and/or radical content), decisions on face-to-face interaction with voters (downsizing investment of time and people in such interaction) and decisions on investing time in public debate with adversaries (restricting time and effort to prepare and actually conduct such debate). All this has major consequences for the quality and the integrity of political discourse and democratic resilience. Second, though microtargeting sounds very precise, it is based on statistics and is often operated by means of bots and botnets that enable the automation, amplification and subversion of political expression, including deliberate targeting with fake news. Even if this may not persuade anybody of anything, it will nevertheless fragment and disrupt individual and societal trust in political parties, journalism, tech platforms and political discourse in general, due to the confusion about who is lying about what.

Human agency is not given, it can be diminished and broken, subverted and overdetermined. A digital unconscious that targets our human unconscious and messes with it, requires redesign to disable such tricks. We cannot expect those who profit from current microtargeting to instigate such redesign. Here we need stringent redress, capable of imposing compliance – combining 'by design' solutions that target the architecture of a rough digital unconscious with practical and effective law enforcement.

THE MODE OF EXISTENCE OF MODERN POSITIVE LAW

MH: Novel Entanglements of Law and Technology

The End(s) has been written for a broad audience, including lawyers, philosophers of law and technology, computer scientists and citizens interested in the implications of the new onli*fe* world they have come to depend on. One of the aims of the book is to highlight the importance of law and the Rule of Law, foregrounding the crucial importance of practical and effective legal protection.

Modern, positive law, *The End(s)* argues, is an affordance of printed text – as modern law is fundamentally text-driven. Based on research into the technologies of the word (Ong 1982), the script and the printing press (Eisenstein 2005), one can conclude that text-driven ICIs have specific affordances for human agents, such as sequential processing of information, systematization in the form of tables of content and of indexes that provide an overview over the content of printed books. As printed text enables authors (legislatures and courts) to reach readers (those under its jurisdiction) beyond the immediacy of face-to-face encounters a triple 'distantiation' takes place, between (1) text and author, (2) author and reader and (3) text and meaning. Apart from extending the reach of the legislator, this triggers a need for iterant interpretation, that can never be taken for granted (Ricoeur 1976, Lévy 1990), and thus generates iterant contestation. This affordance is core to modern positive law, culminating in the Rule of Law. Contestation is what offers legal protection.

Law's performative nature, the so-called 'force of law' (Derrida 1990), is deeply connected with its text-driven nature. Speech act theory shows that law does not depend on propositional logic, but on performative speech acts (MacCormick 2007), such as 'I declare thee husband and wife' or 'husband and husband' or 'wife and wife', depending on what positive law affords. Such declaration has legal effect, e.g. as to inheritance, authority over children or shared assets. In the world we share, such legal effect makes a difference. Legal effect is not a matter of brute force, logical deduction or mechanical application; instead it creates institutional facts (a marriage, a university diploma, the competence to sell one's house). In that sense, law is constitutive of our shared lifeworld.

Computer code may be self-executing, enabling compliance by design. Some may believe that turns behaviours into 'legal by design'. As argued above, this is not the case; if you cannot disobey the law it does not qualify as law. Nevertheless, data-driven cyberphysical applications may take a plethora of decisions that surreptitiously reconfigure our environment. If we do not engage with this challenge, the ensuing choice architectures may overrule text-driven law and the legal protection it affords.

Modern law exists as rooted in text. Its *mode of existence* is text-driven. To the extent that the world that law aims to constitute and regulate is no longer text-driven, lawyers will have to get their act together. Law's *mode of existence* will change, either by (1) understanding code-driven regulation as law, by (2) reducing the role of law in favour of data-driven decision-making, or (3) by envisaging and developing *legal protection by design*.

KOH: Getting Their Act Together

Many characteristically wise words here from Hildebrandt, and I disagree with very little, nothing until the final paragraph. And even then, I'm only not sure. Lawyers will certainly have to get their act together – as, for that matter, will businesspeople, politicians and those in many other arenas for cooperation and the resolution of conflict – in the face of data-driven decisions. Hildebrandt gives us three choices: do they exhaust the possibilities? (Spoiler alert: I don't know).

Law does indeed exist in text, and in oral argument, and in physical space. A witness not only has to present her evidence, she has to do it at a certain time in a certain place. A jury needs to be present, except when it doesn't. Even a judge might have to be kept in ignorance of aspects of the cases over which she presides (e.g. if an offer to settle is made and rejected). Law inhabits the spaces into which it is invited, and it may come into the world of data-driven agency, perhaps as LPbD, perhaps as a type of common law. The problem I foresee with LPbD, as I noted earlier, is that law is often discovered through its collision with the reality of a dispute. The law as remedy, the extrapolation of justice from the relief of the injured, keeps it anchored in our quotidian lives, and away from the abstractions that look good on parchment but are meaningless in a concrete context.

What do the relevant contexts look like? Well, in many of them, we are the playthings of the platforms, as with the Cornell experiment described earlier. Facebook's manipulation was odious to many, as evinced by the loud response, and we need a way of understanding this outrage as a genuine harm for which a remedy is appropriate.

In other areas, however, we need to understand the type of social life afforded by the platforms. I have recently been writing about *social machines* (Shadbolt et al. 2019), computer-mediated interactions enabling communities to respond to modern problems, e.g. of transport, such as Waze,[2] a navigation app which uses community-derived real-time data about incidents such as traffic jams and accidents; crime, such as BlueServo,[3] which crowdsources policing on the Texas-Mexico border, and Onde Tem Tiroteio (Where the Shootouts Are),[4] which uses a network of a million people combining social networking platforms with a special purpose app to provide real-time information about shootings and gang-related crime in Brazil; or health, to enable those suffering from a particular health care problem to pool resources and to offer support and advice to fellow sufferers, such as PatientsLikeMe,[5] or curetogether.[6] Social machines are important enterprises in a connected world; we need to see what does and doesn't help them flourish, and respond when necessary – but this can't simply be programmed in in advance, not least because not all social machines are socially beneficial.

A final thought is the importance of the idea of a data trust (O'Hara 2019). There are many different and not always consistent ideas of what this kind of trust can and should do and be, but the idea that data about one is held in trust, so that, even though one might not be the legal owner/rights-holder of the data one might be the equitable owner. Meanwhile, the data controller would have a fiduciary duty to manage the data for the benefit of the equitable owners (i.e. the data subjects). How this is implemented in law, if it needs to be implemented at all, is a moot point – it could not be a trust in the common law and equity sense (O'Hara 2019) – but, like a standard property trust, the aim is to give everyone confidence that the system works for them, and not for a remote other. The point of law is to drive a wedge between power and authority, and data trusts may be another means of doing that.

CONSERVATISM AND THE QUEST TO PRESERVE PLURALITY AND NATALITY

KOH: Reading Hildebrandt from an Oakeshottian Perspective

Cards on the table: my philosophical position is conservative in the Burkean tradition (not the current horrendous American mangling of the term, applying it to anyone on the right of politics). Burkean conservatism problematizes change, from which it follows that conservatives in different cultures will often believe different things; for instance, in the US, a conservative would believe that a written constitution is essential for liberty, while in the UK, a conservative would think the opposite. Conservatives in Tehran or Beijing would have different ideas again, perhaps not being too bothered by liberty as a value. There is no contradiction in this; societies are different, their histories, settled states, trajectories of change and political standards divergent, their contexts *sui generis*. Unlike most other ideologies, conservatism is not defined with reference to particular ends (such as equality, liberty, free markets or the environment). Of course, conservatives can support these ends (personally, I approve of all but the first of these), but conservative support for them is contingent on their being already embedded in a society. I defend Britain's ancient liberties, not (as liberals do) because they are liberties, but because they are *ancient*. Conservatism, *qua* ideology, pursues no end, other than the continued functioning of a society along lines agreeable to its members (O'Hara 2011).

Conservatism, I believe, is primarily an epistemological position, rooted in the philosophical scepticism of Montaigne and Burke. The essential conservative position can be boiled down to two principles defensible using the resources of public reason (O'Hara 2011). The *knowledge principle* says that society is too complex, interconnected, reflexive and dynamic to be fully described by theory, so that the outcome of any policy intervention or innovation cannot be predicted with confidence. There will be unintended consequences, and the rationalist innovator cannot be sure either that the intended consequences will be realized. The *change principle* says that it follows that any innovation will bring risk (as indeed will stasis). In particular, the rationalist innovator, concerned with righting a wrong or pursuing an opportunity, is blind to the ways in which current practices and innovations implicitly support valuable and valued social interactions, often hidden by familiarity of practice and the absence of evidence. Hence the innovator typically undervalues current institutions. The risk of change is therefore, all things being equal, higher than the innovator's (imperfect) models maintain, and so the burden of proof on the innovator should be greater than ends-focused ideologies generally maintain. Change is more acceptable, and more likely, when a nation, society or culture is troubled, because the risk of change is lower. We should be more accepting of change in Syria, say, than in a peaceful Scandinavian country. Unfortunately, radicals tend to abound in settled, tranquil places, where they are left alone in comfort to theorize, and which they ungratefully wish to disrupt.

Conservatism does not rule out change, but takes its risks seriously. Neither does conservatism predict that change will necessarily be bad, only that the innovator understates the risks, and cannot ensure they will be avoided. *Some* innovations doubtless work very well; we just don't know in advance which ones. Change, when it comes, should be incremental, reversible where possible, and rigorously evaluated.

Note that these two principles don't determine what policies a conservative should pursue. A conservative might have supported Brexit, for instance, because the EU's alien institutional structures and foundations in civil/Roman law have undermined British Parliamentary sovereignty and common law. But equally, another might have opposed it because British politics, society and economics have been deeply shaped by its membership of the EU since 1973, and it cannot be disentangled without risking major harm and instability. A third conservative might (and, I would argue, should) have deplored the use of a referendum, a constitutional concept foreign to the United Kingdom.

Essential is a mutual understanding of the connections forged by a political culture; politics expresses a first-person plural (as Scruton [2005, 2017b, 2017c] puts it), a 'we' determined by pre-political loyalties. A government is 'our' government, and a land is 'our' land. Fashionable politics focuses on inclusion, but politics needs also to encompass exclusion; the trick is to exclude humanely and wisely. As Arendt (1958) argued, we need a common world, a shared human world of institutions and practices which furnishes a durable context for our interaction, collaboration and dispute, which implies some closure to outsiders. This follows from the knowledge principle; when politics is based on pre-political loyalties, the polity will be marked by predictability, stability, legibility and understanding. It will also be valued more highly, and so the risks of change will be correspondingly higher. Conservatism, in these terms of understanding and value, is fundamentally phenomenological, concerned with the *Lebenswelt* of a political culture described relative to human purposes, rather than scientific and social scientific abstractions. The *Lebenswelt* persists through time, as Burke forcefully argued, including history and a continuous thread to the future. Cultures are essentially shared, not only with the living, but with the dead and the not-yet-born, via the enduring institutions that Hegel gathered under the term *Sittlichkeit*.

It is often assumed that data describe the world. No, they are part of the world, and inform our future action. The future cannot be predicted, only imagined. Innovators deal in imaginaries, and the skill of a Zuckerberg or a Schmidt is to make a technological imaginary appear inevitable (I am grateful to an unpublished paper by Susan Halford for the importance of this point). How do we resist this technodeterminism? The radical response is to generate competing imaginaries, but these fall equally foul of the knowledge principle and the change principle. The conservative response is to restore focus on the advantages of the present. As Hildebrandt's *The End(s)* presents history at an inflection point, she defends our plural society with an agonistic reading, accepting, even welcoming conflict between future imaginaries. Yet in its scope, scale and ambition, *The End(s)* reminds me of Michael Oakeshott's *On Human Conduct* (1975), and in many ways updates that statement of liberal conservatism for the twenty-first century. Oakeshott's themes of human behaviour, civil association and modernity's challenges to individuality are revisited in Hildebrandt's work. Both books focus on individual human decision-making and action, the use and purpose of law for constraining action, and the role of the law and the state in creating the circumstances for autonomous, authentic, free individuals to flourish. Resistance to the innovator can involve beating her at her own game, by creating a more persuasive (but equally subjective) imaginary, in a robust world that welcomes diversity and plurality. This, I think, is Hildebrandt's preferred direction. Or we could run with Oakeshott, and demand to know the source of legitimacy of such imaginaries (spoiler alert: there is none, other than public agreement), and work to preserve our common and shared understanding.

MH: The Quest to Preserve Plurality and Natality

My co-editor finds that '[c]onservatism, qua ideology, pursues no end, other than the continued functioning of a society along lines agreeable to its members'. The problem is that its members may disagree about what is agreeable to them and about whether the current functioning is agreeable at all. We must also note that such disagreement may be distributed depending on who wins and who loses. This is where equality (the only value O'Hara does not approve of) comes in and where liberty itself raises questions such as 'whose liberty?' at the cost of 'whose security?' As Jeremy Waldron (2003) famously observed, the trade-off between liberty and security may well involve a trade-off where some are forced to give up part of their liberties to provide others with security. Protecting society against revolutionary change may in point of fact require its members to intervene against a 'continued functioning' that favours the few at the cost of the many and the same goes for a 'continued functioning' that favours a dominant majority at the cost of one or more minorities that have no way to survive in a dignified way.

But I would go further, as I believe that the very values that must be preserved (or conserved if you wish) are those that allow for change. This highlights Arendt's (1958) discussion of 'natality' as pivotal for both human society and the individual person and raises pertinent issues on the cusp of the conservation as well as the reinvention of the 'modern tradition'. This 'modern tradition' indeed thrives on institutions, such as democratic practices, courts and the Rule of Law. These institutions, however, cannot be taken for granted; they require iterant reconstruction in the face of an era built on 'innovative' ICIs and disruptive business models. Other than aficionados of innovation assume, I do not think that just any change will do, or that change should be goal in itself. The questions we urgently need to ask are: (1) what change is required to preserve our relative autonomy and the institutions that enable it? and (2) what must be preserved to afford the freedom to change as core to human agency? If that turns me into a conservative, I am fine; if it labels me as a radical thinker, I am good. The interplay between change and preservation must be discussed in the light of concrete threats to human agency, acknowledging that even to sustain 'continued functioning' may demand either intervention or preservation and more likely both. While also acknowledging that sometimes 'continued functioning' is unacceptable and should be resisted, reversed and transformed. In the case of this book the need for change and preservation will depend on how *the technologies of the subjunctive tense* disrupt capabilities, redistribute risk, obstruct access to justice or otherwise change what we need to preserve. And the 'need to preserve' is not a matter of individual or aggregated preferences. This 'need' cannot depend on a utilitarian calculus that takes human agency for granted; it concerns the extent to which the ICI itself still affords such agency.

Maryanne Wolf (2008, 4) writes about 'the reading brain' in a way that 'celebrates the vastness of our accomplishment as the species that reads, records, and goes beyond what went before, and directs our attention to what is important to preserve'. Based on cultural-historical but foremost on biological and cognitive research into the reading brain, she concludes that (Wolf 2008, 17):

> Within that context, the generative capacity of reading parallels the fundamental plasticity in the circuit wiring of our brains: both permit us to go beyond the particulars of the given. The rich associations, inferences, and insights emerging from this capacity allow, and indeed invite, us to reach beyond the specific content of what we read to form new thoughts. In this sense reading both reflects and reenacts the brain's capacity for cognitive breakthroughs.

This, I have argued in *The End(s)*, is what must be preserved. There, I may be accused of conservatism. But I do not argue for the preservation of the reading brain because it is part of the continued functioning of society. Instead, I argue for such preservation to the extent that it affords us the generative capacity that enhances our agency: our ability to imagine futures while assessing our past; our ability to think along genuinely new lines while still being rooted in older paths; our ability to leap into futures unthinkable to previous generations. And if the latter means entering an era that moves beyond the reading brain we cannot just stand by and – as proper Oakeshottian conservatives – restrict ourselves to incremental responses to whatever ICI develops. Precisely because, as O'Hara writes, the burden of proof should be on the innovator, we cannot sit still and accept whatever 'the innovators' provide us with. Other than O'Hara suggests, this does not leave us with the choice of either resisting 'innovation' or accepting it (hoping the common law will address eventual harm after the fact). It will require a precautionary approach that includes assessments of what new technological infrastructures do to our mind, self and society (Mead and Morris 1962), and it may require re-articulation of text-driven norms in the data- and code-driven environment we face.

'We', however, are not determined by prepolitical loyalties. We are the people that has reinvented itself as constitutive of a political order that is based on democratic participation within the bounds of the Rule of Law. 'We' are not a natural, organic or holistic clan that is bound by kinship, geography or by the subjection to an absolute sovereign. 'We' are the result of an artificial construction, a complex web of speech acts, that institutes what Dworkin has framed as a government that is bound to treat each of its citizens with 'equal respect and concern'. This 'we' cannot be taken for granted, and its iterant institution is partly contingent upon the ICI of the printing press and the resulting 'reading brain'. This ICI generates the plurality 'we' need to foster, precisely because the 'we' is not given, and cannot be assumed to agree on which 'continued functioning' must be preserved. My inspiration here comes from a number of political theorists, legal philosophers and continental as well as Anglo-American philosophers that highlight the need for plurality, agonism and the institutional checks and balances to sustain them, from Dewey (1927) and Radbruch (2006) to Austin (1975), Winch (1958) and MacCormick (2007), from Wittgenstein and Anscombe (2003), Taylor (1995) and Arendt (1958) to Ricoeur (1976) and Mouffe (2000), who weaves many of these strands together.

O'Hara rightly warns against the assumption that LPbD could actually foresee the changes brought about by its well-intended design. However, LPbD – other than techno-regulation – is a *response* to innovative applications that intend to change our *Lebenswelt*, often aiming to disrupt markets while breaking the legal norms that hold together the fabric of human society. And even the unintended consequences of search engines, cloud robotics and social networks disrupt, twist and reconfigure our lifeworld.

LPbD requires that, instead of either rejecting or embracing this type of innovation, we step in to constrain potentially negative implications. To do this we don't have to assume perfect knowledge of the future, but neither should we assume a general scepticism regarding our ability to foresee the consequences of innovation. One could even claim that LPbD will often ensure that 'change, when it comes, should be incremental, reversible where possible, and rigorously evaluated' (O'Hara, above). The point is that such 'change' does not just 'come', but is actively organized by those hoping to benefit (while often framing the unintended consequences for others as collateral damage). LPbD is based on the position that if such change has indirect effects on the redistribution of risk and opportunities it should be co-decided by those who will suffer the consequences, it should include ways to resist its lure and it should not rule out practical and effective access to a court of law.

Finally, the *Lebenswelt* is not – as e.g. Schmitt (1993) portrayed it – a concrete ordering that must be protected against normative claims or activist intervention (Hildebrandt 2015). The *Lebenswelt* is neither a given nor static. Ihde's (1990) postphenomenological analysis of technological mediation demonstrates the extent to which the *Lebenswelt* is an affordance of the prevalent ICI; the text-driven *Lebenswelt* that some of us have been familiar with is already transforming into a data- and code-driven onli*fe* world. If we want to preserve some of the core affordances of the text-driven *Lebenswelt* we will have to work hard to integrate them into the architecture of the onli*fe* world. That is a matter of design, and it is precisely LPbD that should make sure that such design is not monopolized by technology developers and the boards of directors of Big Tech.

So, I may run with Oakeshott insofar as he challenges the legitimacy of technology developers and Big Tech platforms that transform the lifeworld of others, but that is just the beginning. The new onli*fe* world may hold promise, and if it does, we need to make sure it does so in a way that enables plurality and natality based on effective respect for fundamental human rights and freedoms. This, clearly, is no small feat.

NOTES

1. See my ERC Advanced Grant project on 'Counting as a Human Being in the Era of Computational Law' (CoHuBiCoL): <www.cohubicol.com>.
2. <www.waze.com/>.
3. <www.blueservo.net/>.
4. <www.ondetemtiroteio.com.br/>.
5. <www.patientslikeme.com/>.
6. <http://curetogether.com/>.

REFERENCES

Agre, P. E. 1994. 'Surveillance and Capture: Two Models of Privacy'. *The Information Society* 10 (2), 101–27. <https://doi.org/10.1080/01972243.1994.9960162>

Arendt, H. 1958. *The Human Condition*. Chicago, IL: University Press of Chicago

Austin, J. L. 1975. *How to Do Things with Words*. 2nd ed. Boston, MA: Harvard University Press

Bertolotti, T. and L. Magnani. 2016. 'Theoretical Considerations on Cognitive Niche Construction'. *Synthese*, July, 1–23. <https://doi.org/10.1007/s11229-016-1165-2>

Broad, W. J. 1981. 'The Publishing Game: Getting More For Less'. *Science* 211 (4487), 1137–9. <https://doi.org/10.1126/science.7008199>

Brooks, R. 2018. 'My Dated Predictions – Rodney Brooks'. *MIT RETHIMK* (blog). 1 January 2018. <https://rodneybrooks.com/my-dated-predictions/>

Brownsword, R. 2016. 'Technological Management and the Rule of Law'. *Law, Innovation and Technology* 8 (1), 100–40. <https://doi.org/10.1080/17579961.2016.1161891>

Burke, E. 1968. *Reflections on the Revolution in France*. Harmondsworth: Penguin

Calo, R. 2017. 'Technology, Law, and Affordance: A Review of Smart Technologies and the End(s) of Law'. *Critical Analysis of Law* 4 (1). <http://cal.library.utoronto.ca/index.php/cal/article/download/28150>

Dennett, D. 2009. 'Intentional Systems Theory'. In *Oxford Handbook of the Philosophy or Mind*, 339–50. Oxford: Oxford University Press

Derrida, J. 1990. 'Force of Law: The "Mystical Foundation of Authority"'. *Cardozo Law Review* 11, 920–1045

Dewey, J. 1916. 'The Logic of Judgments of Practice Chapter 14'. In *Essays in Experimental Logic*, edited by John Dewey, 335–442. Chicago, IL: University of Chicago

Dewey, J. 1927. *The Public & Its Problems*. Chicago, IL: The Swallow Press

Diver, L. 2018. 'Law as a User: Design, Affordance, and the Technological Mediation of Norms'. *SCRIPTed* 15 (1), 4–41. <https://doi.org/10.2966/scrip.150118.4>

Eisenstein, E. 2005. *The Printing Revolution in Early Modern Europe*. Cambridge; New York: Cambridge University Press

Frankfurt, H. G. 1971. 'Freedom of the Will and the Concept of a Person'. *The Journal of Philosophy* 68 (1), 5–20

Frankfurt, H. G. 2005. *On Bullshit*. 1st edition. Princeton, NJ: Princeton University Press

Gibson, J. 1986. *The Ecological Approach to Visual Perception*. New Jersey, NJ: Lawrence Erlbaum Associates

Gitelman, L., ed. 2013. *'Raw Data' Is an Oxymoron*. Cambridge, MA; London: MIT Press

Hildebrandt, M. 2015. 'Radbruch's Rechtsstaat and Schmitt's Legal Order: Legalism, Legality, and the Institution of Law'. *Critical Analysis of Law* 2 (1). <http://cal.library.utoronto.ca/index.php/cal/article/view/22514>

Hildebrandt, M. 2017. 'Law As an Affordance: The Devil Is in the Vanishing Point(S)'. *Critical Analysis of Law* 4 (1). <http://cal.library.utoronto.ca/index.php/cal/article/download/28154>

Hirschmann, A. O. 1991. *The Rhetoric of Reaction: Perversity, Futility, Jeopardy*. Cambridge, MA: Harvard University Press

Howard, P. N., S. Woolley and R. Calo. 2018. 'Algorithms, Bots, and Political

Communication in the US 2016 Election: The Challenge of Automated Political Communication for Election Law and Administration'. *Journal of Information Technology & Politics* 15 (2), 81–93. <https://doi.org/10.1080/19331681.2018.1448735>

Ihde, D. 1990. *Technology and the Lifeworld: From Garden to Earth*. The Indiana Series in the Philosophy of Technology. Bloomington, IN: Indiana University Press

Ihde, D. 1993. *Philosophy of Technology: An Introduction*. Vol. 1st. Paragon Issues in Philosophy. New York, NY: Paragon House

Kittler, F. 1997. 'There Is No Software'. In *Literature, Media, Information Systems. Essays*, edited by John Johnston, 147–55. Amsterdam: Overseas Publishers Association.

Krogness, K. J. 2011. 'Numbered Individuals, Digital Traditions, and Individual Rights: Civil Status Registration in Denmark 1645 to 2010'. *Ritsumeikan Law Review* 28, 87–126.

Lévy, P. 1990. *Les Technologies de l'intelligence. L'avenir de La Pensée à l'ère Informatique*. Paris: La Découverte

Lippe, P., D. M. Katz and D. Jackson. 2015. 'Legal by Design: A New Paradigm for Handling Complexity in Banking Regulation and Elsewhere in Law'. *Oregon Law Review* 93 (4). <http://papers.ssrn.com/abstract=2539315>

MacCormick, N. 2007. *Institutions of Law: An Essay in Legal Theory*. Oxford: Oxford University Press

Marcus, G. 2018. 'Deep Learning: A Critical Appraisal'. <https://arxiv.org/abs/1801.00631>

Mayor-Schönberger, V. and K. Cukier. 2013. *Big Data: A Revolution that Will Transform the Way We Live, Work and Think*. London: John Murray

Mead, G. H. and C. W. Morris. 1962. *Mind, Self, and Society from the Standpoint of a Social Behaviorist*. Chicago, IL: University of Chicago Press

Mitchell, T. 1997. *Machine Learning*. 1st edition. New York, NY: McGraw-Hill Education

Mouffe, C. 2000. *The Democractic Paradox*. London; New York: Verso

Nissenbaum, H. 2010. *Privacy in Context: Technology, Policy and the Integrity of Social Life*. Stanford, CA: Stanford University Press

Oakeshott, M. 1975. *On Human Conduct*. Oxford: Clarendon Press

O'Hara, K. 2010. *The Enlightenment: A Beginner's Guide*. Oxford: Oneworld

O'Hara, K. 2011. *Conservatism*. London: Reaktion

O'Hara, K. 2015. 'Data, Legibility, Creativity ... and Power'. *IEEE Internet Computing* 19 (2), 88–91. <https://doi.org/10.1109/MIC.2015.34>

O'Hara, K. 2018. 'The Contradictions of Digital Modernity'. *AI & Society*. <https://doi.org/10.1007/s00146-018-0843-7>

O'Hara, K. 2019. *Data Trusts: Ethics, Architecture and Governance for Trustworthy Data Stewardship*. Southampton: Web Science Institute. <http://dx.doi.org/10.5258/SOTON/WSI-WP001>

Ong, W. 1982. *Orality and Literacy: The Technologizing of the Word*. London; New York: Methuen

Radbruch, G. 2006. 'Five Minutes of Legal Philosophy (1945)'. *Oxford Journal of Legal Studies* 26 (1), 13–15. <https://doi.org/10.1093/ojls/gqi042>

Ricoeur, P. 1976. *Interpretation Theory*. Austin, TX: Texas University Press.

Schmitt, C. 1993. *Über die drei Arten des rechtswissenschaftlichen Denkens*. 3. A. edition. Berlin: Duncker & Humblot

Scott, J. C. 1998. *Seeing Like a State: How Certain Schemes to Improve the Human Condition Have Failed*. New Haven, CT: Yale University Press
Scruton, R. 2005. *Philosophy: Principles and Problems*. London: Continuum
Scruton, R. 2017a. *Conservatism: An Invitation to the Great Tradition*. New York, NY: St Martin's Press
Scruton, R. 2017b. *On Human Nature*. Princeton, NJ: Princeton University Press
Scruton, R. 2017c. *Where We Are: The State of Britain Now*. London: Bloomsbury
Shadbolt, N., K. O'Hara, D. De Roure and W. Hall. 2019. *The Theory and Practice of Social Machines*. Cham: Springer.
Taylor, C. 1995. 'To Follow a Rule'. In *Philosophical Arguments*, edited by Charles Taylor, 165–81. Cambridge, MA: Harvard University Press
Tufekci, Z. 2018. 'How Social Media Took Us from Tahrir Square to Donald Trump'. *MIT Technology Review*, no. September/October. <www.technologyreview.com/s/611806/how-social-media-took-us-from-tahrir-square-to-donald-trump/>
Waldron, J. 2003. 'Security and Liberty: The Image of Balance'. *Journal of Political Philosophy* 11 (2), 191–210. <https://doi.org/10.1111/1467-9760.00174>
Winch, P. 1958. *The Idea of a Social Science*. London and Henley: Routledge & Kegan Paul
Wittgenstein, L. and G. E. M. Anscombe. 2003. *Philosophical Investigations: The German Text, with a Revised English Translation*. Vol. 3rd. Malden, MA: Blackwell Pub
Wolf, M. 2008. *Proust and the Squid: The Story and Science of the Reading Brain*. Duxford: Icon Books Ltd
Wright, A. and P. De Filippi. 2015. 'Decentralized Blockchain Technology and the Rise of Lex Cryptographica'. <https://ssrn.com/abstract=2580664>

PART I

3. Data-driven agency and knowledge
Paul Dumouchel

INTRODUCTION

'If it exists, the Master Algorithm can derive all knowledge in the world – past, present and future – from data' (Domingos 2015, xviii). But what exactly does 'derive knowledge from data' mean? How is this to be understood? What does 'all knowledge' refer to here? Everything that can be learned, all forms of cognition or only to knowledge proper – that is, to true and justified beliefs, or only to what we call science? Further, what is or what qualifies as an algorithm in this context? Or to put it otherwise, what does it means to say that a system or machine 'learns'? Clearly, some extremely far-reaching claims are being made concerning what machines can discover from the data they are fed. If data-driven agency is a type of agency where observations are limited to digital data and whose actions result from computational processing of these data, then such agents driven by data processed by machines are apparently driven by what machines have 'learned'. It is therefore important to understand the nature of the knowledge that is mechanically obtained from digital data and what its credentials are.

The question should be made more precise for at least two reasons. First, the terms used when referring to the techniques underlying data-driven agency – for example, AI, computer science, data mining, algorithms, deep learning, big data, machine learning, etc. – are not always well defined and practitioners adopt very different approaches. Second, these methods and techniques are applied in different areas from financial markets to basic physics, from e-commerce to research in genetics. They are involved in profound social and economic transformations and in fundamental science. In the two cases the epistemic value of the results obtained tend to be quite different. The question therefore is not only about the nature of all knowledge that is, or that can be obtained mechanically from digital data, or about the limits of what a machine could (in principle) learn. Rather, 'data-driven agency' should be our guide here. First, because the close relationship between 'knowledge' and 'agency' that it involves is revealing about the nature of the knowledge machines 'learn' and, I suggest, about the nature of scientific knowledge in general. Second, because it is mostly in relation to data-driven (social) agency that imperative and wide-ranging claims are made concerning the knowledge that mechanically guides them.

All claims concerning the promises of big data and cognitive computing[1] are not as ambitious as the passage quoted above, but many authors argue that the very large quantity of data that is now available is radically changing science and our relationship to knowledge.[2] For example, an often quoted book (Mayer-Schönberger and Cukier 2014) identifies three characteristics of big data which, the authors argue, will change the way we live, work and think. First exhaustivity, data sets that can be processed are now large enough to encompass all available data on a phenomenon of interest. Second messiness, data can now be collected from a wide variety of sources which allow researchers to embrace the complex multifaceted nature of the real world unconstrained by prior theoretical or causal hypotheses. The third, closely related characteristic is what the authors term 'the triumph of correlations', that is: data are enough. Given sufficient data spurious correlations, they argue, can be weeded out without the need of theoretical or causal hypotheses. According to Canali (2016) the two central aspects of what is advertised as a new way of 'doing science' are: 1) that big data allow us to make sound predictions and discoveries without recourse to theoretical elements and 2) that correlations found in data constitute knowledge by themselves, immediately, without the need of any causal or theoretical explanations. According to such an understanding, data processed correlations highlighted are all there is to knowledge.

Of course, not all who are active in the fields of computer science, machine learning or big data accept this conception of science and knowledge. The fact, however, is that such claims are viewed as authoritative by many decision-makers, both private and public, and used to justify recourse to data-driven agents in various social contexts. Disputable as they may be, such claims should not be dismissed as simply bad science, that reflect misunderstanding, greed or lust for power, they also correspond to important aspects of the cognitive technologies that are being developed, which it is important to understand.

To begin it may be useful to compare this vision of a new data science to approaches in philosophy of science which it resembles most. Could the claims that 'data are enough' and 'no theory is necessary' be viewed as a radical form of *empiricism*? Empiricists believe that all our knowledge comes from the senses, from observations, sense data that are processed by the brain, as by a computer one may argue. The idea here seems to be that all data whatever its source can be treated in the same way. There are nonetheless two important differences between classical empiricism and the claims that are now being made. First, if empiricists believed that observation could and should be carried out without recourse to prior theory, they also thought that observation should lead to the elaboration of theoretical and causal explanations. Theory was the goal rather than the starting point, while here theoretical and causal explanations are simply dismissed as unnecessary.

Second is the difference between the senses and digital data which can come from many different sources: medical records, internet traffic, financial transactions, GPS, radio telescope observation of distant galaxies, telephone conversation, video games, etc. According to what is claimed, cognitive computing explores regularities and singularities in these data independently of their source or meaning discovering indications of corruption or meaningful correlations with little or no need of information concerning the data's domain of origin. As McQuillan (2018, 261) puts it, 'events in data science are constituted not from experience, but from those traces of experience that can be datafied'. To the opposite, observation is phenomenologically rich. Sound, vision or touch are not only sensuously different but what they reveal about their domain of origin is central to the knowledge gained through observation. In empiricism, observation is not only prior to theory, it is also prior to (its abstraction into) data.

One of the consequences of the focus on algorithms that can explore data independently of their domain of origin, is that the division of science into distinct domains of inquiry becomes less fundamental. This could be viewed as 'reductionism with a vengeance', an extreme form of the 'Unity of Science' project, where one discipline, data science, can provide authoritative answers in all areas of research. Reductionism, however, concerns inter-theoretic relations while here it is precisely the importance of domain specific theories that is being challenged by the idea of an effective procedure that has wide ranging, or even like the master algorithm universal, competence to extract knowledge from data. While reductionism postulated the primacy of basic physics and an epistemological hierarchy of sciences that reflected the ontological structure of the universe, the claims of big data radically challenge both that hierarchy and its underlying ontology.

From these authors' point of view, big data and associated technologies promise a new science that is not hierarchically structured internally, in which there are no fundamental disciplines, only a meta-discipline, data science, where the ability to recognize cancerous cells from benign tumors sits on par with the knowledge of the optimal price of toothpaste relative to dental floss. In this new science the ontology of basic material components is replaced by a dualist metaphysics that has recently been described as a form of Neoplatonism (McQuillan 2018) where mathematical forms are more 'real' than their various concrete instances.

BIG DATA: MACHINE LEARNING AND MACHINE SCIENCE

Big data are associated with data-driven agency because the wealth of data that is now available is considered fundamental to the growing ability of artificial agents to reach intelligent decisions and to the progress of machine learning. It also claims to represent the vanguard of machine learning and of what it can do. This section then will mostly focus on big data, but essential points of the arguments apply to machine learning in general. The term big data is rather ill-defined and the 'big' in big data generally refers to the digital space necessary to record and store the data, which can be of the order of terabytes or even petabytes, though it is often much smaller (Kitchin and McArdle 2016, 6). Big data are also characterized by the methods and technology which allow us to extract valuable results from these sets of data, making big data a part of cognitive computing, data science and what Symons and Alvorado (2016, 2) define as software intensive science (SIS).

Apart from the data sets themselves and the methods for exploring them, the term also refers to practices and strategies motivated by or in relation to the collection and exploitation of these very large sets of data. In most popular presentations the term big data indistinctly refers to all three: the data sets, the mining procedures and the policies/strategies.[3] As Beer (2016) puts it, big data is both a concept and a phenomenon. Two reasons conspire to encourage this double lack of distinction, between the data sets and the procedures on the one hand, and the first two and the associated commercial or social policies on the other. The first reason is conceptual; considering the data as inseparable from the means to obtain knowledge from them is consistent with a conception of knowledge as contained in the data and of deriving knowledge from data as bringing out what is already there. The second is technological; big data cannot exist without the very tools that implement the policies or strategy guided by big data. Data-driven agents are among the instruments that collect the data.

Big data sets are often considered to be a 'by-product' of business and administrative systems, of social networks, and internet traffic.[4] They result from multiform activities which, due to central aspects of modern ICT, leave traces, footprints or trails on the internet or in various data bases. If many of these traces correspond to explicit actions – making a phone call or buying a book – others correspond to what can be described as 'low intentionality acts', like clicking on an ad or viewing a website for a fraction of a second. Such acts are considered 'low intentionality' because they do not always involve a conscious intention. Data sources do not distinguish among clicking on an ad out of curiosity, because one is attracted by the design, because one is interested in the product advertised, or simply sliding the mouse over it by accident. Low intentionality acts are considered as meaningful data, rather than noise. Thus, big data are, it is argued, simply 'found' rather than the product of a specific inquiry, like a census or a sociological questionnaire, and this is viewed as a form of superiority over these classical methods of collecting data. The data sets may be explored with specific hypotheses in mind when they are mined to extract knowledge,[5] but, the argument goes, no such hypotheses presided over the collection of the data. Hence, a high variety, a wide range and diversity of data sources which corresponds to what Schönberger and Cukier (2014) define as the messiness of the data. Because data sets obtained in this way can be upgraded in real time as data are directly and automatically collected from net traffic, phone calls or financial transactions, big data is also defined by its high velocity. Finally, given that the data becomes available as a 'by-product' of other activities, it is cheap and there is no other limit to the quantity of data collected than storing capacities.

These characteristics[6] are viewed as fundamental to what makes big data so special. First, the absence of guiding hypotheses in the collection and exploration of data, the fact that they are a by-product of other activities[7] and often based on low intentionality acts, are central to the frequent claim of its advocates that big data allow us to 'by-pass causality'.[8] Ordinary statistics compile data in view of causal hypotheses concerning interrelations between different variables. They may confirm or infirm these hypotheses, but they are unlikely to discover something new, something that is outside the frame defined by the hypotheses that guided their collection. To the opposite, the variety of sources, the amount of data and the fact that the collection of big data is not constrained by specific hypotheses make it possible to discover surprising and unexpected correlations, when the data are explored by the appropriate algorithm. As Mayer-Schönberger and Cukier (2014, 14) write: 'Big data is about *what* not *why*. We don't always need to know the cause of a phenomena; rather, we can let the data speak for itself'. Second, the fact that the data 'arise' as a by-product of other activities, that traces are collected without agents being aware that they are leaving a trail behind is the basis of the claim that the data can be trusted, that it 'does not lie', which is at the heart of many popular books that extol the revolutionary potential of big data.[9] Unlike responses to polls or questionnaires big data can be trusted, it is claimed, because agents do not have to worry about what others may think or what is the right thing to say; because they do not have any reason, or even the possibility, to hide anything.

These contentions concerning the objectivity, neutrality and trustfulness of the data sets are central to the political positioning of big data as a means to develop sound social knowledge and able to provide new innovative solutions to many existing problems. These characteristics of big data and the idea that it is about the *what* rather than the *why*, and that it can tease out 'valuable recommendations without knowing the underlying causes' (Mayer-Schönberger and Cukier 2014, 52) raise, however, a number of issues.

The first question therefore concerns the 'valuable recommendations' that can be teased out of the data, for even if big data arise as a 'by-product' of other activities it does not follow that their collection is entirely accidental, neither partial nor biased. Big data is retrieved from business and administrative systems, social networks and net traffic in general, but this is not done without any reason. Much of the data are collated, explored and mined in view of specific business and administrative purposes, focusing on the buying habits of internet users, their reactions to different types of advertisement, what they read online, what sites they visit, their on-line friends, the history of their shopping, the relevance of a person's medical record to insurance companies; or on claims made by welfare recipients or on the performance of teachers in schools. Even if the data does 'arise' accidentally and as a by-product of other activities, there clearly is nothing accidental in compiling, storing and treating it. These data are compiled and used for commercial purposes, like marketing, advertisement, fraud protection and differential pricing (Ezrachi and Stucke 2016); for administrative purposes, to evaluate performance (O'Neil 2016); for purposes of governance, to determine who is entitled to social help (Eubanks 2017). As many authors have shown big data can lie, they can misrepresent the world; they are often partial and biased.

The second closely related issue rather than what makes a recommendation valuable, concerns the data themselves. According to Kelleher and Tierney (2018, 77) data science 'encompasses a set of principles, problem definitions, algorithm and processes for extracting nonobvious and useful patterns from large data sets'. Where the data come from is apparently outside the scope of the discipline. Its focus is on the data itself; on how large sets of data can be mined and analyzed to discover non-evident and valuable correlations. As is explicit in the idea of a master algorithm, where the data is from or what it is about is of little importance. Because similar methods and procedures can be used to treat sets of data from widely different domains, there is, especially in the social domain, a temptation to transform this methodological advantage into an ontological truth and to claim that data is enough. However, as data scientists know, what constitutes a valuable correlation, or a useful pattern, is inevitably related to what the data is about, to the domain from which it comes and, as Judea Pearl has long argued, require causal hypotheses.[10]

BIG DATA IN THE NATURAL SCIENCES AND THE SOCIAL DOMAIN

In natural sciences, extremely large sets of data have been around for quite a while, though until recently they were not generally referred to as big data. For example, already in the early 1990s the Diffused Infrared Background Experiment of the NASA Cosmic Background Explorer satellite produced 160 million measurements in a 26 week period and the Human Genome Project (HGP), the mapping of the human genome carried out from 1990 to 2003, involved 500 million trillion base to base comparisons. In current experiments, fluid flow data can be recorded up to every one thousandth of a second (Humphreys 2004, 7). Extremely large sets of data for 30 or 40 years have played a central role in the growth of our knowledge in many natural sciences. A recent article in *Big Data and Society* analyzes the important differences between how big data function in natural science and the way it is used to address social issues.[11] Interestingly, at the core of the authors' argument is the fact that in sciences like high-energy physics or the omic sciences[12] in biology the data which make up the very large sets are not 'found' but 'crafted'.

Very large data sets in natural sciences, as in the social domain, are inseparable from the use of machines. Computers, of course, but also many other machines which are specific to the domain of research from where the data comes, like the robotic synthesis of molecules, automated DNA sequencing, automated data collection and reduction in astronomy, automated detection of particles in accelerators, or magnetic resonance imagery. In biology, in physics, astronomy, medical sciences, big data does not 'arise' by accident. It is explicitly collected using sophisticated methods and machines, instruments that have been designed for that purpose. Furthermore, the data that is 'crafted' is authenticated as sound and relevant in two ways. First, specialists familiar with the domain and its theories either record the data themselves or control measurements or readings, and they collectively have the authority to determine what constitute data and what does not. Second, the data is then transformed by informaticians who either belong to the discipline itself, as in high-energy physics, or have come to constitute a sub-discipline, as have bioinformaticians.[13]

In all cases in the natural sciences, the locus of interpretation of the data remains within the discipline itself. Both what constitutes data and how it should be interpreted are under the collective jurisdiction of specialists of the domain and that final authority is recognized by governments, funding agencies and the general public.

This is not what happens in the social domain. First, the data that is said to be a by-product of other activities is not, as we have previously seen, simply found but explicitly sought for a variety of reasons. It is not however 'crafted' in the sense of being validated and authenticated by the community of concerned researchers. As a consequence, second, anyone who has the necessary technical competence gains the authority to interpret the data, to declare what the data show or prove. When we come to the social field expertise in data science is considered sufficient to make authoritative pronouncements on social issues or to orient policies. To the opposite, in natural sciences informatic competence is viewed as a tool at the service of research and results are interpreted by specialists in the relevant domain of research, not by data experts.[14]

A recent example can help to illustrate the importance of this difference and show that the two phenomena, 'found' data and the displacement of the authority to interpret result from experts in the domain to data specialists, are closely related. In 2016 X. Wu and X. Zhang posted on *arXiv* an article entitled 'Automated Inference on Criminality Using Face Images' which reports results of an experiment where they trained an automated system to recognize criminals from non-criminals based on still images of faces only. They claimed that discriminating features for predicting criminality had been found by machine learning which was free from the biases and prejudices of human observers.[15] Apart from the dubious presuppositions on which this research rests and its many problems, the most egregious mistake concerns the data itself. Wu and Zhang used 1856 facial images of real persons divided in two categories: criminal and non-criminal. The criminal category comprised 730 images of criminals, but we are also told that 330 of them were published as wanted suspects by the ministry of public security of China and it is therefore not entirely clear how many images were of convicted criminals and how many of wanted suspects. Images of the other category were taken from the internet and said to represent a wide variety of professions and social groups. All images are of Chinese males aged 18 to 55. The evident problem is that conviction and criminality are not equivalent (and even less being a wanted suspect). Many criminals are never convicted, and innocents are sometimes convicted. Should we conclude then that machine learning has found discriminating features for predicting criminal conviction?!

As far as social knowledge is concerned – knowledge about criminality – it is impossible to make sense of this result. It is properly meaningless. The data was found on the internet or published by police departments and the result, the ability to automatically predict criminality on the basis of facial images, is deemed to be as evident and factual as the found data. Just as it is obvious that images of convicted criminals are images of criminals and images randomly found on the internet are images of 'ordinary' people, if an automated system can learn to properly classify these images into those two groups and identify discriminating features between them, is it not obvious that it can predict criminality on the basis of facial images? This is not simply the problem identified by the first rule of data science, 'garbage in, garbage out', as the problem is primarily what constitutes data for a specific research, in this case on criminality. It is no accident that among the 40 references of Wu and Zhang's article not one is to a publication in criminology. No other expertise than knowledge of computer science is apparently necessary to claim having developed an automated system able to predict criminality on the basis of facial images.

Beyond this specific article, that some may wish to dismiss as simply bad science, the point is that data need to be interpreted as do results based on them. Data, especially so-called 'found' data does not speak for itself. What can be known with the help of artificial cognitive systems is the result of complex interactions between such machines and scientific communities. Without machines to record them big data would not exists, and without artificial cognitive systems to organize, analyze and present the data in an amenable form, we would not be able to understand it (Humphreys 2004, 7–8). Artificial cognitive systems have brought about an important transformation in the way science is practised and understood: human epistemic abilities have ceased to be the ultimate arbiter of scientific knowledge (Humphreys 2004, 53). However, if human epistemic abilities are not the *ultimate* arbiter of scientific knowledge anymore, nonetheless without these abilities there is no knowledge or at least no science as we have understood it until now. The classifiers developed by Wu and Zhang can discriminate between the two groups of facial images in their data, there is cognition here, the system has learned, but is there knowledge?

WHO KNOWS WHAT AND HOW?

'If evolution can learn us', writes Domingos (2015, 28–9) 'it can conceivably also learn everything that can be learned, provided we implement it on a powerful enough computer'. What does it mean to say that evolution can 'learn' us? What does to 'learn' someone mean? This curious use of 'learn' is revealing. Domingos views evolution as a stunning example of how much a simple algorithm can achieve.[16] However, the algorithm here is not evolution, which rather corresponds to the results, but natural selection, the procedure that brings about evolution. Therefore, in keeping with this image, it would seem more appropriate to say that natural selection can 'learn' us, but to say that natural selection can 'learn' us is simply to say that it can *produce* us. To know or to learn here is to do.

Similarly, a neural network is deemed to have learned when it can produce a certain type of result. For example, when it can 'recognize' with a high level of success pictures that contain a horse. 'Recognize' means to be able to separate pictures which have horses from others where no horse is present. Does that mean that the system knows what a horse is or that it has a concept of a horse? Not anymore than Wu and Zhang's classifiers need to have a concept of criminality. To know, or for a system to have 'learned' is for it to be a *data-driven agent* that successfully performs a given task. The claim that there is nothing else to knowledge than data and that all knowledge can be derived from data without any theories or hypotheses is equivalent to the claim that to know something is to be able to perform a given task.

It is clear that not everyone in the community of data scientists, among those working in computer science and machine learning, share this conception of knowledge which implies the immediate association of knowing and doing. However, the close relationship between machine learning and agency runs deeper. It does not only reflect a conception of knowledge or science that is favoured by some, it is inherent in the artificial cognitive systems that not only profoundly transformed science but also played a central role in the progress of our knowledge during the last 40 or 50 years. Without these artificial cognitive systems our science would be quite different than it is and a lot less performant. There are at least three ways in which these systems tend to identify learning with doing or knowing with the ability to perform a given task.

First is what may be called their epistemic impenetrability. As Paul Humphreys (2004) argues, the many machines and artificial cognitive systems that have become indispensable to contemporary scientific knowledge are not epistemically transparent. There are two reasons why this is the case. One is that we cannot reproduce, to check them, the million lines of calculation a machine does to arrive at a numerical solution of a problem that does not have an analytical solution. The other is that many models, for example in climate change, are so complex, include so many variables, that no one can have a complete representation of the model and know exactly how it works, how it obtains the results it obtains. We need to implement it on a machine and make it run to see what happens.[17] We calibrate the model by using it to make 'predictions' concerning past climate change, but do not always know why modifying this or that parameter brings about better or worse results. The epistemic impenetrability of these systems, machines responsible for automated DNA sequencing or the robotic synthesis of molecules, ultimately forces us to evaluate them on their performance. The fact that they are not epistemically transparent does not mean that they are perfectly obscure, but it does mean that we cannot always provide a reason for why an answer is correct.

The second is what some data scientists named 'insight through opacity' (McQuillan 2018, 257) a phenomenon which reflects a fundamental aspect of artificial cognitive systems. Unlike the opacity that comes from intentional corporate or state secrecy, or that which results from the lack of technical know-how, this form of opacity 'stems from the mismatch between mathematical optimization in high-dimensionality characteristic of machine learning and the demands of human-scale reasoning and styles of semantic interpretation' (Burrell 2016, 2). This opacity corresponds to our inability to understand how the algorithm operates on the data both because of the complexity of the data and because as it learns the algorithm evolves. In consequence, a network will abstract its own hidden features, which can be very effective, but which are by definition hidden from the engineer, and if inspected they may well turn out to be meaningless when 'translated' into human reasoning. In such cases we fail to know how the systems 'knows' or 'learns'; we can only measure its success at performing the desired task.

Finally, algorithms are to some extent strange mathematical objects. Unlike theorems or equations, they cannot be demonstrated, proven or solved. Data analysis is not involved in demonstration from axioms. As Lowrie (2017, 6) writes 'algorithms are developed by their assembly within computational architectures and the social evaluation of their inputs and outputs with respect to some real-world set of tasks'. Ultimately an algorithm either works or it doesn't. It is essentially through its performance as a technical object that we gain knowledge of it as an epistemic object. Whether or not this is because in the final analysis an algorithm is an abstract representation of a task to be accomplished, the main point is that here also performance and knowing appear to be inseparable.

How do machines know then? Clearly, to know for them is to successfully execute a given task. The task has to be rigorously defined and delimited in order for the machine to succeed. What that task means however is – at this point at least – beyond the scope of what the machine 'knows' or can learn. It depends on the community of those who use the machine. On what they want from it and on what they want: knowledge, individually calibrated drug prescription, an augmented sales volume, help in sentencing, etc. In the case of cancer research, of individually calibrated drug prescription and of the biomedical sciences in general, big data is not simply found, it is deeply crafted.[18] This crafting of the data depends on an extensive range of collectively held expertise which authoritatively decide what constitutes data and what cannot be accepted as such. The crafting of data depends on theories, on recognized expertise and the technical competence of specialists in the field.

This is what claims to the effect that the advent of 'big data has rendered the scientific method obsolete' (Anderson 2008) fail to recognize and understand. It leads to short-circuiting the relationship between data and agency, to the illusion that data can speak by itself. Thus, the close relationship between knowing and doing in machine learning has often been interpreted in the social domain as a means of avoiding human judgement. Seeing this escape for human judgement as good, as a way of escaping human biases and prejudices, or as bad, as abandoning our responsibility, misses the point in both cases. The close relationship between knowing and doing that is at the heart of artificial cognitive systems is not an obstacle to human judgement and responsibility or a replacement thereof. Rather, as we can see from the example of the natural sciences, it calls for more elaborate and sophisticated human judgement and interventions. Similarly, in the social domain the growth of data-driven agency should be understood as requiring more rather than less exercise of judgement. Even though this goes against the grain of popular and economic pronouncements concerning this type of technology we should consider its development as providing an opportunity to gain a greater mastery over our future and reflect anew on what it means to know.

NOTES

1. Cognitive computing (CC) refers to technology platforms broadly based on the scientific disciplines of artificial intelligence and signal processing. They encompass machine learning, big data, reasoning, natural language processing, speech recognition and vision (object recognition), human–computer interaction, dialogue and narrative generation, among other technologies. While there is no agreed upon definition of cognitive computing, it seems at present to be the most general term to refer to the various forms of cognitive underpinning of data driven agencies.
2. See for example: Anderson (2008), Clark (2013), Dyche (2012), Mayer-Schönberger and Cukier (2014), Prensky (2009) and Steadman (2013).
3. For example, Domingos (2015), Mayer-Schönberger and Cukier (2014), Seth-Davidowitz (2017), Rudder (2014).

4. See Hammer et al. (2017).
5. According to some authors the absence of such hypotheses is what makes Big Data different from ordinary data mining and machine learning. See Delort (2015).
6. High volume, high variety and high velocity are often described as the three Vs characteristic of Big Data.
7. The term 'by-product' is ambiguous in this context as it may be argued that, for example, the data concerning a financial transaction, or a sale is not a by-product, but a direct result of the operation itself. This is true, but that the data is collated and recorded does not result from some explicit endeavour as in a survey; it is the simple consequence of the fact that the internet automatically keeps traces of all actions, low intentionality or not, that result in web traffic. That is why it is viewed as a by-product, nobody decided that we need to keep or collect this data, that is also why it is cheap and why the only limit to how much data may be recorded and stored is storage space.
8. See Tovar (2016).
9. See note 6 above.
10. See among others, Pearl and Mackenzie (2018) and Pearl (2009).
11. Bartlett et al. (2018).
12. 'Omic sciences' refers to genomics (study of genes), transriptomics (mRNA), proteomics (proteins), metabolomics (metabolites).
13. Bartlett et al. (2018, 5).
14. Bioinformaticians, for example, often agree that they cannot provide a biological interpretation of the result they found. See Bartlett et al. (2018, 12).
15. Wu and Zhang (2016, 4).
16. See also Domingos (2015, 121–42).
17. See Fox-Keller (2002) for a different but complementary analysis of this situation.
18. See for example, Scheuermann et al. (2009) and Arp, Smith and Spear (2015).

REFERENCES

Anderson, C. 2008. 'The End of Theory: The Data Deluge Makes the Scientific Method Obsolete'. *Wired Magazine*, 23 June. <www.wired.com/2008/06/pb-theory/>

Arp, R., B. Smith and A. Spear. 2015. *Building Ontologies with Basic Formal Ontologies*. Cambridge, MA: MIT Press

Bartlett, A., J. Lewis, L. Reyes-Galindo and N. Stephens. 2018. 'The Locus of Legitimate Interpretation of Big Data: Lessons for Computational Social-Sciences from -Omic Biology and High-Energy Physics'. *Big Data & Society* January–June. doi:10.1177/2053951718768831

Beer, D. 2016. 'How Should We Do the History of Big Data?' *Big Data & Society*. January–June. doi:10.1177/2053951716646135

Burrell, J. 2016. 'How the Machine "Thinks": Understanding Opacity in Machine Learning Algorithms'. *Big Data & Society* January–June. doi:10.1177/2053951715622512

Canali, S. 2016. 'Big Data, Epistemology and Causality: Knowledge In and Knowledge Out in EXPOsOMICS'. *Big Data & Society*. July–December. doi:10.1177/2053951716669530

Clark, L. 2013. 'No Questions Asked: Big Data Firm Maps Solutions Without Human Input'. *Wired Magazine*, 16 January. <www.wired.co.uk/news/archive/2013-01/16/ayasdi-big-data-launch>

Delort, P. 2015. *Le Big Data*. Paris: PUF

Domingos, P. 2015. *The Master Algorithm. How the Quest for the Ultimate Learning Machine Will Remake Our World.* New York, NY: Penguin Books

Dyche, J. 2012. 'Big Data 'Eurekas!' Don't Just Happen'. *Harvard Business Review Blog.* 20 November. <http://blogs.hbr.org/cs/2012/11/eureka_doesnt_just_happen.html>

Eubanks, V. 2017. *Automating Inequality. How High-Tech Tools Profile, Police and Punish the Poor.* New York, NY: St Martin's Press

Ezrachi, A. and M. E. Stucke. 2016. *Virtual Competition. The Promise and Perils of Algorithm-Driven Economy.* Cambridge, MA: Harvard University Press

Fox-Keller, E. 2002. 'Models, Simulation and "Computer Experiments"' in *The Philosophy of Scientific Experimentation*, edited by Hans Radder. Pittsburgh, PA: Pittsburgh University Press

Hammer, C. L., D. C. Kostroch, G. Quiros and the STA Internal Group. 2017. 'Big Data: Potential Challenge and Statistical Implications'. *IMF Staff Discussion Note*, September

Humphreys, P. 2004. *Extending Ourselves: Computational Science, Empiricism and Scientific Method.* New York, NY: Oxford University Press

Kelleher, J. D. and B. Tierney. 2018. *Data Science.* Cambridge, MA: MIT Press

Kitchin, R. and G. McArdle. 2016. 'What Makes Big Data, Big Data? Exploring the Ontological Characteristics of 26 Datasets'. *Big Data & Society.* January–June. doi:10.1177/2053951716631130

Lowrie, I. 2017. 'Algorithmic Rationality: Epistemology and Efficiency in the Data Sciences'. *Big Data & Society.* January–June. doi:10.1177/2053951717700925

Mayer-Schönberger, V. and K. Cukier. 2014. *Big Data. The Revolution that Will Transform How We Live, Work and Think.* New York, NY: Mariner Books

McQuillan, D. 2018. 'Data Science as Machinic Neoplatonism' *Philos. Technol.* 31, 253–72. doi:10.1007/s13347-017-0273-3

O'Neil, C. 2016. *Weapons of Math Destruction. How Big Data Increases Inequality and Threatens Democracy.* New York, NY: Crown

Pearl, J. 2009. *Causality, Reasoning and Inference.* Cambridge: Cambridge University Press

Pearl, J. and D. Mackenzie. 2018. *The Book of Why: The New Science of Cause and Effect.* New York, NY: Basic Books

Prensky, M. 2009. 'H. Sapiens Digital: From Digital Immigrants and Digital Natives to Digital Wisdom'. *Innovate* 5(3). <www.innovateonline.info/index.php?view=article&id=705>

Rudder, C. 2014. *Dataclysm. Who We Are When We Think No One's Looking.* New York, NY: Crown Publishers

Scheuermann, R. H., M. Kong, C. Dahlke, J. Cai 1, J. Lee 1, Y. Qian, B. Squires, P. Dunn, J. Wiser, H. Hagler, B. Smith and D.d. Karp. 2009. 'Ontology Based Representation of Metadata in Biological Data Mining' in *Biological Data Mining* edited by J. Chen and S. Lonardi 529–59. Boca Raton, FL: Chapman Hall / Taylor and Francis

Seth-Davidowitz, S. 2017. *Everybody Lies, Big Data, New Data and What the Internet can tell about Who We Really Are.* New York, NY: Dey Street

Steadman, I. 2013. 'Big Data and the Death of the Theorist'. *Wired Magazine*, 25 January. <www.wired.co.uk/news/archive/2013-01/25/big-data-end-of-theory>

Symons, J. and R. Alvarado. 2016. 'Can we trust Big Data? Applying Philosophy of Science to Software'. *Big Data & Society.* July–December. doi:10.1177/2053951716664747

Tovar, E. 2016. 'Measuring Socio-Spatial Justice. From Statistics to Big Data – Promises and Threats'. *Justice spatiale – Spatial justice*, Université Paris Ouest Nanterre La Défense, <https://halshs.archives-ouvertes.fr/halshs-01507168/document>

Wu, X. and X. Zhang 2016. 'Automated Inference on Criminality Using Face Images' *arXiv.org digital archives*, November 2016, the latest version with response to their critics is from May 2017 arXiv:1611.04135v3

4. The emergent limbic media system
Julie E. Cohen

INTRODUCTION

The emergence of the platform as the core organizational logic of the networked information economy (Cohen, 2019) and the accompanying proliferation of infrastructures for data harvesting, predictive profiling and behavioural microtargeting have profoundly reshaped both patterns of information flow and capabilities for participation in social and commercial life. The changes upend settled ways of understanding the nature and social function of media technologies – and therefore challenge conventional wisdom about the appropriate roles(s) for law in relation to media and information.

For several hundred years, political philosophers and legal theorists have conceptualized media technologies as 'technologies of freedom' (De Sola Pool 1983), arguing that access to information and to the means of communication promotes reason, self-determination and democratic self-government. Internet policy research and activism have overwhelmingly adopted that framing. Certainly, access to information, the capacity for reason, self-determination and democratic self-government are inescapably interrelated, but other aspects of the interrelationship between media technologies, reason and democracy have changed beyond recognition. As communications theorist Mark Andrejevic (2013, 9–10) explains, our most deeply rooted instincts about the role of information in a democratic society 'took shape during an era of relative information scarcity', and so many defining political battles 'revolve[d] around issues of scarcity and the restriction of access to information'. Today's networked digital information infrastructures have different and more complicated affordances. In contemporary conditions of infoglut – of 'an unimaginably unmanageable flow of mediated information ... available to anyone with Internet access' (ibid, 2–3) – new political and epistemological dilemmas flow instead from abundance and algorithmic intermediation. The problem is not scarcity but rather the need for new ways of cutting through the clutter, and the re-siting of power within platforms, databases and algorithms means that meaning is easily manipulated.

The quest for data-intensive surplus extraction that characterizes the surveillance economy (Cohen 2018, Zuboff 2015) has spurred development of a fast-evolving collection of techniques designed to undercut the exercise of informed reason by users of networked information services. Contemporary, platform-based information infrastructures and ecosystems are being optimized to detect behavioural cues and to appeal to motivation and emotion on a subconscious level. That gradual but seemingly inexorable shift has begun to produce object lessons in the law of unintended consequences. Widespread dispersal of personal information and lack of control over the conditions for its storage and access have engendered unprecedented vulnerability to fraud, harassment and sabotage. Algorithmically-mediated processes designed to create tight stimulus-response feedback loops have exposed and deepened social divides on a variety of cultural and political issues, fostering unprecedented politicization of public discourse and rapid erosion of the will to find or make common ground. The result is an information environment that magnifies the vulnerability of ordinary citizens to reputational and financial harm, manipulation and political disempowerment.

This chapter, adapted from my recent book on legal institutions and the political economy of informationalism (Cohen, 2019), explores the patterns of information flow within the platform-based, massively-intermediated information environment. Both to structure that exploration and by way of provocation, I offer the following analogy: the operation of the digital information environment has begun to mimic the operation of the collection of brain structures that mid-twentieth-century neurologists christened the limbic system and that play vital roles in a number of precognitive functions, including emotion, motivation and habit-formation.[1] I do not mean to suggest that anything about the configuration or operation of the digital information environment is natural or organically determined. I seek simply to focus the reader's attention on the mismatch between the 'technologies of freedom' frame that dominates legal discussions about media law and policy and the kinds of responses that platform-based, massively-intermediated information infrastructures work to produce. In *The End(s)* (at 40), Mireille Hildebrandt posits the formation of a new 'digital unconscious' that constitutes the field of operation for the emergence of 'data-driven agency' – agency that is 'mindless,' algorithmically generated and directed toward 'ubiquitous anticipation' (ibid, 67). Those characteristics also make the digital unconscious a field of operation for precognitive activation and manipulation at scale.

REPUTATION AS CAPITAL AND STIGMA

Within the platform-based, massively intermediated information environment, reputation has emerged as an explicit locus of self-management, a powerful motivator and a persistent source of anxiety. Self-presentation is an enduring human concern (Goffman 1959). Individuals have always devoted time to reputation work of one sort or another, building, cementing and sometimes undermining their standing in their communities. In the networked information age, however, reputation has become increasingly quantified and datafied, and reputational data and metrics are widely dispersed, flowing through channels far removed from individual control. As those shifts have occurred, the mechanisms for building and maintaining reputational capital and attempting to repair reputational damage have changed almost beyond recognition.

Today's quantified, datafied reputation metrics trace their origins to two mid-twentieth-century developments. The first was the emergence of the consumer reporting industry. The earliest consumer reporting entities were simply clearinghouses for collection and exchange of the sorts of information traditionally monitored by local lenders – salary, repayment history, and so on. As the volume of information mushroomed and as technological development produced new methods for storing and processing the information, market actors began to experiment with more efficient ways of formulating and expressing judgements about consumer creditworthiness and reliability (Lauer 2008, 2010). Those efforts led ultimately to metrics for quantified credit scoring (Poon 2007). Today, the revolution in processing power that began during the late-twentieth century has put the necessary computing resources to engage in consumer scoring within general reach, and the emergence of networked information architectures and the reconfiguration of those architectures to enable pervasive tracking and personalization have made flows of personal information ubiquitous and easy to capture. Contemporary consumer reputation metrics include a wide range of correlations, inferences and predictions generated by data mining and analysis (Robinson + Yu 2014).

Another historical precursor of contemporary quantified, datafied reputation metrics was the ratings systems developed during the mid-twentieth century to demystify markets in consumer goods and services. As mass-marketed goods and services increasingly displaced more local options, and as those goods and services became increasingly more complex and difficult for consumers to evaluate at the point of purchase, ratings systems such as those developed by *Consumer Reports* and *Good Housekeeping* emerged (Carsky et al. 1998, Rao 1998, Strach and Russell 2003). Those systems, often consisting of simple, five-point scales for communicating the results of more complicated product testing, are the conceptual antecedents of the customer satisfaction ratings that today are seemingly everywhere. Like credit scoring, however, ratings production is no longer the sole province of trained experts. Contemporary ratings systems claim a different kind of epistemic authority, located in the personal experiences of consuming subjects. Information businesses – including both general-purpose platforms such as Google and Yelp and specialized sites like TripAdvisor and OpenTable – compete with each other to develop crowd-sourced ratings and present them to consumers as valuable sources of information.

Within platform-based information environments, however, the ratings craze has spread beyond businesses and products to individuals themselves. An early pioneer in this regard was eBay, which developed the first widely-publicized system for aggregating user feedback on buyers and sellers (Knobel and Lankshear 2002). Contemporaneously, news and information sites like Slashdot began using feedback systems to help users make sense of the rapidly proliferating participatory universe. Slashdot designed its interface both to push more highly-rated comments to the top and to identify those users whose postings tended to be rated more highly (Bruns 2005, 31–52). Both models spread rapidly to other platform-based commercial and discussion fora, which developed variants suited to their own purposes. Meanwhile, computer scientists and legal academics have gravitated to the idea of crowd-sourced, peer-produced ratings as a panacea for a wide variety of social coordination problems ranging from driving to dating (Masum et al. 2011).

Both the personal data used for consumer reputation scoring and publicly-available reputation metrics are increasingly widely dispersed, and that has made network users vulnerable to new kinds of reputational harm. Crowd-sourced ratings systems and similar participation metrics are expressly designed to enable reputation-at-a-distance; for exactly that reason, though, such systems create new possibilities for gaming and abuse. The design and operation of social networking platforms also magnifies reputational vulnerability. Although in recent years social networking platforms such as Facebook have allowed users to indicate their preferences about sharing certain items and about identification and tagging in photos posted by others, it is impossible to prevent information posted to a social network from spreading beyond its point of origin.

Neither the growing importance of datafied reputational constructs nor the new vulnerabilities they generate have been lost on network users. Literatures from marketing to self-help to media studies reflect the emergence of an acutely reputation-inflected sensibility of self-presentation. Social media updates, for example, are less spontaneous and more carefully curated to accentuate the positive and enviable. Younger, 'born digital' network users in particular have developed and internalized elaborate rules of self-presentation (boyd 2014, Marwick and boyd 2014). Many older users, meanwhile, cultivate techniques of online reputation building that are highly instrumentalized, straightforwardly acknowledging that their point is to craft reputation as a factor of production. In part, that approach reflects the changing nature of production in the informational economy. Self-promotion is an essential survival skill for freelance information workers, and new data-based metrics of reputation – numbers of followers on Twitter or Instagram, numbers of views on YouTube, and so on – matter for success. It has become common to see self-proclaimed experts on self-management and self-promotion tutoring their readers on the best ways of maximizing and refining their own public exposure.

The paradoxical combination of heightened reputational sensibility and diminished control over reputational development creates and feeds a continual need for reputational maintenance and repair (Woodruff 2015). Predictably, maintenance and repair themselves have become business models. A new industry euphemistically titled 'search engine optimization' has emerged to serve the needs of both individuals and businesses seeking to burnish their public images and improve their visibility. Another industry, dedicated to credit monitoring and credit repair, responds to the increasing datafication of reputation and the prevalence of identity theft by offering individuals the promise of protection for a small monthly fee.

Although the language of reputation management and self-management is the language of individual choice, the new economies of reputation and reputation modelling distribute reputational authority and vulnerability unevenly. Information about reputation is plentiful, but decoding and effective intervention require specialized expertise. The technologies of curation and repair that offer to return some measure of control also change the nature of that control. Prior to the era of datafied, dispersed reputation, repairing damaged commercial and social reputation demanded sustained relational and communal engagement. The new processes of curation and repair substitute an individualized, commodified vision of reputation management as a market-centred activity pursued by individual neoliberal subjects (Brown 2003, May and McWhorter 2015).

SURVEILLANCE AS PARTICIPATION AND VIRTUE

Platform-based, massively-intermediated environments optimized for commercial surveillance also mobilize the digital unconscious to motivate enrolment and participation in the surveillance economy. Within commercial surveillance environments, the themes of play, games and participation are increasingly prominent.[2] The forms of play and gaming are highly organized and strategic and revolve around the idea of gamification, defined in business texts as the application of concepts and techniques from games to drive consumer 'engagement' that promotes business objectives in other areas of activity (Paharia 2013, Zichermann and Linder 2013). In gamified commercial surveillance environments, personal information is collected from subscribers both at enrolment and on a continual basis during the course of play, and that information is used not only to deliver rewards, but also and more importantly to engage in various forms of targeted marketing.

FourSquare, a social networking application used for sharing information about one's whereabouts, is generally credited with popularizing the idea of gamification as a data collection technique. For the first four years of its existence, FourSquare offered subscribers opportunities to compete for rewards, which took the form of badges that might designate a subscriber 'Mayor' of her favourite bar (for being a regular visitor) or 'Player Please' (for checking into the bar with three or more members of the opposite sex). That initial experiment inspired a broad and durable shift toward marketing strategies incorporating elements of play and game-based competition. For example, discount fashion retailer H&M, in partnership with an online gaming company, has used gamification to bring customers off the street and into its stores, offering those who are playing the game virtual items that can be scanned in the store to generate discounts. Nike+, a personal fitness tool, uses gamification to help its users set fitness goals, monitor their own progress and track their progress relative to that of other users.

As these examples illustrate, the gamification of commercial surveillance has roots in customer loyalty programmes that are decades old, but gamification rewards customer loyalty in a way that generates public, social recognition. The field of crowd-sourced promotion has its cautionary tales. Facebook's ill-fated Beacon service, which automatically coopted its members' social updates as promotion tools, sparked outrage that led to high-profile class action litigation (Singel 2008). Contrast, however, the experience of gamified promotion ventures that are shopping-oriented first and foremost. Groupon, a social shopping site, uses gamification – in the form of an anthropomorphic icon named 'Clicky' that entices users to pursue access to additional content and exclusive discounts – to incentivize bargain-hunters to visit the site more frequently. Groupon's early success can be traced to its founders' recognition that customers could absorb producer surplus and reveal information about their resources, their patterns of discretionary spending and their social networks at the same time.

After settling the Beacon litigation, Facebook used its newly developed 'Like' button to similar (but far more wide-ranging) effect (Zuboff 2018, 160–1, 457).

The gamification of commercial surveillance also has roots in the Quantified Self (QS) movement, which was founded in 2007 by a group of technology evangelists seeking better living through data; at the same time, however, it represents a significant cooptation of that movement. The initial impetus behind the QS movement was aggressively populist. QS entrepreneurs and communities offered participants the opportunity to shift control of health, diet and fitness away from impersonal providers offering cookie-cutter recommendations and back toward individuals (Wolf 2010, Singer 2011). Predictably, however, commercial providers of QS technologies and applications entered the field, offering services like the Nike+ fitness tracker described above. As they have done so, the dialogue around QS has shifted, deemphasizing control over data and emphasizing instead the need to provide and share data to gain tools for controlling other aspects of one's life, including health, diet and fitness, but also work habits, sex life, sleep patterns, and so on. Where the populist QS discourse was earnest and geeky, commercial QS products speak to lifestyle concerns in the language of marketing.

At its core, the gamification dynamic is a technique for supply chain management that aims to keep the commercial surveillance economy's data harvesting pipelines full and flowing. FourSquare emerged as social networking platforms were migrating into the economic mainstream and seeking sources of financing in capital markets. Its use of rewards as incentives for participants was both a strategy for achieving market penetration and a way of responding to potential investors' demands for a plausible revenue model. Here FourSquare is a cautionary tale because its gamification strategy proved unable to hold subscriber interest, and in 2013 it announced that it was abandoning its badge system (Rodriguez 2014). A different and more durable example of gamification within a social networking platform is the unending competition for followers, favourites and retweets on Twitter, which leverages a more intrinsic motivation for recognition and influence.

Gamification motivates enrolment in commercial surveillance environments by making surveillance participatory and pleasurable. Gamified surveillance environments are not games, but they are like games. They manifest both actions taken by the subject of gamified surveillance to perform the in-world rituals of gameplay – for example, to unlock benefits or 'level up' membership – and background machine actions that establish the environment for gameplay – for example, the repetitive background displays of status updates from other users or ticker updates offering a continual stream of discount opportunities (cf. Galloway 2006, 6–8). They also establish an external frame of reference for the gameworld – for example, by establishing a process for enrolment, defining tiers of membership and corresponding benefits, and imposing 'gamic death' upon logout (ibid).[3] But there are also profound differences between games and gamified surveillance environments. The gameworld purports to be the social world, or some segment of it, but its focus is on targeting and nudging patterns of discretionary spending and leisure mobility. Gamification techniques reconfigure their participants as depoliticized, neoliberal subjects who achieve both self-expression and self-realization through the purposive and playful exercise of consumptive freedom (Brown 2003, May and McWhorter 2015).

Gamified surveillance environments therefore also represent powerful mechanisms for behavioural conditioning. The 'token economies' characteristic of gamified surveillance environments have been used as a form of behaviourist therapy for psychiatric patients, preparing them for reintegration into society by giving them sets of situation-specific rituals to perform (Raczkowski 2013). In commercial surveillance environments, gamification takes on a similarly ameliorative gloss, inculcating repetitive behaviour patterns oriented toward self-betterment. As Jennifer Whitson (2013, 169) describes it, 'becoming the victorious subject of gamification is a never-ending leveling-up process, guided by a teleology of constant and continual improvement, driven by an unending stream of positive feedback and virtual rewards, and fuelled by the notion that this process is playful'. Additionally, both the dominant platforms that sit atop data harvesting ecologies and lesser designers of app-based services use insights gleaned from addiction research to design interfaces that will maximize user engagement (Alter 2017; Lewis 2017).

THE RISE OF BEHAVIOURAL MICROTARGETING

Other marketing and promotional activities, meanwhile, mobilize the digital unconscious to detect, prime, amplify and exploit emotional responses to informational content. From one perspective, such activities are broadly consistent with marketing's decades-long effort to claim for itself the status of a behavioural science (Bartels 1974, Jones and Shaw 2002). From another, new techniques for behavioural marketing, 'consumer neuroscience' and content optimization for 'user engagement' represent radical departures. Such techniques increasingly bypass persuasion and even awareness in favour of data-driven sensing and manipulation, and they target not only consumptive preferences but also cultural, political and religious affiliations and even basic frames for scientific, historical and journalistic understanding.

Marketers have long sought to appeal to consumers' emotions, and have long recognized that branding is powerful in part because of its capacity to encode subconscious appeal. As social beings, humans use behavioural and linguistic cues to signal their status and their affiliation with different economic, cultural and ideological tribes (Bourdieu 1984). Brand-related signalling continues those patterns but refracts them through an ethos of consumerist participation, creating de facto sumptuary hierarchies (Beebe 2010) through which consumers can signify their socioeconomic status and lifestyle preferences. Platform-based, massively-intermediated environments enable brands to become even further detached from the goods and services to which they notionally refer and to take on expressive lives of their own. The modern corporation does not simply advertise its wares. It develops a 'social media presence' on platforms like Facebook and Twitter, streaming updates to its followers about developments that might implicate its market or enhance its brand cachet. It also uses social media to develop gamified promotional strategies designed to recruit individual consumers as brand evangelists and reward them for their successes. Whereas individual reputation increasingly is expressed in quantified metrics that require specialized expertise to decode, the content of modern branding is memetic and compelling. It is propagated by means of compact, graphically intensive signifiers and catchy slogans and soundbites carefully designed to take root in consumers' subconscious minds.

Ultimately, however, brand-related strategies for consumer surplus extraction confront inherent limitations. First, consumers are not simply passive recipients of brand-related messaging. Some simply resist brand-related messaging, while others appropriate and remix logos, jingles and other promotional material to subvert such messaging in powerful and creative ways (Coombe 1998). The same platform-based media infrastructures that enable businesses to reach consumers also enable consumers to assign new meanings to brands and advertising copy and distribute their own messages widely. Second, even highly effective brand-related messaging must contend with contemporary conditions of infoglut, which make even those messages that (some) consumers want to receive difficult to distinguish from the millions of other pieces of information competing for their attention. As David Murakami Wood and Kirstie Ball (2013, 57) have explained, the certain access to consumer preferences that databases combining demographic information with information about buying behaviour appeared to promise is in important respects a mirage; like other techniques of governance, the constructed 'brandscapes' informed by such databases remain 'messy, contingent, and subject to failure'.

New techniques for behavioural microtargeting promise solutions to these problems. In other work (Cohen 2018; see also Zuboff 2018) I have described the emergence of data-intensive activities of profiling and predictive analysis and noted information businesses' increasingly heavy reliance on sensors embedded in browsers, smart objects and mobile devices to collect consumer data. The two sets of practices are mutually reinforcing. Within the predominantly behaviourist frame that animates contemporary practices of data-based surplus extraction, unmediated behavioural data – i.e., data that are not self-reported or otherwise subject to conscious manipulation by consumers – are the holy grail, promising previously unequalled accuracy in predictive forecasting and commensurate levels of profit. That logic dictates continuous experimentation with technologies for sensing, tracking and measuring consumer interests and activities within both physical and networked spaces. As Joseph Turow (2017) has described, supermarkets in particular have been pioneers in the use of techniques for tracking consumers' progress through physical stores and correlating patterns of movement and browsing with coupons and other offers. Online, both platform firms like Amazon, Facebook and Google and specialized digital advertising firms are continually experimenting with techniques designed to detect and record the minutest of pauses on a pageview or news item or the movements of a cursor hovering over a link. The resulting detailed simulacra of attention patterns can be folded into existing systems of predictive analytics and used to infer interests and personality traits. Mirroring these commercial experiments, academic literatures in marketing (Venkatraman et al. 2012, Plassmann et al. 2015), psychology (Kosinski et al. 2013, Youyou et al. 2015), and computer science (Huang et al. 2011) describe new research programmes designed to develop and test such techniques.

Other new marketing practices attempt to detect users' mental and emotional states and personalize promotional messages accordingly (Glenn and Monteith 2014, Pang and Lee 2008). Facebook in particular has acknowledged conducting various experiments involving use of linguistic analysis to detect users' emotional states. In 2014, a paper coauthored by a Facebook data scientist (Kramer et al. 2014) described a massive experiment in which Facebook varied items in users' newsfeeds and then used automated discourse analysis tools on those users' own subsequent posts to gauge the effects of the newsfeeds on their emotional states. In 2014, Facebook acknowledged having served different advertisements to teenaged girls and young women based on considerations such as detected levels of depression and dissatisfaction with self-image (Armstrong 2017).

Providers of online content, who earn advertising revenues in proportion to clicks and page views, have pursued methods of competing for attention and mindshare that harness both the insights of behavioural psychology and the properties of network organization. The reigning strategy, pioneered by the founders of sites like BuzzFeed and UpWorthy, involves content optimization for user engagement using teasers colloquially known as clickbait – 'a style of headline that explicitly tease[s] readers, withholding just enough information to titillate them into reading further' (Foer 2017, 139). Clickbait exploits a particular dimension of human curiosity: the dislike of being uninformed about something that everyone else already knows (Loewenstein 1994, 91). Users will engage with the content by clicking through the headline in order not to be left out of the loop, and they will share what they find after clicking with their networks as a way of signalling inclusion to others. They will stay on the platform longer and disconnect more rarely, if at all. In the wake of platform-driven cycles of consolidation and retrenchment in the print media industry, even long-established outlets for news and commentary now rely on services like Chartbeat, a platform for tracking clicks, likes and retweets, to help them refine their abilities to drive web traffic (Foer 2017, 144–6). One result is that media outlets of all types increasingly rush to cover the same topics, lean heavily on techniques for manufacturing instant outrage, and frame their appeals for attention in the same breathless, you-won't-believe-what-happened-next tone.

Platform-based providers of search, content aggregation and social networking services operate at the intersection of behavioural microtargeting and content optimization for engagement. So, for example, Google's search engine uses behavioural cues together with its accumulated wealth of data about users to anticipate the type of content users want to find and adjust both autocomplete recommendations and search results accordingly. Its content aggregation platform YouTube uses similar information to target video content; social networking providers like Facebook and microblogging platforms like Twitter function as de facto aggregators for a wide range of content and deliver feeds optimized to everything that is known or inferred about particular users' opinions and beliefs. That is where the law of unintended consequences kicks in. Within platform-based, massively-intermediated environments, the digital unconscious becomes a device for manipulating and activating subjectivity at scale (cf. Stark 2018, Couldry and Hepp 2017, 187). Platform-based intermediation alters collective behaviour in ways that have begun to produce large-scale societal effects.

AMPLIFYING COLLECTIVE UNREASON

Some of the most transformative effects of networked, platform-based media infrastructures concern the ways that they alter and amplify the capabilities and behaviours of groups. Networked, platform-based architectures enhance the ability to form groups and share information among members, to harness the wisdom and creativity of crowds, and to coalesce in passionate, powerful mobs. They also, however, magnify the dark side of each of these forms of affiliation, collective meaning-making and collective action. The spread of behavioural microtargeting techniques into the domains of political and civic discourse heightens the volatility of interactions in networked spaces, reinforcing tribal patterns of affiliation and exclusion, amplifying conspiracy theories and junk science, and driving the rapid propagation of narratives about ethnic nationalism, white supremacy and racial violence.

Platform-based digital infrastructures' affordances for collective meaning-making and collective action are widely recognized. Just as networked digital platforms have lowered the costs of identifying and connecting with commercial counterparties, so they also have lowered the costs of forming affinity groups of all kinds. Like their counterparts in real space, online affinity groups provide friendship, intellectual and emotional affirmation, and shared organizational capacity, but online affinity groups can extend over great distances and also can bridge other kinds of divides, connecting many who otherwise would not have met. The Internet era has witnessed the emergence of a vast, diverse and eclectic range of peer-based cultural production, ranging from open source software developed according to the maxim 'given enough eyeballs, all bugs are shallow' (Raymond 1999, 30) to wikis and fanworks reflecting multiple contributions. The landscape of networked collective action encompasses everything from spontaneous flash mobs to social action campaigns coordinated via Facebook pages, Twitter hashtags or reddits to digital infrastructures for facilitating both traditional charitable giving and new types of 'pay-it-forward' generosity. Networked information and communication technologies also have enabled the rapid organization of mass protests, such as those mobilized by the Occupy Wall Street and Black Lives Matter movements and by pro-democracy activists during the political uprisings of the Arab Spring (MacKinnon 2012, Freelon et al. 2016, Tufecki 2017).

The dominant cultural narratives about these cultural and political effects of platform-based interconnection have been celebratory, but other implications of the platform-based digital environment's affordances for affinity group formation, distributed peer production and collective action are less rosy. Distributed communities of peers have created and sustained robust and seemingly impermeable alternate realities rooted in conspiracy theories and virulent forms of ideological extremism. Crowd-based judgements about the relevance, credibility and urgency of online information can create cascades that lend sensationalized, false and hatred-inciting online material extraordinary staying power (Barton 2009, Kuran and Sunstein 1999), and those cascades can engender behaviours that cause both private and social harms.

Because of the way that platform-based, massively-intermediated environments work, networked spaces both expose and intensify political and ideological polarization around multiple, assertedly equivalent truths. That result stands in jarring contradiction to the utopianism of the early Internet pioneers, who assumed that expanded access to information online would usher in a new era of cosmopolitanism and enlightened tolerance. Platform-based intermediation promotes cosmopolitanism only to those users already inclined in that direction; to other users, it promotes other values. A wealth of social science research shows that more homogenous groups – whether online or off – more readily become polarized in both their beliefs and their perceptions of reality (Sunstein 2009). Algorithmic mediation of information flows intended to target controversial material to receptive audiences intensifies in-group effects, reinforcing existing biases, inculcating resistance to facts that contradict preferred narratives, and encouraging demonization and abuse of those who hold opposite beliefs and political goals (Quattrociocchi et al. 2016). People do encounter other perspectives online, but exposure to opposing views is more likely to trigger automatic, instinctual rejection and anger than it is to promote reasoned engagement. And platform affordances for volatility, engagement around sensationalized content and ideological polarization have fuelled the emergence of vast media ecosystems organized around extreme political views (Faris et al. 2016, Keegan 2016).

Relatedly, platform-based information feeds flatten communicative hierarchies in a way that underscores the relative unimportance of claims to objective and/or empirical authority. A Facebook or Twitter feed, for example, presents the reader with a continuous stream of content within which all sources are (or appear to be) equivalent. This diminishes the privileged position once held by major broadcast networks and national newspapers of record and invites both relativization and rejection of the possibility of objectivity; 'all so-called experts are biased, any account partial, all conclusions the result of an arbitrary and premature closure of the debate' (Andrejevic 2013, 12). Relativization fortifies alternate realities such as climate change denialism and anti-vaccination crusades and the echo chambers that support them (Wong 2019). At the same time, information abundance generates new types of power asymmetries that revolve around differential access to data and to the ability to capture, store and process it on a massive scale. Under such conditions, techniques of critique and deconstruction increasingly become tools of powerful interests seeking to advance their own agendas (ibid, 15–18, Albright 2018).

Platform affordances for cascade-based diffusion, polarization and relativization are easily manipulated and weaponized. As is now widely known, in the months preceding the 2016 US presidential election, websites peddling 'fake news' stories – such as allegations that Democratic candidate Hillary Clinton and her campaign manager, John Podesta, were running a child pornography ring out of the basement of a Washington DC pizza restaurant (Graham 2016) – earned their distributors millions of dollars in advertising revenues. According to their own statements, some distributors had no particular political axe to grind, but instead were simply exploiting the affordances of the network for profit (Subramanian 2017). Other stories were sponsored by hostile state actors, and still others were sponsored by wealthy and highly motivated domestic interests seeking to reinforce and widen existing partisan divides (Solon and Siddiqui 2017, Cadwalladr and Graham-Harrison 2018). As they had hoped, groups predisposed to believe the worst of Clinton and her team shared, up-voted and retweeted the stories. Experts in election law and digital voting, watching carefully for signs of fraudulent tampering with digital voting machines, were unprepared for new kinds of digital tampering that took aim directly at voters' minds. Arguably, no-one should have been surprised; both the earlier 'Brexit' vote in the United Kingdom and the Russian military and political incursions in Ukraine had followed a similar pattern (Cadwalladr 2017, Paul and Matthew 2016).

Platform affordances also have fuelled upsurges in identity-based harassment, nationalism and organized hate. Affordances for networked collective action enable the rapid, ad hoc formation of angry, vengeful mobs, eager to shame real or apparent transgressors. Pioneering works by Danielle Citron (2014) in law and by Whitney Phillips (2015) in media studies explore the ways that networked, massively-intermediated spaces reinforce and magnify the power of crowds to target selected individuals and groups. More generally, investigations by multiple teams of researchers have shown that ethnic nationalism and organized hate against racial and religious minorities are on the rise, aided by algorithmic processes that amplify bigoted diatribes, magnify conspiracy theories and propel coded memes into the limelight (Angwin et al. 2017, Marwick and Lewis 2017, Potok 2017). Nativist hate-mongering bleeds inexorably into political discourse and public life. The pro-Brexit vote was influenced in part by narratives about the cultural and economic consequences of uncontrolled migration, and similar themes continue to shape elections across Europe (Polakow-Suransky 2016). In the Trump-era US, nationalist and white supremacist ideologies have burst into the open, adopting sophisticated and ironic new forms, gaining in strength as outraged responses generate new information cascades, and fuelling the rise of the self-designated 'alt-right' as a political force (Nagle 2017).

The increasingly unreasoning and often vicious character of interaction in online, platform-based digital environments complicates accounts of the democratizing potential of information networks. Networked, platform-based information and communication technologies are crowd-enhancers; they boost the amplitude of collective actions and counter-actions. Undeniably, such technologies have important affordances for bottom-up organizing, collective creativity and crowd-sourced, democratic action. Collective meaning-making and collective action, however, can be directed toward a variety of ends. The particular configurations that networked digital information infrastructures have assumed within the political economy of informational capitalism also make them sites of extraordinary divisiveness and manipulability, creating new risks to the human project of democratic, inclusive, sustainable coexistence.

CONCLUSION

The scope and content of media law and policy are contested for a wide variety of reasons that are beyond the scope of this chapter. An essential first step in making sound media policy for the networked information era, however, is understanding the ways that platform-based, massively-intermediated information infrastructures function and the range of effects they produce. This chapter has highlighted interrelated sets of effects that should concern law- and policy-makers. Rather than predominantly stimulating the development and exercise of conscious and deliberate reason, today's networked information flows are gradually being optimized for subconscious, affective appeal. Some processes originating in the 'digital unconscious' produce new subjectivities oriented toward consumerist self-care; others leverage and reinforce fear and anger, producing new subjectivities and collectivities oriented toward polarization and tribalism. All portend far-reaching collateral effects on the emerging information society and the subjects who inhabit it.

NOTES

1. For an overview, see MacLean (1955). Current models of the nervous system have moved beyond rigid functional segregation to recognize that, for example, the neurological processes that produce learning and memory extend across multiple brain regions (e.g., McGaugh et al. 1996). Within those models, however, the structures in the limbic region remain pivotal.
2. This section is adapted from Cohen (2016).

REFERENCES

Albright, J. 2018. 'Untrue-Tube: Monetizing Misery and Disinformation'. *Medium*, 25 Feb. 2018, <https://medium.com/@d1gi/untrue-tube-monetizing-misery-and-disinformation-388c4786cc3d>

Alter, A. 2017. *Irresistible: The Rise of Addictive Technology and the Business of Keeping Us Hooked*. University Park, PA: Penn State University Press

Andrejevic, M. 2013. *Infoglut: How Too Much Information Is Changing the Way We Think and Know*. New York: Routledge

Angwin, J, M. Varner and A. Tobin. 2017. 'Facebook Enabled Advertisers to Reach 'Jew Haters,' *ProPublica*, 14 Sept. 2017, <www.propublica.org/article/facebook-enabled-advertisers-to-reach-jew-haters>

Armstrong, P. 2017. 'Facebook Is Helping Brands Target Teens Who Feel "Worthless"'. *Forbes*, 1 May 2017, <www.forbes.com/sites/paularmstrongtech/2017/05/01/facebook-is-helping-brands-target-teens-who-feel-worthless/#77160232344e>

Bartels, R. 1974. 'The Identity Crisis in Marketing'. *Journal of Marketing* 38(4), 73–6

Barton, A. M. 2009. 'Application of Cascade Theory to Online Systems: A Study of Email and Google Cascades'. *Minnesota Journal of Law, Science, and Technology* 10(2), 473–502

Beebe, B. 2010. 'Intellectual Property Law and the Sumptuary Code'. *Harvard Law Review* 123(4), 809–89

Bourdieu, P. 1984. *Distinction: A Social Critique of the Judgement of Taste*. trans. Richard Nice. Cambridge, MA: Harvard University Press

boyd, d. 2014. *It's Complicated: The Social Lives of Networked Teens*. New Haven, CT: Yale University Press

Brown, W. 2003. 'Neo-Liberalism and the End of Liberal Democracy'. *Theory & Event* 7(1) 15, <http://muse.jhu.edu/journals/theory_&_event/>

Bruns, A. 2005. *Gatewatching: Collaborative Online News Production*. New York, NY: Peter Lang

Cadwalladr, C. 2017. 'The Great British Brexit Robbery: How Our Democracy was Hijacked'. *Guardian*, 7 May 2017, <www.theguardian.com/technology/2017/may/07/the-great-british-brexit-robbery-hijacked-democracy>

Cadwalladr, C. and E. Graham-Harrison. 2018. 'Revealed: 50 Million Facebook Profiles Harvested for Cambridge Analytica in Major Data Breach'. *Guardian*, 17 Mar. 2018, <www.theguardian.com/news/2018/mar/17/cambridge-analytica-facebook-influence-us-election>

Carsky, M. L., R. L. Dickinson and C. R. Canedy, III. 1998. 'The Evolution of Quality in Consumer Goods'. *Journal of Macromarketing* 18(2), 132–44

Citron, D. K. 2014. *Hate Crimes in Cyberspace*. Cambridge, MA: Harvard University Press

Cohen, J. E. 2016. 'The Surveillance-Innovation Complex: The Irony of the Participatory Turn'. In *The Participatory Condition in the Digital Age*, eds. Darin Barney et al., 207–26. Minneapolis, MN: University of Minnesota Press

Cohen, J. E. 2018. 'The Biopolitical Public Domain: The Legal Construction of the Surveillance Economy'. *Philosophy & Technology* 31(2) 213–33

Cohen, J. E. (2019) *Between Truth and Power: Legal Constructions of Informational Capitalism*. New York, NY: Oxford University Press

Coombe, R. J. 1998. *The Cultural Lives of Intellectual Properties: Authorship, Appropriation, and the Law*. Durham, NC: Duke University Press

Couldry, N. and A. Hepp. 2017. *The Mediated Construction of Reality*. Malden, MA: Polity

De Sola Pool, I. 1983. *Technologies of Freedom*. Cambridge, MA: Harvard University Press

Faris, R., H. Roberts, B. Etling, N. Bourassa, E. Zuckerman and Y. Benkler. 2017. 'Partisanship, Propaganda, and Disinformation: Online Media and the 2016 U.S. Presidential Election,' Berkman Klein Center for Internet and Society at Harvard University, <https://cyber.harvard.edu/publications/2017/08/mediacloud>

Foer, F. 2017. *World Without Mind: The Existential Threat of Big Tech*. New York, NY: Penguin

Freelon, D., C. D. McIlwain and M. D. Clark. 2016. 'Beyond the Hashtags: #Ferguson, #BlackLivesMatter, and the Online Struggle for Offline Justice,' Center for Media & Social Impact, <http://cmsimpact.org/wp-content/uploads/2016/03/beyond_the_hashtags_2016.pdf>

Galloway, A. 2006. *Gaming: Essays on Algorithmic Culture*. Minneapolis, MN: University of Minnesota Press

Glenn, T. and S. Monteith. 2014. 'New Measures of Mental State and Behavior Based on Data Collected from Sensors, Smartphones, and the Internet'. *Current Psychiatric Reports* 16(12), 523–32, doi: 10.1007/s11920-014-0523-3

Goffman, E. 1959. *The Presentation of Self in Everyday Life*. New York, NY: Anchor Books

Graham, D. A. 2016. 'The "Comet Pizza" Gunman Provides a Glimpse of a Frightening Future'. *The Atlantic*, 5 Dec. 2016, <https://www.theatlantic.com/politics/archive/2016/12/the-inevitability-of-more-comet-pizza-incidents/509567/>

Hildebrandt, M. 2015. *Smart Technologies and the End(s) of Law: Novel Entanglements of Law and Technology*. Northampton, MA: Edward Elgar

Huang, J., R. W. White and S. Dumais. 2011. 'No Clicks, No Problem: Using Cursor Movements to Understand and Improve Search,' in *Proceedings of the SIGCHI Conference on Human Factors in Computing Systems*, 1225–34. New York, NY: ACM

Jones, D. G. B. and E. Shaw. 2002. 'A History of Marketing Thought'. In *Handbook of Marketing*, eds. Barton A. Weitz and Robin Wensley, 39–65. Thousand Oaks, CA: SAGE Publishing

Keegan, J. 2016. 'Blue Feed, Red Feed: See Liberal Facebook and Conservative Facebook, Side by Side'. *Wall Street Journal*, 18 May 2016, <http://graphics.wsj.com/blue-feed-red-feed>

Knobel, M. and C. Lankshear. 2002. 'What Am I Bid? Reading, Writing, and Ratings at eBay.com'. In *Silicon Literacies: Communication, Innovation and Education in the Electronic Age*, ed. Ilana Snyder, 15–30. New York, NY: Routledge

Kosinski, M., D. Stillwell and T. Graepel. 2013. 'Private Traits and Attributes Are Predictable from Digital Records of Human Behavior'. *PNAS* 110(15), 5802–5

Kramer, A. D. I., J. E. Guillory and J. T. Hancock. 2014. 'Experimental Evidence of Massive-scale Emotional Contagion through Social Networks'. *PNAS* 111(24), 8788–90

Kuran, T. and C. R. Sunstein. 1999. 'Availability Cascades and Risk Regulation'. *Stanford Law Review* 51(4), 683–768.

Lauer, J. 2008. 'From Rumor to Written Record: Credit Reporting and the Invention of Financial Identity in Nineteenth-Century America'. *Technology and Culture* 49(2), 301–24.

Lauer, J. 2010. 'The Good Consumer: Credit Reporting and the Invention of

Financial Identity in the United States, 1840-1940'. *Enterprise and Society* 11(4), 686–94.

Lewis, P. 2017. '"Our Minds Can Be Hijacked": The Tech Insiders Who Fear a Smartphone Dystopia'. *The Guardian*, 6 Oct. 2017, <https://www.theguardian.com/technology/2017/oct/05/smartphone-addiction-silicon-valley-dystopia>

Loewenstein, G. 1994. 'The Psychology of Curiosity: A Review and Reinterpretation'. *Psychological Bulletin* 116(1), 75–98

MacKinnon, R. 2012. *Consent of the Networked: The Worldwide Struggle for Internet Freedom*. New York, NY: Basic Books

MacLean, P. D. 1955. 'The Limbic System ("Visceral Brain") in Relation to Central Gray and Reticulum of the Brain Stem: Evidence of Interdependence in Emotional Processes'. *Psychosomatic Medicine* 17(5), 355–66

Marwick, A. and d. boyd. 2014. '"It's Just Drama": Teen Perspectives on Conflict and Aggression in a Networked Era'. *Journal of Youth Studies* 17(9), 1187–204

Marwick, A. and R. Lewis. 2017. 'Media Manipulation & Disinformation Online'. *Data & Society*, <http://datasociety.net/pubs/oh/DataAndSociety_MediaManipulationAndDisinformationOnline.pdf>

Masum, H., M. Tovey and Y.-C. Zhang, eds. 2011. *The Reputation Society*. Cambridge, MA: MIT Press

May, T. and L. McWhorter. 2015. 'Who's Being Disciplined Now? Operations of Power in a Neoliberal World'. In *Biopower: Foucault and Beyond*, eds. Vernon W. Cisney and Nicolae Morar, 245–58. Chicago, IL: University of Chicago Press

McGaugh, James L., L. Cahill and B. Roozendaal. 1996. 'Involvement of the Amygdala in Memory Storage: Interaction with Other Brain Systems'. *PNAS* 93(24), 13508–14.

Nagle, A. 2017. *Kill All Normies: Online Culture Wars from 4Chan and Tumblr to Trump and the Alt-Right*. Winchester, UK: Zero Books

Paharia, R. 2013. *Loyalty 3.0: How Big Data and Gamification Are Revolutionizing Customer and Employee Engagement*. New York, NY: McGraw Hill

Pang, B. and L. Lee. 2008. 'Opinion Mining and Sentiment Analysis'. *Foundations and Trends in Information Retrieval* 2(1–2), 1–135

Paul, C. and M. Matthew. 2016. 'The Russian "Firehose of Falsehood" Propaganda Model: Why It Might Work and Options to Counter It'. RAND Corporation: Perspectives, <www.rand.org/pubs/perspectives/PE198.html>

Phillips, W. 2015. *This Is Why We Can't Have Nice Things*. Cambridge, MA: MIT Press

Plassmann, H., V. Venkatraman, S. Huettel and C. Yoon. 2015. 'Consumer Neuroscience: Applications, Challenges, and Possible Solutions'. *Journal of Marketing Research* 52(4), 427–35

Polakow-Suransky, S. 2016. 'The Ruthlessly Effective Rebranding of Europe's New Far Right'. *The Guardian*, 1 Nov. 2016, <https://www.theguardian.com/world/2016/nov/01/the-ruthlessly-effective-rebranding-of-europes-new-far-right>

Poon, M. 2007. 'Scorecards as Devices for Consumer Credit: The Case of Fair, Isaac & Company Incorporated'. *The Sociological Review* 55(s2) 284–306.

Potok, M. 2017. 'The Year in Hate & Extremism'. Southern Poverty Law Center: Intelligence Report, <http://splcenter.org/fighting-hate/intelligence-report/2017/year-hate-and-extremism>

Quattrociocchi, W., A. Scala and C. R. Sunstein. 2016. 'Echo Chambers on Facebook'. John M. Olin Center for Law & Economics, Harvard Law School,

Discussion Paper No. 877, <www.law.harvard.edu/programs/olin_center/papers/pdf/Sunstein_877.pdf>

Raczkowski, F. 2013. 'It's All Fun and Games...: A History of Ideas Concerning Gamification'. In *Proceedings of DiGRA 2013: DeFragging Game Studies*, 344–54. Atlanta, GA: Digital Games Research Association

Rao, H. 1998. 'Caveat Emptor: The Construction of Nonprofit Consumer Watchdog Organizations'. *American Journal of Sociology* 103(4), 912–61

Raymond, E. S. 1999. *The Cathedral and the Bazaar*. Sebastopol, CA: O'Reilly Media

Robinson + Yu. 2014. 'Knowing the Score: New Data, Underwriting, and Marketing in the Consumer Credit Marketplace'. <www.teamupturn.com/static/files/Knowing_the_Score_Oct_2014_v1_1.pdf>

Rodriguez, S. 2014. 'Meet Swarm: 5 Things You Need to Know About Foursquare's New App'. *Los Angeles Times*, 15 May 2014, <http://beta.latimes.com/business/technology/la-fi-tn-foursquare-swarm-app-5-things-20140515-story.html>

Singel, R. 2008. 'Facebook Beacon Tracking Program Draws Privacy Lawsuit'. *Wired*, 14 Aug. 2008, <www.wired.com/2008/08/facebook-beacon>

Singer, E. 2011. 'The Measured Life'. *MIT Technology Review*, 21 June 2011, <www.technologyreview.com/s/424390/the-measured-life/>

Solon, O. and S. Siddiqui. 2017. 'Russia-Backed Facebook Posts "Reached 126m Americans" During U.S. Election'. *Guardian*, 31 Oct. 2017, <www.theguardian.com/technology/2017/oct/30/facebook-russia-fake-accounts-126-million>

Stark, L. 2018. 'Algorithmic Psychometrics and the Scalable Subject'. *Social Studies of Science* 48(2), 204–31

Strach, L. and M. Russell. 2003. 'The Good Housekeeping Seal of Approval: From Innovative Consumer Protection to Popular Badge of Quality'. *Essays in Economic & Business History* 21, 151–66.

Subramanian, S. 2017. 'Inside the Macedonian Fake-News Complex'. *Wired*, 15 Feb. 2017, <www.wired.com/2017/02/veles-macedonia-fake-news/>

Sunstein, C. 2009. *Going to Extremes: How Like Minds Unite and Divide*. New York, NY: Oxford University Press

Tufecki, Z. 2017. *Twitter and Tear Gas: The Power and Fragility of Networked Protest*. New Haven, CT: Yale University Press

Turow, J. 2017. *The Aisles Have Eyes: How Retailers Track Your Shopping, Strip Your Privacy, and Define Your Power*. New Haven, CT: Yale University Press

Venkatraman, V., J. A. Clithero, Gavan J. Fitzsimons and Scott A. Huettel. 2012. 'New Scanner Data for Brand Marketers: How Neuroscience Can Help Better Understand Differences in Brand Preferences'. *Journal of Consumer Psychology* 22(1), 143–53.

Whitson, J. 2013. 'Gaming the Quantified Self'. *Surveillance & Society* 11(1–2), 163–76.

Wolf, G. 2010. 'The Data-Driven Life'. *New York Times*, 28 Apr. 2010, <www.nytimes.com/2010/05/02/magazine/02self-measurement-t.html>

Wong, J.C. 2019. 'How Facebook and YouTube Help Spread Anti-Vaxxer Propaganda'. *The Guardian*, 1 Feb. 2019, <https://www.theguardian.com/media/2019/feb/01/facebook-youtube-anti-vaccination-misinformation-social-media>

Wood, D. M. and K. Ball. 2013. 'Brandscapes of Control? Surveillance, Marketing, and the Co-construction of Subjectivity and Space in Neoliberal Capitalism'. *Marketing Theory* 13(1), 47–67

Woodruff, A. 2015. 'Necessary, Unpleasant, and Disempowering: Reputation

Management in the Internet Age'. In *Proceedings of the SIGCHI Conference on Human Factors in Computing Systems*, 149–58. New York, NY: ACM

Youyou, W., M. Kosinski and D. Stillwell. 2015. 'Computer-Based Personality Judgments Are More Accurate than Those Made by Humans'. *PNAS* 112(4), 1036–40

Zichermann, G. and J. Linder. 2013. *The Gamification Revolution: How Leaders Leverage Game Mechanics to Crush the Competition*. New York, NY: McGraw Hill

Zuboff, S. 2015. 'Big Other: Surveillance Capitalism and the Prospects of an Information Civilization'. *Journal of Information Technology* 30, 75–89

Zuboff, S. 2018. *The Age of Surveillance Capitalism: The Fight for a Human Future at the New Frontier of Power*. New York, NY: Public Affairs

5. Smart technologies and our sense of self: Going beyond epistemic counter-profiling
Sylvie Delacroix and Michael Veale[1]

INTRODUCTION

Pervasive and complex digital profiling practices have moved from niche concern to global debate.[2] International scandal has raged around the fine-grained and supposedly influential political profiling undertaken by firms such as Cambridge Analytica, powered by covertly obtained data and facilitated by the lax respect for privacy and data protection by technology giants. The chair of the relevant UK House of Commons oversight group, the Digital, Culture, Media and Sport (DCMS) Committee, claimed the online broadcast of one of their evidence sessions was 'the biggest ever live-streamed audience that parliament has ever had' (Helm 2018). While social media content is now under increased scrutiny, similar and perhaps more invasive industries are emerging to process data collected from sensors in homes, environments, and even on our bodies. Given these developments, such scandals are likely to be relatively commonplace in the years to come.

To approach these problems, we must define them. Researchers and practitioners in this field have tended to work with some canonical problem framings to think about societal implications. A typical framing sees a large data controller[3] using machine learning techniques on personal data to build a model to predict something consequential: whether someone will pay back a loan, buy a product or commit a crime. They query this model with new input data relating to a particular individual to make or support a decision concerning them. The opacity of the decision system limits an individual's ability to contest it (for example, under equality law). That individual might have an instrumental or an intrinsic claim to a right to transparency, as recognized by freedom of information laws; algorithmic information provisions in administrative law, such as recent French law (Edwards and Veale 2018); the common law 'duty to give reasons' in English law (Elliott 2011, Oswald 2018); and transparency rights and obligations in relation to automated decision-making systems present in European data protection law (Edwards and Veale 2017).

These rights have occupied much of the debate around algorithmic systems. They broadly attempt to rectify epistemic imbalances: a powerful entity knows or understands something concerning an individual that they themselves do not. This knowledge asymmetry can be exploited in a way that the individual is powerless to prevent. All the rights and obligations mentioned above (from transparency to freedom of information) stem from a general effort to mitigate the effects of unprecedented epistemic imbalances. These efforts are far from new in computing: explanation facilities have a long history in expert systems research (Guidotti et al. 2018). However such facilities have primarily been aimed at decision-support users, rather than affected individuals (Binns et al. 2018). The perceived need for the latter – for 'algorithmic accountability' – has motivated a range of new research communities to consider the extent to which such 'downstream transparency' can – and should (Weller 2017) – be provided. Alongside the latter have been cautious voices, arguing that the transparency ideal is rife with limitations (Ananny and Crawford 2016), and that solely focusing on transparency rights may further individualize responsibility for ensuring systems are socially aligned, a 'transparency fallacy' which fails to give individuals meaningful control just as the 'notice and choice' paradigm failed in the past (Edwards and Veale 2017).

Information flows between actors are key to Mireille Hildebrandt's understanding of the risks of computational profiling in *The End(s)*. Hildebrandt draws on a range of scholarship, including G. H. Mead and Helmuth Plessner, to consider how an individual's behaviour – and process of identity formation – is shaped by a range of mutual expectations. Such expectations are multilateral in nature: individuals do not just internalize a set of rules that constitute a role, nor seek to get inside another actor's head, but must intuitively internalize expectations that an entire social framework generates of themselves in relation to those around them, and of those around of them in relation to each other. Non-human agents must build similar understandings if they are to integrate seamlessly in our lives too, and generally must do so in a different way than we can. We must do the same to navigate a world that contains sophisticated non-human actors capable of analysis and adaptation. Hildebrandt is concerned that, faced with highly granular profiling systems (insofar as they achieve their intended predictive functions at all), individuals will be unable to effectively anticipate the way they will be read, and therefore are left in an unequal and problematic situation which may harm them as well as the broader social fabric.

To address this, in *The End(s)* Hildebrandt proposes the mechanism and frame of 'counter-profiling'. This consists of 'conducting data mining operations on the behaviours of those that are in the business of profiling, whether "those" are humans, computing systems or hybrid configurations' (*The End(s)*, 223) to help redress the imbalances generated by machine learning systems. Hildebrandt does not see this as a necessarily individual activity, but one which could be undertaken collectively, akin to the means by which media organizations currently hold important systems to account in constitutional democracies. Such counter-profiling organizations have been proposed at different scales, from the use of 'super-complaint'-style powers in Article 80 of the GDPR to empower NGOs (Edwards and Veale 2018), platforms to facilitate stories on machine learning systems in journalism (Trielli et al. 2018), or the collective use of data protection rights with the purpose of aggregating the results and potentially 'reverse engineering' consequential systems (e.g. Mahieu et al. 2018, Palmetshofer and Semsrott 2018).

Counter-profiling might generate an array of types of knowledge. In recent years, there has been a heightened focus on procedures to obtain information about the decision-logics of predictive systems due to the tendency of such systems to utilize undesirable proxies for use in decision-making. Typically, a decision-system might be using only seemingly non-sensitive data as input, but inferring some latent class or variable which has not been explicitly measured, such as race, disability, or social status, and using this to, in part, determine outcomes (Barocas and Selbst 2016, Calders and Žliobaitė 2013). At an individual level explanation facilities are another way in which counter-profiling can be operationalized. Often, these proceed by creating a simplified version of a model (such as the area around a decision-point), or snapshot part of its logic (such as a sensitivity analysis) to provide further information to a user. This information might serve a variety of purposes: from increasing trust (or a sense of due process), to enabling users to react and take certain actions, or to detect 'bugs' and errors in a deployed system.

Such forms of counter-profiling seem focused on *epistemic* imbalances. One side 'knows' more than the other, even if this knowledge is not expressed in a semantic or otherwise interpretable form (Burrell 2016): rectifying this imbalance is the core purpose of such counter-profiling endeavours. The latter are mostly concerned with the models themselves, rather than also turning to consider the sociotechnical systems they inhabit and co-create.

Yet when we profile each other in the world, the heuristics and intuitions we develop along the way go beyond what is required to build a simple model of a single person. The problem is that explanation facilities within machine learning systems proceed from precisely this 'simple model' perspective, aiming to simplify a system in a way that allows humans to understand it. Even where these explanation facilities are designed to prescribe reaction or foster response (e.g. for an individual to know how she should change her input data, if she can, to get different results from a machine), their overarching objective is still to simplify a single software object so that a human can understand or interpret it.

In *The End(s)*, by contrast, Hildebrandt describes counter-profiling as a wider endeavour. Individuals are not assumed to be simply seeking information about biases, or explanations of software: instead they might be working together (as they do in purely human interactions) to understand 'hybrid configurations' (*The End(s)*, 223). The focus is on re-enabling mutual anticipation, rather than simply balancing knowledge. As noted by Hildebrandt, efforts to regain mutual anticipation across society that are stuck in the simplistic '[opening] the skull of another person' (*The End(s)*, 222) perspective seem likely to stall before they make significant progress.

We too are doubtful that a focus on epistemic rebalancing will meaningfully address the societal issues stemming from sophisticated profiling systems. In this chapter, we elaborate on one challenge that epistemic counter-profiling fails to consider: to what extent is our commitment to equality imperilled by our insatiable appetite for optimization via cheap, ubiquitous sensors and actuators?

PERVASIVE PROFILING AS SOCIAL CRUELTY

To understand the fundamental nature of the commitment to equality we are concerned about, it is helpful to start by considering instances when this equality is most clearly negated. What do rape, genocide, torture and slavery have in common? They are, following Andrea Sangiovanni (2017, 76), all paradigmatic instances of *social cruelty*: '[S]ocial cruelty involves the unauthorised, harmful, and wrongful use of another's vulnerability to attack or obliterate their capacity to develop and maintain an integral sense of self'.

How can the seemingly benign, profile-based endeavour to optimize the way we spend our time (along with the food we eat, the people we meet, and the news we read) be even *remotely* connected to practices as abhorrent as genocide? It helps to start by considering what makes genocide distinctively wrong. Sangiovanni (2017, 77) articulates this by reference to: 'the reasons for mass murder, which are grounded in an ideology that singles out a group of people as deserving extermination in virtue of who they are ... Those affected can no longer appear in public without fear or maintain a social self that is (partially) defined or controlled by them'.

No matter what kind of person the member of a group targeted for genocide may have been aspiring to become, being targeted in such a way renders those aspirations and efforts of self-definition irrelevant (just like the efforts of the person subjected to rape or torture).

Even in mundane circumstances, retaining some sense of ownership over the way one projects oneself, both socially and through one's body, is never easy. To do so requires, minimally, a to-and-fro movement between the process of definition of one's 'self' from *without*, such as the effects of natural events and human encounters, and from *within* – how one appropriates such events and encounters. This to-and-fro movement is easily imperilled. Events such as a grave illness (or prosecution) can leave one with the sense that one no longer knows how to continue (and hence appropriate such events), given who one was (Delacroix 2018). In those cases, the threat to the to-and-fro movement is exogenous. What would a threat from *within* look like?

We posit that the invisible, profile-based optimization of our environment may, in the longer term, undermine our capacity to develop and maintain an integral sense of self *to such an extent* as to fall within the scope of Sangiovanni's definition of social cruelty. This endangers our commitment to *moral* – not merely epistemic – equality.[4] How so? Just like the slave-owner (or the authorities behind a genocide) not only does not need, but precludes any active input from the person the slave (or member of a group targeted for genocide) is trying to be, data-controllers can 'read' me, build a profile that accurately anticipates my upcoming moves, desires and risks without any need for active input on my part. In the data-controller's 'eyes' – and consequently in the eyes of other users of the profile-based technology – I am merely becoming the person anticipated by that profile.

Given the impact of this definition of self *from without*, my ability to resist or contest this extraneous definition, already under pressure, will be increasingly compromised as those profile-based, ubiquitous computing applications leverage recent advances in affective computing (rebranded in recent years as 'Emotional AI'). Profiling systems which anticipate desires and preferences based on physiological indicators of nascent emotions may all too easily compromise the 'counter-process' of definition *from within* by making any effort of appropriation seemingly redundant. Rather than experiencing the tension(s) between nascent feelings (such as those leading to anger) and one's meta-preferences or aspirations (for instance the type of parent one strives to be), the individual may be presented with an instantly 'optimized' environment that either removes or masks the cause of one's upcoming anger. While such optimization would probably make for smoother interpersonal relationships, at least in the short term, it may also leave us with poorer versions of ourselves, ones that are deprived of the chance to learn from and grow through the experience of such tensions.[5] Most worryingly, this fine-tuned optimization of our environment makes it considerably more likely that we will end up conforming to the profile-based, extraneous definition of ourselves, thus turning such profiles into self-fulfilling prophecies.

Hildebrandt does allude to this concern, stating that such smart technologies

> may thus 'read' our emotions before we have a chance to develop our own reflection and response to our own emotional state . . . [i]f we cannot contest the way we are being 'read' and steered and thus if we cannot resist the manipulation of our unconscious emotional states, we may lose the sense of self that is pre-conditional for human autonomy. Not having a chance to develop feelings, we may actually become the machines that smart technologies take us to be. (*The End(s)*, 71–72)

Here, we wish to unpack this insight further, and propose mechanisms and practices which might help avoid this undesirable end.

AFFECTIVE COMPUTING AND THE NEW BEHAVIOURISM

Affective computing, more recently rebranded as 'emotional AI', is one of the technologies that play a central role in the optimization endeavours above. It is defined as 'computing that relates to, arises from, or deliberately influences emotions' (Picard 1997, 249). One of the domain's early proponents, Rosalind Picard, argued strongly for the consideration of the functions that emotions play in processing and problem-solving – that computers 'do not need affective abilities for the fanciful goal of becoming humanoids; they need them for a meeker and more practical goal: to function with intelligence and sensitivity' (Picard 1997, 247). As well as considering the role of emotions *in* computing, a major strand of affective computing surrounds affect *detection* through a range of modalities including face, posture, blood volume pulse, skin conductivity, vocal tone, spoken or written text, and more (see generally Calvo et al. 2015). Fuelled in particular by heavy commercial interest in using these systems to understand consumers in a marketing context, research in this field has been plentiful and well-funded. Such research has gone far beyond the question of whether digital affect detection is even possible (e.g. Healey and Picard 1998) to attempt to computationally parse 'micro-expressions': involuntary and near-invisible muscle movements thought to betray us; expressions researchers believe are 'capable of revealing the actual emotions of subjects even though such leaks are unintentional' (Xu et al. 2017). These are involuntary leakages or flags which might indicate deception: laughing at an unfunny joke, smiling while angry, or the like. Such flags have been of research interest for nearly half a century (Ekman and Friesen 1969), and, with the ease of computation and cheapening of high resolution, high frame-rate cameras that can capture these transient involuntary signals, has led to a range of datasets and predictive benchmarks (see e.g. Yan et al. 2014). Richer and more confident understanding of affect might also be gleaned from fusing multiple sources of information such as posture (Gunes and Piccardi 2005) or data from wearables (Gunes and Hung 2016).

Coupled with what Antoinette Rouvroy terms 'data behaviourism' – the belief (rightly or wrongly) that human actions can be well-anticipated through inductive methods applied to large amounts of data (Rouvroy 2013) – this would seem to leave data subjects quite open to pre-emption and interpretation by data controllers in ways data subjects have limited practical ability to control or mitigate. Such pre-emptive approaches are already receiving publicity and drawing concern. In 2018, a spate of news stories surrounded a new patent filed by the firm Amazon, which owns and controls the 'Echo' or 'Alexa' voice assistant ecosystem. While many firms patent technologies that never go on to enter production, they are often deemed indicative of a firm's thinking or internal research spend. This patent, *Voice-based Determination of Physical and Emotional Characteristics of Users*, sought to understand whether users were experiencing an 'emotional abnormality' and aimed to take some form of corrective action. The illustrative example provided (Figure 5.1) shows a woman who appears to be ill or upset being asked whether she would like a recipe for chicken soup.

While the validity of this approach requires strong behaviourist assumptions, in practice incorrect or miscalibrated inferences will have tangible effects on how individuals act and are expected to act – and indeed on their very capacity for 'action'.

As that through which we 'make our appearance' (Arendt 1958), revealing who – rather than what – we are, action is inherently unpredictable. Hannah Arendt reminds us of this in at least two respects. As the vehicle through which each and every citizen exercises her agency – her capacity to start something new – true action presupposes an element of surprise. 'The fact that man is capable of action means that the unexpected can be expected from him, that he is able to perform what is infinitely

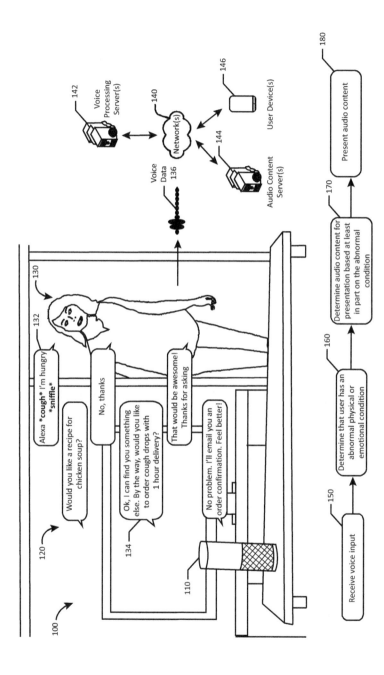

Source: United States Patent and Trademark Office, <www.uspto.gov> (public domain).

Figure 5.1 Patent no US010096319, Amazon Technologies Inc.

improbable' (Arendt 1958, 178). Action is also unpredictable to the extent that we cannot anticipate exactly what kind of self we will reveal through it, nor how that self will be read and narrated by those who surround us.

This unpredictability inevitably generates anxiety, and Arendt deplores the progressive shrinking of the public sphere (*polis*) (concomitant with the widespread withdrawal to the private pursuit of economic interests) as Modernity's regrettable coping mechanism. The advent of profile-based optimization tools that aim to mitigate (or possibly cancel altogether) the unexpectedness inherent in action goes one significant step further, as an 'unpredictability coping mechanism'. By potentially short-circuiting *thought* itself (that space where *I* am called to balance conflicting feelings, aims and aspirations), the smooth, profile-based optimization of our environment may ultimately render us incapable of *judgement*. Without the latter, without some ability to question deeply internalized habits of thought and action, there is no *polis*: only a large number of what Arendt refers to as the pre-political 'homo faber' – who are focused on the production of artefacts – working side by side at best (or, at worst, a series of thoughtless 'Eichmanns') (Arendt 1994).

FOSTERING SELF-DEFINITION

The downstream regulation of profiling practices, with its ex-post remedies, such as transparency rights after-the-fact, seems an unlikely answer to the dystopian future described above. Not only might these remedies be too little, too late, but these rights after-the-fact also require a capacity for reflexive action. Reflection theorists have highlighted the need to create appropriate settings and 'scaffold' simple information provision in order to enable it to have a transformative effect on individuals, and it is unclear whether such characteristics are built into the rights and provisions discussed above (Slovák et al. 2017). Furthermore, it is possible that highly granular profiling processes themselves might systematically undermine the ability to reflect. It is furthermore highly unclear what these ex-post remedies would be ex-post *of*: an individual profiling instance? Systematic exposure and behaviour change over many months, or years? A sudden, regretful action that an individual attributes to her environment? There may well be individual uses for these remedies, but they are no panacea, and at best they will need to be augmented with other means and measures.

Here we instead focus on upstream design interventions. We see two main avenues through which political and ethical agency might be preserved alongside some of the benefits that personalization and pre-emption might bring. We review these in the context of some connected efforts in the relevant research literature – particularly in human–computer interaction – and highlight their opportunities, as well as their unresolved gaps and pitfalls, which are in dire need of future research and practice.

PASSIVE INTERVENTIONS: PROFILES IN PERSPECTIVE

Much interface design has centred on ideas of 'seamlessness' (Weiser 1994), where the functioning of a system (such as utilized profiling practices) are hidden to the user to better let them focus on the task they want to achieve. While this can help users with certain tasks, in many cases, it can also obscure the way that a given system works, and individuals might lose perspective as a result.

To counterbalance this, some researchers have explored means of giving users greater perspective on how their experience of a system relates to others' experience of a system. In some forms, this might resemble the counter-profiling efforts we were perhaps unduly critical of above. Give users a better understanding of how a system works, and they might want to work differently with it, against it, or customize it to their needs (Ekstrand and Willemsen 2016). Yet it is not required for an individual to understand how a system works and 'perceives' them (epistemic equality) to be given the opportunity to reflect, and something to reflect upon. Here, building on *The End(s)* (see 222–3), we consider interventions which do not seek to *explain* the profiling system, but instead provide perspective in other ways and with more consideration of the sociotechnical context and other actors involved. Might such perspective provide the moral jolt required to keep the to-and-fro of self-definition going?

One interesting approach has been to focus on many different users at once, and giving individuals perspective upon how *others* might be seeing a platform or recommender system. Webster and Vassileva (2007) propose a news recommender system with a twist: it is accompanied by a visual map of yourself in relation to other users in your social network, whom you can place closer or farther away from yourself to change their own influence on what you see, as well as take a glimpse into the kinds of recommendations they will be getting. Kang et al. (2016) propose a similar system for Twitter users to explore content 'popular just beyond a user's typical information horizon'. Here, the focus is less on 'why did I get this recommendation?', than on 'what are others using this system experiencing?'.

This approach appears promising, but also contains pitfalls. While some primarily public platforms like Twitter already support basic ways to see the timelines of other users, it is not easy or intuitive for users to access this functionality. Moreover, much content is private in nature, so putting yourself in someone else's shoes is limited by the streams and viewpoints you are authorized to access, for example on platforms like Facebook. Furthermore, when moving beyond the recommender system paradigm, systems can be personalized in more functional ways. The way that individuals have configured their smart home, or series of smart devices, might be fundamentally incompatible with the profiles of other individuals. Short of engaging in a lifestyle swap, with hardware and software included, it is hard to see how this approach translates neatly into many newly datafied areas of life. Lastly, it is not at all a given that seeing other users – who may indeed be subject to personalization just as deeply, and their own reflective capacities equally challenged – will provide the stimulus needed to help a user retain ownership over the process of identity formation and self-definition.

A different approach surrounds users not with the data or information of others, but accumulated information on *themselves* which they may not have mentally logged or been aware of. The *Balancer* web extension, for example, displays a stick figure in the browser carrying a load (with a carrying pole) which would become more lopsided the less ideologically diverse the media consumed was (Munson et al. 2013). The use of this tool appeared to have a small observed effect on encouraging more diverse media consumption. Other tools aim to encourage users to directly take perspectives, such as develop pro/con lists (Kriplean et al. 2012a), reflect upon other users' perceptions (Kriplean et al. 2012b), or mapping out user comments onto axes of values to prompt users to navigate across them more broadly (Faridani et al. 2010). What users might *not* have done could also be of interest, and in some ways, more challenging to convey. Tintarev et al. (2018) presented users with visualizations of their profiles, and found evidence that some were effective in helping users identify 'blind-spots'.

In the physical world, this approach echoes *personal informatics*, also referred to as self-tracking or the 'quantified self' movement. This area primarily concerns fitness wearables at present but does have a range of applications (and adherents) more broadly. Research in this field has emphasized that users do not reflect on the data trails they collect as a result of using these devices and systems in straightforward and uniform ways, but instead their practices are highly task and goal dependent (Li et al. 2011). While relevant data with reflective potential might be able to be logged, to encourage heterogeneous users to reflect upon it in ways that are usable, useful and meaningful to them is likely to be challenging. While there may be ways to introduce information into a user's environment (e.g. through ambient interfaces displaying data designed to be 'processed in the background of awareness' (Wisneski et al. 1998)), whether such passive approaches, often based on lights or sounds and lacking depth or complexity (e.g. Houben et al. 2016), would be effective at promoting moral reflection is a question for empirical research.

ACTIVE INTERVENTIONS: SURPRISES AND APPROPRIATION

If passively illustrating highly personalized systems to users is not enough to encourage reflection and behaviour change, might more active interventions hold promise? Are there ways of building reflectivity-inducing tools that would prompt end-users to question the deeply ingrained habits of thought and action that make their behaviour as end-users suitable for profiling in the first place?

In the research field of recommender systems, there has long been interest in understanding how or why simple metrics, such as accuracy on training data, do not appear to relate fully with users' satisfaction with systems. This suggests that other values or constraints, aside from accuracy, may be pertinent in the design of such systems. Two are of particular interest in this context. The first is the notion of *serendipity*. Coined by Horace Walpole in 1754, over time serendipity has become used to describe an accidental, unplanned, but valuable discovery, often in a scientific context (Merton and Barber 2011). In human-computer interaction, it has generally been seen as a novel prediction that triggers a positive emotional response from a user. Another, related, notion is *unexpectedness*. Unexpectedness does not restrict itself to *novel* (totally unseen) predictions or actions, but instead draws upon a model of what the user is expecting. Those predictions that are outside a user's expected range, but not so far outside to be irrelevant, are considered 'unexpected' (Adamopoulos and Tuzhilin 2014).

The notions of serendipity and unexpectedness as they have been explored in the recommender systems literature share two problematic assumptions in relation to the issues described in this paper.

First, they take an individual's preferences as simply not fully known, rather than malleable or not fully formed. A similar assumption is shared by microeconomics, where even complex consumer preferences are static and do not depend on the options at hand (cf. Dietrich and List 2013). This might be reasonable in trivial domains, but quickly becomes controversial in consequential cases, particularly morally charged ones. There is a wide array of literature in the field of political science on how individuals' value-laden preferences change in response to actions, messages, sources of information and under different conditions of knowledge (for a review, see Druckman and Lupia 2000). It is these types of techniques which might be deployed, even automatically, to give individuals moments of moral reflection, or to attempt to stir them from the routines they take for granted. Those designing and maintaining predictive systems might think themselves archaeologists, uncovering individuals' preferences, but might they be sometimes better described as architects shaping and developing them (Bettman et al. 1998, Gregory et al. 1993)?

Understanding how individuals' preferences change would be an ethically challenging area of research and practice. Intervention-based, habit forming research is relatively uncontroversial when the aim is known by the participant and agreed to – for example, to form habits commonly thought of as healthy, such as changing eating patterns or exercising more. Where issues of concern have heavier moral or political dimensions, it becomes less so. Facebook attracted significant criticism for its experimental intervention, without informed consent, to test the 'emotional contagion' hypothesis, whereby individuals' emotional states are influenced by those around them. Researchers attempted (and claimed to succeed in) manipulating individual behaviour by altering the composition of the content they were exposed to (Kramer et al. 2014). These kind of methods – the A/B testing common to technology firms today – form the basis of 'agile' development of software systems. Such practices have been highlighted in the context of how they transform privacy concerns and necessary governance (Gürses and van Hoboken 2018), or how they might engage concerns typically found in research ethics (Bird et al. 2016). Quasi-experimental methods (which require no active random intervention) might be useful, but given that they tend to require particular fortuitous setups, they are notoriously difficult to apply generally, and would therefore be unlikely to see easy uptake with regard to the day-to-day development of systems.

Second, both serendipity and unexpectedness are typically introduced as constraints aimed at maximizing user satisfaction or perceived utility. Serendipity in particular (given its potential emotional underpinnings) has yet to be considered as a possible reflexivity-inducing, habit-distancing tool meant to foster agency, not just user satisfaction. To understand how serendipity and political/ethical agency may be related, it is useful to consider the extent to which habit all too easily compromises the latter. Our capacity for what Arendt calls 'judgement', i.e. our capacity to call into question widely accepted practices when they are wanting, indeed presupposes an ability to step back from the habitual, to query seemingly routine values or practices. This capacity cannot be taken for granted: challenging as it is to maintain such critical distance in an 'offline world', it becomes even more so when the technology we interact with is designed to be habit-inducing to a much greater extent than the 'natural' objects that structure our quotidian habits.

To what extent can we – and should we – design the profiling systems we so extensively rely on in our daily lives to sometimes 'work backwards', and periodically prompt us to reconsider the very traits and habits that feed our respective profiles? Can we design such systems in such a way as to shake us out of deeply ingrained habits through surprise? Such suggestions have been made in particular for decision-support systems (Delacroix 2018), and it is worth considering how this logic might extend into ubiquitous computing applications. For such surprises to have that agency-enabling, habit-shaking effect, they would have to go beyond 'trivial' prediction failures, and lead us to reconsider our understanding of the world, and our place within it. Given this likely axiological component, would such 'surprise-based' interventions amount to covert paternalistic interventions? Not if their goal is not so much to 'nudge' us towards a particular choice (Sunstein and Thaler 2003), but instead to enable us to creatively make choices for ourselves, rather than blindly adhering to old habits. Instead of narrowing down choice to a particular goal or target, the aim could be to open it up more widely, and celebrate diverse uses of technology. Here one may usefully leverage recent research on the factors that impact upon individuals' different levels of creativity (Zabelina et al. 2011) – these factors include 'fluency' and 'flexibility' – and endeavour to counter the effects of routinization with applications that are not that dissimilar to those used in the context of art and mathematics (Boden 2010) as well as business (Adam et al. 2006).

Yet for such efforts to be genuinely agency-enabling, one would need to move beyond the overwhelmingly passive role which end-users are typically endowed with, and design systems that carve them an active role within the learning loop (this approach is sometimes referred to as 'interactive machine learning' or 'IML' (Wallach and Allen 2008)). An explicit requirement to keep monitoring the results of the learning process, combined with a demand for regular, creative input on the part of end-users, indeed has the potential to not only improve the system's learning performance; it may also keep thoughtless torpor at bay by encouraging an 'ethical feedback loop'.

Related to this are a range of calls that ask designers not to design products for imagined users, but to give individuals space to define and purpose technologies themselves (see e.g. Hildebrandt 2019). Dix (2007) calls this 'designing for appropriation', arguing designers should take a principled approach to allow for interpretations, provide visibility and avoid overemphasis on seamlessness, expose the intentions of particular features or routines, seek to support users rather than control them, allow coupling, chaining and modular expansion, and encourage sharing and learning. This echoes calls in a range of fields, such as mobile health (mHealth) to consider technologies which go beyond paternalistic prevention to encourage 'self experiments and reflective practice' (Churchill and schraefel 2015, 63). This is accompanied in regulatory terms by the nascent but growing 'right to repair' movement, which seeks to enshrine the ability to tinker, fix and have access to replacement parts for objects that are increasingly difficult for users to open and mend (Koebler 2017). All of these directions appear to head for active efforts for users to engage in the systems they are part of, and the introduction, growth or enforcement of any one of them may bring spillover effects to support the causes we have outlined above.

CONCLUSION

Our appetite for control and predictability is far from new. The sophisticated profiling endeavours attempting to personalize our choices can be read as merely extending the scope of this long-standing appetite. Personalization does have clear benefits: aside from reducing cognitive load, it is essential to developing technologies which are more tailored and accessible to individual needs, and navigating and making sense of the swelling mass of digitized information. Yet the extent to which, just like any tool (and perhaps more so than any other tool), it will end up *changing* its users must be considered critically. Here, we have argued that our current regulatory focus on addressing epistemic imbalances (e.g. through 'explainable' systems) is, on its own, inadequate, and additional approaches and tools are needed.

This chapter focused on the extent to which sophisticated profiling techniques may insidiously imperil the fragile movement of to-and-fro that is essential to any person's endeavour to continuously re-define her sense of self in a way that commands respect, both from herself and from others. This respect for each and every person's need to preserve a gap between the self that we present to the world and the self that we conceal is at the heart of our commitment to moral equality. It presupposes a certain degree of opacity, an opacity threatened by our supposedly strengthening ability to infer future desires and preferences from past behaviour and/or physiological indicators. But the challenges raised by profiling techniques go further than the need to preserve opacity respect. It is our very ability to step back and call into question existing practices (what Arendt would refer to as 'judgement') that is potentially at stake. Pushed to its limit, the smooth optimization of our environment may indeed prevent us from ever experiencing the tensions or emotional discomforts that prompt us to step back and reconsider practices we took for granted. An optimally personalized world may not ever call for any 'action' as Arendt understands it.

Can systems be designed to personalize responsibly? Greater time and research needs to be invested in designing viable 'perspective widening' tools that leverage the knowledge we have acquired on the mechanisms underlying habit-formation and transformation. Encouraging users to reflect on the use of systems by themselves and others – for example, by making usage logs compellingly visible – has been suggested, but heavily burdens the individual with little guarantee of meaningful engagement. More active approaches, such as the concepts of serendipity and unexpectedness developed in recommender systems and information retrieval seem initially promising, but also come with their own sets of flaws. Primarily, they are still modelling and catering to user satisfaction, and underestimate the extent to which individuals' preferences are themselves malleable. Any approach that tries to predict what users might like, or even what might change their views, risks the same pitfalls as any other form of personalization we have described.

Instead, we argue that perhaps the most promising avenue seems to be to push technologists to aim for their systems to be diversely used, and measure success at least partly on that basis. Inviting appropriation and repurposing, and exploring how it can be supported, would help keep users engaged in systems of data collection and profiling. This would not be a straightforward task, and may at times be in tension with traditional measures, such as accuracy. Yet simple, technical fixes that sit neatly alongside existing evaluation paradigms are unlikely to be fixes at all. For designers and developers to appreciate that is the first important step to understanding how to navigate this new risk in a world of 'smart' technologies.

NOTES

1. Michael Veale acknowledges funding from the Engineering and Physical Sciences Research Council (EPSRC) [grant number EP/ M507970/1]. Both Sylvie Delacroix and Michael Veale are supported by the Alan Turing Institute under EPSRC grant number EP/N510129/1. Thanks go to Mireille Hildebrandt and a further anonymous reviewer for comments on this work which shaped the final version.
2. The GDPR, in Article 4(4), defines profiling as 'any form of automated processing of personal data consisting of the use of personal data to evaluate certain personal aspects relating to a natural person, in particular to analyse or predict aspects concerning that natural person's performance at work, economic situation, health, personal preferences, interests, reliability, behaviour, location or movements'.
3. A data controller is a natural or legal person who, jointly or alone, 'determines the purposes and means of the processing of personal data' (Article 4(7), GDPR).
4. As for why the latter is best understood as a commitment to the absence of social cruelty, see Sangiovanni (2017).
5. On the value of anger, see Srinivasan (2018).

REFERENCES

Adam, F., P. Brezillon, S. Carlsson and P. Humphreys. 2006. *Creativity and Innovation in Decision Making and Decision Support*. London: Ludic Publishing

Adamopoulos, P. and A. Tuzhilin. 2014. 'On Unexpectedness in Recommender Systems: Or How to Better Expect the Unexpected'. *ACM Transactions on Intelligent Systems and Technology* 5 (4), 1–32

Ananny, M. and K. Crawford. 2016. 'Seeing Without Knowing: Limitations of the Transparency Ideal and its Application to Algorithmic Accountability'. *New Media & Society* <https://doi.org/10.1177/1461444816676645

Arendt, H. 1958. *The Human Condition*. Chicago, IL: The University of Chicago Press

Arendt, H. 1994. *Eichmann in Jerusalem: A Report on the Banality of Evil*. New York, NY: Penguin

Barocas, S. and A. D. Selbst. 2016. 'Big Data's Disparate Impact'. *California Law Review* 104, 671

Bettman, J. R., M. F. Luce and J. W. Payne. 1998. 'Constructive Consumer Choice Processes'. *The Journal of Consumer Research* 25 (3), 187–217

Binns, R., M. Van Kleek, M. Veale, U. Lyngs, J. Zhao and N. Shadbolt. 2018. '"It's Reducing a Human Being to a Percentage"; Perceptions of Justice in Algorithmic Decisions', *Proceedings of the ACM SIGCHI Conference on Human Factors in Computing Systems (CHI'18)* <https://doi.org/10.1145/3173574.3173951>.

Bird, S., S. Barocas, K. Crawford, F. Diaz and H. Wallach. 2016. 'Exploring or Exploiting? Social and Ethical Implications of Autonomous Experimentation in AI', *Presented at the 3rd Workshop on Fairness, Accountability and Transparency in Machine Learning (FAT/ML 2016), 18 November 2016, New York City, New York* <https://papers.ssrn.com/sol3/papers.cfm?abstract_id=2846909>

Boden, M. 2010. *Creativity and Art: Three Roads to Surprise*. Oxford: Oxford University Press

Burrell, J. 2016. 'How the Machine "Thinks": Understanding Opacity in Machine Learning Algorithms'. *Big Data & Society* 3 (1) <https://doi.org/10.1177/2053951 715622512>

Calders, T. and I. Žliobaitė. 2013. 'Why Unbiased Computational Processes Can Lead to Discriminative Decision Procedures'. In B. Custers, T. Calders, B. Schermer and T. Zarsky (eds), *Discrimination and Privacy in the Information Society: Data Mining and Profiling in Large Databases*. Berlin, Heidelberg: Springer Berlin Heidelberg, 43–57

Calvo, R. A., S. D'Mello, J. Gratch and A. Kappas. 2015. *The Oxford Handbook of Affective Computing*. Oxford: Oxford University Press

Churchill, E. F. and m. c. schraefel. 2015. 'mHealth + Proactive Well-being = Wellth Creation'. *Interactions* 22 (1), 60–3.

Delacroix, S. 2018. *A Vulnerability-Based Account of Professional Responsibility* <https://doi.org/10.2139/ssrn.2840864>

Delacroix, S. 2018. 'Taking Turing by Surprise? Designing Digital Computers for morally-loaded contexts' *arXiv preprint arXiv:1803.04548 [cs.CY]* <https://arxiv.org/abs/1803.04548>

Dietrich, F. and C. List. 2013. 'Where Do Preferences Come From?'. *International Journal of Game Theory* 42 (3), 613–37

Dix, A. 2007. 'Designing for Appropriation', in *Proceedings of the 21st British*

HCI Group Annual Conference on People and Computers: HCI. . .But Not As We Know It – Volume 2, Swindon, UK: BCS Learning & Development Ltd., 27–30

Druckman, J. N. and A. Lupia. 2000. 'Preference Formation' *Annual Review of Political Science* 3 (1), 1–24

Edwards, L. and M. Veale. 2017. 'Slave to the Algorithm? Why a "Right to an Explanation" is Probably Not The Remedy You Are Looking For'. *Duke Law and Technology Review* 16 (1), 18–84

Edwards, L. and M. Veale. 2018. 'Enslaving the Algorithm: From a "Right to an Explanation" to a "Right to Better Decisions"?'. *IEEE Security & Privacy* 16 (3), 46–54 <https://doi.org/10.1109/MSP.2018.2701152>

Ekman, P. and W. V. Friesen. 1969. 'Nonverbal Leakage and Clues to Deception †'. *Psychiatry* 32 (1), 88–106

Ekstrand, M. D. and M. C. Willemsen. 2016. 'Behaviorism Is Not Enough: Better Recommendations through Listening to Users'. In *Proceedings of the 10th ACM Conference on Recommender System (RecSys'16)*. New York, NY: ACM Press, 221–4

Elliott, M. 2011. 'Has the Common Law Duty to Give Reasons Come of Age Yet?'. *Public Law* (Jan), 56–74

Faridani, S., E. Bitton, K. Ryokai and K. Goldberg. 2010. 'Opinion Space: A Scalable Tool for Browsing Online Comments'. In *Proceedings of the 28th International Conference on Human Factors in Computing Systems – CHI'10*. New York, NY: ACM Press, 1175

Gregory, R., S. Lichtenstein and P. Slovic. 1993. 'Valuing Environmental Resources: A Constructive Approach'. *Journal of Risk and Uncertainty* 7 (2), 177–97.

Guidotti, R., A. Monreale, F. Turini, D. Pedreschi and F. Giannotti. 2018. 'A Survey Of Methods For Explaining Black Box Models', *arXiv Preprint 1802. 01933v [cs. CY]*

Gunes, H. and H. Hung. 2016. 'Is Automatic Facial Expression Recognition of Emotions Coming to a Dead End? The Rise of the New Kids on the Block'. *Image and Vision Computing* 55, 6–8

Gunes, H. and M. Piccardi. 2005. 'Affect Recognition from Face and Body: Early Fusion vs. Late Fusion', in *2005 IEEE International Conference on Systems, Man and Cybernetics*, vol. 4, IEEE, 3437–43

Gürses, S. and J. van Hoboken. 2018. 'Privacy after the Agile Turn'. In E. Selinger, J. Polonetsky and O. Tene (eds), *The Cambridge Handbook of Consumer Privacy*, 1st edn., Cambridge: Cambridge University Press, 579–601

Healey, J. and R. Picard. 1998. 'Digital Processing of Affective Signals'. In *Proceedings of the 1998 IEEE International Conference on Acoustics, Speech and Signal Processing, ICASSP'98*, IEEE, 3749–52

Helm, T. 2018. 'Was the Brexit Poll Compromised? We May Need a Public Debate About That', *The Guardian*, 14 April <www.theguardian.com/uk-news/2018/apr/14/damian-collins-mp-interview-need-reform-electoral-law-digital-age> accessed 15 April 2018

Hildebrandt, M. 2015. *Smart Technologies and the End(s) of Law*. Cheltenham, UK: Edward Elgar

Hildebrandt, M. 2019. 'Privacy As Protection of the Incomputable Self: From Agnostic to Agonistic Machine Learning'. *Theoretical Inquiries in Law* 19 (1) <https://doi.org/10.2139/ssrn.3081776>

Houben, S., C. Golsteijn, S. Gallacher, R. Johnson, S. Bakker, N. Marquardt,

L. Capra and Y. Rogers. 2016. 'Physikit: Data Engagement Through Physical Ambient Visualizations in the Home'. In *Proceedings of the 2016 CHI Conference on Human Factors in Computing Systems*, ACM, 1608–19

Kang, B., N. Tintarev, T. Höllerer and J. O'Donovan. 2016. 'What am I Not Seeing? An Interactive Approach to Social Content Discovery in Microblogs'. In: Spiro E. and Ahn, Y. Y. (eds.) *Proceedings of the Conference on Social Informatics (SocInfo 2016)*. Springer, Cham, 279–94

Koebler, J. 2017. 'Source: Apple Will Fight "Right to Repair" Legislation', <https://motherboard.vice.com/en_us/article/mgxayp/source-apple-will-fight-right-to-repair-legislation> accessed 16 May 2018

Kramer, A. D. I., J. E. Guillory and J. T. Hancock. 2014. 'Experimental Evidence of Massive-Scale Emotional Contagion through Social Networks'. *Proceedings of the National Academy of Sciences of the United States of America* 111 (24), 8788–90

Kriplean, T., J. Morgan, D. Freelon, A. Borning and L. Bennett. 2012a. 'Supporting Reflective Public Thought with Considerit'. In *Proceedings of the ACM 2012 Conference on Computer Supported Cooperative Work – CSCW'12*. New York, NY: ACM Press, 265

Kriplean, T., M. Toomim, J. Morgan, A. Borning and A. Ko. 2012b. 'Is This What You Meant?: Promoting Listening on the Web with Reflect'. In *Proceedings of the 2012 ACM Annual Conference on Human Factors in Computing Systems – CHI'12*. New York, NY: ACM Press, 1559

Li, I., A. K. Dey and J. Forlizzi. 2011. 'Understanding My Data, Myself: Supporting Self-Reflection with Ubicomp Technologies'. In *Proceedings of the 13th International Conference on Ubiquitous Computing – UbiComp'11*, New York, NY: ACM Press, 405

Mahieu, R. L. P., H. Asghari and M. van Eeten. 2018. 'Collectively Exercising the Right of Access: Individual Effort, Societal Effect'. *Internet Policy Review* 7 (3) <https://doi.org/10.14763/2018.3.927>

Merton, R. K. and E. Barber. 2011. *The Travels and Adventures of Serendipity: A Study in Sociological Semantics and the Sociology of Science*. Princeton, NJ: Princeton University Press

Munson, S. A., S. Y. Lee and P. Resnick. 2013. 'Encouraging Reading of Diverse Political Viewpoints with a Browser Widget', in *ICWSM*, aaai.org <www.aaai.org/ocs/index.php/ICWSM/ICWSM13/paper/viewFile/6119/6381>

Oswald, M. 2018. 'Algorithm-Assisted Decision-Making in the Public Sector: Framing the Issues Using Administrative Law Rules Governing Discretionary Power'. *Philosophical Transactions of the Royal Society A: Mathematical, Physical and Engineering Sciences* 376 (2128), 20170359

Palmetshofer, W. and A. Semsrott. 2018. 'Get Involved: We Crack the Schufa!' <https://okfn.de/blog/2018/02/openschufa-english/> accessed 15 April 2018

Picard, R. W. 1997. *Affective Computing*. Cambridge, MA: The MIT Press

Rouvroy, A. 2013. 'The End(s) of Critique: Data Behaviourism Versus Due Process'. In *Privacy, Due Process and the Computational Turn*. London: Routledge, 157–82.

Sangiovanni, A. 2017. *Humanity without Dignity: Moral Equality, Respect and Human Rights*. Cambridge, MA: Harvard University Press

Slovák, P., C. Frauenberger and G. Fitzpatrick. 2017. *Reflective Practicum: A Framework of Sensitising Concepts to Design for Transformative Reflection*. New York, NY: ACM Press, 2696–707

Srinivasan, A. 2018. 'The Aptness of Anger'. *The Journal of Political Philosophy* 26 (2), 123–44

Sunstein, C. R. and R. H. Thaler. 2003. 'Libertarian Paternalism Is Not an Oxymoron'. *The University of Chicago Law Review* 70 (4), 1159

Tintarev, N., S. Rostami and B. Smyth. 2018. 'Knowing the Unknown: Visualising Consumption Blind-Spots in Recommender Systems'. In *Proceedings of the 33rd ACM/SIGAPP Symposium On Applied Computing. Pau, France 9–13 April 2018*

Trielli, D., J. A. Stark and N. Diakopolous. 2018. *Algorithm Tips: A Resource for Algorithmic Accountability in Government* <https://perma.cc/3ER3-49FE> accessed 15 April 2018

Wallach, W. and C. Allen. 2008. *Moral Machines: Teaching Robots Right from Wrong*. Oxford: Oxford University Press

Webster, A. and J. Vassileva. 2007. 'The Keepup Recommender System'. In *Proceedings of the 2007 ACM Conference on Recommender Systems – RecSys'07*, New York, NY: ACM Press, 173

Weiser, M. 1994. 'The World is Not a Desktop'. *Interactions* 1 (1), 7–8

Weller, A. 2017. 'Challenges for Transparency'. In *2017 ICML Workshop on Human Interpretability in Machine Learning (WHI 2017)*

Wisneski, C., H. Ishii, A. Dahley, M. Gorbet, S. Brave, B. Ullmer and P. Yarin. 1998. 'Ambient Displays: Turning Architectural Space Into an Interface Between People and Digital Information'. In *International Workshop on Cooperative Buildings*. Berlin: Springer, 22–32

Xu, F., J. Zhang and J. Z. Wang. 2017. 'Microexpression Identification and Categorization Using a Facial Dynamics Map'. *IEEE Transactions on Affective Computing* 8 (2), 254–67

Yan, W.-J., X. Li, S.-J. Wang, G. Zhao, Y.-J. Liu, Y.-H. Chen and X. Fu. 2014. 'CASME II: An Improved Spontaneous Micro-Expression Database and the Baseline Evaluation'. *PloS One* 9 (1), e86041

Zabelina, D., D. L. Robinson, D. Council, J. R. Michael and K. Bresin. 2011. *Patterning and Nonpatterning in Creative Cognition: Insights From Performance in a Random Number Generation Task* <https://doi.org/10.1037/a0025452>

6. Rethinking transparency for the Internet of Things

m.c. schraefel, Richard Gomer, Enrico Gerding and Carsten Maple[1]

INTRODUCTION

A key aspect of the onli*f*e world that Diana inhabits is the extent to which technology, with agency, is built into the environment. Toma, her Personal Digital Assistant (PDA), not only communicates with other PDAs that represent individuals, but with agents that control physical infrastructure – heating, lighting or access – or oversee an array of business processes, such as advertising or data gathering. These embedded agents – which we'd refer to as the Internet of Things (IoT) – are programmed with priorities and agendas that represent the interests of their owners; making trade-offs (for instance) between comfort and energy efficiency, or security and ease-of-access; some may co-operate with Toma to help fulfil Diana's needs or to respect her preferences about (for instance) being shown targeted advertising, but that co-operation is by no means guaranteed. In some cases – as is so often the case today – Diana may be faced with the choice of either submitting to surveillance by an IoT environment, or foregoing access to particular spaces or services altogether. In other cases, it may not even be apparent – to Toma or to Diana – that this embedded technology, and the agency that it exhibits, even exists at all.

Human–Computer Interaction (HCI) and AI are well placed to imagine tomorrow's IoT-enabled environment (and today's personal data sharing) as a more equitable, negotiable and sustainable practice than either the take-it-or-leave-it, agree-or-not approach that is so pervasive in 2018 or a dystopian future in which we are subjected to the agency and surveillance of IoT devices without any kind of control or perhaps even awareness. This chapter focuses on how, with the IoT about to explode, it is essential that HCI, along with AI, embrace this space, and design it from a human-centred, human-valued perspective. We propose several concepts and questions to help envision the IoT as such a consentful, human-centred space.

The Internet of Things, we are told, is about to achieve epic scale, with Cisco and Ericsson (Dave Evans and Hans Vestburg, respectively) having predicted that there will be 50 billion devices connected to the Internet by 2020 (though each have since revised their estimates down to 30 billion and 28 billion). Their ecosystem is wildly heterogeneous. A multitude of devices, working in isolation and as networked constellations, will collect data and use it to alter the environments around us; in service of a diverse range of stakeholders and subject to varied terms and conditions. One of the key concerns of the IoT and its high-speed cousin, the Internet of Vehicles, is just how that data may be captured, shared and used not only within one fixed environment like a home, but across environments, from the wired High Street, to a smart healthcare environment, to our own homes, and in the transport infrastructure that connects those places together.

In other words, as the objects of our environment become more connected to the Net, do we simply become another internet-connected thing ourselves, and thereby reduce our privacy, our control over the environment around us and our civic values, in the name of everything from convenience to counterterrorism? Likewise, given the vast scale, speed and heterogeneity of this expanding ecosystem, are we creating new risks to our personal and national security, both as citizens and as societies – not even from wilful hacking but just because the scale of our IoT reach will exceed our grasp of all the necessary protections – like rights to privacy, freedom of expression, to be safe from surveillance to name but a few – that we assume are ours in a civil society?

INSIGHTS

In response to the current data status quo and in anticipation of this changing ecosystem, new rules for data sharing have been established; for example, the European Union's General Data Protection Regulation (GDPR). Some of these principles have been put in place well in advance of the technical means to sustain their implementation. For instance, despite years of research into how to present privacy notices, few people – if anybody – would argue that they actually provide meaningful transparency to citizens; responding to citizens' right of access is still a labour-intensive manual process in most organisations; and new rights to data portability or the right to be forgotten throw up thorny technical problems relating to data interchange and offline backups, respectively. Consequently, there is a key moment for HCI and User Experience (UX) research and design to influence society for good: not just to design wonderful devices for the IoT, but also to consider the wicked problems of how to make the mechanisms and personal-data-driven assumptions that enable the IoT apparent and accountable to developers, designers, businesses, policymakers and citizens. By this deliberate engagement we can help surface the implications of the pervasive requirement that we share our data in order to engage with services. From this foundation, we can develop models of how people understand data, their social expectations about how data behaves or may be used, and means for developers to know their designs comply with these expectations – and for citizens and policymakers to be able to trust that they do. Because of HCI's expertise in human-centred approaches to design, HCI researchers and designers have a key role to play in informing the shape of these exchanges and to create an ecosystem that supports social, technical, meaningful consent at IoT scale.

To better see these opportunities for the future, let's consider the status quo of consent to data-sharing in the current digital economy.

CITIZEN CONSENT IN DATA SHARING

The Internet has made liars of us all. No one has used a browser, a social media site or a smartphone app without encountering a box that says, before continuing, that A) we have read the terms and conditions of a service and B) we agree to them. We click 'agree' when we haven't a clue if we do or don't really agree. In other words, in a world where our personal data is largely the oil that greases the wheels that keep the Internet running, we have very little meaningful say in what data is collected and how it's used, and no real understanding of why we may wish to limit it, or for that matter, give it away in buckets. Given the current (some might say insulting) approach to consent, this status quo is not surprising. Regulation, unfortunately, has to date created only a veneer of consent – a legal illusion of choice and control – but design has not delivered interactions that support genuine informed and meaningful choices that laws such as the GDPR call for.

The stats are very clear about how broken terms and conditions (T&C) pages are: if we were to read these 'agreements' it would be nearly a full-time job (McDonald and Cranor 2008). More disturbingly, these terms are generally written to require a sophisticated level of reading comprehension – beyond the norm for the population using these services (Moran, Luger and Rodden 2014). So even if we did read these T&Cs, most of us wouldn't understand them. When we make decisions in such an environment, they are uninformed, and, when we give our consent under such conditions, it isn't meaningful.

The timing of consent decisions is also problematic. We are also asked to consider complex terms at exactly the moment that work in HCI on task interruption has shown is the wrong time (Trafton and Monk 2007): when that request gets in the way of our primary task. We click the 'agree' button because clicking it gets rid of the interruption so that we can get on with posting our cat video, or uploading a draft of our paper to a co-editing site, or synchronizing our calendar with a cloud service, not because by clicking the button we agree with the stated terms.

Many of us became acclimatized to this meaningless box clicking around installing software: yes, yes we don't own it, uh huh we're just leasing it, and no we won't make copies of it. Sure. In those days, however, it was rare for software to call home to the mothership to report on our usage or check our ongoing entitlement to use it. Now, it is commonplace for software to be deployed as a service that knows exactly where it is and how many copies have been authorized. But that service, especially when deployed on phones or mobile devices, gathers far more information for many more very amorphous reasons than just software licensing. More troubling, as has been shown when installing apps on phones: few people are even aware that the app is (re)setting permissions to access personal data not needed for its operation (Shih, Liccardi and Weitzner 2016), such as gathering up our contacts and text messages. There is also the belief that this personal-data capture is a trade with the developer, and that if one pays for the app then that data trade is closed. Not so. Some apps take even more liberties in the paid version. Consent is not meaningless in this context – it's non-existent.

In the app case, research suggests that few people are aware that data-access permissions can be set per app to limit access to that data (Shih, Liccardi and Weitzner 2016). And why would a person consider whether it's OK for an app to access some of their data if they have no awareness this data is being accessed in the first place? Indeed, the situation is not much different on the Web. For people in some areas of computing, we may take it for granted that unless we use services like ad blockers or virtual private networks, we are being tracked across interlocking webs via mechanisms like fingerprinting and cookies. For instance, every time we put a URL into a social media feed and it is shortened by that service, that URL reflects its path through the network – who has used it, who has looked at it, where they've gone after visiting it, and so on (Gomer et al. 2013). Our social networks and beliefs are effectively exposed. New research-based services like TrackMeNot (Howe and Nissenbaum 2009) run randomized Web searches from our browsers in order to confuse this profile that is constructible from our footsteps through these pathways of the Net. Problematically, however, the few studies that have looked at how tracking is perceived show that only a small number of people in the general public are aware of the degree to which they are being followed online, or that their Internet traffic is being shared among various, mostly commercial entities. The data suggests that when people do learn of this tracking, they characterize it as creepy (Ur, Leon and Cranor 2012) and want to find ways to control it (Melicher et al. 2016).

We see this awareness effect in other data-related transactions: once people are aware of what is happening to their data without their consent, they demand better conditions. What of the privacy paradox, then? In the privacy paradox, people say they're concerned about privacy, but if you put a form in front of them and request personal data, they readily hand it over. As more researchers have now shown, this response is not a contradiction. We are a sense-making people: if we are asked for something – especially tied to something we want – we assume there must be a rationale for it. We assume the best. When responses are probed, however, many people who provide very personal data to a service do so without a clear model of how that data may be used by the service itself; how that data may be used by other people accessing that service; what of that data is actually necessary for the service to function, and the risks associated with sharing that data. We are busy: it is easier to trust there is a good reason for this data request, it seems, than to stop and check if we're being scammed. Indeed, we need only consider the outrage when those who do stop and look raise a red flag about terms and conditions. Doing so, however, has required the work of what we might call social interpreters to translate the language of the revised terms and conditions, moving it out of the abstract and into concrete terms that are meaningful to people. These changes otherwise remain opaque, again making our consent socially meaningless.

TOWARDS APPARENCY AND SEMANTIC/ PRAGMATIC TRANSPARENCY

Just from the above scenarios, we can see numerous opportunities for interaction research and design to change the status quo around data consent from meaningless to meaningful. Fundamental to any change, however, is to see a need for it. This is what we've been calling apparency. One may have very well-defined terms and conditions, but if people don't even know that their contacts are being accessed by a puzzle game they downloaded, if this use is not apparent in the first place, transparency about the terms of an unperceived process is at best meaningless.

As designers, we can help to develop the means to make such data processes apparent in order for the terms to be meaningfully transparent.

In the context of ubiquitous computing, Matthew Chalmers (Chalmers and Galani 2004) framed the exposure of making the properties of a system apparent as 'seamfulness', as opposed to seamlessness or, more particularly, sameness. For instance, rather than hiding which cellphone tower a phone may be using, it might be better to make this information available. Some people might find it useful and empowering: being able to look under the hood of a system at various levels of detail, specifically in order to engage with it and change it, is a valuable property.

In data-driven services – like most of those on the Internet – one can point to the terms and conditions and label them as either transparent or opaque, based on the language used and the specificity of descriptions. But such transparency refers largely to only an acknowledgement that data is being collected and that it may be used to 'improve the quality of the service' – as cookie notices on websites in the EU constantly assert without explanation of what or how, exactly. Apparency would seek to make those connections clear and traceable toward meaningful transparency. For example, there are no cues to the user of a downloaded game that make it apparent that there are personal-data settings associated with this app and that changing them (or not) will have an effect on risks of burglary (GPS access), identity theft (contacts access), workplace harassment (enabling anyone online to see pictures from social occasions), job-selection discrimination (social media commentary being available), or preferential or discriminatory pricing (Hannak et al. 2014). Nor is it readily apparent that shared data is churned into use for targeting advertisements, not only on the site where the data is initiated but also from that site to other sites, and through a network of brokers and advertisers, as a person surfs the Web (Gomer et al. 2013). The simple act of touching these sites is of course itself valuable data that is both unapparent and untransparent.

Indeed, we might reframe a progressive scale from apparency to transparency, in which we have apparency, semantic transparency and pragmatic transparency. Let's call it apparency to s/p transparency. Apparency reflects how an activity – in this case a data activity – is signalled. Semantic transparency addresses whether we know what the terms of the apparent activity are and mean; pragmatic transparency reflects the degree to which we know what these data actions actually do or entail.

The idea that elements of an artefact or system should be communicated through the form or appearance of an artefact is well established in interaction design; most notably through Norman's re-purposing of the concept of Affordance from Ecology. In an ecological sense, an affordance is something that an environment provides (positive or negative) to an organism. In design, Affordance takes on a suggestive sense: an affordance is a use or feature that an object suggests it could be used for – a common example would be the use of underlining to indicate that a hyperlink can be followed, or the use of a drop shadow to suggest that part of a touch-screen can be used as a button. HCI's repurposing of affordance draws an important distinction between what is possible and what is perceptible; and it follows that good design is the art of communicating possible actions, and their outcomes.

HCI has largely been concerned with how the users' own possible actions can be communicated through design, though. Concerns around privacy – or more generally those of personal agency – are bound up in more complex multi-stakeholder systems, replete with power dynamics and potentially competing objectives. Apparency is as much about communicating the actions of those other parties – to intercept communications, or to collect and process personal data – as it is about communicating the actions that the immediate user might take themselves.

There are already lovely examples of apparency and s/p transparency design online. A padlock icon in a web browser's address bar is used to indicate a secure channel. If one is unfamiliar with the padlock, clicking on it usually displays text to make more of the semantics of the process apparent: that data is being transmitted over an encrypted channel. For pragmatic transparency, these claims can be explored and tested. Most web cams now have a built in LED that illuminates to indicate when the camera is active, making the otherwise imperceptible recording process apparent; and, in many web browsers, a browser tab that is accessing the camera is indicated by an additional icon, allowing camera use to be interrogated further. These are signifiers of apparency, seams that can be exposed and tested in terms of semantic and pragmatic transparency. We can decide how far we wish to probe those signifiers, but with them, the resources are there to make a more informed judgement about the channel. The padlock is an elegant, apparent expression that makes the semantic and pragmatic transparency of a binary state richly available.

Relatively few examples of such apparency and transparency exist for the Internet of Things, though. IoT devices that are embedded into the environment rather than held in one's hand may lack any means of interacting with us at all; it may be contingent on other pieces of technology, like Toma, to make these hidden systems apparent to us – or to convey our preferences to them – as we move into their proximity.

Apparency for the properties that would inform a consent decision are potentially nuanced and variable. A meaningful consent decision for some people might take into account whether the requesting party had a good record of keeping personal data secure, whether they had an ethical approach to handling personal data, or perhaps even knowledge about whether they were avoiding tax. Our aim in building apparency is not just (or, possibly, even) to convey technical properties of a system, but to support people in making decisions and exerting their own agency in a way that reflects their values and concerns. Such a framing leads us to consider, beyond apparency and transparency, notions of controllability and accountability.

CONTROLLABILITY AND ACCOUNTABILITY

It would be a considerable step forward to reflect, in an interface, the actions of another party both apparent, and transparent, but then what? In support of agency, we must consider not only whether things are apparent, but whether the people to whom those processes are now visible are able to exert any control over them. In design terms, we would like to create new affordances – new means of interacting – that (for instance) allow one to engage, disengage or shape the processes that have been made apparent.

For example, knowing about ad blockers allows someone who does not wish to be tracked by ad networks to turn that tracking off. In order to do so, that tracking must be apparent, but the possibility of acting to control it must also be afforded somehow.

In our own experiments with a prototype system called the Web Mirror, we've observed that detailed semantic transparency is often no more effective than telling people about possible tracking countermeasures – a finding that suggests showing pragmatic ways to *disagree* might support our notion of consent more effectively than focussing on detailed transparency and agreement.

In the case of consent, at least so far as it is understood in laws such as the GDPR, apparency, transparency and controllability are tightly coupled at the point at which someone signals their consent to something. A consent interaction is, in itself, a means of exerting control – of accepting or rejecting a proposal. Where consent fails, such as the much maligned 'cookie banners' that are now prevalent across the web, it's often because important aspects of cookie use (like tracking) are not made apparent, and there's no practical means of rejecting what's proposed.

Apparency, transparency and controllability are future-oriented concepts, though. They refer to an ability to understand and shape what's happening now, or what could or will happen in the future. Where something can, and is, made apparent and controllable in advance then those concepts might arguably be sufficient. What about scenarios where something is not apparent or controllable in advance, though? Or where that apparency or control is insufficient, incorrect or even deliberately ignored?

To deal with those issues, we turn towards accountability – the idea that it should be possible to inspect past actions, and to seek redress in response to mistakes or malicious actions. Accountability is a key part of privacy regulation such as GDPR (Urquhart, Lodge and Crabtree 2018). Accountability builds on ideas of apparency and transparency, in the sense that it involves an element of being clear about what has taken place; and on controllability, in the sense that it engenders some form of acting. Unlike how those concepts are often understood, pro-active and in advance, in the case of accountability those concepts are also meaningfully applied to actions in the past. In order for an IoT system to be accountable, it may be necessary to interrogate where and when data was collected or processed, and what outcomes that processing led to (pragmatic transparency). Moreover, it might be necessary to correct erroneous past actions somehow; either to prevent them from happening again in the future, or to make up for damage that has been caused.

Accountability is particularly important when it comes to consent because many of the restrictions set during a consent exchange – such as purpose limitation – can't be enforced through technical means; accountability provides a mechanism for individuals to check whether their trust in a data controller to honour their wishes was warranted, as well as providing a pressure to encourage data controllers to be honest.

TIMING

As stated earlier, we know from HCI research on interruption that when we're asked to consider anything that takes us away from our primary task, it's simply not going to get our full attention, especially when it's something as abstract as data permissions or terms and conditions. Just get out of our way! Decoupling decisions, in time, from the point that those decisions are required by a system also overcomes practical implications of the IoT, where many devices will lack a means of interacting directly with users and hence will become dependent on other devices that do.

When we look, there are multiple examples of such asynchronous transactions all around us in the physical world. Consider making purchases. Each time we withdraw cash from a bank machine or use a debit or credit card, we get a receipt of the transaction – and that's about it. We are not asked to review our purchasing history at the time of the transaction. Instead, we receive a monthly statement both as a record of our spending and debts, and as a log we are encouraged to review in case of errors. That monthly statement itself is a review process, but it is a data trail of what has happened with our various assets, from cash on hand to credit lines.

The statement, however, along with our receipts, fits into a larger practice of personal money management, including tasks like setting a budget, saving for a purchase, investing, and so on. Insurance purchasing is part of a similar genre of practices where we consider the terms and conditions of a policy as best we can, well before we actually need the policy – in fact, it's required that we have a policy before we need it. We may consider the terms and prices of the policy, if these change, before we renew, and then start shopping around again.

In other words, for many kinds of existing and important transactions, we have established practices to review attributes from the transaction history as well as the terms and conditions. These reviews fit into a larger mechanism that informs our quality of life, from how we manage debt with financial planning to how we manage risk with insurance provisions. A key point, however, is that even though not all citizens practice such fiscal hygiene, the data is there to enable those processes. Such is not the case for personal-data transactions on the Internet. Surely in HCI we can draw on these analogous practices to better design our engagement with the terms and conditions of data consent, and with auditing consent transactions. And surely in the development of policy we can leverage the strengths and weaknesses of these analogous practices to help us reflect on how better to value and deliver on such transactions.

NEGOTIATION/AUTOMATION

Of course, one of the reasons for reviewing our financial transactions is to see if the terms of service are fair and competitive. We use these terms to evaluate and select service providers. After all, when we agree to terms and conditions, we engage in a contract with the supplier. In the data-driven world, however, these contracts are one way and binary. We as the consumers of the services can say only yay or nay. Sometimes, saying nay can feel impossible: if one's whole community is making use of a service, it's hard to be the lone holdout.

Once again, if we turn to real-world examples, negotiation is a key part of just about any other agreement of exchange between parties. We negotiate everything from our contract with employers or staff to our fee for network access. Many of us can't walk out of a shop without either talking a price down or haggling for extras at no cost. Negotiation is ubiquitous – except on the Internet. Why?

We have been exploring how we might be able to automate consent in terms of negotiable data-sharing preferences using autonomous agents (Baarslag et al. 2017), and thus begin to create richer, non-binary terms for data exchange and service provision. In this approach, a person can say under which conditions or for which types of services they may be willing to share their text messages but not their images, their browsing history but not anything else, and so on.

In our studies we see that people are willing to share more data on average when they can negotiate the data-sharing terms. Our studies also demonstrate that a negotiation-oriented approach to permission management better enables people to align their data-sharing practices with their actual privacy preferences. Our recent work (in submission) perhaps not surprisingly shows that permissions are not sufficiently context-sensitive for meaningful consent: sharing photos is far too broad; sharing photos of public spaces with health services is more appropriate. Being able to trace and retract those images is also important.

We have touched on only two designs around consent: 1) our work with mirroring back a Web tracker's reflections of us, and 2) offering asynchronous opportunities to set responsive terms about sharing conditions to automate consent. There are many more mechanisms HCI designers can offer to support richer, more nuanced engagement with a data-sharing ecosystem. It's important to be clear within these design explorations that there is a distinction between privacy and sharing. People are not averse to sharing some personal data. Much to our surprise, we often found people keen to share data (sometimes their friends' contact information but not their own) in exchange for services when they understood the terms and they had a say in that exchange. In other words, where apparency to s/p transparency was supported, data-sharing quality improved and often increased. Likewise, not all businesses are driven to grab out on personal data wherever possible. At our workshops with researchers, policymakers and industry members, we have been delighted to find that some businesses would like to see how a nuanced data policy for negotiating these terms could work for new services and be a business differentiator.

THE INTERNET OF TERMS AND CONDITIONS (OF THINGS)

We already experience what has been called consent fatigue when we are regularly asked to agree to effectively meaningless terms and conditions. Likewise, when terms and conditions change – and we see such notices – it seems gratuitous to ask us to say we agree to new terms when, what is our choice if we do not yet we wish to buy an app from a developer that is available only through this one vendor site? The number of times UK/EU citizens see 'this site uses cookies' – when there are no options not to accept them – has caused more annoyance than engagement. The current state of the art for consent, therefore, is meaningless consent. But at least we might say we are asked. We see a screen. We hit a button.

In the Internet of Things (IoT), the predicted number of devices that we will encounter in our homes, on the way to work, at work, at play and on the road is, to use a biblical term and all it entails, legion. In the IoT, every fridge will know your name, but many things will not have interfaces through which consent can be requested and given – or not.

Interactions will be handed off from one infrastructure to another. As we move between districts in our autonomous vehicles, our consent may be either assumed unnecessary or implied as given, yet the data terms and conditions that apply when moving from one infrastructure to another – and the guarantees of data protection – may be different. Many may recall the problems of Google Street View taking pictures with identifiable people in the images: no consent was obtained. This case was a brilliant example of the usually opaque becoming very apparent against a background of social expectations of privacy: it was quickly established that such exposure of identifiable faces in Street View was not acceptable.

Likewise, there are recent examples in subways, malls and museums in the UK, and airports in the US, where the MAC address of a mobile phone is tracked without any requests for consent or any options to shut off access to this information that was never intended for these purposes, the assertion being that MAC addresses are not tied to the individual. Both legal and technical experts (McIntyre 2010) would argue that this assertion is at best dubious, and further that such data is all too easy to combine with one or two other seemingly innocuous data bits to de-anonymize someone.

These kinds of seemingly anonymous though personal data-tracking contexts are key examples of how HCI expertise can help shape policy: we are part of the dialogue around identifying the art of the possible for interactive technology to support citizens' well-being. Ours is the community with insight into what is possible for interactive technology to do now, or in the near future, to help shape approaches to laws for individual and social interaction.

Fundamentally, if, as a civil society, we assert a right or belief or ethical principle that we have a stake in the use of the data we generate as citizens, and a right to strong protection of data about us, whether about what we read or where we sit to read it, then we need mechanisms that can negotiate our consent on our behalf at both IoT scale and IoT speed. It is eminently possible to build such infrastructures of consent. But for them to be effective, HCI has a key contribution to make to ensure that the approaches are both meaningful and sensible. Here we discuss just a few of the questions HCI research can help address.

THE SHAPING OF THE SHAPE OF THINGS TO COME: BAKING-IN APPARENCY

How do users model IoT apparency and s/p transparency? The IoT is still largely terra incognita. We mainly hear about its failures. For example, IoT devices have been hacked to create denial-of-service attacks on domain-name servers, thus cutting off Internet communications (Woolf 2016). Or you may recall the TVs that track every word we speak in their presence, where the terms and conditions say this is all fair game.

Where HCI can lead is to develop scenarios of interaction and models of people's understanding of IoT interaction. Plainly, without understanding what we as citizens think is happening with these devices – and in particular with the data we enable them to capture – we can't design safer, more usable experiences. For instance, trust and risk are concepts often discussed as putting the IoT project itself at risk. People may wrongly trust a service, such as online baby monitors, when the user experience maps to one's expectations: look, I can see my child. Success. But there could be a lack of what we might call risk apparency in what was happening with the data being made available. What if the service managing the connection between the camera and one's phone was snooping? Here the perception of trust is inappropriately high, and of risk, inappropriately low. How interaction design can help connect with potentially autonomous agents to help users come to more informed understandings of these systems' interactions within an IoT ecosystem is a new kind of interaction design challenge.

Without understanding what we as citizens think is happening with these devices, we can't design safer, more usable experiences.

Where do users' and designers' models diverge, and how should we design for this? There is fundamental work to be done to engage with industries that want to deliver smart homes, cities, hospitals and cars to connect those aspirations with citizens' understanding and expectations. In 2016, Nest 'bricked' its smart hubs, devices that cost roughly $300. It was a blunt lack of apparency toward consumers who had made a purchase in good faith – and who believed, based on experiences with other devices in their homes, that Nest would continue to function as long as it was turned on, like a lamp or a router. Would a smart car be shut off by its developers if it too were construed to be always and only the property or IP of its service provider? This is a new model of how we think about physical devices. While we may be accustomed to buying software licences, this approach to hardware is unexpected; when we buy something physical we are used to owning it. We need to explore whether we need new design languages or at least new semantics to signal these new properties – not just to accept them but also to be able to make choices about whether we wish to invest in them or to negotiate their terms. We also need apparency around the data flows between devices in these environments in order to understand, agree or disagree with, or change them.

For instance, the majority of fitness trackers are tied to a particular vendor's software service. The vendor accesses all the data. They may have Application Programming Interfaces (APIs) to enable other services to access that data as well under certain terms, but then both services have an individual's data. The individual can't simply buy the hardware and set up their own software server to track their own data. Likewise, a software service can't come along to map to the hardware in order to create an open data repository of step counting from any tracking source. This could act as a public good or a research archive, or could support citizen science to explore who does the most stepping in what age group at what time of day. If we buy the hardware, the current model allows us to talk only to its software service or cloud. One might call this a kind of consent choice, but again, when all trackers play by these rules, one is not choosing among data models but rather among colours. This example is just of one device. Apple's proprietary ecosystem with its home and health kits promises to be the infrastructure that bridges between devices, providing analytics and a common voice-enabled interface. The apparency to consumers of how data flows behind this convenience is largely occluded. We don't mean to say that the ecosystem is evil, but rather that without these flows and constraints being apparent, we can't truly consent to data about us flowing into the common pool of these ecosystems; without controllability, we can't meaningfully exert any agency or choice; and without accountability we can't check whether our trust in services is well placed. In these circumstances, innovation is throttled, not enabled.

Can users form adequate models of device ecosystems and their infrastructure? In order to make meaningful regulations, policymakers need high data apparency to be modelled as part of the data flows across intersecting or competing infrastructures or local ecosystem boundaries. By way of example, right now if we go from one coffee shop to another to access the Internet, we may be asked at each one to sign in and agree to the terms and conditions. Our access to sites at these locations may be faster or slower or perhaps time-limited, but the experience is largely similar. And yet, without data apparency, it is impossible to tell whether different data is being captured and what additional tracking is being added to the sites we visit.

There is in these interactions a lack of another type of apparency signalling – what can happen to our data over time. To return to the apparency of the padlock icon, it signals a steady state process: the channel is either secure or it isn't. There is only a 'now' to that signal. But our captured data can be so multi-purpose and can contribute to so many other ways of constructing a pattern. Time – in particular the future – is an unmet, open challenge. For example, in our current negotiation models, we test only those conditions where the data stays within a particular time frame. But what happens to collected data when the company is sold or closes and sells off its assets? The EU GDPR tries to take these kinds of future-proofing scenarios into account, but how do we represent these decisions in terms of interactions, from apparency to semantic and pragmatic transparency, to help consumers, businesses and policymakers make choices? With rich apparency to s/p transparency interactions in which time is one of the variables to make apparent, consent for data use can be far more meaningful.

Apparency of these conditions can also enable developers and businesses to have new markets and can create new and valuable differentiators. For instance, hardware developers may create open trackers that output open data to a health or storage device or service of their choice, where people themselves offer up their data for open studies, in which, like open software, access to the data used by any third party must remain open. Likewise, controllability will enable people to engage – or disengage – to the extent that they are comfortable, or only to the point that the benefits to them begin to diminish. Supported by accountability, trustworthy products and services can build a reputation that erodes the all-too-common feeling that services are creepy or even adversarial.

CONCLUSION

If we do not have apparency-to-accountability models of how data about us is actually being used now and in potential futures, or how the IoT systems around us are operating, we can't consent – or not – in a meaningful way that allows us to protect our interests and exert our own agency.

To consider whether or not we consent – assuming we can have a clearer sense of consent terms – we need a prime time in which to consider the terms of our consent policy, as we would our bank statements or insurance.

To have consent, we need greater apparency of what will follow as a result of our consent. For the scale and speed of the IoT, this apparency/consent decision will need to be automated on our behalf; there is rich potential to create nuanced human-centred services with our colleagues in AI that can leverage the negotiation of consent/sharing terms.

Having strong, clear apparency, controllability and accountability as a backbone to meaningful consent will also help clarify risks within the data flows of large-scale, heterogeneous IoT infrastructures, from homes to cities to national infrastructure.

Overall, by improving apparency to accountability, we make meaningful consent possible. When meaningful consent becomes part of a system, entirely new kinds of services may be imagined that create value based on visible, shareable data. We can also make services more resilient. To get there, we need the design acumen of HCI researchers and UX practitioners to help design, deliver and evaluate apparency interactions at IoT scale.

NOTE

1. The work informing this paper is supported by the Engineering and Physical Science Research Council UK projects Meaningful Consent in the Digital Economy (EP/K039989/1) and Cyber Security and the Internet of Things (EP/N02298X/1). We are grateful to Simone Barbosa, who in discussions of apparency helped tease out and name the two ways we use transparency as semantic/pragmatic.

REFERENCES

Baarslag, T., A. Alan, R. Gomer, M. Alam, C. Perera, E. Gerding and m. schraefel. 2017. 'An Automated Negotiation Agent for Permission Management'. Proc of the 16th International Conference on Autonomous Agents and Multiagent Systems (AAMAS 2017)

Chalmers, M. and A. Galani. 2004. 'Seamful Interweaving: Heterogeneity in the Design and Theory of Interactive Systems'. *ACM Designing Interactive Systems* (DIS2004). doi:10.1145/1013115.1013149

Gomer, R., E. Mendes Rodrigues, N. Milic-Frayling and m. schraefel. 2013. 'Network Analysis of Third Party Tracking: User Exposure to Tracking Cookies through Search'. *2013 IEEE/WIC/ACM International Joint Conferences on Web Intelligence (WI) and Intelligent Agent Technologies (IAT)*, 549–56. IEEE. doi:10.1109/WI-IAT.2013.77

Hannak, A., G. Soeller, D. Lazer, A. Mislove and C. Wilson. 2014. 'Measuring Price Discrimination and Steering on E-Commerce Web Sites'. *Proceedings of the 2014 Conference on Internet Measurement Conference – IMC'14*. doi:10.1145/2663716.2663744

Howe, Daniel C. and H. Nissenbaum. 2009. 'TrackMeNot: Resisting Surveillance in Web Search'. *Lessons from the Identity Trail: Anonymity, Privacy and Identity in a Networked Society*.

McDonald, A. M. and L. F. Cranor. 2008. 'Cost of Reading Privacy Policies, The'. *ISJLP* 0389:=, 1–22. <http://heinonlinebackup.com/hol-cgi-bin/get_pdf.cgi?handle=hein.journals/isjlpsoc4&section=27>

McIntyre, J. J. 2010–11. 'Balancing Expectations of Online Privacy: Why Internet Protocol (IP) Addresses Should Be Protected as Personally Identifiable Information'. *DePaul L. Rev.* 60, 895. <http://heinonlinebackup.com/hol-cgi-bin/get_pdf.cgi?handle=hein.journals/deplr60&section=37>

Melicher, W., M. Sharif, J. Tan, L. Bauer, M. Christodorescu and P. G. Leon. 2016. '(Do Not) Track Me Sometimes: Users' Contextual Preferences for Web Tracking'. *Proceedings on Privacy Enhancing Technologies* 2016 (2), 135–54. doi:10.1515/popets-2016-0009

Moran, S., E. Luger and T. Rodden. 2014. 'Literatin: Beyond Awareness of Readability in Terms and Conditions'. *UbiComp*, 641–46. doi:10.1145/2638728.2641684

Shih, F., I. Liccardi and D. J. Weitzner. 2016. 'Privacy Tipping Points in Smartphones Privacy Preferences'. Proc. of the 2015 ACM Conference on Human Factors in Computing Systems. doi:10.1145/2702123.2702404

Trafton, J. G. and C. A. Monk. 2007. 'Task Interruptions'. *Reviews of Human Factors and Ergonomics.* doi:10.1518/155723408X299852

Ur, B., P. G. Leon and L. F. Cranor. 2012. 'Smart, Useful, Scary, Creepy: Perceptions of Online Behavioral Advertising'. *Proceedings of the Eighth . . .* <http://dl.acm.org/citation.cfm?id=2335362>

Urquhart, L., T. Lodge and A. Crabtree. 2018. 'Demonstrably Doing Accountability in the Internet of Things'. ArXIv. <https://arxiv.org/pdf/1801.07168.pdf>

Woolf, N. 2016. 'DDoS Attack That Disrupted Internet Was Largest of Its Kind in History, Experts Say'. *The Guardian*

7. From the digital to a post-digital era?
Charles Ess

INTRODUCTION

This most important book develops fine-grained analyses of the drivers and benefits behind Big Data, coupled with its multiple threats – most centrally, to human autonomy and constitutional democracy – along with two concrete proposals for countering these threats. There is much here that I will support in especially ethical directions.

Following a summary of central elements of Hildebrandt's arguments, I take up three major intersections between Hildebrandt and (1) Media and Communication Studies (MCS) and (2) Information and Computing Ethics (ICE). First, Medium Theory (MT) helps clarify and support her understanding of the complex relationship between print technology and the Rule of Law. Second, I introduce virtue ethics in ICE in order to show how Hildebrandt's accounts overlap with key components of this ethical framework: virtue ethics thus powerfully reinforces and enhances certain aspects of Hildebrandt's normative accounts and argument. Finally, I suggest how Hildebrandt's accounts and argumentative trajectory likewise cohere with an emerging shift from a digital to a post-digital era (MCS). These three intersections both strengthen her arguments and show how her work is deeply relevant to not only legal scholarship and philosophy, but also to Media and Communication Studies and Information and Computing Ethics.

CORE POINTS AND ARGUMENTS

To begin with, I find the philosophical foundations and approaches to soundly ground the overarching trajectory of argument and core aims of the book. These start with phenomenological accounts of the lifeworld, coupled with Don Ihde's post-phenomenological account of technology (*The End(s)*, 171). This phenomenological background foregrounds *embodiment* in human knowing and navigating of our world (*Welt* and

Umwelt, as Hildebrandt helpfully explicates). This emphasizes non-dualistic understandings of the mind–body relationship that are then exemplified in Hildebrandt's use of notions of embodied and embedded mind, along with the importance of embodied tacit knowledge (*The End(s)*, 28f., 35). Hildebrandt further conjoins her phenomenology with hermeneutics, most explicitly in conjunction with the discussion of different types of philosophy of law (*The End(s)*, 7.2.3, 140ff.).

In ethical terms, Hildebrandt's core, primarily deontological emphasis on human autonomy is critical: this foregrounds individual (but also relational) human freedom (and identity building as one of its primary tasks) and thereby the grounding of modern constitutional democracies. Particularly helpful here is Hildebrandt's account of the Nature and Rule of Law in modern constitutional democracies as including 'Self-rule, disobedience and contestability' as their hallmarks (*The End(s)*, 10). Even better, Hildebrandt takes up some version of *relational autonomy*: she makes clear several compelling grounds for doing so – and I would add support by way of recent feminist philosophy (e.g., Veltman and Piper 2014). Hildebrandt also sees an immediate connection between this conception of human autonomy and Helen Nissenbaum's account of privacy as 'contextual integrity' (Hildebrandt 2014, 83f.). I and many others find this account to be essential to contemporary ways of conceptualizing privacy and efforts to defend it (e.g., Ess 2015). More broadly, Hildebrandt properly utilizes deontology and utilitarianism as ethical frameworks that, for example, ground many of the deep differences between US and EU approaches to privacy and privacy protections. By the same token, the discussion and thought experiment of Japanese understandings of selfhood as relational, coupled with animistic traditions that sharply differ from Western ones are, to my knowledge and understanding, well informed and absolutely useful.

Still more broadly, Hildebrandt clearly and consistently focuses throughout on the role of utilitarian interests in profit and benefit as primary drivers in the development of smart technologies – especially as these drivers often threaten to override deontological emphases on basic rights implied and required by autonomy. Recognizing this tension is a major component of her argumentative strategy. Most simply, rights such as privacy and freedom of expression, coupled with norms such as equality, justice and fairness, are foundational to constitutional democracy. Seeking to override these rights in the name of utilitarian considerations – whether national security (e.g., as justifying surveillance and correlative privacy violations in the name of the greater good) or economic efficiency and greater profit – is a core problem in the history of modern technology in general (Ess 2017) and in digital media ethics in particular (Ess 2013).

Hildebrandt's close analysis of the emergence of smart technologies and their threats to deontological rights – specifically as these are at the heart of the Rule of Law – stands as a current, most urgent example of and thus contribution to these debates.

Most broadly, the analyses of Big Data and its threats are helpful in especially three ways. One, Hildebrandt provides throughout the book compact accounts of various aspects of Big Data, along with related technologies such as AI and social robots. Two, to recall Neil Postman's (1985) famous juxtaposition of the two major types of dystopias confronting us – namely, the more obvious terrors of an Orwellian Big Brother vis-à-vis the more subtle and thereby more pernicious dangers of Aldous Huxley's *Brave New World* ([1932] 2006) – Hildebrandt's focus certainly includes both: but her work is especially salutary as it foregrounds the latter sort of dangers posed by Big Data. Third, Hildebrandt's two concrete proposals for countering these threats – namely, counter-profiling and morphological computing – inspire hope for sustaining modern law and democracy.

A FIRST COMMENT: THE PRINTING PRESS AND THE RULE OF LAW VIS-À-VIS MEDIUM THEORY

In my view, a central strength of Hildebrandt's argument is its incorporation of Medium Theory. I will show this by briefly introducing Medium Theory, a prominent theory within Media and Communication Studies (MCS) – and thereby clear away a common oversimplification of Medium Theory that could be read into one passage in the book. I use this background to thus pre-empt a potential misreading, to help undergird central components of her argument, and show the relevance of Hildebrandt's work for MCS.

Hildebrandt explicitly invokes key figures of Medium Theory – namely, Marshall McLuhan, Walter Ong, and Elisabeth Eisenstein (e.g. *The End(s)*, 48–50, 178): these are primary resources in both her account of technology versus technique (*The End(s)*, 160) and her account of the deep dependencies of the Rule of Law upon the printing press as a communication technology. This second component forms in turn a central premise for one of Hildebrandt's most compelling concerns – namely, the possibility of the Rule of Law being left behind in the transition from the era of print to the era of digital technologies, specifically including the rise of Big Data and pre-emptive computing.

Briefly, the Rule of Law entails key connections to justice, norms of equality and respect for persons, and the specific possibility of our *contesting* how we are 'read' by others, including digital machineries: all of these cluster about core Modernist and, most centrally, specifically deontological emphases on human (relational) autonomy as in turn justifying and requiring constitutional democracy to defend the basic rights that flow from this autonomy, including privacy and rights to due process. Clearly enough, the Rule of Law depends essentially on the printing press and its affordances (as is argued most centrally in *The End(s)*, sections 8.3.1 and 8.3.2). Equally clearly, the transition from (analogue) print to the digital world raises profound differences from the ICI (Information Communication Infrastructure) of print: these differences undoubtedly threaten the affordances of the print ICI underpinning the modern Rule of Law (argued most centrally in *The End(s)*, section 8.3.3).

To understand the argument here properly, however, requires clarifying two different understandings of the relationship between what Medium Theory takes as the communication technologies of *literacy-print* vis-à-vis the communication technologies of electric and electronic media, coupled with what Ong characterized as the *secondary orality* of electronic media (1988). On the one hand, popular receptions of McLuhan taken up in the 1990s vis-à-vis the Internet emphasized a simple 'either/or' understanding of the relationship between literacy-print and secondary orality. For example – as Hildebrandt notes – John Perry Barlow's (in)famous 'Declaration of the Independence of Cyberspace' (1996) insisted that the emergence of the Internet as the exemplar technology of electronic media and secondary orality meant the end of literacy-print and all the institutions it inaugurated and fostered. Either one or the other – but not both. By contrast, most Medium Theorists argue a 'both/and' understanding of these relationships. As Klaus Bruhn Jensen has put it: 'Old media rarely die, and humans remain the reference point and prototype for technologically mediated communication' (2011, 44; cf. *The End(s)*, 43). Most obviously, once literacy was invented, we did not stop talking (e.g. *The End(s)*, 217). This means that instead of an either/or between (literacy-) print and an electronic/digital era – our movement towards the latter will certainly bring much of the previous era's communication technologies and correlative institutions and practices in its train, however much these may be significantly transformed by the transition (cf. Ess 2014).

My worry is that Hildebrandt may be misunderstood by readers who presume the either/or understanding, as in some places the tension between print and digital ICIs is presented as more of an either/or – for example, in her discussion of the relationship between printing and the Rule of Law in *The End(s)*, section 8.3. Certainly, I have no quarrel here regarding the facts that Hildebrandt takes up: the case made here for strong correlations between print technology and the Rule of Law is very strong. And, as we will see in the next section, there is a particular element of this case – namely, the role of text in requiring *judgement* – that I foreground in conjunction with what I see as her resonances with virtue ethics. Most importantly, Hildebrandt's point here is to make clear how the ICI of pre-emptive computing profoundly threatens the affordances of print that make the Rule of Law possible: again, no quarrel. But it would be easy for a reader primed with a (1990s') presupposition of an either/or between literacy-print and an electronic/digital era to (mis-) read Hildebrandt here as suggesting an exclusive opposition between print and digital ICIs.

Happily, such a misinterpretation will be countered by numerous other passages that clearly square with the more nuanced understanding that old media are transformed rather than extinguished in the transition to a new medium. This is perhaps most explicit towards the close of the book, where Hildebrandt observes just that 'the spoken word and unwritten law were transformed by their relationship with text' (*The End(s)*, 217). Indeed, this emphasis on a transformational relationship between print and digital ICI is exemplified in Hildebrandt's foregrounding the possibility of saving the core elements of the Rule of Law through the ICI of pre-emptive computing: 'This need not be the end of law if we develop new ways to preserve what differentiates law from administration and techno-regulation' (*The End(s)*, 218). This is, in fact, her central point – one pursued in the concrete suggestions of how to develop a Legal Protection by Design (*The End(s)*, section 10.2.3 onward).

In this light, Hildebrandt's sharp contrasts between print and digital ICIs should be understood *not* along the lines of 1990s' mis-readings of Medium Theory, but rather as forcefully arguing how digital ICI deeply threatens the Rule of Law. And where she echoes the more prevailing emphasis in Medium Theory on transformation (rather than extinction) of old media in new media epochs, Medium Theory thereby helpfully articulates and undergirds precisely Hildebrandt's optimistic possibilities of our preserving the Rule of Law in a digital (or, as I will finally argue, a post-digital) era, despite the threats of a digital ICI.

VIRTUE ETHICS

A second way of undergirding Hildebrandt's argument is to explore its intersections with virtue ethics. To be sure, Hildebrandt is focused on law, not ethics (personal communication). At the same time, however, reading many of her important points and insights through a virtue ethics lens thereby elaborates and strengthens them. The point is not to suggest that Hildebrandt is somehow a closet virtue ethicist: she is explicitly not an ethicist at all. It is rather to show how virtue ethics, especially as increasingly central in Information and Computing Ethics (ICE), including the *design* of ICTs, thereby directly supports Hildebrandt's arguments, and further makes them salient beyond her primary audience of legal philosophers and scholars.

I review here elements of virtue ethics traditions that are most salient to Hildebrandt's work. We will see in the next section how these components of virtue ethics will then specifically reinforce Hildebrandt's analyses and arguments seeking to sustain the Rule of Law in a (post-) digital era.

Partly in conjunction with the rise of feminist philosophies and ethics of care, virtue ethics has re-emerged over the past few decades as an increasingly important complement to the (formerly) more prevailing modern ethical frameworks of consequentialism (including utilitarianism) and deontologies. Several factors drive this renaissance. First, virtue ethics is a genuinely global tradition, one rooted in the ethical traditions, norms and practices of such ancients as Socrates, Plato and Aristotle; Confucian, Buddhist and Hindu traditions; and multiple indigenous traditions. Especially Greek virtue ethics grounds core components of the Abrahamic religions and then the more secular ethical norms and trajectories of Enlightenment rationalism (Ess 2013, 207–12). As we will see, Enlightenment versions of virtue ethics in turn become definitive for the strands of Information and Computing Ethics (ICE) that intersect most closely with Hildebrandt's analyses and arguments.

Virtue ethics is usually indexed by four key concepts: contentment (*eudaimonia*), judgement or practical wisdom (*phronēsis*), and flourishing or thriving – as these are core constituents, finally, of the good life. Virtue ethics begins with what would seem to be a (near-) universal human interest: what must I do – and then, become – to be(come) *content* with my life, as an individual who is simultaneously entwined across an array of social and larger (including natural and 'supernatural') relations? 'Content' here translates the Greek notion of *eudaimonia* – literally, well-spiritedness or a sense of well-being. Here, virtue ethics invokes experiences of contentment or well-being that follow from our taking up a difficult challenge or practice, such as the skills or excellent abilities (virtues) of musicianship or a craft – or, more fundamentally, the virtues required for *friendship*. Specifically, empathy, patience and perseverance are virtues essential for deep human communication and thus friendship (Vallor 2015, 2016). Such virtues – like the skills of musicianship or craft – do not come 'naturally'. Rather, they are difficult to learn, acquire and improve upon, most especially at the beginning. But our sense of contentment and flourishing or thriving centrally depend upon our pursuit and improvement of such virtues, both as individuals (e.g., by becoming better musicians after years of practice) and as relational beings (e.g., as the friendships and intimate relationships central to good lives depend upon several virtues).

Specifically, virtue ethics forms the foundations of Information and Computing Ethics as articulated by Norbert Wiener. In *The Human Use of Human Beings* ([1950] 1954), Wiener explores both the dangers and potentials of emerging computational technologies, arguing that these potentials are best pursued by designing and appropriating these technologies in service to the larger Enlightenment project of emancipation and liberation. Wiener foregrounds 'liberté' from the motto of the French Revolution, taking it to mean 'the liberty of each human being to develop in his freedom the full measure of the human possibilities *embodied* in him' ([1950] 1954, 106; emphasis added, CE).

A central component of virtue ethics is a specific form of ethical judgement – *phronēsis*. *Phronēsis* is a form of reflective judgement, in contrast with determinative judgement. Determinative judgements begin from specific general principles or (quasi-) universal norms. By contrast, *phronēsis* begins 'on the ground', i.e., thick in the middle of a range of possible choices vis-à-vis a number of context-specific details and features. Ideally, determinative judgements deduce clear, final, unambiguous and single conclusions from given norms or principles. *Phronēsis*, by contrast, must first struggle to discern which norms or principles, among an array of many implicated by a given context and possible choices, are most salient – and among these, which take priority over others. These multiplicities of possible norms – and possible prioritizations thereof – mean that multiple phronetic judgements can be made and rationally justified. *Contra* a (relatively) clear, deductive, univocal determinative judgement, phronetic judgements are thereby marked by uncertainty and ambiguity. As the phrase 'judgement call' suggests, we understand that such judgements can legitimately vary not only between person to person, but also, so to speak, intra-personally: the same person may make a different judgement in similar contexts but at a later time, and thereby from the standpoint of greater, or at least different, insight, experience, etc.

As Shannon Vallor (2016) as well as feminist ethics of care and more recent work on notions of relational autonomy (e.g. Veltman and Piper 2014) suggest, phronetic judgement, as something of a first virtue, is acquired and practised precisely as we are members of larger communities. To borrow from Carol Gilligan (1982), phronetic judgements are frequently oriented towards sustaining and enhancing our 'webs of relationships'. Moreover, in part because of the complexities of these webs of relationships, especially as dynamic and frequently changing, phronetic judgement is frequently mistaken. These mistakes, moreover, are not simply recognized in some sort of theoretical or abstract way: they are often *felt* in directly embodied ways, e.g., the sense of guilt experienced as a pang in the stomach, regret felt – literally – as a *heart*ache, and so on. At the same time, it is just these mistakes and their felt consequences that point to self-correction as a critical feature of *phronēsis*: simply, we learn from our mistakes and thereby improve our practice of *phronēsis* as a virtue.

Indeed, this capacity for ethical self-correction is a key feature of *phronēsis* in Plato – and subsequently in Wiener. Plato uses the κυβερνήτης (*cybernetes*) – a steersman, helmsman or pilot – as a primary exemplar of *phronēsis*: 'An outstanding pilot [*cybernetes*] or doctor is aware of the difference between what is impossible in his art and what is possible, and he attempts the one, and lets the other go; and if, after all, he should still trip up in any way, he is competent to set himself aright' (*Republic*, 360e–361a). The *cybernetes'* capacity for self-correction is manifestly the inspiration for 'cybernetics' as taken up by Wiener as 'the science of messages' ([1950] 1954, 77).

Specifically, Wiener's focus on the virtue ethics project of unfolding 'the full measure of the human possibilities *embodied*' in us ([1950] 1954, 106; emphasis added) highlights how our acquiring and practising virtues, beginning with *phronēsis*, precisely implicate *embodied*, and thereby, often *tacit* forms of learning and experience. Hubert Dreyfus provides several examples of how we learn these more tacit and embodied dimensions of judgement-making – namely, only by close, face-to-face experience with more experienced human being(s), e.g., medical students on rounds with a senior physician or the younger musician 'hanging out' (my phrase) with a more experienced one (Dreyfus 2001, see Ess 2016a).

Especially critical for Hildebrandt's overall argument, including her use of Hannah Arendt (*The End(s)*, 116), is the argument that *phronēsis* is *not* reducible to computational technologies and techniques, e.g., the title of Joseph Weizenbaum's seminal volume, *Computer Power and Human Reason: From Judgment to Calculation* (1976). Weizenbaum partly grounds his account of judgement on Arendt's descriptions of policy makers in the US military establishment who presumed a quasi-mathematical understanding of reason, and human political and historical realities as reducible to laws as mathematically expressible and necessary as those of the natural sciences. Arendt notes specifically: '[They] did not *judge*; they calculated ... An utterly irrational confidence in the calculability of reality [became] the leitmotif of the decision making' (Arendt 1972: 11ff.; cited in Weizenbaum 1976, 13f.; see Ess 2016b, 62). Weizenbaum contrasts human judgement explicitly with what is calculable (1976, 44) – a distinction further elaborated in more recent work arguing that *phronēsis* is not computationally tractable (Gerdes 2014, see Ess 2016b, 62–65). These understandings of the virtue of *phronēsis* thus reinforce

Hildebrandt's account of what especially relationally autonomous human beings are capable of, specifically in the age of the Rule of Law, and what the technologies of pre-emptive computing can*not* do.

VIRTUE ETHICS IN HILDEBRANDT

We can now see how these central elements of virtue ethics intersect with Hildebrandt's work.

First, in a number of places Hildebrandt articulates what I would couch in terms of *phronēsis* and judgement more broadly. Second, Hildebrandt's account of the role of feelings in our deliberations and identity building can again be straightforwardly correlated with both foundational Enlightenment virtues and more contemporary accounts of the role of virtues – including loving itself as a virtue – in friendship and intimate relationships that contribute to the good life more broadly.

In numerous places Hildebrandt either describes or refers to what I mean by especially *phronēsis* but also judgement more generally – though she does not always explicitly name the processes involved as such. As a first example, consider the first full paragraph in *The End(s)*, on p. 39, including:

> We must learn, as humans with newly extended minds, when these assumptions hold or do not matter and when they are crucially wrong. ... We need to reorganize our intuitions and realign our inclinations to develop a new kind of constructive distrust of what computing systems tell us and arrange for us ...

I may be badly overreading here (where such (mis-)interpretation is itself a form of phronetic judgement at work in hermeneutics) but these lines strongly remind me of the capacity for self-correction as a primary feature of *phronēsis*.

In addition, I would argue that *phronēsis* and an allied capacity – analogical reasoning (cf. Ess 2016b, 63) – are in play in several of the hermeneutical moments that come to the foreground in Hildebrandt's analyses. This argument can be made in conjunction with a second example – Hildebrandt's wonderful analysis of how double mutual anticipation, as so critical to human experience and our shared *Welt*, is threatened by the pre-emptive computing examples drawn from the Diana narrative. In this context she observes (*The End(s)*, 67):

> In being double – anticipating how one is anticipated – and mutual – expecting that others do the same – the ensuing uncertainty is reciprocal; people guess how they are being profiled by others doing the same. This is

what provides for the ambiguity inherent in human communication, sustaining predictability while cherishing the open character of meaning production. Ambiguity leaves room for creative misunderstandings, it nourishes the fragility of the Welt – but it also fosters its potential for novel perspectives and thus its flexibility and robustness in the long run. *Ambiguity does not imply the absence of meaning or direction; it hinges on a limited set of possible meanings that may require incompatible responses, thus forcing those involved to make a choice in favour of one interpretation rather than another.* This is how we get on in life, *guessing what is expected from us and intuiting how our actions are 'seen' or 'read' by others. Most of this requires no conscious effort and does not depend on following a set of preconceived rules. We thrive on ambiguity by tacitly following hunches that operate smoothly beyond our deliberate control.* (emphasis added, CE)

By my lights – especially as informed, to begin with, by an understanding of diverse forms of 'controlled' or 'systematic' ambiguity identified initially by Aristotle as standing between pure univocity and the sorts of sheer (and vicious) forms of ambiguity or equivocation that we rightly worry about (Ess 1983) – the processes invoked here of attempting to interpret our ambiguous communications, both explicit and tacit (proxemics, gaze, gesture, etc.), are hermeneutical processes that invoke both determinative and *phronetic* or reflective judgement in at least two ways. One, to use Hildebrandt's later example of a thumb's up – we learn to understand what this gesture can mean over time: in part, I would argue, as we sometimes *mis*-interpret the (essentially ambiguous) gesture, taking it to mean one thing, only to find out it means something else. This entails the capacity for self-correction that defines phronetic judgement: at the same time, precisely because the judgements here are *not* determinative – i.e., as depending on '*a set of preconceived rules*' – they must be reflective or phronetic judgements. Secondly, such judgements – as with the other virtues – when practised become literally incorporated or embodied: and in this way they operate at the more tacit levels suggested here in Hildebrandt's language of 'hunches' that involve no conscious effort or deliberative control.

The intersection with the focus on virtues as practices that are critical to our becoming human appears in an especially powerful way in connection with Hildebrandt's subsequent discussion of the role of feelings in our ethical decision-making – in contrast with AIs as devices that, to paraphrase, can only fake emotions, not feel them (*The End(s)*, 70f.). Hildebrandt's account of the role of feelings is especially forceful here (*The End(s)*, 71):

Feelings emerge when humans become aware of their emotions. Feelings allow for and thrive on conscious attention to and reflection on one's emotional responses. They enable us to develop a personality that is not entirely intuitive, not completely dependent on whatever emotion overwhelms us. Feelings integrate awareness, deliberation and an interior monologue on our emotional habits. *They thus enable us to grow and mature into the kind of person we want to be.* (emphasis added, CE)

The last sentence clearly overlaps the primary sense of virtue ethics, especially following the Enlightenment and Wiener's emphasis on *liberté* as the freedom to become our best selves. This overlap is extended as Hildebrandt considers the dangers of the absence of such feelings in AIs (and, I would add, specifically robots – Ess 2016b). She writes (*The End(s)*, 71f.):

> The most prominent threat, however, that connects with concerns over autonomy, identity and digital sorting, occurs if we cannot defend ourselves. If we cannot contest the way we are being 'read' and steered and thus if we cannot resist the manipulation of our unconscious emotional states, *we may lose the sense of self that is pre-conditional for human autonomy. Not having a chance to develop feelings, we may actually become the machines that smart technologies take us to be.* (emphasis added, CE)

To put this in the language and conceptual vocabulary of virtue ethics: feelings, to begin with – including, perhaps most centrally, the feelings of love and desire – are *not* simply 'passions', as (some) Romantics would have it, i.e., powers from beyond that overwhelm our rationality and autonomy. Rather, as Sara Ruddick (1975) has described (also drawing on phenomenology), whatever the vagaries of desire, love itself is a *virtue*: love as experienced and taken up in the context of long-term relationships of friendship and intimacy requires cultivation and practice. Moreover, Ruddick's account of 'complete sex' foregrounds how loving as a virtue intertwines with the sorts of Kantian deontological emphases we see in Hildebrandt's account as well, beginning with (relational) autonomy and consequent ethical norms of equality and respect (Ess 2016b).

By contrast, in virtue ethics language and conception, our failure to acquire, practice, and cultivate such virtues is often described in terms of an ethical 'de-skilling' (Vallor 2015). Building on the virtue ethics work of Ruddick and Shannon Vallor (2015, 2016), I have argued precisely the point raised here by Hildebrandt, but with a specific focus on questions of love and sex with robots. Most briefly, much suggests that AIs/robots, however sophisticated, will not acquire a first-person phenomenal awareness of themselves as embodied beings – an awareness that is pre-conditional for any sense of genuine desire for an Other. Simply put, the best they can do is fake it. While some have argued that fake emotions from AIs/robots will be sufficient conditions for human love (e.g. Levy 2007), Ruddick's account of complete sex shows how such experiences rather require the mutuality and equality of desire. Such mutuality means not simply that I desire the Other and the Other desire me: moreover, we desire that the Other desire our desire. This seems strongly overlapping with Hildebrandt's use of Harry Frankfurt's account of a person as 'an agent capable of having a desire about her own desires, an intention about her own intentions' (*The End(s)*, 91). In both cases, the absence of first-person phenomenal consciousness and genuine desire (along with other emotions), means that a sexbot (a) is incapable of such second-order reflections on its desires and intentions, and so it (b) could offer us only zombie sex: all of the motions, including the gestures of faked emotion – but no presence of a first-person, relationally autonomous and feeling person who thereby calls me to practise the virtues of loving, equality and respect. Echoing Sherry Turkle's warnings along these lines (2011), falling for the trap of fake emotions and the ease of sex on command from a robot may have its normative place (e.g., in therapeutic contexts). But if doing so thereby draws us from the work of acquiring and cultivating the virtues of loving (along with other requisite virtues such as patience, perseverance, empathy, trust, and so on), we are thus threatened with a profoundly dangerous deskilling of the virtues and practices central to human friendship and intimacy. Bluntly, we risk becoming the zombie 'lovers' we accept in place of human beings (Ess 2016b). This would instantiate Hildebrandt's worry, as argued above, that 'we may actually become the machines that smart technologies take us to be' (*The End(s)*, 71f.).

Central additional points in the volume inspire similar observations. For example, the work of identity building to be protected by privacy rights (*The End(s)*, e.g. 86f.) sounds like a virtue practice to me: our identity is to be cultivated through the acquisition of a variety of practices, including the sorts of boundary control described here and then in the Japanese context (*The End(s)*, 6.4, 114ff.). Indeed, virtue ethics is central to Japanese culture: so it is not surprising that a version of *phronēsis* shows up here, namely in the tasks of a relational self attempting to exercise *Wakimae*, 'situated discernment' – what my Japanese students explain to me as 'reading the atmosphere': this is the strongly hermeneutical exercise of constant interpretation of the dynamically changing, fine-grained context constituted by others' feelings, interests, needs, etc., especially as expressed in tacit, embodied ways, as the basis for one's own judgements of what the next best move, comment, action, etc. may be, in order to contribute to the specific harmony of the group here and now. In particular: of course, mistakes will be made, requiring the self-correcting capacity of *phronēsis* for on-going cultivation and maturation of one's abilities as a social/relational being.

As a last example: Hildebrandt foregrounds the role of judgement and, at least implicitly, relevant virtues in her discussion of 'The Hallmarks of Modern Law' (*The End(s)*, 176ff.) Here Hildebrandt takes up no less than seven ways in which the rise of the printing press and the affordances of print shape the emergence and features of modern law. The sixth is how 'the proliferation of printed text . . . reinforces the need for reiterate interpretation that [in turn] greatly enhances the role of the lawyers as stewards of a coherent web of legal texts (legislation, administrative and judicial decisions)' (*The End(s)*, 178). Predictably, this shift in authority and thus power to lawyers as civil servants resulted in significant conflict with traditional aristocratic authority – in this case, King James I, who attempted to intervene in 'the application of the law' (*The End(s)*, 179). Chief Justice Coke's counterargument in 1608 is telling (*The End(s)*, 179):

> . . . causes which concern the life, or inheritance, or goods or fortunes of his [Majesty's] subjects, are not to be decided by natural reason but by artificial reason *and judgement of law, which law is an art which requires long study and experience, before that a man can attain to the cognizance of it.* (emphasis added, CE)

This last emphasis on 'long study and experience' coheres perfectly with judgement as *phronēsis* – first of all as such judgement is acquired over time and through the kind of apprenticeship Dreyfus (2001) has described, i.e., in which we learn from both explicit instruction but also via the tacit and embodied cues and reflections of *phronēsis* possible only through proximate embodied interaction between apprentice and master.

Judgement is likewise at work in Hildebrandt's discussion of the seventh affordance of print and text (*The End(s)*, 180):

> . . . *the need to interpret* a written norm in the light of the web of applicable legal norms and in the light of the case at hand requires suspending judgment. Interpretation must take into account the legal effect that a decision will have on similar cases, while paying keen attention to how the same norm has been applied in preceding case law. (emphasis in the original)

What I espy here is that this suspension of judgement is a precondition for exercising the judgement at work in this process, beginning with the work of *phronēsis* in particular in seeking to discern from the contexts of a particular case just which larger norms and extant cases are indeed relevant.

Again, I'm not arguing that Hildebrandt is a closet virtue ethicist who needs to be more explicit about her use of core virtue ethics notions and insights. Again, Hildebrandt has rightly pointed out the importance of our maintaining the clear distinctions between law, on the one hand, and ethics on the other (personal communication). At the same time, however, insofar as law is inevitably shaped and undergirded by diverse ethical norms, principles, and frameworks, my argument is that much of her most significant analyses and insights powerfully overlaps with key insights and understandings from virtue ethics. Insofar as these overlaps are coherent and consistent, virtue ethics can thus be invoked as supporting and, in some instances, elaborating on a number of Hildebrandt's key points and arguments. Especially given its increasing role and significance in contemporary ethics and in Information and Computing Ethics more specifically, such support and elaboration serve as strong allies in defending and elaborating several of Hildebrandt's core points and argumentation, as well as make her work directly relevant to Information and Computing Ethics (ICE).

CONCLUDING REMARKS: FROM THE DIGITAL TO THE POST-DIGITAL

To begin with, I can only heartily endorse Hildebrandt's invocation of the essential importance of retaining *reading* as affiliated with the ICI of print as critical to her larger project of sustaining human autonomy, respect, privacy, and the other core elements of the Rule of Law. Here she draws primarily on the work of Maryanne Wolf (*The End(s)*, 49) and then comments in the conclusion of ch. 8 (*The End(s)*, 183f.):

> Law – as we know it – requires deliberation as well as binding decisions. The core idiosyncrasy, a critical quality of the Rule of Law, is tied to the linearity of the reading mind, to its acquired habit of sequential processing, as explained and elaborated by Maryanne Wolf in her work on the reading brain. This chapter proposes that if we stop reading and start behaving like digital natives, we may lose the need to reflect, to consider, to hesitate, to delay our judgement. If we are no longer forced to confront contradictory texts, why should we hesitate? I am not sure that interactions with the smart ICI of the onli*f*e world afford much self-conscious deliberation. This raises a final, twofold concern that relates to, on the one hand, the possibility that the affordances of the onli*f*e world will lead to an instrumentalization of the law, and, on the other hand, to the possibility that the ICI of pre-emptive computing takes a deterministic turn.

Against these critical threats, the first good news, from my perspective, is just that there is increasing recognition of the importance of reading and writing as analogue and embodied experiences vis-à-vis their more virtual/digital counterparts (e.g., Wollscheid, Sjaastad and Tømte, 2016). This attention to the embodied and analogue dimensions of learning are in turn part and parcel of an emerging understanding that we have entered a post-digital era. Very briefly, we have focused on 'the digital' in all of its manifestations and impacts for some three decades – as documented within the Onlife Project, for example, as an effort to, in turn, re-engineer the primary concepts underlying the digital era, including precisely the online/offline binary. Arguably, the all but exclusive focus on 'the digital' has been necessary, largely beneficent, and profoundly transformative. At the same time, however, Medium Theory reinforces the point that it is simply mistaken to assume, *à la* Barlow and others in the 1990s, that digital technologies necessitate a series of stark either/ors between, e.g., the offline or the online or the digital or the analogue (cf. Ess 2011).

To be sure, the Onlife Project itself rejected these binaries – a rejection that grounds Hildebrandt's book and her use of 'onli*fe*' as a key term. And there are certainly extensive empirical as well as theoretical grounds for doing so (Ess and Consalvo 2011). Indeed, it is worth noting that resistance to these binaries began as early as 1991, with Allucquere Roseanne Stone's (1991, 113) warning 'that virtual community originates in, and must return to, the physical. . . . Forgetting about the body is an old Cartesian trick'. Following more than a decade of feminist and phenomenological insistence that embodiment cannot be ignored or forgotten, Brian Massumi (2002) forcefully pointed out the central danger of these binaries and the on-going Cartesian privileging of mind over body: to focus exclusively on 'the digital' is to ignore the role of the analogue in defining and shaping the human sensorium.

Within the domain of the digital humanities, David Berry (2014) attributes the term 'post-digital' to Kim Cascone (2000) as a way of thinking about the digital and the analogue as inextricably interwoven. Berry further draws on Bernard Stiegler's dire warnings (2013) that the focus on the digital in the name of Digital Humanities threatens 'the development of attention, memory, concentration, and intelligence', and thereby the core humanities' projects of learning to think for ourselves for the sake of pursuing a life worth living (entailing, as we have now seen, autonomy and the good life in virtue ethics terms). Berry then takes up the term 'post-digital' to indicate *not* the rejection of digital technologies but rather a move beyond the 1990s' opposition between digital and analogue. More recently, media sociologist Simon Lindgren (2017, 298) likewise observes this broad shift from the digital to the post-digital as 'an era where the digital is no longer new and exciting, but something that is commonplace and assumed'.

The post-digital, then, appears to be more than reactionary nostalgia (against which Hildebrandt also rightly warns), something restricted to niche phenomena such as a growing preference for analogue film and vinyl records over their digital counterparts. Rather, the body and the analogue, so to say, are enjoying a kind of resurrection following their entombment in the digital era. Hildebrandt's call for morphological computing in particular and for sustaining the Rule of Law more broadly cohere with and importantly instantiate these shifts from a digital to a post-digital era.

In short: in parallel with exploiting Medium Theory and virtue ethics to elaborate and defend key elements in Hildebrand's work – contextualizing her project vis-à-vis the post-digital likewise suggests still further groundings and reinforcements. Simultaneously, I see her utterly crucial intention to preserve human relational autonomy, privacy, equality and the Rule of Law more broadly as a core pillar in the transformation into a post-digital era.

REFERENCES

Arendt, H. 1972. *Crises of the Republic*. New York: Harcourt, Brace, Javonovich.

Barlow, J. P. 1996. 'A Declaration of the Independence of Cyberspace'. <https://projects.eff.org/~barlow/Declaration-Final.html>.

Berry, D. 2014. 'Post-Digital Humanities: Computation and Cultural Critique in the Arts and Humanities'. *Educause Review*, May 19. <http://er.educause.edu/articles/2014/5/postdigital-humanities-computation-and-cultural-critique-in-the-arts-and-humanities>

Cascone, K. 2000. 'The Aesthetics of Failure: "Post-Digital" Tendencies in Contemporary Computer Music'. *Computer Music Journal* 24(4), 12

Dreyfus, H. 2001. *On the Internet*. New York, NY: Routledge

Ess, C. 1983. *Analogy in the Critical Works: Kant's Transcendental Philosophy as Analectical Thought*. Dissertation, Pennsylvania State University

Ess, C. 2011. 'Self, Community, and Ethics in Digital Mediatized Worlds'. In C. Ess and M. Thorseth (eds.), *Trust and Virtual Worlds: Contemporary Perspectives*. Oxford: Peter Lang, 3–30

Ess, C. 2013. *Digital Media Ethics*, 2nd edition. Oxford: Polity Press

Ess, C. 2014. 'Selfhood, Moral Agency, and the Good Life in Mediatized Worlds? Perspectives from Medium Theory and Philosophy'. In Knut Lundby (ed.), *Mediatization of Communication* (vol. 21, Handbook of Communication Science). Berlin: De Gruyter Mouton, 617–40

Ess, C. 2015. 'New Selves, New Research Ethics?' In H. Ingierd and H. Fossheim (eds), *Internet Research Ethics*. Oslo: Cappelen Damm, 48–76. Retrieved from Open Access: <http://press.nordicopenaccess.no/index.php/noasp/catalog/book/3>

Ess, C. 2016a. 'Ethical Approaches for Copying Digital Artifacts: What Would the Exemplary Person (*Junzi*) / a Good Person [*Phronemos*] Say?' In Reinold Schmücker and Darren Hick (eds), *The Aesthetics and Ethics of Copying*. London: Bloomsbury, 295–313

Ess, C. 2016b. 'What's Love Got to Do with It? Robots, Sexuality, and the Arts of Being Human'. In M. Nørskov (ed.), *Social Robots: Boundaries, Potential, Challenges*. Farnham: Ashgate, 57–9

Ess, C. 2017. 'God Out of the Machine?: The Politics and Economics of Technological Development'. In A. Beavers (ed.), *Macmillan Interdisciplinary Handbooks: Philosophy*. Farmington Hills, MI: Macmillan Reference, 83–111

Ess, C., and Consalvo, M. 2011. 'What is "Internet Studies"?' In M. Consalvo and C. Ess (eds), *The Handbook of Internet Studies*. Oxford: Wiley-Blackwell, 1–8

Gerdes, A. 2014. 'Ethical Issues Concerning Lethal Autonomous Robots in Warfare'. In J. Seibt, R. Hakli and M. Nørskov (eds), *Sociable Robots and the Future of Social Relations: Proceedings of Robo-Philosophy 2014*. Berlin: IOS Press, 277–89

Gilligan, C. 1982. *In a Different Voice: Psychological Theory and Women's Development*. Cambridge, MA: Harvard University Press

Huxley, A. [1932] 2006. *Brave New World*. New York, NY: Harper

Jensen, K. B. 2011. 'New Media, Old Methods – Internet Methodologies and the Online/Offline Divide'. In M. Consalvo and C. Ess (eds), *The Handbook of Internet Studies*. Oxford: Wiley-Blackwell, 43–58

Levy, D. 2007. *Love and Sex with Robots: The Evolution of Human-Robot Relationships*. New York, NY: Harper Collins

Lindgren, S. 2017. *Digital Media and Society*. London: Sage

Ong, W. 1988. *Orality and Literacy: The Technologizing of the Word*. London: Routledge

Postman, N. 1985. *Amusing Ourselves to Death: Public Discourse in the Age of Show Business*. New York, NY: Penguin

Ruddick, S. 1975. 'Better Sex'. In R Baker and F Elliston (eds), *Philosophy and Sex*. Amherst, NY: Prometheus Books, 280–99

Massumi, B. 2002. *Parables for the Virtual: Movement, Affect, Sensation*. Durham, NC: Duke University Press

Plato. 1991. *The Republic*, trans. Allan Bloom, with notes, an interpretive essay and a new introduction. New York, NY: Basic Books

Stiegler, B. 2013. *What Makes Life Worth Living: On Pharmacology*. Cambridge: Polity Press

Stone, A. R. 1991. 'Will the Real Body Please Stand Up? Boundary Stories about Virtual Cultures'. In M. Benedikt (ed.), *Cyberspace: First Steps*. Cambridge, MA: MIT Press, 81–118

Turkle, S. 2011. *Alone Together: Why We Expect More from Technology and Less from Each Other*. New York, NY: Basic Books

Vallor, S. 2015. 'Moral Deskilling and Upskilling in a New Machine Age: Reflections on the Ambiguous Future of Character'. *Philosophy of Technology* 28, 107–24

Vallor, S. 2016. *Technology and the Virtues: A Philosophical Guide to a Future Worth Wanting*. Cambridge, MA: MIT Press

Veltman, A. and Piper, M. 2014. 'Introduction'. In Andrea Veltman and Mark Piper (eds), *Autonomy, Oppression and Gender*. Oxford: Oxford University Press, 1–11

Weizenbaum, J. 1976. *Computer Power and Human Reason: From Judgment to Calculation*. New York, NY: W. H. Freeman

Wiener, N. (1950) 1954. *The Human Use of Human Beings: Cybernetics and Society*. Garden City, NY: Doubleday Anchor

Wollscheid, S., Sjaastad, J. and Tømte, C. 2016. 'The Impact of Digital Devices vs. Pen(cil) and Paper on Primary School Students' Writing Skills – a Research Review'. *Computers & Education* 95 (April 2016), 19–35. doi:10.1016/j.compedu.2015.12.001

PART II

8. Do digital technologies put democracy in jeopardy?
Gerard de Vries

INTRODUCTION

In 1996, John Perry Barlow argued that if the governments of the industrial world would leave the internet alone, 'we will create a civilization of the Mind in Cyberspace'. He envisioned 'a world where anyone, anywhere may express his or her beliefs, no matter how singular, without fear of being coerced into silence or conformity'. As governments had already started to interfere, Barlow wrote: '[w]e must declare our virtual selves immune to [their] sovereignty, even as we continue to consent to [their] rule over our bodies'. He proclaimed the independence of Cyberspace.

Two decades later, rather than a civilisation of the Mind, we face 'chaotic pluralism' (Margetts et al. 2016) – a turbulent world of political activism on social media, of hate-speech, echo chambers and social division, filter bubbles created by algorithms, trolls distributing fake news, and botnets building up the appearance of momentum behind online campaigns. Citizens are profiled on the basis of data harvested from social media to be 'micro targeted' with cleverly designed and extensively tested emotions-triggering content to influence their views on political issues and their voting behaviour. A whole array of new, digital tools for spreading propaganda, manipulating publics and influencing elections has emerged.

In a way, we should have anticipated this. After the advent of radio and television, political organizations soon discovered how to exploit these media; it should not come as a surprise that digital technologies are used for political gains too.

Radio and television have changed the way politics works in many ways, but they did not bring democracy to an end. This time is different, it is claimed: digital technologies pose an existential risk to democracy.

A FEW SCANDALS OR AN EXISTENTIAL CRISIS?

By mid-2018, we knew that Russian trolls had tried to influence the US elections in favour of Trump. Facebook had to concede that the privacy of an estimated 87 million Facebook users has been breached; their data had been used by the firm Cambridge Analytica to enable micro-targeting voters in the 2016 US election. In the UK EU-referendum pro-leave campaigns have used the same tools; according to whistle-blowers, data from an insurance company and a price comparison site have been used without consent. The UK Electoral Commission has reported that for having coordinated their finances to pay for their online strategies, nominally distinct pro-leave campaigns have violated UK electoral law.

That Facebook has breached the privacy of its users is a scandal; that the pro-leave campaigns have used data without consent and have violated UK electoral law is a scandal too. But do a scandal or two really put democracy in the UK and US at risk? Trump and pro-leave organisations are not the only ones who have employed online strategies extensively for their campaigns; so did the Obama and Clinton campaigns, and so does every modern political organization worth its salt. Were it not for Trump's presidency and Brexit, would we have a discussion about the impact of digital technologies and the future of democracy at all?

In a democracy, when a scandal is reported, one expects oversight authorities and law enforcement agencies to look into the matter; if illegal action is suspected those responsible should be brought to justice. If established laws are deemed insufficient to keep the advances of technology in check, in a democracy one calls for legislators to introduce better regulation. By now, all of that has been set in course. UK authorities and the US Senate and Congress have looked into the scandals that have been reported. To give control back to citizens over their personal data, the European Union enforced its General Data Protection Regulation by 25 May 2018. So, may we be reassured?

To understand why democracy is at risk and in fact is facing an existential crisis, we should look at the bigger picture, Zuboff (2015) has argued. With big data and artificial intelligence, a new, 'deeply intentional and highly consequential logic of accumulation' is introduced, which will establish 'a ubiquitous networked institutional regime that records, modifies, and commodifies everyday experience from toasters to bodies, communication to thought, all with a view to establishing new pathways to monetization and profit'. We have entered the age of what Zuboff calls 'surveillance capitalism', an age in which – compared to the capitalism of former times – the relations between companies, the population and states will substantially be transformed. 'Surveillance capitalism establishes a new form of power in which contract and the rule of law are supplanted by the rewards and punishments of a new kind of invisible hand'. A new regime is about to be established, she claims, 'a sovereign power of a near future that annihilates the freedom achieved by the rule of law'.

Big words, indeed. But perhaps we may perceive already some foreshadowing of the new regime that Zuboff envisions. To claim the 'right to be forgotten' the European Union grants EU-citizens, they have to petition Google to erase their personal data from its search engine's database; so, the EU has outsourced the execution of judicial due process to a large extent to the company which has given rise to the problem. To tackle disinformation online, the European Commission has formulated in April 2018 a similar strategy. To ensure (among other things) transparency about sponsored content, in particular political advertising, as well as to restrict targeting options for political advertising and to reduce revenues for purveyors of disinformation, the EC proposed that online platforms should develop and follow a common Code of Practice. Again, the detailed formulation of a key public policy and its execution are laid primarily in the hands of private platforms.

One may of course react pragmatically to such developments. Digital technologies are a recent development; it will take some time for democracies to sort out how to manage their risks. As Runciman (2013) has argued, democracy is remarkably resilient. Over the last hundred years, its history shows repeated patterns of behaviour when democracy is faced with crises: misapprehension, confusion, brinkmanship, experimentation and recovery. Do digital technologies and the business models that are grafted on them really present a bigger threat to democracy than challenges of the past, like the rise of steel and oil monopolies, economic crises, mass unemployment, and even war? This is not the first challenge democracy has to face and it will not be the last one either. One should give policymakers some time, the pragmatist thinks.

Nevertheless, fundamental questions may be raised. 'Invent the printing press and democracy is inevitable', Carlyle (cited in Dewey 1954 [1927], 110) wrote; modern law – and hence the rule of law – is contingent on the printing press, Hildebrandt (2015, 177ff.) has argued. So, it's quite reasonable to wonder – more or less nervously – what kind of political regime we may expect to emerge in an age in which the online world rapidly evolves, to the point of by now having permeated almost all of social life.

However, the evolution of the online world takes place while democracy is also challenged in other ways. In the past decades, populism and autocracy have been on the rise; the traditional legitimacy of the democratic order has decreased; a new kind of demand for democratic legitimacy is on the rise, with increased emphasis on image and communication,

Rosanvallon (2011) has argued. How to determine the weight of digital technology among the various developments that are claimed to be at the root of our present political predicament? Would the desire to answer that question not add just another nightmare – a methodological one?

We had better change focus. Instead of trying to detect the 'impact' of digital technologies and the business models of surveillance capitalism on democracy and to figure out their weight relative to all other factors that can be listed to account for Trump, Brexit, populism and the rise of autocracy, it's more productive to ask how, where and why democracy might be *vulnerable* to digital technologies. We need to get a view on the conditions that are required for democracy to continue functioning properly. After that, we may be in a better position to assess whether digital technologies pose a serious threat to it.

HOBBES' LEGACY

Today, democracy is associated with almost anything that is conceived to be politically desirable: freedom, justice, security, deliberation, accountability, the rule of law. At the same time, and sometimes by the same people, democracy is loathed for its endless disputes, the rule-mania of politicians and for the wasting of public money by governments.

To discuss a system's vulnerability, one should put one's normative judgements on hold, to set off with a conception that is as minimalist as possible. For that, we may turn to Schumpeter (1942), according to whom democracy is just a system in which rulers are selected by competitive elections; to Popper (1962: vol. I, 124), who defended democracy as the only system in which citizens can get rid of governments without bloodshed; or simply to the *Oxford English Dictionary*, which defines democracy as 'a form of government in which the power resides in the people and is exercised by them either directly or by means of elected representatives'.

All three 'vote-centric' (Kymlicka 2002, 290) conceptions of democracy leave one key term unexplained: what does it mean 'to rule', what is a 'government'? The OED comes to the rescue. It informs us that 'government' means, among other things, 'continuous exercise of authority over subjects' and 'the action of governing the affairs of a state'. The combination of the two cited lemmas presents a puzzle however: how is it conceivable that in a democracy on the one side 'the power resides in the people', whereas, on the other side, in acting to take care of the affairs of a state, government means 'continuous exercise of authority over subjects'?

This puzzle was solved by Hobbes, who formulated the modern conception of the state (Skinner 1989). Hobbes (1968 [1651]) conceived the state as a union in which – by a hypothetical covenant in which they have traded some of their rights for safety and security – the many have become One, a single agent, an artificial man, the sovereign, to whom an act can be attributed. An organic metaphor, the 'body politic', which Hobbes used as a synonym for the state, accounts for the idea that multiple parts can integrate and function as one actor. The idea is famously captured by the frontispiece of *Leviathan*. The many make up the body politic; its soul, and so its animating force, is the sovereign who keeps watch over city and countryside and who has been authored the right to rule, to exercise authority over the many.

Who figures as the sovereign, who actually governs? In a monarchy, the people make up the body politics and the king its soul, its animating force. In a democracy, both the state's body and its soul are made up by the people. As the OED definition suggests, they exercise sovereign power either directly or – in states with large numbers of people – by means of elected representatives. In the latter case, elections serve as an aggregation mechanism for translating the preferences of the people into a decision who will have the right to govern, that is, to rule with authority until the next election. By conflating a *technique of decision* and a *principle of justification* (Rosanvallon 2011, 2), democratic elections present the answer to the problem how the idea that in a democracy power resides in the people can be reconciled with the idea that a government exercises authority over its citizens. Without elections, in larger states there can be no democracy.

Given the key role of elections in our minimalist conception of democracy, we can identify three kinds of potentially democracy-violating events: 1) the people are manipulated (by either an internal faction, or a foreign power) to incite them to vote in ways that do not express their true will; 2) the integrity of elections is breached; and 3) an unelected group of people grabs government power. Let's shortly review how digital technologies may materialize these potential threats.

First, manipulation of voters' preferences. Bots, trolls and techniques like the micro-targeting of voters are available to influence public opinion and hence the electorate. However, under our minimalist conception of democracy, all of this is of little relevance. In a democracy, elections, not opinion polls, register the people's will. What counts are the *results* of an election, not what has happened, or may have happened, prior to it. Voters may have been bombarded with carefully targeted propaganda and they may have changed their opinion in the weeks before the election or even in the polling booth; what matters are the votes casted at a polling station, or registered in another official way; they, and they alone, express the people's sovereign will.

In the past, more traditional campaigning strategies have been used to trigger the same effects for which digital techniques are employed. Smearing opponents is an old, well-established political trick; to build up the image of their candidates and to gather momentum, political parties have organized big rallies, tailored for favourable television coverage; that politicians promise more than they will ever be able to deliver when elected, is not something new either. For reaching out to much larger numbers of voters, bots, trolls and spreading propaganda by micro-targeting techniques may cause more turbulence and social division than traditional strategies. They may put *society* in jeopardy. But they don't put *democracy* at risk. The polling stations remain open, and people will still be able to cast their votes, to elect their representatives and hence to exercise the sovereign power that resides in them.

Second, tampering with the integrity of elections. Where electronic voting machines are used, it might be possible to hack into them. However, solutions are available to reduce this risk; one can either rely on more technology (better firewalls) or on less technology (by going back to the old paper and pencil ballot practice). Of course, the algorithms used for counting votes and for calculating who has won seats should be checked for accuracy and fairness, but this holds for more traditional systems as well. Sufficient oversight will guarantee the integrity of elections; apart from lawyers, people with intimate knowledge of IT will have to sit on oversight boards. In fact, their task may be easier than with some of the older systems; just remember the disarray after the Bush/Gore 2000 US Presidential election (Lynch et al. 2005).

Third, to prepare the ground for a *coup d'état*, fake-news may have been distributed on the internet to delegitimize the sitting government and to cause social division. To stay in power, the new rulers may have to arrest print-journalists and to park some tanks in front of the radio and TV studios. However, to prevent people to mobilize against them, they will have to either shut down the internet or – like the Chinese government does (King et al. 2017) – devote extensive financial and human resources to manage and control social media and the web – resources that a sitting government may have, but which those who staged the coup unlikely will have immediately available. For those who plan to launch a *coup*, digital technologies are likely to be a greater threat than for democracy.

Finally, consider the situation Zuboff points at. Now that we have driverless cars, the idea of a 'driverless government', of algorithmic regulation, comes into view – the prospect of a society in which the people's preferences are harvested from their behaviour on the internet and other sources, and processed by artificial intelligence to provide the ruling and services the people want. When the people's preferences change, the system will adapt automatically. Big private companies provide the necessary technologies. Would that be a threat to democracy? Sure, if the company that provides this service has a monopoly. The markets on which they operate should be competitive. But we trust market operators to provide key services like the provision of food, energy, finance and telecom. They already use big data techniques to optimize their services. So why wouldn't we trust market operators to deliver the service to provide for a far more efficient, real-time form of democratic rule, than a government, elected in the old way, can ever provide?

Under the minimalist conception of democracy of Schumpeter, Popper and the OED, there is little reason to think that the use of digital technologies for political gains will put democracy at risk. Yes, we may expect more turbulence, more pluralism, more voices calling loudly for attention, and probably more social division too. But was democracy not precisely intended for governing societies that acknowledge and embrace pluralism?

Indeed. But can a democracy *continue* to function in a society that is deeply divided? Hobbes didn't think so and for that reason he opted for the monarchy. So, apart from providing elections, the key-mechanism for *establishing* a democratic government, does *continuity* of its functioning not depend on some conditions as well?

A FALLACY OF MISPLACED CONCRETENESS?

In a hilarious video-installation the German philosopher Peter Sloterdijk ironically made the point that a functioning democracy will require much more than just a mechanism for collecting and expressing the will of the people. In the video, Sloterdijk impersonated a businessman eager to sell an inflatable, 'pneumatic' parliament that could be dropped from an airplane to offer 'instant democracy' anywhere, even in a desert state (Sloterdijk and Mueller von der Haegen 2005). As the 'coalition of the willing' had to discover in Iraq, things don't work out quite that way.

So, perhaps the 'vote-centric' conception of democracy is a bit too minimalistic. In adopting it, we may have committed what Whitehead (1967 [1925], 51, 58) has called the 'Fallacy of Misplaced Concreteness'. We may have taken an abstraction as if it is a complete description.

Is the vote-centric conception of democracy an 'abstraction' indeed? The OED defines democracy in terms of 'the people', and 'government', that is, in terms of given social entities that have the power to (inter-) act. This is plain common sense; this is how we conceive society, the social world, to be made up: a mixture of micro-actors (individuals) and macro-actors (organizations and institutions) which interact with each other.

Hobbes' organic metaphor for relating the micro- and macro-level may be conceived as out-of-date; twentieth century sociologists have discussed at length how to integrate individual social behaviour and institutions, micro- and macro-levels, theoretically and methodologically. But in conceiving democracy along the OED-lines, all of that we may ignore. In this case, we know exactly how the micro- and the macro-level, the people on the one hand and government on the other, are related, namely by the humble aggregation mechanism of an election. To call this an 'abstraction' seems to be quite far-fetched.

However, in speaking in this way about 'government' as a macro-actor, we have taken for granted that a government has the *legitimacy* to rule. In Hobbes' conception of the state, the hypothetical covenant is supposed to provide for that: the many have *authorized* the sovereign to rule on their behalf. In less hypothetical form, it is captured by the idea that a democratic government needs legitimacy: to be able to act, to function and to rule it needs the people's assent. The minimalist conception of democracy assumes that the outcomes of an election provide for this, till the next election.

In a wide-ranging historical study of democratic legitimacy, Rosanvallon (2011, 8–9) notes that this was sufficient for a view from the 'outside' – for the utopian ideologies that once gave solidity to the democratic order. But sociologically, it is naive: it is based on a view which conceives 'the people' as a social generality, rather than a collection of individuals with conflicting opinions about what they expect from their government – what one will encounter once one enters any society and gets an 'inside' view. For this reason, Rosanvallon (2011, 8–9) suggests, legitimacy should be conceived, like trust between individuals, rather as an 'invisible institution', a 'tissue of *relationships* between government and society', on which the social appropriation of political power depends. By deconstructing the idea of social generality, Rosanvallon opened the way to study in historical detail how – gradually, from the early nineteenth century up to the present time – new forms of democratic legitimacy have emerged. He notes that although for a long time elections have provided both the *technique* for electing governments and the *justification* for the legitimacy of governments, by now, although we still use this technique, the justification it is supposed to provide has waned.

We need to get a better view on what Rosanvallon calls a 'tissue of relationships between government and society'. We need to 'unscrew' Hobbes' Leviathan (Callon and Latour 1981). To get there, we need to depart from the ontology that is implied in common sense and in the way Hobbes framed his theory of the state. Instead of conceiving society to be made up by given micro- and macro-entities – 'the people' and 'government' – which are able to act and to enter into relations with each other, in our analyses we need to give relations pride of place.

To view the world by giving relations pride of place may seem to be a quite uncommon way to do. But as Latour (2005, Latour et al. 2012) has argued, in our experiences on the Web we have learned to view the world through this lens. Nowadays, if we encounter the name of – say – a scholar we haven't heard of before, we open our browser. The Web informs us about what she has published, and in which university she is based. What we get is a list of links. If we follow the links, the Web provides more links. But by continuing to follow these links, gradually, we will get a pretty good idea of who this scholar is. We get a view of a network of relations – to research interests, colleagues, grants, etc. Who is she? The network of links identifies her. What about her university? Again, by following links, we identify the institution in terms of a network of links – to employees, grant organizations and subjects of research. So, on the Web, we identify entities (like individuals and institutions) in terms of *networks of relations*. There is no implicit hierarchy, no 'micro-' and 'macro-level'; everything is on the same plane, connected by links. On the Web, a site that does not link to other sites and that is not linked to by other sites, is simply non-existent. On the Web, one exists and continues to exist only as long as one is *linked* to others.

The Web presents a *relationist* conception of the world, that is, an ontology in which relations, rather than entities or essences, take pride of place. Whereas common sense suggests that the world is made up by entities (like individuals and organizations) with pre-given essences and identities, in a relationist ontology whatever exists is defined by the relations in which it has become entangled. In this conception of the world the existential question any existent faces is not 'to be or not to be', but 'to be or *no longer* to be' – a double question, in fact: 1) to exist, to be, an existent has to be *related* to other existents; and 2) to *continue* its existence, these relations will have to remain in place because continuity of existence is not guaranteed by some essence (Latour 2013, De Vries 2016, 135 ff., 169 ff.).

Hence, to define or describe something, a relationist ontology suggests two different tasks: first, one should trace how the network of relations that makes up its existence is set up; second, one has to study why – that is, under which conditions or by deploying which means – this network of relations remains stably in place. This double task is the key to the kind of analysis of the social world that has become known as 'actor-network theory' (Latour 2005).

Once this double task is apprehended, it becomes clear in which sense the minimalist definition of democracy is based on a 'fallacy of misplaced concreteness': it answers the first question (by pointing to elections that set up the relation between the people and the government), but fails to address (and, hence, 'abstracts from') the second one – the question under which conditions elections as a technique to *set up* a democratic government *continues* to provide the justification of that government's legitimacy, which it needs to act with authority and to maintain itself.

To avoid this fallacy, we will have to redescribe democracy in relationist terms. As Montesquieu and Dewey have done so in the past, they may guide us. Once this is done, we may reconsider the question whether – and if so, on which points – democracy is vulnerable to digital technologies.

A RELATIONIST ACCOUNT OF DEMOCRATIC GOVERNMENT

Montesquieu's *De l'esprit des lois* was published in 1748.[1] It is a long, often perplexing, comparative study of various kinds of government which integrates philosophy, empirical material and political commentary. Four different types of government are discussed: monarchies, democratic republics, aristocratic republics and despotic states. As the aristocratic republic comes halfway between monarchy and democracy, for our purpose it can be left out of the discussion.

The types of government which are compared have conventional names. However, whereas the tradition of political theory identified each of them by the *source* of the ruler's power (like brute force, the way succession is regulated, the ruler's virtuousness, or – in Hobbes' case – a hypothetical covenant), Montesquieu put the spotlight on how in each type of government power is *exercised*. His reason: in both despotic states and monarchies a single person rules; but a despot rules according to his will and whims, whereas a monarch rules according to fixed or established laws, which will involve mediate institutions. The same source of rule can exercise his power in such different ways that the types of government must be said to be different.

Therefore, Montesquieu defined the *nature* of a government – that is, what it *is* – not by the *source* of the ruler's power, but by the way power is *exercised*. The various kinds of government are distinguished by whether or not the relation between ruler and ruled is established by laws and mediate institutions. In a despotic state, one alone rules, without law; monarchs govern according to established laws; in a democracy, the people have sovereignty and the exercise of their power is regulated by electoral laws that set out how, by whom, for whom, and on what issues votes should be cast. They determine the nature of democratic government.

Montesquieu conceived laws, 'taken in the broadest meaning', to be 'the necessary *relations* deriving from the nature of things'. He applied this idea to *any* law – regardless of what one might believe to be its author: God, nature or man. For this concept of law, he took his lead from natural philosophy, the physics of his time.

Abandoning the Aristotelian paradigm, seventeenth century natural philosophers had started to describe the physical world in terms of laws of nature that state relations between moving bodies. Observing that 'the world, formed by the motion of matter and devoid by intelligence, still continues to exist, its motions must have invariable laws', Montesquieu argued that 'if one could imagine another world than this, it would have consistent rules or it would be destroyed'. Without being related according to the laws of nature, everything would fall apart; the world would not *continue* to exist. Whereas most philosophers interpret the laws of nature in epistemological terms (as stating *known* relations between observed phenomena), Montesquieu used natural philosophy's concept of law to introduce a *relationist* ontology.

The laws of nature he assumed to apply with invariable necessity; but he noted that the laws men create themselves impose a lesser degree of necessity. As an intelligent being, man can guide himself, he wrote; but men are limited beings, prone to lapsing into ignorance and error. So, men have to be stimulated in one way or another to follow their own rules and to be called back to their duties. This defined his research agenda. He set out to study how governments are *established* and how they are able to act and *maintain* themselves by inciting men to follow their rule.

Governments do not fall out of blue sky and they do not operate in a vacuum. They are established in a region where the people are already related to each other in many ways – by sharing geographical and climatic conditions, by their manufacturing and trade, their religion, morals and manners, et cetera. Establishing a government means establishing ways to exercise power, and thus to introduce new relations *in addition to* the ones that already are present, namely relations between ruler and subjects. As the ruler will have to exercise his power *in* the world, the way his power is exercised will have to relate to the mundane – physical and social – conditions of the society that has to be governed. Hence, to establish a government these conditions have to be translated into the way power is exercised.

However, it is not sufficient to establish a government. Because men are limited beings, for a government to act and to *maintain* itself, men need some incitement to follow the ruler's orders. Therefore, apart from its nature, Montesquieu identified for each kind of government what he called its *principle*, a specific kind of passion that sets a government in motion and enables it to maintain itself. He argued that in a monarchy, honour makes all the parts of the body politic move; 'its very action binds [the nobles], and each person works for the common good, believing he works for his individual interests' (Montesquieu 1989 [1758]: III, 7). The principle of democracy is identified as virtue, that is, love for the republic and a continuous preference of the public's interest over their own. The principle of despotism is fear: when the people no longer fear his ever-raised arm and fury, the despot is lost. As – apart from fear – these passions do not come about spontaneously, education and civil and criminal laws will have to be introduced to incite and support the appropriate passions. They play a pivotal role in maintaining a government. 'The corruption of each government almost always begins with that of its principles', Montesquieu (1989 [1758]: I, 8) observed.

A large part of *De l'esprit des lois* – hundreds of pages – is devoted to discuss in detail how various kinds of government have to relate to the mundane conditions of the societies they govern. The discussion covers ancient Greece and Rome, various European countries, Islamic states and the Far-East, based on evidence collected from a wide range of sources: the works of ancient authors, travel reports and Montesquieu's own ad hoc observations in various European countries. Given that *De l'esprit des lois* was published in 1758, it is not surprising that Montesquieu's handling of empirical material – which takes up the larger part of the book – doesn't meet modern standards. Later history has shown him to be wrong on many points. Nevertheless, his analysis of how governments are established, operate and succeed to maintain themselves remains of great value.

In contrast to Hobbes, Montesquieu did not have to suppose some hypothetical covenant that has lifted men out of the state of nature when there was a war of all against all. He considered despotism to be the default condition of mankind. Despots rule by exercising brute force, over timid, down-beaten people, who live in fear of his ever-raised arm. Despotism 'leaps to view, so to speak', he wrote. '[I]t is uniform throughout; as only passions [i.e. fear] are needed to establish it, everyone is good enough for that' (Montesquieu 1989 [1758]: V, 14).

However, not all people live in fear. In monarchies and republics, the exercise of power is mediated by laws and institutions. This brings *reflection* into the business of government, he argued. If the exercise of power is channelled by law, before a ruler's orders are executed, they will have been discussed, reviewed, checked and if necessary amended. Hesitation being explicitly organized, the result will be a *moderate* government that offers security of one's person and property. To guarantee political *liberty* as well, Montesquieu argued, additional constitutional provisions to prevent abuse of power are necessary: the legislative, executive and judiciary powers have to be separated. The latter argument made him 'the father of [modern] constitutions' (Shklar 1987, Chpt. 6).

Moderate governments are complex, fragile political constructions. They do not come into being just because men love liberty and hate violence – also people who live under the yoke of a despot will share those feelings. They are established by introducing *laws*; they are 'masterpiece[s] of legislation that chance rarely produces and prudence is rarely allowed to produce' (Montesquieu 1989 [1758]: V, 14).

Montesquieu's theory of government offers two profound lessons.

First, to *establish* a *moderate* government, laws have to be *added* which translate the already existing mundane conditions of life. Whereas in Hobbes' *Leviathan* (as its famous frontispiece depicts) the sovereign raises *above* city and countryside, Montesquieu's conceives governments to be established *in* a world in which people are already related. Hence, when the mundane conditions of their lives change, to maintain a moderate government, its laws will have to be adapted.

Second, to act and maintain itself, a moderate government needs a principle – 'virtue' in the case of democracy. Proper civil and criminal laws and education should support it. When this principle becomes corrupted, despotism looms.

To assess democracy's vulnerability in the digital age, we have to take these two lessons to heart. We will have to consider, first, whether the arrival of digital technologies will require adapting the laws that establish democracy. As elections are key to the establishment of a democracy (on this Montesquieu agrees with the minimalist conception), we will have to review electoral laws. Subsequently, we will have to assess whether in the age of digital technologies the principle of democracy is vulnerable.

Before we get into this assessment, however, we need to substantiate this principle, which Montesquieu identified as the 'love for the republic' and a 'continuous preference of the public interest over one's own'.

That most people still 'love' democracy is beyond question. In opinion-polls, in large majority, they continue to express their support for it. That they still prefer 'public interests' over their own, however, is less clear. But before getting lost in gloomy thoughts about the rise of egotistic individualism, we had better clarify the term 'public interest'. Montesquieu left it unexplained. For a substantial clarification, we may turn to Dewey. He is a lesser writer than Montesquieu, but they are on common ground. Both analysed government in relationist terms.

In accounting for the state, Dewey wrote, '[m]en have looked in the wrong place. They have sought for the nature of the state in the field of agencies, in that of doers of deeds, or in some will or purpose back of the deeds. They have sought to explain the state in terms of authorship'. In a democracy, 'the public' is supposed to authorize the government. But 'we shall not . . . find the public if we look for it on the side of the *originators* of voluntary actions' (Dewey 1954 [1927], 17–18). To account for the notion of 'public interest', one should not look at the intentions or preferences of individual actors; but rather consider their *relations*.

Dewey distinguished two kinds of arrangements persons make with one another: 'those which affect only the persons directly engaged in a transaction, and those which affect others beyond those immediately involved as well'. In this distinction, he explained, 'we find the germ of the distinction between the private and the public. When indirect consequences are recognized and there is effort to regulate them, something having the traits of a state comes into existence' (Dewey 1954 [1927], 12). He therefore defined 'the public' to consist of

> all those who are affected by the indirect consequences of transactions to such extent that it is deemed necessary to have those consequences systematically cared for. . . . Since those who are indirectly affected are not participants in the transaction in question, it is necessary that certain persons be set apart to represent them, and to see to it that their interests are conserved and protected. (Dewey 1954 [1927], 15–16)

This is the task of the officials of the democratic state, of representatives who as guardians of custom, as legislators, as executives, judges, etc. have to organize 'the public' and to care for its especial interests by methods intended to regulate the conjoint actions of individuals and groups (Dewey 1954 [1927], 35).

Two important consequences follow. First, the distinction between the private and the public should not be taken for the one between the 'individual' and the 'social'. Many private arrangements are 'social'; reversibly, the public cannot be identified with the socially useful either: whether it is socially useful to regulate the indirect consequences of transactions or not, may be highly controversial and the subject of debate. Second, like Montesquieu, Dewey emphasized that the state is a specific form of social life which is *added* to other forms of social life, like transactions on the market, or relations among friends. The democratic state consists of government officials and the public. In a democracy, citizens have therefore 'dual capacity': as *voters*, they are 'government officials' who exercise sovereign power by way of their elected representatives; but they also make up '*the public*' that a government organizes and cares for.

On this reading, the idea of having 'a continuous preference of the public interest over one's own' acquires a precise meaning. It does *not* refer to a preference for something 'socially useful', shared values, or some higher purpose. In a democracy, people will disagree about all of that. 'A continuous preference of the public interest over one's own' simply means to accept democracy and the rule of law as the proper way to exercise power and to care for the interests of those who are affected by the consequences of transactions they are not engaged in.

DEMOCRACY'S VULNERABILITY IN THE DIGITAL AGE

Montesquieu's relationist theory of government and Dewey's notion of 'public interest' suggest that to consider democracy's vulnerability in the digital age, we have to assess to which extent digital technologies may either 1) corrupt the *nature* of democracy – that is, the way citizens exercise their sovereign power as voters – or 2) corrupt the idea of 'public interest', the core of what Montesquieu called the *principle* of democracy.

For the first challenge – the challenge to what Montesquieu called a government's *nature* – we have to turn our attention to the way in a democracy people exercise their sovereign power, that is, to the electoral *laws* and the electoral *system*. The two need to be distinguished (Farrell 2011, 3). Electoral *laws* regulate the process of elections: from the calling of elections, through the process of candidate nomination, party campaigning and funding, up to the stage of counting votes and determining the actual election result. They open up a space for public debates about nominations, party programs and the future of the country. The electoral *system* determines how results are calculated, that is, how the votes that have been cast are translated into seats won and lost.

Fake-news disrupts the public debate; bots build up momentum to incite voters to jump on the band-wagon; micro-targeting voters allows candidates and parties to approach the electorate – split up in groups of voters with similar profiles – with messages and promises, tailored to the selected groups' supposed interests, emotions and preferences. As mentioned above, more traditional campaign strategies have been used widely to achieve similar effects. However, the traditional tricks – like smearing opponents, organizing rallies, and deceiving the electorate – are performed in the public eye; the press may report about them; they may become the subject of public debate. Online campaign strategies, and especially the use of bots and micro-targeting voters, are much harder to detect. They operate under the radar of the public eye, unchecked.

The specific challenge digital campaign strategies pose for democracy is therefore *not* that they offer means for manipulation, deception and distributing disinformation; politicians knew how to manipulate and deceive the electorate long before the internet. Online campaign strategies allow circumventing the counter-power that *public* scrutiny of campaign strategies affords. They limit the discussion and reflection that electoral law is supposed to bring into the business of establishing a democratic government. They challenge a keystone of the *nature* of democracy, its electoral laws.

The electoral system should be considered as well. As the outcome of elections in non-proportional electoral systems (like the UK's 'first-past-the-post' system) are usually determined in a limited number of swing constituencies where two main parties compete for votes, they encourage micro-targeting the electorate of those constituencies. Electoral systems that introduce proportional representation (especially where the entire country is the constituency) are arguably less susceptible for them. So, for countries with a non-proportional electoral system, the spread of digital campaign strategies should be a reason to reconsider the electoral system.

The second challenge, the one to the *principle* of democracy – 'love of the republic and a continuous preference of the public interest over one's own' – deserves a somewhat longer discussion.

The number of publications that point to the spread of an individualistic, ego-centred culture must run into the thousands. However, many of them precede the internet, the web and social media. In fact, concerns about the decline of shared social values date back to the end of the nineteenth century, when early sociologists started to discuss the transformation of society associated with industrialization and urbanization as a shift from *Gemeinschaft* to *Gesellschaft* and as a transformation in the nature of social solidarity. How these social changes affected the political order and the notion of public interest is anything but clear, however. About the same time early sociologists discussed the evanishment of shared social values, universal suffrage and modern parties-based representative democracy were established and democratic legitimacy became solidly anchored in the institution of elections.

However, Rosanvallon's (2011) historical study of the changes in democratic legitimacy suggests that around 1980 a new guiding principle of the democratic ideal, 'legitimacy by proximity', emerged. Increasingly, citizens expected their representatives to show compassion and to communicate directly with them about their particular interests. Social media may have boosted this development when they appeared about two decades later. A lot of what is expressed on social media belongs to the genre one may call – with the title of Norman Mailer's 1959 book – 'Advertisements for Myself'. However, social media are extensively used to call attention for public issues and to shape collective action as well (Margetts et al. 2016). How the balance plays out is impossible to establish. Contexts, and the range of time considered, matter. The impact of technologies on society often depends on the range of time one takes into consideration: effects on the short-term and the long-term may differ radically (Kranzberg 1986).

To be more precise, we have to leave the debate about culture, values and expectations; we need to focus on what Dewey called the role of citizens as 'the public' a government has to care for. We have to reconsider Zuboff's claims about 'surveillance capitalism'. Where 'the public' was once – to cite Dewey – 'organized and made effective by means of representatives who as guardians of custom, as legislators, as executives, judges, etc., care for its especial interests by methods intended to regulate the conjoint actions of individuals and groups', surveillance capitalism organizes the public by way of big data and artificial intelligence. Law is replaced by code. It changes the way the public is organized. The government officials who used to take care of the public are replaced by more efficient means. Private platforms will provide for it. Efficiency, the quality for which markets are praised, takes pride of place.

However, the qualities for which democracy should be loved are moderate government and liberty, not efficiency. It's quite ironic that what is often conceived as the downside of democratic politics – its endless disputes, the time it takes to agree on a decision, the bureaucracy that comes with law-based government – is precisely what makes democracy stand out: the reflection and hesitation which precedes the execution of power when power is exercised in accordance to the law. Beyond question, decisions of an autocratic, despotic ruler will be executed faster; it would also save a lot of time and money if police officers could impose punishments directly, on the spot, without going through the whole circus of court procedures and legal assistance. But by that time, we have left democracy and entered a despotic police state.

It would be wrong to call 'surveillance capitalism' a despotic police-state however. The rule of law is replaced by the rewards and punishments of a new kind of invisible hand, not by the whims and will of a despot. The people still make up the body politic, but they have delegated the exercise of their power to digital technologies. Their private interests are registered and collected as big data and coordinated by AI-algorithms. In this world, there is no place for the idea of some 'public interest' above, or next to, the interests of one's own. In an age of surveillance capitalism, there is no place for the virtue of 'continuous preference of the public interest over one's own'.

Replacing law by algorithms strikes at the root of the *nature* of democracy and will corrupt its *principle*. Zuboff is right: it would 'annihilate the freedom achieved by the rule of law'. But the reason she gives for this conclusion is misdirected. Not the fact that power is transferred to the hands of a few private companies annihilates freedom, but the fact that the hesitation and reflection which exercising power in accordance to the law affords are evaded, when power is exercised by code. If the question whether a state is democratic or not is decided on the basis of who *has* power, one may doubt whether we have ever lived in a democracy. As every government will have to acknowledge, private companies in sectors like energy and finance exert enormous power. What makes a democracy stand out is the way power is *exercised* by law and mediate institutions. In a democracy, the people, as well as companies, enjoy liberty *not* because they have power and can do what one wants, but because their actions are bound by laws. 'Liberty is the right to do everything the laws permit; and if one citizen could do what they forbid, he would no longer have liberty because the others would likewise have the same power', Montesquieu (1989 [1758]: XI, 3) wrote. One should not confuse having *power* with *liberty*.

CONCLUSION

Is democracy vulnerable in the age of digital technologies and surveillance capitalism? Not surprisingly, the answer depends on one's conception of democracy. In this chapter, two conceptions have been reviewed: the OED's one (with its underlying Hobbesian theory of the state) and Montesquieu's conception of democratic government, amended with some ideas from Dewey.

In a democracy, the people exercise sovereign power by electing or rejecting those who rule on their behalf. On that, Schumpeter, Popper, the OED, Montesquieu and Dewey agree.

Perceived from the Hobbesian point of view, digital technologies do not put democracy seriously at risk. That these technologies allow spreading disinformation widely and effectively is a problem for society, not for democracy. Producing and distributing politically sensitive disinformation is not illegal; to outlaw it would limit the freedom of speech a democratic government is supposed to respect and protect. The hands of a democratic government are tied. Any attempt to limit the distribution of disinformation should therefore be organized outside government, by civil society organizations and by platforms for reasons of their corporate *social* responsibility. That private platforms effectively take over services to execute power is no problem to democracy either, provided they operate on competitive markets, with sufficient oversight. It may take some time and some experimentation to find effective means to keep the challenges of digital technologies in check. But history shows that democracies are resilient and can be trusted for performing this task.

Montesquieu's conception of democracy reframes the problems democratic societies face in the digital age. It shifts the attention from the question who has power to the question how power is exercised. If the exercise of power is delegated to algorithms, the reflection and hesitation which law introduces into the exercise of power is substantially reduced and may even be eliminated. Moderation and political liberty then may become at risk. Producing and distributing disinformation may be old political tricks; but if digital technologies are introduced for this purpose they pose a new and serious problem because they operate under the radar of the public eye. The reflection and hesitation that electoral laws introduce in political campaigns is disrupted. On Montesquieu's conception of democracy, digital technologies do indeed present a serious challenge to the democratic process.

Montesquieu's conception of democracy not only points to vulnerabilities that remain hidden in the Hobbesian conception. It opens a view on policy-options for managing these vulnerabilities as well.

First, in a democracy, it is the task of government officials, rather than private companies, to care for what Dewey calls 'the public', that is, those who have to face the consequences of transactions they were directly not engaged is. Laws should provide for this. The idea to allow big data and AI algorithms to decide on matters that affect the public (like judicial ones and social security) should be met with reluctance. Code is *not* law. If for reasons of efficiency, part of the process of exercising power is delegated to digital technologies, this should be explicitly done under the law and with appropriate public oversight. That under EU regulation, one has the right to have any automatically produced decision to be reviewed by a human actor, is only a very meagre way to restore the function that law is supposed to perform.

Second, the issues that are discussed as problems of spreading 'disinformation' need to be reformulated. Spreading disinformation by digital means is not only a challenge to society, but to the nature and principle of democracy as well. Once this is understood, there is room for considering other policy options beyond the ones the EC has proposed. To maintain itself in the digital age, democracies will have to reconsider both their electoral law and their electoral system.

To put political messages distributed on social media to various groups of voters back into the public eye, electoral law should include the obligation for candidates, political parties, as well as their affiliates (e.g. PACs) to publicize an online, searchable and up-to-date registry of all the messages that they have sent and are sending out during an election campaign.

It would open up their online strategies for inspection, criticism and debate, provide civil society organizations and the press with the necessary counter-power and would stimulate the political debate.

Moreover, as argued above, the arrival of online campaign strategies gives reason to reconsider existing electoral systems (in particular the first-past-the-post system).

Montesquieu's theory of government acknowledges that government do not operate in vacuum. When social relations change – which is evidently the case now digital technologies have permeated almost all of social life – to *maintain* democratic government its laws will have to relate to the new conditions. Surely, democracy is a resilient system; but it is also a fragile one, and it may become corrupted.

So, Barlow was wrong. To have 'a world where anyone, anywhere may express his or her beliefs, no matter how singular, without fear of being coerced into silence or conformity' requires democracy and the rule of law, not the independence of Cyberspace.

NOTE

1. Some of the material in this section is drawn from De Vries (forthcoming).

REFERENCES

Barlow, J.P. 1996. 'A Declaration of the Independence of Cyberspace', available at <www.eff.org/cyberspace-independence>

Callon, M. and B. Latour. 1981. 'Unscrewing the Big Leviathan: How Actors Macro-Structure Reality and How Sociologists Help Them To Do So'. In Knorr-Cetina, K. and A.V. Cicourel (eds.), *Advances in Social Theory and Methodology – Towards an Integration of Micro- and Macro-Sociologies*. London: Routledge and Kegan Paul, 277–303

De Vries, G. 2016. *Bruno Latour*. Cambridge: Polity Press

De Vries, G. (forthcoming). 'Politics is a "Mode of Existence"'. In Felski, R. and S. Muecke (eds.), *Latour and the Humanities*. Baltimore, MD: Johns Hopkins University Press

Dewey, J. 1954. [1927]. *The Public and its Problems*. Athens, OH: Swallow Press-Ohio University Press

Farrell, D. M. 2011. *Electoral Systems*. 2nd edn. Houndsmill, Basingstoke: Palgrave MacMillan

Hildebrandt, M. 2015. *Smart Technologies and the End(s) of Law*. Northampton, MA: Edward Elgar Publishing

Hobbes, T. 1968. [1651]. *Leviathan*. Ed. with an Introduction by C. B. Macpherson. Harmondsworth: Penguin Books

King, G., J. Pan and M. E. Roberts. 2017. 'How the Chinese Government

Fabricates Social Media Posts for Strategic Distraction, Not Engaged Argument'. *American Political Science Review* 111 (3), 484–501

Kranzberg, M. 1986. 'Technology and History: Kranzberg's Laws'. *Technology and Culture* 27, 544–60

Kymlicka, W. 2002. *Contemporary Political Philosophy*. Oxford: Oxford University Press

Latour, B. 2005. *Reassembling the Social – An Introduction to Actor-Network-Theory*. Oxford: Oxford University Press

Latour, B. 2013. *An Inquiry into Modes of Existence*. Cambridge, MA: Harvard University Press

Latour, B. and P. Weibel (eds.). 2005. *Making Things Public – Atmosphere of Democracy*. Cambridge, MA: MIT Press

Latour, B., P. Jensen, T. Venturini, S. Grauwin and D. Boullier. 2012. 'The Whole is Always Smaller Than Its Parts. A Digital Test of Gabriel Tarde's Monads'. *British Journal of Sociology* 63 (4), 591–615

Lynch, M., S. Hilgartner and C. Berkowitz. 2005. 'Voting Machinery, Counting and Public Proofs in the 2000 US Presidential Election'. In Latour, B. and P. Weibel (eds.), *Making Things Public – Atmosphere of Democracy*. Cambridge, MA: MIT Press, 814–25

Margetts, H., P. John, S. Hale and T. Yasseri. 2016. *Political Turbulence*. Princeton, NJ: Princeton University Press

Montesquieu. 1989. [1758]. *The Spirit of the Laws*, translated and edited by A. M. Cohler, B. C. Miller and H. S. Stone. Cambridge: Cambridge University Press

Popper, K. R. 1962. *The Open Society and its Enemies*. London: Routledge, 2 volumes

Rosanvallon, P. 2011. *Democratic Legitimacy – Impartiality, Reflexivity, Proximity*. Princeton, NJ: Princeton University Press

Runciman, D. 2013. *The Confidence Trap*. Princeton, NJ: Princeton University Press

Schumpeter, J. 1942. *Capitalism, Socialism, and Democracy*. New York, NY: Harper & Brothers

Shklar, J. N. 1987. *Montesquieu*. Oxford: Oxford University Press

Skinner, Q. 1989. 'The State', In Ball, T., J. Farr and R. L. Hanson (eds.), *Political Innovation and Conceptual Change*. Cambridge: Cambridge University Press

Sloterdijk, P. and G. Mueller von der Haegen. 2005. 'Instant Democracy: The Pneumatic Parliament'. In Latour, B. and P. Weibel (eds.), *Making Things Public – Atmosphere of Democracy*. Cambridge, MA: MIT Press, 952–7

Whitehead, A. N. 1967. [1925]. *Science and the Modern World*. New York, NY: The Tree Press

Zuboff, S. 2015. 'Big Other: Surveillance Capitalism and the Prospects of an Information Civilization'. *Journal of Information Technology* 30, 75–8

9. In defence of 'Toma': Algorithmic enhancement of a sense of justice[1]
David Stevens

INTRODUCTION

'Toma' is a piece of advanced computational software that employs algorithms to predict, structure and alter the attitudes, behaviour and choices of Diana, its human user (*The End(s)*, 1–10). Toma is dispersed across a number of platforms – handheld device, home, car, office computer system – and links with other Personal Data Assistants (PDAs), as well as third-party service providers, including government. Toma illustrates the potential that, in combination with Big Data, algorithms can significantly enhance human decision-making. Humans are 'hackable': by correcting for familiar flaws that beset human reasoning, algorithms can enable individuals to better fulfil their preferences, act in accordance with their values or promote their well-being. Toma also balances the interests of Diana against the interests of third parties, potentially harmonizing and optimizing outcomes by shaping beliefs, desires and choices.

Part of the Toma story illustrates the various concerns about algorithmic transparency, accountability, agency and bias. In this chapter I set aside such concerns about the background conditions that might lead us to worry about the practical implications of employing algorithms, and concentrate instead on the positive transformative effects of algorithms for enhancing human well-being via the structuring of choices and behaviour. My focus, specifically, is on the normative question of what limits there are over the state's use of algorithms to steer our unconscious minds. In particular, I focus on the permissibility of the state using algorithms to influence the *moral* beliefs, attitudes and behaviour of its citizens for socially beneficial ends. With governments increasingly interested in alternatives to traditional methods of gaining compliance with public policies (incentives and coercive threats), algorithms increasingly offer ways of bringing citizens to socially beneficial moral attitudes and behaviour (Wilkinson 2013, 341). Faced with the threat of a range of serious political issues that call for large-scale coordinated action – such as global warming – finding workable methods for gaining compliance is pressing (see Persson and Savulescu 2012, Rosa 2013). Increasingly sophisticated algorithms, that is, offer benefits in multiple directions: individuals benefit because their well-being is improved by optimizing choices that will better achieve their own ends; society benefits by having its members adopt attitudes and behaviours that are conducive to peaceable social cooperation; and taxpayers benefit by governments using less costly means to achieve the same ends.

Despite such positive benefits, there exist very real concerns about the manipulation that increasingly powerful algorithms will facilitate. Even when algorithms work perfectly, normative concerns remain that such manipulation is undermining of autonomy or dignity. The central question addressed here is whether it is morally permissible for the state to use this technology to interfere in society to promote individually and socially beneficial ends. In what follows, I argue for a two-fold conclusion: that there are principled reasons for the state to refrain from seeking to maximize the well-being of its citizens, but that it is permissible for the state to seek to develop in citizens a sense of justice that would underpin socially cooperative behaviour. If the state were to employ technologies such as algorithms to promote the well-being of its citizens – by shaping their goals, beliefs and choices – then it would undermine the fundamental interest that citizens have in deciding for themselves what goals or ends to pursue. However, this kind of independence depends upon a scheme of social and political institutions that are only capable of being maintained if citizens possess the right kinds of attitudes regarding those institutions and the proper treatment of others; a sense of justice. Employing technology to shape these attitudes is, I argue, a morally permissible role of the state.

This chapter has the following format. I begin by exploring some of the transformative possibilities that algorithms promise. Second, I consider some familiar justifications that might block the state's use of algorithms to promote individual well-being. I reject these on the basis that they do not work in the case of algorithms. Third, I point to other grounds that might block state interference in the ends that citizens pursue on grounds that it undermines the freedom of citizens to plan, revise and pursue ends they choose for themselves, regardless of whether this promotes their well-being. Fourth, I develop this account in terms of political morality – about the proper relationship between citizen and state. Finally, I argue that although the state is not permitted to promote particular ends, it can employ technological enhancements to bring about attitudes and beliefs in citizens regarding a sense of social justice and cooperation.

THE POTENTIAL OF ALGORITHMS FOR ENHANCEMENT

Let us flesh out the Toma story. Diana employs Toma to help organize her life more efficiently and effectively. Toma is highly sensitive to the needs, moods, physical state and preferences of Diana. Toma shapes and controls many features of Diana's world by filtering information, balancing competing claims on her time and attention and adjusting her environment. Toma 'reads' Diana, anticipating her responses based on previous actions and a wealth of external data (*The End(s)*, 59–61). Toma's computer system is *autonomic*: unsupervised learning algorithms and neural networks that employ forms of artificial intelligence, advanced statistical methods, and machine learning (*The End(s)*, 23–6, Hildebrandt 2016). It is trained on, and works in tandem with, Big Data: vast quantities of data distributed across multiple datasets (*The End(s)*, 31–40, Pasquale 2015, 19–58, Hildebrandt 2013, 2–7). As Hildebrandt (*The End(s)*, viii–ix) writes:

> Our lifeworld is increasingly populated with things that are trained to foresee our behaviours and pre-empt our intent. These things are no longer stand-alone devices, they are progressively becoming interconnected via the cloud, which enables them to share their 'experience' of us to improve their functionality. We are in fact surrounded by adaptive systems that display a new kind of mindless agency.

Toma goes beyond prediction. Toma exhibits a form of agency, actively altering Diana's beliefs, attitudes and behaviour, enabling her to make better decisions in line with what it takes to be her wider interests. Toma operates at two levels: first, it influences the actual *choices* Diana makes by restricting the feasible option set, or making it more likely that a better option will be selected from the set. In this, algorithms ameliorate familiar flaws in human reasoning that cause individuals to depart from fully rational decision-making, such as myopia, framing, loss aversion and overconfidence (see Persson and Savulescu 2012, 12–41, Savulescu and Maslen 2015, 80–81, Kahneman 2011, 278–374, Sunstein 2014, 8–13). In this, Toma performs tasks similar to 'nudging': structuring the background against which individuals can be led to make better (more optimal) choices, given their desires (see Sunstein 2014, Hausman and Welch 2010). Toma 'frames' choices, and 'primes' Diana.

Second, Toma operates directly on the very *beliefs* and *desires* Diana has. It filters information, and it induces or forestalls emotional responses by regulating various features of the environment or Diana's physiology that impact on her attitudes and decision-making. In this, it is akin to 'bioenhancement': the introduction of chemicals – such as serotonin – into the brain, or the control of nutrition, sleep, exercise and stressors that directly alter the beliefs and desires of individuals (see Persson and Savulescu 2012, Sparrow 2014, Baccarini 2014, Savalescu and Maslen 2015, Clayton and Moles 2018). Toma also alters Diana's interests to bring them into harmony with societal and third party interests. For example, Toma removes certain decisions from Diana, preventing her from driving when her stress levels reach a certain threshold, reporting to her insurance company and government agencies on her behaviour, and from acting in ways that undermine socially cooperative efforts, such as denying options that would increase her carbon footprint. Toma does all of this behind Diana's back; she has no access to the processes by which Toma makes these changes, and they often occur via the 'reading' and altering of subtle patterns regarding Diana's behaviour that she is unaware of (*The End(s)*, 27, 51), as discussed in *The End(s)*, at 11:

> Technologies regulate our behaviours by making certain behaviours possible and constricting others. The regulations that stem from technological artefacts is less obvious than enacted legal norms, and not enacted by a democratic legislator. Its regulative force depends on how engineers, designers and business enterprise bring these artefacts to the market and eventually how consumers or end-users engage with them. Its material and social embedding has a way of inducing or inhibiting certain behaviour patterns, such as sharing personal data. Depending on their design and uptake, technologies can even enforce or rule out certain types of behaviour.

Toma is of course fictitious, but it is not wildly fantastical. Distributed computing is now a significant feature of our daily existence, and increasingly so. Algorithms are now widely employed – criminal justice and policing, traffic and air-traffic control, finance, environmental monitoring, healthcare, insurance and education – and their use being extended and diversified. As Hildebrandt has observed, algorithms exhibit a form of *autonomic* decision-making that operates in a manner akin to human decision-making (*The End(s)*, 54–7; see also Hildebrandt 2016). One of the features laid bare by behavioural psychology is that most of our choices are not based on deliberative reasoning, as we may have hoped (*The End(s)*, 56, Kahneman 2011, 19–30, Haidt 2012, 32–56). Rather, our decisions are often based on emotional responses, and simple pattern recognition. Our bounded rationality can only cope with a small amount of information, so most functions are performed by our unconscious minds or nervous systems (*The End(s)*, 56–7). If sophisticated reasoning enters the picture at all, then it does so as a form of post hoc rationalization – an attempt to persuade our self or others of the rightness of our actions (*The

End(s), 56, Haidt 2012, 55). In particular, our moral decision-making is like an elephant and its rider (Haidt 2012). The emotional elephant goes where it wants, and the rider constructs a rationale. Although the rider can, given enough time and effort, alter the course of the elephant, it is rarely in control. If this picture is correct, then the notion of individuals as self-governing, autonomous subjects is a fiction (*The End(s)*, 56). Consequently, where algorithmic computing, such as Toma, exercises this influence over our lives, then the line that separates the two becomes blurred. Like Michael Gilhaney in Flann O'Brien's *The Third Policeman*, who has ridden the same bicycle for 30 years, the atoms have become intertwined, making him almost half bicycle. When not riding, Gilhaney can often be found propped against a wall by his elbow or standing on one leg at the kerb (*The End(s)*, 56):

> The autonomic nervous system does not require our explicit consent to raise blood pressure or increase the breathing speed to adjust our internal environment. Similarly, the autonomic computer system could adjust our external environment in order to do what it infers to be necessary or desirable for our well-being.

This blurring of the lines between autonomic systems raises, as Hildebrandt shows, questions about the extent to which humans can be said to be autonomous. One such concern is that when our beliefs, attitudes and choices are influenced and altered behind our backs, then it undermines notions of freedom and dignity. If it is generally preferable that we hold beliefs because we recognize the force of the reasons behind them, then we should be concerned about non-rational belief formation. When algorithms manipulate beliefs and desires, and the choices that flow from them, it seems like indoctrination. In doing so, it may be thought to fail to treat us with the kind of respect owed to independent human agents. It is not clear where the bicycle ends and the person starts (see also Hildebrandt and Koops 2010, 436).

TYPES OF INFLUENCE

To unravel what is objectionable, consider an extension of Toma's story.[2] Toma judges that Diana's well-being is being hampered by her poor diet and, after reviewing all the available evidence and options, tailored to Diana's physical and psychological composition, concludes that her diet would be much improved by not eating meat. Toma also concludes that changing Diana to a vegetarian diet will have important positive environmental and social impacts that go beyond her own well-being. Diana's earnings are not sufficient for Toma to be able to replace her current poor-quality meat with organically and humanely reared meat, nor is her psychological makeup one that would allow a severe reduction in meat consumption without constantly testing her will-power. The easiest path to better nutrition is for Toma to bring about vegetarianism. Toma is also aware that Diana harbours certain negative emotional reactions to animal suffering and uses this to create leverage. Consequently, Toma: removes meat options from on-line shopping suggestions, replacing them with attractive vegetarian ones; guides Diana toward vegetarian recipes and hides away meat recipes; selects routes, shops and restaurants that have few or no meat options and well-reviewed vegetarian ones; streams adverts and information to her smartphone about animal suffering; adjusts the image in her smart spectacles to make meat look repulsive; enrols her onto social media pages of those who oppose animal suffering; administers a small, imperceptible, electrical current via her smart watch that causes nausea whenever Diana's desire for meat threatens to surface. After a short time Diana no longer desires to eat meat. Her well-being improves, and she is pleased to no longer be a meat eater because of the suffering it causes. Moreover, if presented with the steps taken by Toma, Diana would agree that it is better that Toma took those steps.

What, if anything, is objectionable in this story? One familiar line of argument is that such choosing for others undermines their well-being, either by replacing an individual's judgement about what is in their interests with a less accurate judgement, or in supplanting that judgement it treats that individual a less than fully morally capable being. Both lines of defence face strong objections. Let us consider each in turn.

First, we might think that our choices have *instrumental* value (Scanlon 1998, 251). That is, I am just more likely to judge what is in my interest than some third party, such as the state or its representatives. When I visit a restaurant it is generally better if what appears on my plate is what I selected from the menu, even if the waiter thinks I will enjoy another dish more (Scanlon 1998, 251–2). The waiter is less likely to match my tastes to the options than I am. This account, however, rests on an empirical claim that the increasing power of algorithms has shown to be seriously flawed. What algorithms show is that in some instances I may not be the best judge of my own interests. I may, for example, be swayed by a desire to impress my friends with my knowledge of Greek cuisine and make a choice that I will not enjoy as much as if I had not been swayed by that consideration. Deferring to Toma's authority would prevent me from departing from the rational pursuit of my ends. Algorithms may know us better than we know ourselves.

Second, our choices might have *representative* value (Scanlon 1998, 252): our choices say something about us, even when those choices are less than optimal for our well-being (*The End(s)*, 71). When you pick a gift for your mother it matters that it is *you* that picks it (Scanlon 1998, 252). It matters because of what it says about how you view your mother and the relationship between you, even if she would have picked a better gift (one more in line with her preferences) for herself. When Toma makes these choices it removes the opportunity for realizing this value.

It is not clear, however, that this account blocks algorithmic enhancement. In fact, algorithms might enhance it by providing more opportunities for the exercise of such choices. If choice has this value, then we have an interest in having more instances of it. Toma is capable of shaping beliefs and behaviour in ways that prevent us from closing off opportunities to make such choices, and of opening up new opportunities. By denying Diana the opportunity to eat meat, it creates a series of future choices with regard to animal welfare, as well as a healthier lifestyle, that she might not otherwise have had.

A further observation is that this account depends upon a controversial view of freedom, one that many reasonable people reject. Many are untroubled by their life plans lacking high levels of choice so long as their ends are the 'right' ones (Quong 2011, 99). It is more important for many that they lead good lives or hold the correct beliefs, and less important how they come to lead it or hold those beliefs. Such independence has a less privileged place in their conceptions of morality. Such individuals might welcome algorithmic enhancement because it makes them more likely to succeed in pursuing what they take to be a good life. Deferring to Toma would be a useful instance of pre-commitment – like Ulysses tying himself to the mast – in order to remove options now that would make the selection of other options at a later point more certain (Elster 1979, 37–47).

If the state can reliably improve the well-being of citizens by utilizing algorithms to push them towards better ends, or steer them away from detrimental ends, then there is little in this line of reasoning to block such paternalistic interference. Yet, this seems intuitively implausible. If it were not, then it would commit us to saying there is no difference between Diana coming to act upon reasons that she finds, upon reflection, to be sufficiently weighty to motivate her actions, and acting merely as a result of some unseen external, but benign, force (Clayton and Moles 2018). But, there does seem a difference between Diana rejecting a meat option because she weighs the animal suffering involved as an overwhelming reason not to take a bite, and a feeling of nausea induced by an electric current triggered by her smartwatch. There is something valuable in recognizing for oneself the moral requirements that are applicable to us.

SOME CONCERNS OVER INFLUENCE AND SELF-DETERMINATION

In this section I lay out some concerns that algorithmic enhancement poses that rely not on their ability to promote well-being, but that operate in spite of this ability. These concerns stem from the idea of self-determination or independence.

It is helpful, following Elster, to distinguish several forms of influence over our beliefs and desires (1979, 81–83). First, a *voluntary choice* is one where a person desires, on the basis of good reasons, x over y, and does x for those reasons. At the opposite end of the continuum is *coercion*. Coercion takes place when a person desires x over y, and continues to do so even when a third party forces her to do y. Between these two poles, other forms of influence exist. *Seduction* is where a person initially prefers x over y, but comes to prefer y over x once she has been coerced into doing y. *Persuasion* occurs when a person who initially prefers x over y is led, by a series of short-term improvements, to prefer y over x. At each step in the process of persuasion the person sees the reasons for change, and comes to accept those reasons *as reasons* for the change.

Diana's vegetarianism looks like a case of seduction: a series of steps that exploit various 'intrapsychic mechanisms' in order to lead her to a desire not to eat meat (Elster 1979, 82). These mechanisms take place behind Diana's back. As such, they differ from persuasion. As Raz writes: 'Manipulation, unlike coercion, does not interfere with a person's options. Instead, it perverts the way the person reaches decisions, forms preferences or adopts goals' (1986, 377–8). Even if Toma is accurate in terms of the benefits to Diana's health in changing diet, it does not seem to act permissibly. Given the choice, Diana may still refrain from switching. This possibility makes it the case that when Toma acts behind Diana's back, it does so impermissibly. This would not be the case if Diana's friend, Charles, were to attempt to change her mind by arguing with her face-to-face – laying out the various health benefits, environmental impacts and animal welfare considerations. When Charles engages Diana in such a conversation it is with the explicit intention of changing her mind. Moreover, Diana can argue back, contributing further evidence, or proposing a different relative weighting of the evidence and moral considerations (Elster 1979, 83–4, see also Taylor 1971, Taylor 1976).

It is also worth noting that this form of influence renders Diana's desires unstable. If option a is removed from the choice set (a, b, c) by Toma, and a was Diana's preferred option, when left with b and c, Diana might come to view a as lacking any real value now it is no longer available (Elster 1983, 112–25). The 'coming to view' element occurs behind Diana's back, perhaps through a psychological process such as the tendency to reduce cognitive dissonance. If this is the case, then it is difficult to determine if any part of the process is autonomous; desires are *adaptive* (Elster 1983, 110–11). When Diana comes to desire vegetarianism via Toma's processes, it is unclear whether she would revert to being desirous of meat eating if Toma were to reverse the process. If Toma were able to cause Diana's desires to flip-flop in this manner, adapting to the available options, then we could be fairly certain that these are not, in any meaningful sense, Diana's actual desires or choices. This would be different from the case where, through learning and experience of, say, her dietary needs or moral concerns about animal suffering, Diana comes to desire vegetarianism.

THE ACCEPTABILITY REQUIREMENT

These concerns provide us with some reason to reject the employment of algorithms where they run the risk of influencing the desires and beliefs of individuals, even where such influences might be thought to improve well-being. Whilst some features of algorithms may enhance our capability to pursue freely chosen ends, when they set what ends we should pursue they undermine our independence. Such manipulation fails to respect the fundamental interest individuals have in the capacity to plan, revise and rationally pursue their own ends. Such manipulation demeans or diminishes this moral status. Even if governments were certain that some course of action (such as vegetarianism or a specific physical exercise programme) would maximize the well-being of the vast majority of its citizens, implementing a change of belief or desire amongst its citizenry via algorithmic tweaking, would be impermissible because it undermines the respect for independence owed to its citizens. Thus, governments have principled reasons not to take a stand on certain issues regarding the ends that individuals may choose.

This notion of independence also raises issues, as Sparrow (2014, 26) notes, of *political* morality – about the proper relationship of citizen and state. We are born into and inhabit societies governed by a set of legal, socioeconomic and political institutions and arrangements that coercively impose various kinds of actions upon us. This raises what Rousseau termed the 'fundamental problem' of political society: how to reconcile individual freedom with the constraints necessary to guarantee the security of individuals (Rousseau 1997, 49–50). As free and equal individuals we all have a claim to live under conditions of freedom. But, we also, for our security and prosperity, need to live in societies that are well-ordered – that is, governed by legal constraints (*The End(s)*, 10). Part of Rousseau's solution is that our freedom is preserved only if we live under rules that we, ourselves, endorse. When a person endorses the law, we can consider that person as regarding those constraints as self-imposed rules of self-determining, free, individual (Rousseau 1997, 50–1, Rawls 1996, 68).

In Rawls (1996), the view is that citizens are free and equal in virtue of their possession of two moral powers: a capacity for a sense of justice, and a capacity for a conception of the good. A sense of justice is the capacity to understand, apply and act from a public conception of justice. It supports just political and legal institutions and underpins the proper treatment of others in accordance with what kinds of behaviour we owe them. A capacity for a conception of the good is the capacity to form, revise and rationally pursue a conception of one's rational advantage. Rawls states that, in virtue of these two moral powers, persons are free, and that their 'having these powers to the requisite minimum degree to be fully cooperating members of society makes persons equal' (Rawls 1996, 19, see also *The End(s)*, 74–5).

Consequently, we have duties to arrange our institutional framework such that it provides a fair distribution of the various benefits and burdens of social cooperation. This will include the provision of various familiar rights, freedoms and opportunities, and the distribution of socioeconomic goods such that everyone has the means to pursue the ends they choose.

When individuals are free to form their own views, it is inevitable that they will arrive at different judgements about what roles, relationships or goals are desirable or worthy of pursuit. Even reasonable citizens who are committed to treating each other fairly and with appropriate respect will come to different conclusions about what comprehensive ends are valuable. But, this is *reasonable* disagreement, because each citizen retains the fundamental commitment to the idea of treating each other as free and equal, as well as to an ideal of social unity where citizens see themselves as 'ready to propose fair terms of cooperation and to abide by them provided others do' (Rawls 1996, 54, 63–6, Quong 2011, 291).

What follows from this is that the state should be guided by a conception of political morality that is acceptable to free and equal citizens. This 'acceptability requirement' claims that laws and policies lack justification to the extent that citizens can reasonably reject the moral ideals and principles that guide it (Clayton and Stevens 2018). If we have reasons to arrange our institutions in ways that preserve or maintain independence, then when the state appeals, in justification of a law or policy, to the worth of any particular comprehensive end, then its reasons are likely to be rejected by those citizens who do not share that conception of the good. As Hildebrandt argues, this does not result in a view that eschews all constraints on freedom, but only *unreasonable* constraints (*The End(s)*,

80). Reasonable constraints are those that are acceptable to reasonable citizens, given the myriad of convictions about comprehensive ends that are an inevitable outcome of the exercise of practical reason under free, democratic institutions. In other words, the justification of the state's powers to coerce citizens or to prevent certain actions must proceed in terms that do not deny the assumptions, ideals or conclusions of the diversity of doctrines held by reasonable citizens, that is, citizens who respect the rights and interests of others.

If the state were to mandate the use of algorithms to interfere in society in order to promote the well-being of its citizens behind their backs, then it would be at odds with the acceptability requirement. It would be at odds with it because it would be seeking to promote ways of living or conceptions of what constitutes human flourishing by cultivating certain comprehensive beliefs and shaping the choices of individuals in accordance with those ends. Such conceptions would be controversial and subject to rejection by some reasonable citizens. Consider the following examples of governments using algorithms to manipulate the desires of citizens to improve their well-being or to bring about socially beneficial ends: First, the de-emphasizing of consumerism over eco-friendly lifestyles by making some options (public transport, recycling) more visible, or by altering the physical or psychological environment to make the formation of beliefs and desires contrary to the state-mandated ones less likely. Second, the promotion of certain diets via the mechanisms considered above with the aim of improving health and for reducing environmental impacts. Third, the promotion of a Christian lifestyle and beliefs because it is considered not only true but that a shared set of religious values is socially beneficial for achieving peace and stability.

If the above seem far-fetched, then we need only recall how extremely simple adjustments to both our external environments and our psychological mechanisms can have significant impact on our beliefs, desires and behaviour. For example, bitter tastes can trigger moral disgust and sweet tastes can trigger more favourable moral judgements (Eskine et al. 2011). Physical touch can trigger higher levels of trust and monetary sacrifice between strangers (Morhenn et al. 2008). Priming individuals with favourable images and stories of individuals from different cultural backgrounds mitigates discriminatory tendencies such as anti-immigrant prejudices (Motyl et al. 2011). Dopamine levels and the number of friends an individual has are, in combination, correlated to political views (Settle et al. 2010). The use of emotive words can lead to the same moral statements being judged differently (Van Berkum et al. 2009). Poorly lit environments lead to increases in cheating and self-interested behaviour (Zhong et al. 2010a). Physical cleanliness leads to more severe moral judgements immediately after the process of cleaning (Zhong et al. 2010b). All of these are easily manipulated by smart technology. Yet, in taking any of these actions, the state seemingly endorses views that, though they might be conducive to either individual well-being or socially beneficial ends, rely on controversial claims, such as the causes and relative weighting of reasons for climate change and the processes necessary for combating it, the importance of animal welfare and the moral necessity of vegetarianism, or the plausibility of a religious doctrine and the appropriateness of its values for social cohesion.

CULTIVATING A SENSE OF JUSTICE

The acceptability requirement is a stringent test for laws and policies to pass, and it rules out many possible uses of technology, such as policies aimed at promoting the well-being of citizens. It does not, however, rule out all forms of moral enhancement. I argue in this section that the use of such technology to cultivate a sense of justice in citizens is morally permissible.

A sense of justice is the capacity to understand, apply and act from a public conception of justice. It supports just political and legal institutions and underpins the proper treatment of others in accordance with what kinds of behaviour they are owed by us. A sense of justice is necessary if we are to lead independent lives. Without the appropriate limits on our behaviour that a sense of justice brings, the pursuit of our own ends would undermine the independence of others. A sense of justice does not set the whole content of what is owed to others, it only sets limits on what is permissible in terms of actions that would make it more difficult for others to realize their own interests.

To see this, we can note that the acceptability requirement does not, and cannot, apply to all moral rules. For example, where there are rules or laws prohibiting the deliberate harming of others, it is irrelevant whether an individual to whom they apply endorses them or not. That is, there are morally enforceable duties – to do or refrain from doing certain things – that are not subject to reasonable agreement. Whilst it may be valuable for individuals to endorse such rules, their non-acceptance does not provide grounds for thinking those rules lack validity, as all the rules do is ensure that the individual does what she is morally required to do. Only in those cases where an individual is not under an enforceable moral duty not to act in a certain way or another is that individual's freedom violated if she is subject to laws she reasonably rejects.

Belief formation plays a vital role in helping citizens to develop an effective sense of justice and a conception of citizenship. A form of education that cultivates such attitudes is not ruled out by the acceptability requirement. Even those, such as children, who cannot consent are reasonably subject to a state-mandated curriculum that attempts to cultivate such beliefs and attitudes. As Rawls (1996, 199) writes, the role of education will include:

> [A] knowledge of their constitutional and civic rights so that, for example, they know that liberty of conscience exists in their society and apostasy is not a legal crime, all this is to ensure that their continued membership when they come of age is not based simply on ignorance of their basic rights or fear of punishment for offenses that do not exist. Moreover, their education should also prepare them to be fully cooperating members of a society and enable them to be self-supporting; it should also encourage the political virtues so that they want to honor the fair terms of social cooperation in their relations with the rest of society.

Part of this function of education is *directive*: to bring individuals to a set of beliefs about the value of social unity and to instil attitudes about the proper treatment of others. Cultivating this sense of justice is part of the role of education, and it does so, often at a young age, behind the backs of individuals via the use of non-rational mechanisms such as rewards and punishments, issuing prescriptions and modelling the behaviour of others. However, education for these ends has had limited success. Some people fail to cultivate certain beliefs, desires and forms of behaviour to a sufficient degree. Where this is the case, the state's use of technological enhancement to better secure the uptake of these beliefs, attitudes and norms of behaviour may be permissible. The kinds of autonomic computing systems that power Toma might be brought to bear on such matters. Using the same range of options, algorithms might be employed to combat latent discriminatory tendencies, on grounds such as race, gender, sexuality or age, and to pre-empt desires to deliberately harm others or conduct gratuitous violence. By filtering information such that the user is less likely to encounter, say, extreme racist or homophobic literature, images or video, or by managing meals, diet and surrounding temperatures, noises and sleep patterns, some influence can be exercised over the resulting attitudes.

TWO OBJECTIONS

The above argument raises two immediate criticisms, the exploration of which allows for the view defended to be fleshed out in more detail, although the observations will be necessarily brief.

The first objects that the asymmetric treatment conceptions of the good and a sense of justice is not sustainable on principled grounds. If the state may not impose, or appeal to, particular comprehensive ends in its justification of its policies, because these ends are subject to reasonable disagreement, the criticism runs, then similar disagreement exists with regards to what justice requires. After all, individuals do not simply disagree about what makes their lives go well, they disagree about almost every value, including freedom, equality and justice itself. Political debate about matters of justice, such as taxation, healthcare and social security, seem as intractable and deeply motivated as debates about abortion, fox hunting or prayer in schools. This suggests there are no shared reasons or uncontroversial views that would form the foundation for state policies about what justice requires. When the state, say, enacts policies to reduce economic inequality, some citizens will be subject to laws and constraints they think lack validity in just the same manner as if the state had implemented a Christian view of morality on atheistic citizens.

This presents a dilemma. Either we admit that reasonable disagreement applies to matters of justice and retract a partisan commitment to cultivating a sense of justice amongst citizens; or, we deny that questions of justice are subject to reasonable disagreement, and extend this to matters of the good. Either horn of the dilemma would undo the view defended above. Grasping the first horn would make the use of algorithms to supplement moral learning impermissible. Grasping the second would commit us to a perfectionist account of political morality that I have been at pains to avoid because it would permit (all else equal) the use of algorithmic enhancement to advance particular state-mandated versions of human flourishing.

The response to this objection is that it ignores the fact that the acceptability requirement appeals only to *reasonable* views, not to views *tout court*. A reasonable view, on Rawls's conception, is marked out by its being willing to propose and abide by fair terms of social cooperation, and to view citizens as free and equal. A reasonable conception of justice is, in turn, marked out by several criteria, including the provision and protection of a familiar set of rights and liberties, certain opportunities, a specific division of wealth and income, universal healthcare, and the state being employer of last resort. These goods are necessary in order for individuals to pursue their self-chosen ends and to cultivate and act from a sense of justice. This means that some views – such as Nozick's (1974) libertarian view – would be excluded as unreasonable because they deny certain all-purpose resources as necessarily accompanying liberties in order that individuals can make full use of those liberties. Nozick's view claims, instead, that the unfettered market is the appropriate mechanism for setting the baseline distribution of such resources.

The response to the asymmetry objection, then, is not to deny the existence of disagreement about justice, but to point to the fact that much actual disagreement is unreasonable, and thereby irrelevant to the permissibility of the state deploying its coercive power. Reasonable disagreement will still occur over justice – for example, Rawls's own conception, 'justice as fairness', is but one reasonable conception amongst a range of reasonable conception, but the scope of the disagreement will be narrower. Consequently, there would still be some latitude for argument and debate over what the content of a sense of justice could be promoted through algorithmic enhancement.

The second objection is that in seeking to bring about beliefs and desires conducive to a sense of justice or social unity, the state undermines its own legitimacy. It does so, this objection claims, because the sense in which an individual can be said to freely consent to the authority of the state is weakened when the state itself shapes the political motivations of its citizens. If beliefs and desires are shaped in this way, then we cannot, as we have seen, be certain that they are genuine, rather than adaptive. It would be unsurprising if citizens whose political motivations are shaped by the state come to endorse the view of justice on which the state is based. This is a criticism brought against education for a sense of justice in general by Brighouse (1998). To ward against this Brighouse claims that such endorsement must: 1) be based on political arrangements which citizens would consent to if those citizens were reasonable, possessed sufficient information and capable of reasoning in a manner. However, Brighouse worries that this hypothetical consent is too easily attained, so he adds: 2) there must be sufficient *actual* consent, and this too must be free, informed and rational (Brighouse 1998, 723).

In response I offer two brief observations. First, actual consent is too high a bar. Brighouse claims that actual consent is the 'usual' criterion for a theory of political morality to meet. But, this is not the case if he means that the most plausible accounts do, or must, include this requirement. The views of Rawls, Raz and Dworkin (to name some of the most prominent) do not consider consent to be a requirement of a view's legitimacy. To require this would be to impose a threshold that no view could meet. There are always those – nihilists, free-riders, the infirm and the bloody-minded – who would withhold consent. Rawls, for example, relies upon a 'natural duty of justice' to generate legitimacy (Rawls 1971, 114–17). Dworkin adopts an account of associative duties to ground consent (1986). And, Raz employs a mechanism to generate an obligation to obey the law based on the idea that consent exists where compliance with a given law thereby enables a person to better act upon her reasons for action than not complying with it (1988).

Second, the claim that hypothetical consent is too easily obtained is also open to challenge. A plausible view of political morality rests on stringent ideals of justice and democracy. These will place significant demands on political principles and institutions, not ones that are weak and easy to meet (Clayton 2006, 134). Rawls's natural duty of justice is a case in point. The duty to bring about, support and comply with just institutions and laws is a significant requirement that places considerable demands on citizens, including the duty to obey laws because they are laws brought about by just institutions. That such features must be present for the state to be legitimate imposes a high threshold on what would count as hypothetical consent.

Because of this high threshold we can see why many of the problems in advancing justice are collective action problems that require the coordination of all citizens and the assurance that the benefits and burdens of this cooperation are distributed fairly. The natural duty of justice generates an obligation to obey the law when this better enables us to conform with the requirements of justice than if we each, individually, acted according to our own judgements about how to realize justice. Because of this, cultivating a sense of justice supportive of just institutions is crucial. Moreover, this must be true for a sufficient number of citizens. If the number of citizens who possess a sense of justice is too small, then it becomes counter-productive: those who act from a sense of justice would be taken advantage of by those who would free-ride. Whilst we should prefer methods, such as formal education, where individuals come to adopt a sense of justice based on an understanding of the reasons, if a sufficient number of citizens adopting a sense of justice cannot be achieved in this way, then some supplementary options such as algorithmic enhancement are, at least in principle, permissible.

CONCLUSION

Despite familiar worries, algorithms offer significant opportunities for enhancing human well-being. They can provide ways of improving decision-making, selecting and advancing valuable goals. They offer ways of enabling governments to better advance the well-being of their citizens by providing alternatives to legal constraints and incentives. In this contribution I have argued that, despite such purported benefits, there are principled reasons for governments to refrain from employing technology to these ends. Governments, I have argued, cannot promote comprehensive goals or ends without undermining their own legitimacy. Instead, laws and policies must be acceptable to citizens who will, necessarily, disagree about the value or importance of these comprehensive ends. I have also argued, however, that this does not apply to the promotion of a sense of justice. In order to maintain just and stable political institutions it is necessary that a sufficient number of citizens come to adopt and abide by the appropriate attitudes and forms of behaviour. Where traditional methods of belief formation, such as educational institutions and informal methods of socialization, fall short, then algorithmic enhancement can permissibly pick up some of the slack.

NOTES

1. For discussions on the subject-matter of this essay I thank Matthew Clayton, Carlos Lopez-Benitez, Kieron O'Hara, Rebecca Orton and Patrick Tomlin. For their most helpful comments on an earlier draft I thank Kieron O'Hara and, in particular, an anonymous reviewer.
2. I thank an anonymous reviewer for suggesting the following example.

REFERENCES

Baccarini, E. 2014. 'Public Reason and Moral Bioenhancement'. *Ethics and Politics* Vol XVI, 2, 1027–41

Brighouse, H. 1998. 'Civic Education and Liberal Legitimacy'. *Ethics* 108, 719–45

Clayton, M. 2006. *Justice and Legitimacy in Upbringing*. Oxford: Oxford University Press

Clayton, M. and A. Moles. 2018. 'Neurointerventions, Morality and Children' in D. Birks and T. Douglas (eds.), *Treatment for Crime: Philosophical Essays on Neurointerventions in Criminal Justice*. Oxford: Oxford University Press, 235–51

Clayton, M. and D. Stevens. 2018. 'What's the Point of Religious Education?' *Theory and Research in Education* 16, 65–81

Elster, J. 1979. *Ulysses and the Sirens: Studies in Rationality and Irrationality*. Cambridge: Cambridge University Press

Elster, J. 1983. *Sour Grapes*. Cambridge: Cambridge University Press

Eskine, K., N. Kacinik and J. Prinz. 2011. 'A Bad Taste in the Mouth: Gustatory Disgust Influences Moral Judgment'. *Psychological Science* 22 (3), 295–9

Haidt, J. 2012. *The Righteous Mind: Why Good People are Divided by Politics and Religion*. London: Penguin

Hausman, D. and B. Welch. 2010. 'Debate: To Nudge or Not to Nudge?' *The Journal of Political Philosophy* 18 (1), 123–36

Hildebrandt, M. 2013. 'Slaves to Big Data. Or Are We?' *IDP. REVISTA DE INTERNET, DERECHO Y POLÍTICA* 17, 7–44. Available at: <www.raco.cat/index.php/IDP/article/viewFile/303366/393038>

Hildebrandt, M. 2015. *Smart Technologies and the End(s) of Law: Novel Entanglements of Law and Technology*. Cheltenham: Edward Elgar Publishing
Hildebrandt, M. 2016. 'The New Imbroglio: Living with Machine Algorithms' in L. Janssens (ed.), *The Art of Ethics in the Information Society*. Amsterdam: Amsterdam University Press, 55–60
Hildebrandt, M. and B.-J. Koops. 2010. 'The Challenges of Ambient Law and Legal Protection in the Profiling Era'. *The Modern Law Review* 73 (3), 428–60
Kahneman, D. 2011. *Thinking, Fast and Slow*. London: Penguin
Mittelstadt, B., P. Allo, M. Taddeo, S. Wachter and L. Floridi. 2016. 'The Ethics of Algorithms: Mapping the Debate'. *Big Data and Society* July-September, 1–21
Morhenn, V., J. Park, E. Piper and P. Zak. 2008. 'Monetary Sacrifice Among Strangers is Mediated by Endogenous Oxytocin Release after Physical Contact'. *Evolution and Human Behavior* 29, 375–83
Motyl, M., J. Hart, T. Pyszcynski, D. Weise, M. Maxfield and A. Siedel. 2011. 'Subtle Priming of Shared Human Experiences Eliminates Threat-Induced Negativity Towards Arabs, Immigrants, and Peace-Making'. *Journal of Experimental Psychology* 47, 1179–84
Nozick, R. 1974. *Anarchy, State and Utopia*. New York, NY: Basic Books
Pasquale, F. 2015. *The Black Box Society: The Secret Algorithms that Control Money and Information*. London: Harvard University Press
Persson, I. and J. Savulescu. 2012. *Unfit for the Future: The Need for Moral Enhancement*. Oxford: Oxford University Press
Quong, J. 2011. *Liberalism Without Perfection*. Oxford: Oxford University Press
Rawls, J. 1971. *A Theory of Justice*. Oxford: Oxford University Press
Rawls, J. 1996. *Political Liberalism*. New York, NY: Columbia University Press
Rawls, J. 2001. *Justice as Fairness: A Restatement*. Cambridge, MA: Harvard University Press
Raz, J. 1986. *The Morality of Freedom*. Oxford: Clarendon Press
Rosa, H. 2013. *Social Acceleration: A New Theory of Modernity*. New York, NY: Columbia University Press
Rousseau, Jean-Jacques. 1997. *Rousseau: 'The Social Contract' and Other Later Political Writings*. Unknown edition. Cambridge; New York, NY: Cambridge University Press
Savulescu, J. and H. Maslen. 2015. 'Moral Enhancement and Artificial Intelligence: Moral AI?' In J. Romportl, E. Zackova and J. Kelemen (eds), *Beyond Artificial Intelligence: Topics in Intelligent Engineering and Informatics*, vol. 9. Springer, Cham, 79–95
Scanlon, T. 1998. *What We Owe to Each Other*. Cambridge, MA: Belknap Press
Settle, J., C. Dawes, N. Christakis and J. Fowler. 2010. 'Friendships Moderate an Association between a Dopamine Gene Variant and Political Ideology'. *The Journal of Politics* 72 (4), 1189–98
Sparrow, R. 2014. 'Better Living Through Chemistry? A Reply to Savulescu and Persson on "Moral Enhancement"'. *Journal of Applied Philosophy* 31, 1
Sunstein, C. 2014. *Why Nudge? The Politics of Libertarian Paternalism*. London: Yale University Press
Taylor, C. 1971. 'Interpretation and the Sciences of Man'. *The Review of Metaphysics* 25 (1), 3–51
Taylor, C. 1976. 'Responsibilities for Self' in A. O. Rorty (ed.), *The Identities of Persons*. Berkeley, CA: University of California Press, 281–99

Van Berkum, J., B. Holleman, M. Mieuwland, M. Otten and J. Murre. 2009. 'Right or Wrong? The Brain's Fast Response to Morally Objectionable Statements'. *Psychological Science* 20 (9), 1092–99

Wilkinson, T. M. 2013. 'Nudging and Manipulation'. *Political Studies* 61, 341–55

Zhong, C.-B., V. Bohns and F. Gino. 2010a. 'Good Lamps Are the Best Police: Darkness Increases Dishonesty and Self-Interested Behavior'. *Psychological Science* 21 (3), 311–14

Zhong, C.-B., B. Strejcek and N. Sivanathan. 2010b. 'A Clean Self Can Render Harsh Moral Judgment'. *Journal of Experimental Social Psychology* 46, 859–62

10. The conservative reaction to data-driven agency

Kieron O'Hara and Mark Garnett

INTRODUCTION

In this chapter we consider the conservative response to the world of data-driven agency (*The End(s)*, 22–3) and the 'onli*f*e world' (*The End(s)*, 1–15). Even on the most simplistic understanding of conservatism – that is, a generalized opposition to change – it is apparent that conservatives will be deeply concerned about these technological developments. However, the task of understanding conservatives' responses has a number of complications.

In particular, the meaning of conservatism itself has been vigorously contested (O'Hara 2011, Garnett 2017), which makes the task somewhat harder. The word is increasingly abused, particularly but not only in journalistic discourse, and particularly but not only in the United States, where it has been applied to anyone on the right of politics, thereby yoking libertarians such as Rand Paul, those devoted to big government such as Ronald Reagan and George W. Bush, Christian traditionalists such as Phyllis Schlafly, and foreign policy hawks such as John Bolton, together with people whose principles are somewhat indeterminate, such as the Forty-Fifth President of the United States. The term is also abused in political psychology, where many experiments which purport to demonstrate psychological differences across the political spectrum (again, typically performed in the US) are based on self-identification as 'conservative' or 'liberal' (e.g. van der Toorn et al. 2017).

Conservatism itself is a sceptical philosophy, towards both the claims of science and social science (Oakeshott 1991), and the perfectibility of human nature (Quinton 1978). The conservative argues that rationalist social engineers systematically undervalue functioning institutions and traditions in society, while overvaluing their own abilities to reshape society and people to their preferred blueprint (Burke 1968); furthermore, they lack the legitimacy to impose their blueprint upon society (Oakeshott 1975). Consequently, the aim of conservatism is not to prevent or block change, but rather to place the burden of proof on the innovator, and to ensure that social change is (a) incremental, (b) reversible where possible and (c) rigorously evaluated (O'Hara 2011).

The conservative tradition therefore centred around the defence of long-established institutions, opposing the efforts of rationalists to 'modernize' them. Some of this tradition atrophied into a backward-looking reactionary nostalgia (as, for instance, in the thinking of Joseph de Maistre or Evelyn Waugh), but many others maintained a sprightly rearguard action against universal rationalist ideas, such as twentieth century communism.

In the present chapter, we look at ways in which conservative thinkers have approached questions of technological and social change, focusing on 'traditional conservatism' – exemplified here by Edmund Burke (1730–97) – and 'modern conservatism', of which Michael Oakeshott (1901–90) is recognized as a leading exponent. In between we also include the ideas of Alexis de Tocqueville (1805–59), whose position was informed by his epic study of the egalitarian assumptions of the new American democracy. All three of these figures exemplify a brand of conservatism, yet all have commitments to a liberal society as well.

Data-driven agency, particularly as manifested in the major companies of the surveillance economy, is often criticized on three grounds: the disproportionate amount of power that such companies wield because of the scope of their data collection; the externalities imposed on network members, such as privacy breaches and issues with mental health and addiction; and the externalities imposed on wider society, such as fake news and trolling. These criticisms, all of which are important, have emerged because the problems are usually viewed through the lens of liberalism: how do different claims to freedom stack up against each other? How do they resolve my privacy (freedom from intrusion) and your freedom of speech? Are we able to say that Facebook users have freely 'chosen' membership when they would experience non-membership as a serious handicap in their social and working lives? Should we have the freedom to spread fake news? Or to spread fake news using bots? When are algorithms discriminatory?

In this chapter, we consider data-driven agency through a different lens, that of modernity in its digital manifestation (O'Hara 2018a). To that end, we can begin to gather conservative resources, both critiques and defences of modernity. To anticipate the outcome, the rise of data-driven agency was not predicted by conservatives, who generally expect challenging innovations to come from government, not the private sector. Yet conservatism can give us a new perspective on the phenomenon by highlighting the tensions between innovations and settled patterns of practice, and the need to respect the institutional and conceptual superstructure upon which innovations are built (what Nissenbaum [2010] calls contextual integrity). O'Hara (2018b) has looked at the specific issue of privacy through this lens, as one aspect of the debate about data-driven agency. At the moment, though, conservative philosophy provides the means for diagnosing problems, without clear policy guidance for addressing them.

BURKE: THE MYSTICAL STATE

Though Burke never called himself a conservative, his writings were highly influential among those members of the British Tory Party who adopted the name 'Conservative' in the 1830s (Jones 2017), and made a considerable impact on continental European thinkers. Burke's main message, given its most eloquent expression in his *Reflections on the Revolution in France* (Burke 1968, first published 1790), was that gradual reform was preferable to radical change. From this viewpoint he predicted that, unless they were checked, the French Revolution, and more widely the drive to re-shape politics, morals and society in accordance with the presumed dictates of abstract reason would prove a potent threat to European civilization.

For the present purpose, Burke's predictions and prescriptions are less important than his underlying assumptions. He argued that human behaviour was at best unpredictable, since humans are creatures of emotion more than reason. Civilized existence thus depends on recognized chains of authority, culminating in the state to which Burke referred in quasi-mystical terms. On Burke's premises, the state and more widely the rule of law play a crucial role in saving individuals from the consequences of their own unruly instincts. Those who apply abstract principles to question the state's authority may have good intentions, but if their ideas take hold they will trigger a catastrophic collapse of authority. All serious constraints on behaviour will be removed, creating the ideal conditions for demagogues and dictators who will first flatter the people, then enslave them (Burke 1968, 183–4).

Burke did not consider the state infallible. Principles of governance needed to be attended to, and Burke had supported the American Revolution in 1776, because he considered the unrepresented American population was being used by the British colonial powers unfairly as a cash cow, in breach of Parliament's responsibilities. Burke also spent many years unsuccessfully attempting to prosecute Britain's first *de facto* Governor-General of India, Warren Hastings, for various crimes committed on his watch, arguing that the historic and natural rights of Indians had been neglected by the imperial authorities in the 1770s and 1780s. The difference between these cases, and that of the revolutionary fervour of the 1790s, was that in the later period it was the revolutionaries who were threatening social order, rather than the state abusing its power by neglecting natural justice and its own traditions of orderly government, as it had in America and India.

The government crackdown on 'seditious' writings in the 1790s, targeting publishers as well as incendiary authors like Thomas Paine, was warmly supported by Burke and his parliamentary allies (Bourke 2015, 857–62). On this basis, it would be reasonable to suppose that Burke would have approved government surveillance of the Internet, and would have urged state agents to maintain close and constant vigilance, even in peaceful times. In the troubled 1790s, the British government relied heavily on a network of spies and informers, and, at least in that context, Burke was on the side of authoritarian order against the principle of free speech. A Burkean today would certainly understand the need for surveillance in the face of the threat from fundamentalist Islamist terror (which many commentators, including conservative ones, already argue is a by-product of modernity and technological change – Scruton 2002, Gray 2003, Roy 2004). Whether such a modern-day Burkean would condone mass untargeted surveillance of the kind exposed by Edward Snowden, is more of a moot point.

Despite his prescient views on the likely course of the French Revolution, Burke was certainly not an infallible prophet of social developments. In his view, the 'unmerited' hierarchy of his day still rested on personal contact between individuals in what could be described as an 'organic' society; it might not have been a system that one would have designed *ab initio*, but as it had grown up slowly over centuries, its quirks and irrationalities were part of the assumed and unquestioned background of civic life. To remove them without warning, however 'rational' the new order might appear on paper, would suddenly undermine the stock of certainties and meanings that the vast majority of people relied upon to make sense of their position in the world, and to calibrate their own behaviour as cooperative and social beings (Burke 1968, 185).

The industrial revolution transformed this picture. By 1845, despite the efforts of enlightened industrialists like Robert Owen, the alienation caused by the hollowing out of previous relationships between rich and poor had become so glaring that a conservative novelist (and future British Prime Minister), Benjamin Disraeli, could depict them as inhabitants of 'two nations'. Meanwhile, the spread of democracy post-1832 entailed a radical change in the nature of the state. Instead of being a guardian which saved the public from the consequences of its own unfettered instincts, it would henceforth be a point of contestation between rival groups of demagogues who flattered 'the people' into thinking that their untutored emotions deserved the same respect as the mature judgements of qualified observers (like Burke himself).

For anyone trying to apply Burke's ideas to twenty-first century Britain, these considerations give rise to mixed feelings about the appropriate role of the state in regulating the new forms of media. On the one hand, the need for an authority which could exercise some kind of oversight seemed more urgent than ever. In his 'Discourse on the Art of Political Lying' (1713), Jonathan Swift wrote that 'falsehood flies, and truth comes limping after; so that when men come to be undeceived, it is too late, the jest is over'. This quotation brings the contrast between liberal and conservative views on the value of 'pluralism' into sharp focus; John Stuart Mill and his admirers would argue that limping truth always wins in the end, as with Aesop's hare and tortoise. But the Internet has jet-propelled the hare of falsehood, without lending noticeable assistance to the tortoise of truth. Furthermore, developments in the technology of death mean that the effects of falsehood can be far more deadly than in Swift's day. The persecution of the Muslim Rohingya people of Myanmar in 2016–18, before the army stepped in to complete the job, was coordinated to a large extent on Facebook, while academically, research shows that falsehoods travel faster in some online conditions; on Twitter, for example, falsehoods are retweeted by more people, and faster (Vosoughi et al. 2018).

Faced with the threat of subversion in the 1790s, Burke eulogized the state as the ultimate bulwark against socio-political disorder. But in the age of the Internet, following so many radical changes which would have been disagreeable to Burke, it is doubtful whether the state can any longer be trusted with the kind of supervisory powers which he had recommended at the time of the French Revolution. The idea that a hollowed-out or disintermediated state, capable of generating fear but not respect, should increase its scope for intrusion at this point could be supported by admirers of Thomas Hobbes, but not by Burkeans. Furthermore, supervisory powers of this kind have not typically been of the sort that the state has wished to take on. 'Solutions' to the 'fake news' controversy tend to come in one of two guises: either a technical solution, with automated detection of activity associated with fakery such as retweeting botnets, or alternatively an abdication of responsibility, in which the problem is handed over to those private sector oligarchs (Facebook, Google, etc.) deemed to have sufficient market clout to make a difference. Indeed, one of the reasons why fake news and other forms of post-truth behaviour have made such significant inroads into democratic political culture is that the oligarchs are protected from the consequences of publishing such statements; they are treated legally not as publishers, but rather as conduits of information, with little or no responsibility for what goes out under their aegis. By sharp contrast, in Burke's time the publishers of radical tracts were only too easy to identify and to prosecute. Joseph Johnson, who published the first part of Paine's radical *Rights of Man*, refused to issue the second part for fear of prosecution (Keane 1995, 304–5).

Since Burke's ideas conflict sharply with so many of the received wisdoms of the democratic age, it is somewhat ironic that controversy over government's regulatory role – the question of whether or not it should enjoy a 'snooper's charter' – coincided with growing interest in Burke's ideas in the higher ranks of Britain's Conservative Party (e.g. Norman 2013). The attempt to revive Burke was usually associated with his invocation of 'little platoons' – groups which, according to some Conservative politicians, could be equated with intermediate institutions which should be cherished and defended against both heavy-handed state interference and excessive individualism. In this debate, Burke could (with some ingenuity) be re-painted as a great thinker whose, in the last resort, would always have thrown his weight into the libertarian scale. However, his exaltation of the little platoons – beginning with the family, and providing 'the first link in the series by which we proceed towards a love to our country, and to mankind' – took for granted the inescapability of a face-to-face society (Burke 1968, 135). These were precisely the organic relationships which have been eroded since the industrial revolution, and whose fragmentary remains are most at risk in the age of the Internet, which offers irresistible opportunities for individualists to disintermediate everyday interactions, such as visiting a bank or buying groceries from a real shop staffed by (increasingly harassed) employees.

Burkeans might be inclined to take refuge in their hero's pronouncement that 'The individual is foolish... but the species is wise, and when time is given to it, as a species it always acts right' (Burke 1999). On this view, misuse of the Internet would gradually subside, as people recognized which of its attractions were spurious, and inauthentic. However, in this speech, he was taking it for granted that human relationships would still be conducted on the 'organic' basis with which he was familiar. In an earlier passage, he had contrasted 'the species' with an aggregate of unconnected individuals. Calling the latter 'the multitude', he wrote that this body 'for the moment is foolish, when they act without deliberation'. The Internet is the best medium so far devised for inspiring a 'multitude' – an assemblage of individuals lacking meaningful connections or respect for qualified opinion – to 'act without deliberation', with consequences which can be far more than momentary when a state has surrendered its law-making authority, to produce what Helen Margetts et al. (2016)

describe as 'chaotic pluralism'. The rise of populist political actors, disdainful of representative politics, might be presented by the Burkean as the likely consequence of the undermining of the elitist principles of the liberal architects of our modern democratic infrastructure such as Madison and Hamilton, not only by social change (Bimber 2003, O'Hara in press), but also by the rejection and by-passing of the idea of top-down political expertise and authority (McGinnis 2013), exacerbated by the tendency of some Western academics and politicians to argue that the system that nurtured them and their contrarian talents is a cesspool of oppression. These changes have been welcomed by political entrepreneurs from Donald Trump downwards (cf. e.g. Carswell 2012). It has also been argued that centres of power haven't really changed that much during the Internet century (Hindman 2009); but from the Burkean perspective while the state might have seen an immense accretion of formal power since 1945, in itself it has become far less deserving of respect, and in any event the increasingly-varied forces ranged against it have greatly increased in potency.

TOCQUEVILLE: THE DISINTERMEDIATED COMMUNITY

The importance of organic connections between individuals, or what social scientists call 'strong ties', has long been a theme in conservative thinking. Such connections tend to be given rather than chosen, serve a number of purposes rather than being transactional, semi-permanent rather than temporarily formed around a mutual advantage or exchange, involve taking on responsibilities to the other rather than based on reciprocity, and often bring with them assumptions of asymmetric authority or status rather than equality (Scruton 2006). Such relationships are likely to come in useful at various times, but endure just as strongly through the times when they are not. They need no justification; we often construct our identities in terms of our strong ties. Think of the relationships between a parent and a child, a clergyman and his flock, a community leader and community members, two friends, two neighbours, comrades in a regiment, a doctor and her patients, or even two natives of the same country or district. Far from oppressing us with the inequalities and possibly unearned authority that they distribute, these organic connections protect us, in conservative thought, from the all-powerful states and corporations whose operations tend to reduce us to indistinguishable ciphers. Our strong ties make us individuals, whereas our weak ties merely reflect our immediate preferences and context.

These strong organic interpersonal connections contrast with the weak ties, with no substantial significance, transactional connections based on a temporarily-constituted mutual advantage, which are supported very well by the Internet, which can divest a relationship of all but the material essentials required to achieve that advantage, leaving neither intimacy nor emotional intensity. Compare the relationship that a villager used to have with the village shopkeeper, where the nature of the villager's wants would be learned and catered for by the shopkeeper possibly over a period of decades, while the shopkeeper would also act as a conduit for news and discussion (and gossip), with the immediate gratification of an eBay transaction, which requires nothing more than a mail drop and a PayPal account number. It has been argued, of course, that weak ties are more conducive to information flow and therefore innovation than strong ties (Granovetter 1973), because they are the sources of more novel information; those with whom we have strong ties tend to share much of our social network, and so tend not to surprise us (Baer 2010). For the conservative, this is an advantage, not a disadvantage, and indeed some of the trust relationships important in knowledge transfer are more commonly found in relationships with strong ties (Levin and Cross 2004).

It is also worth pointing out that strong ties can ameliorate conflict, in that one is generally accountable for aggressive action in a context where one has strong ties to others. Weak ties support such modern-day phenomena as trolling and shaming. There are few social norms to discourage us to keep our noses out of someone else's business, and indeed an ideological parody of democracy supports everyone's right to comment on everything – hence the Twitterstorms when someone has said something in bad taste or that would be better kept private (Goldman 2015, Ronson 2015, Laidlaw 2017, Kasra 2017). The act of retweeting a complaint is the work of a second, takes no risk and requires no commitment.

What would a conservative make of a world of weak ties? As it happens, we have an example of a philosopher who considered this question: Tocqueville. Reacting against Rousseau's concept of a society in which all relationships are justifiable, egalitarian and designed, Tocqueville produced a vision of what the world would be like without the undesigned, strong ties which provide so much of the scaffolding for our moral lives. What is extraordinary is how Tocqueville's warnings conjure up the decontextualized individual of the onli*f*e world, with smartphone, personal agent and portable infotainment, whisked from home to office to airport by driverless car, geographically close to but spiritually remote from his fellows. This passage (Tocqueville 2003, vol.2, part 4, chapter 6, 805) from 1840 describes the new kinds of soft despotism we might expect in the new democracies:

I wish to imagine under what new features despotism might appear in the world: I see an innumerable crowd of men, all alike and equal, turned in upon themselves in a restless search for those petty, vulgar pleasures with which they fill their souls. Each of them, living apart, is almost unaware of the destiny of all the rest. His children and personal friends are for him the whole of the human race; as for the remainder of his fellow citizens, he stands alongside them but does not see them; he touches them without feeling them; he exists only in himself and for himself; if he still retains his family circle, at any rate he may be said to have lost his country.

This vision prefigures Hildebrandt's own argument that data-driven agency brings a new type of perception in which 'even our immediate surroundings are being mediated, especially when engaging with mobile applications that provide us with "augmented reality"' (*The End(s)*, 50). Tocqueville was suspicious of democracy. Hildebrandt embraces it, as do most modern conservative thinkers, but recognizes the importance of resisting the slide into the condition Tocqueville describes. Can she square the circle? There will certainly be costs and benefits to any kind of shift away from the current model of surveillance capitalism (Zuboff 2019), but Hildebrandt is clear that only 'after determining what normativity we need to survive as reasonably free and reasonably constrained individual persons, we can decide how to distribute the costs as well as the benefits' (*The End(s)*, 15).

The stakes are certainly high. In a continuation of the above passage, Tocqueville (2003, 805–6) describes the opportunity for a peculiar type of power that emerges in the name of an egalitarian 'justice':

Above these men stands an immense and protective power which alone is responsible for looking after their enjoyments and watching over their destiny. It is absolute, meticulous, ordered, provident, and kindly disposed. It would be like a fatherly authority, if, fatherlike, its aim were to prepare men for manhood, but it seeks only to keep them in perpetual childhood; it prefers its citizens to enjoy themselves provided they have only enjoyment in mind. It works readily for their happiness but it wishes to be the only provider and judge of it. It provides their security, anticipates and guarantees their needs, supplies their pleasures, directs their principal concerns, manages their industry, regulates their estates, divides their inheritances. Why can it not remove from them entirely the bother of thinking and the troubles of life?

Thus, it reduces daily the value and frequency of the exercise of free choice; it restricts the activity of free will within a narrower range and gradually removes autonomy itself from each citizen. Equality has prepared men for all this, inclining them to tolerate all these things and often even to see them as a blessing.

Whereas Burke thought the state could protect us from the multitude, Tocqueville switches the thought round to worry about the state neutering the multitude (which includes all of us). But he was still thinking in terms of the state as major actor; he never anticipated that this amount of power could devolve to a private actor (cf. *The End(s)*, 75). There is no reason that it shouldn't, as the power Tocqueville envisages is not coercive in the traditional sense. Surveillance capitalism requires only a powerful enough body to spread itself across most aspects of the lives of most people – it could be a private company, but no-one anticipated Google until Google appeared. As Tocqueville predicted, such powers are not judgemental; Google and Facebook are quite pleased for people to be happy, want them to be, and do not judge the means by which they are made happy (it could be watching opera or porn), as long as they are the agents and arbiters of the happiness.

We are increasingly approaching a reality in which many options in law are closed down or marginalized by technology. Hildebrandt worries about the adequacy of written law to cope in this new world (*The End(s)*, 177). Once more, this need not be the state in operation, but a private service provider working for governments; one well-known example of this is Google's own policing of the right to be forgotten following the Google Spain ruling of 2014 (Bygrave 2015). Tocqueville (2003, 806) anticipates the operation, but not the locus, of power:

> Thus, the ruling power, having taken each citizen one by one into its powerful grasp and having molded him to its own liking, spreads its arms over the whole of society, covering the surface of social life with a network of petty, complicated, detailed, and uniform rules through which even the most original minds and the most energetic of spirits cannot reach the light in order to rise above the crowd. It does not break men's wills but it does soften, bend, and control them; rarely does it force men to act but it constantly opposes what actions they perform; it does not destroy the start of anything but it stands in its way; it does not tyrannize but it inhibits, represses, drains, snuffs out, dulls so much effort that finally it reduces each nation to nothing more than a flock of timid and hardworking animals with the government as shepherd.

Now we hear the cadences of Lessig's *Code* (1999), or Zittrain's *The Future of the Internet* (2008), where architecture intervenes to constrain humanity in pleasant, carefully constructed walled gardens. Technology undercuts law in such private spaces. First, design and coding (even open source code) is not controlled by a democratic (or otherwise) legislator, and we never get to vote on it. Second, whereas we have a right to violate the law without dissociating ourselves from our fellow citizens (think of Gandhi's *satyagraha* or the suffragettes), side-stepping the design of a technological device takes us out of the association that exists on or via that device. Third, it is hard if not impossible to contest the effects of technological architectures, because they are often invisible, certainly extremely complex, and not least because there is nowhere to contest them. In such a world, the rule of law itself – the keystone of the solid Burkean society – is under threat.

OAKESHOTT: DEFENDING PLURALITY

Conservatives resisting the advent of modernity since Burke and Tocqueville may be felt to be wasting their time – that particular horse has bolted, and the pragmatic conservative position should be the defence of modernity against the encroachment of the particular structures of digital modernity (O'Hara 2018a). Like Tocqueville, Michael Oakeshott was a thinker on the borderline between liberalism and conservatism, often claimed as a liberal (Gray 1993). In this section, we explore some of the parallels between Oakeshott's major work *On Human Conduct* (1975) and Hildebrandt's *The End(s)*, and argue that it may be that, in order to gain political traction in a world of digital modernity, the conservative must already have accepted a good deal of the innovation characteristic of the twentieth century, and even the twenty-first. Nevertheless, once this acceptance has taken place, the close connections between Hildebrandt's agonistic view and Oakeshott's conservatism indicate one possible coalition which twenty-first century conservatives might begin to build.

Plurality, Agency and Practice

Oakeshott's starting point was the pluralism of a modern society, where citizens, groups, associations, enterprises, religions and ideologies compete for attention, defending their own practices, gathering resources and persuading others of their merits. A healthy society could easily be quite fractious, and Oakeshott's purpose was to understand how a plurality could sustain and reproduce itself, without imposing consensus, even as society members were in perpetual conflict. Influenced by his own Hegelian idealism (Oakeshott 1933), Oakeshott argued that this cacophony could not be aggregated to produce a God's-eye view (Oakeshott 1975, 12): 'where conduct is the choice and pursuit of substantive conditions of things every achievement is evanescent' (Oakeshott 1975, 84). In practical life so much is going on that it will make little sense from any perspective other than the specific subjective and partial position of individuals.

He distinguished between a collected state of affairs, which is merely a concatenated list of the interactions between individuals or civic groups, and a collective, which involves ordering or 'making sense' of these interactions, which Oakeshott thought to be inherently totalitarian and inimical to pluralism (1975, 86–7). We might add that, in technology-mediated modernity, our perceptions of reality are altering all the time, so that hyperconnectivity is reconfiguring our perceived environment and the set of choices we can make (cf. 1975, 50). The data that these choices create are the digitized collected state of affairs, whereas running algorithms over the data to produce inferences or derive policies is the digital version of the sensemaking collective.

Oakeshott called the ability to act within a collected state of affairs effective *freedom* or *liberty*, founded in the abilities of individuals to negotiate the collected state of affairs, understand its affordances, interpret their own interests within it, and develop coalitions of allies (perhaps via debate and effective advocacy of their own position), in order to adapt their satisfactions to better achieve them (cf. O'Hara in press). Within this picture, practices and norms have two crucial functions: they give individuals a palette of actions and behaviours which facilitate the negotiation of the complexities of plural existence; and they provide a locus for the individual to enact himself as a virtuous and social person, able to play a full part as a trustworthy member of civil associations.

These are important for Hildebrandt too. 'Roles, institutions and cultural patterns [roughly what Oakeshott referred to as practice] are tied up with predictions; they help to predict how other agents will probably behave' (*The End(s)*, 58). She notes the distancing effect of the printed word in the development of practice, and how what Oakeshott called effective freedom depends on 'specific mental skills, such as sound argumentation, sustained sequential reasoning and the willingness to give an account of one's choices by providing reasons' (*The End(s)*, 58). One needs to embrace autonomy, control and accountability in the post-Gutenberg world. She adds that technology that predicts, aggregates and pre-empts our choices and actions will forever change that world; a new set of practices is being subtended so that effective freedom may require a whole new set of skills (*The End(s)*, 59ff.), and will be protected only partially by data protection rights (*The End(s)*, 187).

In the onli*fe* world, Hildebrandt argues that a system that takes one's first order preferences for granted, catering for them before one is aware of them, diminishes one's capacity to reflect on habits and desires, and therefore one's capacity to remake oneself in order to improve as a person (by one's own standards) (*The End(s)*, 92). Data for profiling and pre-emption is much more easily available for the owner of the databases and software than the individual data subject, which is crucial because the data will produce non-obvious knowledge about matters such as creditworthiness, health or employability (*The End(s)*, 101), again creating an asymmetrical position. The actual affordances of technology matter, not those that are perceived, as some of the former may be hidden (*The End(s)*, 170). In such a world legal expertise is displaced by data expertise, which is worrying because, unlike lawyers who are paid to advise clients who are fully aware of their involvement in a legal case, data scientists are generally funded by the data consumers, thereby exacerbating the asymmetry (*The End(s)*, 182). Furthermore, important social protections – such as the socialization of risk via insurance or related industries (*The End(s)*, 194) – may disappear, replaced by individual responsibility calculated from data trails.

Individuality, for Oakeshott, goes beyond agency; it involves embracing the possibilities of agency and taking up opportunities for adventure and exploration (Oakeshott 1975, 237). This condition contrasts with that of what Oakeshott called the '*individual manqué*' (Oakeshott 1975, 275), who longs 'for the shelter of a community', distrusts his own instincts, and recedes into a heteronomous condition where his desires and satisfactions are set out for him by external agencies. The *individual manqué* is a moral failure, and a danger to plurality, resentful of the difference which will follow from ignoring the authorities for and sources of his own desires and beliefs. Hildebrandt is similarly concerned about fallen individuals damaged by pre-emption of actions and patterns of action, 'handy and comfortable' though it may be (*The End(s)*, 51). However, she is more sympathetic towards *individuals manqués* than Oakeshott, and an interpretation of her thesis is that recession into heteronomy is happening covertly via technologies which 'conflate time and space into a synchronized environment that allows for "always on" real-time accessibility' (and cf. Ekbia and Nardi 2017). As in Huxley's *Brave New World*, the *individual manqué* has been suckered into his supine position, rather than meekly surrendering.

Law, Authority and the State

Oakeshott's main purpose in *On Human Conduct* was to describe how individuals can form into groups without losing the plurality inherent in their pursuit of their own satisfactions. To that end, he introduced the key concept of civil association (Oakeshott 1975, 108–84), a self-sufficient, rule-based relationship of equal free agents (Oakeshott 1975, 110). Oakeshott maintained that the state is, at bottom, a civil association (not a machine or a managerial entity), that through history has taken two different forms. The state as *societas* provides security and creates the conditions for the individual to flourish. It holds the ring between different citizens, and attempts to make it possible for plurality, dispute and dispute resolution to occur, via well-understood traditions and practices. The state as *universitas* instead pursues particular enterprises (policies), and subordinates individuality to those policies. Such a state has a cause, a purpose or an aim.

The rules governing the manner of its members' interactions and pursuits make up the law. The civil association is created precisely through recognition of the law as authoritative. For Oakeshott, there is no narrative about law beyond this. Hildebrandt agrees that law should neither be 'sterilized' as an independent construct, nor instrumentalized for economic or political purposes (*The End(s)*, 147). Law, for Oakeshott, does not oblige anyone to do anything specific, but rather creates obligations to act in a manner consistent with the law. In this sense, law acts adverbially (Hildebrandt: 'law does not prescribe or describe; it predicts what legal effect will be attached to what event, action or state of affairs' – *The End(s)*, 157). As Hildebrandt notes, complying with law is also consistent with challenging it in a court of law, and understanding, interpreting, extending and changing operative legal norms (*The End(s)*, 10, 173); the nature of law as printed text encourages interpretation and disagreement (*The End(s)*, 177).

Oakeshott argued that the law laid down by a civil association should understand the state as *societas*, not *universitas*. The law, ideally, will avoid prescriptions about behaviour that cannot easily be enforced because they conflict with norms of civil conduct (Oakeshott 1975, 178). Second, the law should ideally only have substantive effects on behaviour which has the capacity to harm others (Oakeshott 1975, 179). This simulacrum of Mill's harm principle subtends a private sphere for the individual. Third, innovation should be within the capacity of the association to absorb it (Oakeshott 1975, 178).

The modern goal-based state (*universitas*) has a tendency to address tricky, even insoluble, problems, such as 'the problem of the poor', which reconceptualized poverty from an issue of embarrassment for a nation, to the unproductive use of human 'assets' – a reconceptualization that helped bring about the enlightened managerial state (Oakeshott 1975, 303ff., and cf. *The End(s)*, 173). More modern examples might be the wars against crime, drugs and terror, as well of course as highly technologized 'real' warfare itself (Oakeshott 1975, 272–4). In such a world, where the state takes on such responsibilities, the citizen inherits a duty to render herself legible to the state so she can be deployed effectively (Scott 1998). In order to (appear to) control the big issues of poverty, crime etc., the state categorizes us, and makes us take certain actions. Inevitable failure to achieve a partially-specified goal requires remedial action on the part of the state, further extending its powers and assumed responsibilities, and a vicious circle is in operation.

Bulk data gathering, in such contexts, is justified in terms of efficiency, but for Oakeshott this is a *non sequitur*: the state need not be efficient because it is not there to *do* anything efficiently or badly other than provide the conditions for civil society. Hildebrandt does not share Oakeshott's scepticism, but neatly states the dilemma of machine learning (*The End(s)*, 25):

> If the assumptions [of machine learning] restrict the capability of the agent to respond to relevant changes in its environment, it will come up with incorrect, irrelevant or ineffective solutions. . . . However, the problem is that if those who pay for these systems believe in their objectivity, and act upon their predictions, we may not easily learn about the inadequacy.

Hildebrandt weighs in against citizens being addressed, not as members of a civil association defined by law, but 'as entities whose behaviour must change to achieve some greater good', complaining that 'the language has shifted from regulating the *actions* of legal subjects, to regulating the *behaviour* of groups of individuals' (*The End(s)*, 164–5). As O'Hara has argued, if behavioural economics can show that certain correlations occur under laboratory conditions, the temptation for paternalistic policy-makers is to reproduce the laboratory conditions in the world (O'Hara 2015). The response to a prediction (e.g. that someone is likely to be a criminal or terrorist) may inadvertently help to bring the prediction to pass (*The End(s)*, 196–7).

In this context, Oakeshott's description of the therapeutic state (Oakeshott 1975, 308ff.), which emerges when the state as *universitas* adopts the goal of the health of its citizens, and uses its authority to enforce behaviour consistent with its own definition of health, is prescient. The state becomes a 'sanatorium from which no patient may discharge himself by a choice of his own', eerily reminiscent of the 'nudge' programme which has become popular amongst paternalistic *faux*-liberal governments (Halpern 2015). Big data provide a ready source of evidence against which citizens can be pronounced ill in this sense – illness here need only consist in being a sufficiently large number of standard deviations away from 'the norm'.

Law is not, on the Oakeshottian view, a means to an end, however good the end; people should not be treated as rational agents despised by a system which nudges them into doing what they ought to do. Hildebrandt's slogan remains salutary: *my behaviour should not be redressed without first addressing me about it* (*The End(s)*, 185). For many, this is an issue of human dignity, but for the Oakeshottian conservative, it is because no-one has the legitimacy to erect a standard against which my behaviour can be judged, or the competence to redress my behaviour without unintended consequences.

DISCUSSION

As we have moved from pre-modernity to modernity to digital modernity, conservative thinkers have resisted. Sometimes the resistance is mere reactionary nostalgia, but the more constructive thinkers have emphasized the important, often hidden or indeterminate, support that existing institutions and practices provide for innovations. If those innovations threaten the supporting institutions, then they cannot be sustainable (at least in the form they were originally presented), and may risk damaging social resources of independent value (O'Hara 2018a).

As we have seen, much conservative thinking has revolved around the state and its dialectic with the people (or the masses, or the multitude), and indeed the state is an important client of data-driven agency (Halpern 2015); most states have digital strategies and ambitions to grow the digital economy. Burke saw the state as a protection against the unruly mob, while Tocqueville anticipated that it would go too far in atomizing it. Oakeshott wanted a state without purpose other than to sustain and support civil society, and disliked the historical trend toward a state with goals, even a therapeutic state that worked for the good of 'the people' (as the state would inevitably determine what that 'good' would be). As society became more liberal, conservatives, reflecting that change, became less tolerant of the state and more protective of the people it governed.

Yet the digital revolution has been largely a creation of the private sector, and so conservatism may need to revert to a Burkean frame in order to manage the rapid technological change of the twenty-first century. The externalities imposed on society by the tech giants have generally been countered by government, particularly the federal government in the US and the European Commission, which for example have each launched several trustbusting investigations. The EU's General Data Protection Regulation is also becoming highly influential worldwide as a restriction on data processing. The call for offline social norms to be mirrored online (Nissenbaum 2010) would surely demand policing from the state as much as protection from the state.

Furthermore, we have seen how our admittedly small sample of conservatives has become more sensitive to the concerns of the individual over time. Much of Oakeshott's argument in particular rested on an individualistic idea of agency. Oakeshott stressed the contribution made by individual agents, whereas in a modern civil association legitimacy and responsibility are quite often distributed around the system and hard to locate at a particular person or point. Collective interests and governmental purposes are tricky to disentangle from collected interests of individuals and the optimal conditions for civil society (Flathman

2005), and Oakeshott's ideas need to be augmented with a more realistic account of the use of authority and the affordances of the Hobbesian state (Galston 2012), and of the social machines, are formed by individuals on the fly to achieve collective goals at scale (Shadbolt et al. 2019), that may become the twenty-first century's 'little platoons'. An individual's cognition, when augmented with social resources, becomes socialized and less individual as a result.

However, like Tocqueville, Oakeshott never considered in any detail the ways in which private data-collecting social networks could subvert these distinctions. Social networks have no powers to compel, so it is hard to characterize them as a kind of *universitas*. Yet network effects (Farrell and Klemperer 2007) mean that resisting the massive benefits of being part of a giant connected network is extremely hard, especially as many social networks are beginning to provide services for governments, or in education, banking or identity management. No doubt membership of such networks is not strictly speaking coerced, but the pressures to join are immense, and the costs of leaving correspondingly so (Ekbia and Nardi 2017).

The genius of the technologically-enabled social networks with their unprecedented data collection, however, means that they present the Oakeshottian with a dilemma. Either the onli*f*e world as described by Hildebrandt is indeed a genuine plurality (and therefore unobjectionable, despite the power wielded by the tech giants), or the Oakeshottian critique of unfreedom needs to be augmented – on the diagnostic side – by an account of how individuals can be illegitimately constrained by exogenous technological forces, and – on the constructive side – what role the state can legitimately play in defending the 'multitude' against these private sector actors.[1]

NOTE

1. The authors would like to thank Martin Beckstein for rigorous comments on an earlier draft of this chapter.

REFERENCES

Baer, M. 2010. 'The Strength-of-Weak-Ties Perspective on Creativity: A Comprehensive Examination and Extension'. *Journal of Applied Psychology* 95(3), 592–601, <https://doi.org/10.1037/a0018761>

Bimber, B. A. 2003. *Information and American Democracy: Technology in the Evolution of Political Power*. Cambridge: Cambridge University Press

Bourke, R. 2015. *Empire and Revolution: The Political Life of Edmund Burke*, Princeton, NJ: Princeton University Press

Burke, E. 1968. *Reflections on the Revolution in France*. Harmondsworth: Penguin

Burke, E. 1999. 'Speech on the Reform of the Representation of the Commons in Parliament (1782)'. In *Select Works of Edmund Burke Volume 4: Miscellaneous Writings*, Indianapolis, IN: Liberty Fund

Bygrave, L. A. 2015. 'A Right to be Forgotten?' *Communications of the ACM* 58(1), 35–7, <https://doi.org/10.1145/2688491>

Carswell, D. 2012. *The End of Politics: and the Birth of iDemocracy*. London: Biteback

De Tocqueville, A. 2003. *Democracy in America*. London: Penguin

Ekbia, H. R. and B. A. Nardi. 2017. *Heteromation: and Other Stories of Computing and Capitalism*. Cambridge, MA: MIT Press

Farrell, J. and P. Klemperer. 2007. 'Coordination and Lock-In: Competition with Switching Costs and Network Effects'. In Mark Armstrong and Robert K. Porter (eds.), *Handbook of Industrial Organization Vol.3*. Amsterdam: North-Holland Elsevier, 1967–2072, <https://dx.doi.org/10.2139/ssrn.917785>

Flathman, R. 2005. *Pluralism and Liberal Democracy*. Baltimore, MD: Johns Hopkins University Press

Galston, W. A. 2012. 'Oakeshott's Political Theory: Recapitulation and Criticisms'. In Efraim Podoksik (ed.), *The Cambridge Companion to Oakeshott*. Cambridge: Cambridge University Press, 222–44

Garnett, M. 2017. 'Conservatism'. In Paul Wetherly (ed.), *Political Ideologies*. Oxford: Oxford University Press, 65–96

Goldman, L. M. 2015. 'Trending Now: The Use of Social Media Websites in Public Shaming Punishments'. *American Criminal Law Review* 52, 415–51

Granovetter, M. S. 1973. 'The Strength of Weak Ties'. *American Journal of Sociology* 78(6), 1360–80, <https://doi.org/10.1086/225469>

Gray, J. 1993. 'Oakeshott as a Liberal'. In *Post-Liberalism: Studies in Political Thought*. London: Routledge, 40–46

Gray, J. 2003. *Al Qaeda and What it Means to be Modern*. London: Faber & Faber

Halpern, D. 2015. *Inside the Nudge Unit: How Small Changes Can Make a Big Difference*. London: W.H. Allen

Hildebrandt, M. 2015. *Smart Technologies and the End(s) of Law*. Cheltenham: Edward Elgar

Hindman, M. 2009. *The Myth of Digital Democracy*. Princeton, NJ: Princeton University Press

Jones, E. 2017. *Edmund Burke and the Invention of Modern Conservatism 1830–1914: An Intellectual History*. Oxford: Oxford University Press

Kasra, M. 2017. 'Vigilantism, Public Shaming and Social Media Hegemony: The Role of Digital-Networked Images in Humiliation and Socio-Political Control'. *The Communication Review* 20(3), 172–88, <https://doi.org/10.1080/10714421.2017.1343068>

Keane, J. 1995. *Tom Paine: A Political Life*. London: Bloomsbury

Laidlaw, E. B. 2017. 'Online Shaming and the Right to Privacy'. *Laws* 6(1), <http://dx.doi.org/10.3390/laws6010003>

Lessig, L. 1999. *Code and Other Laws of Cyberspace*. New York, NY: Basic Books

Levin, D. Z. and R. Cross. 2004. 'The Strength of Weak Ties You Can Trust: The Mediating Role of Trust in Effective Knowledge Transfer'. *Management Science* 50(11), 1477–90, <https://doi.org/10.1287/mnsc.1030.0136>

Margetts, H., P. John, S. Hale and T. Yasseri. 2016. *Political Turbulence: How Social Media Shape Collective Action.* Princeton. NJ: Princeton University Press

McGinnis, J. O. 2013. *Accelerating Democracy: Transforming Governance Through Technology.* Princeton, NJ: Princeton University Press

Nissenbaum, H. 2010. *Privacy in Context: Technology, Policy and the Integrity of Social Life.* Stanford, CA: Stanford University Press

Norman, J. 2013. *Edmund Burke: Philosopher, Politician, Prophet.* London: William Collins

Oakeshott, M. 1933. *Experience and its Modes.* Cambridge: Cambridge University Press

Oakeshott, M. 1975. *On Human Conduct.* Oxford: Clarendon Press

Oakeshott, M. 1991. 'Rationalism in Politics'. In *Rationalism in Politics and Other Essays.* Indianapolis, IN: Liberty Fund, 5–42

O'Hara, K. 2011. *Conservatism.* London: Reaktion Books

O'Hara, K. 2015. 'Data, Legibility, Creativity ... and Power'. *IEEE Internet Computing* 19(2), 88–91, <https://doi.org/10.1109/MIC.2015.34>

O'Hara, K. 2018a. 'The Contradictions of Digital Modernity'. *AI and Society*, <https://doi.org/10.1007/s00146-018-0843-7>

O'Hara, K. 2018b. *Where Shall We Draw the Line? Conservatism, Privacy and Digital Modernity*, SSRN, https://ssrn.com/abstract=3262386

O'Hara, K. In press. 'Burkean Conservatism, Legibility and Populism'. *Journal of Political Ideologies*

Quinton, A. 1978. *The Politics of Imperfection: The Religious and Secular Traditions of Conservative Thought in England From Hooker to Oakeshott.* London: Faber & Faber

Ronson, J. 2015. *So You've Been Publicly Shamed.* London: Pan Macmillan

Roy, O. 2004. *Globalised Islam: The Search for a New Ummah.* London: Hurst

Scott, J. C. 1998. *Seeing Like a State: How Certain Schemes to Improve the Human Condition Have Failed.* New Haven, CT: Yale University Press

Scruton, R. 2002. *The West and the Rest: Globalization and the Terrorist Threat.* London: Continuum

Scruton, R. 2006. *Arguments For Conservatism: A Political Philosophy.* London: Bloomsbury

Shadbolt, N., K. O'Hara, D. De Roure and W. Hall. 2019. *The Theory and Practice of Social Machines.* Cham: Springer

Van der Toorn, J., J. T. Jost and B. Loffredo. 2017. 'Conservative Ideological Shift Among Adolescents in Response to System Threat'. *Zeitschrift für Psychologie* 225, 357–62, <https://doi.org/10.1027/2151-2604/a000299>

Vosoughi, S., D. Roy and S. Aral. 2018. 'The Spread of True and False News Online'. *Science* 359(6380), 1146–51, <https://doi.org/10.1126/science.aap9559>

Zittrain, J. 2008. *The Future of the Internet: And How to Stop It.* New Haven, CT: Yale University Press

Zuboff, S. 2019. *The Age of Surveillance Capitalism: The Fight for a Human Future at the New Frontier of Power.* London: Profile

11. Artificial intelligence, affordances and fundamental rights
Christoph B. Graber[1]

INTRODUCTION

The expansionism of giant platform firms has become a major public concern (The Economist 2018, Zuboff 2015, 85), an object of political scrutiny (Council of Europe 2018) and a topic for legal research (Pasquale 2016, Cohen 2017a). As the everyday lives of platform users become more and more 'datafied' (Mayer-Schönberger and Cukier 2013, chap. 5; Cohen 2017a, 140; Esposito 2017, 252), the 'power' of a platform correlates broadly with the degree of the firm's access to big data and artificial intelligence (AI). From a constitutional law perspective, a question of primary importance is whether technology-enabled actions of mega platforms interfere with an effective use of fundamental rights online.

However, legal doctrine faces problems in addressing the key conceptual challenges of fundamental rights on the Internet. This is because the classic liberal approach conceives fundamental rights as constitutional norms protecting the individual against the power of the nation state. However, mega platforms such as Facebook and Google/YouTube, that together amass more than 60 per cent of global digital advertising revenues (Fortune 2017) and combine 'the functions of conduits, content providers, and data brokers' (Pasquale 2016, 512) for billions of people around the world, do not fit the triad of individual, power and state. What is more, classic fundamental rights doctrine does not provide for classifications that would permit conceptually including technologies, physical objects or materialities in general (for a discussion, see Cohen 2017b).

As organizations that are enabled by networked technologies, platforms raise new fundamental rights questions which are related to the material preconditions of an effective individual or social enjoyment of fundamental rights. An example highlighted in this text is platforms using AI-driven personalization technologies in opaque ways to manipulate flows of information. Such practices have been criticized as interfering with subjective individual rights, including data privacy, physical and mental personal integrity and free speech. However, as far as *subjective individual rights* are concerned, the absence of a fundamental rights accountability of platforms is not a problem in my view. One does not need fundamental rights for this; ordinary regulations of state law such as statutes of private law (liability or tort law), penal law and data protection law will do (see Council of Europe 2018). The real fundamental rights issue lies at the *trans-individual (discursive) level*. From the perspective of sociological systems theory (which methodologically informs this text), platforms are perceived as expansive social systems entailing the risk of thwarting society's autonomous self-reproduction (Graber 2018, 242–6).[2] Hence, a true fundamental rights question to ask would be whether, for example, the effects of non-transparent online content personalization affect the autonomy of the political discourse. Research by Cass Sunstein and others suggests that the extended use of AI-powered personalization technologies by platform firms is reinforcing the already existing trend towards 'filter bubbles' (Pariser 2011, see also Cavender 2017) and fragmented public spheres (Sunstein 2017). This opens the worrying prospect that communication – including about political issues – is increasingly taking place only between like-minded parties, and requires us to think more deeply about the future of political autonomy and democracy in the digital ecosphere.

In this chapter I would like to focus on a particular aspect of this topic that is almost entirely overlooked in the current fundamental rights debate. It is about the difficult relationship *between the social and the material* in fundamental rights theory. How does the materiality of technology facilitate or limit the institutionalization of fundamental rights online? Questions of this kind are caused, for example, by personalization technologies that may corrode a user's trust in the integrity of the infrastructure she is using for online communication. Smart personalization technologies put the platform in a position to materially interfere with the communication process and technically manipulate the global flows of social knowledge – often without people's awareness (International Panel on Social Progress 2016, 66). An effective use of communicative freedom online depends, inter alia, on preconditions that are technological. People will only then be effectively able to communicate freely if they have confidence in the integrity of the communicative process.

This thesis is supported by empiric evidence. As a consequence of the 2013 Snowden revelations, a wider public became aware that the US National Security Agency (NSA) was systematically monitoring all communication on the Internet (Greenwald 2014). As a broad study has shown for the case of Wikipedia, users' realization of the widespread surveillance practices, in which Google, Facebook, Twitter, Apple, Microsoft and their like cooperated secretly with the NSA,[3] led to a 'chilling effect' (Penney

2016). The 'chilling effect' theory generally describes how certain state acts may deter people from exercising their free speech rights (see e.g. Penney 2016, 126).[4] Here, the concept is used more specifically to refer to a situation where users who lose trust in the integrity of the Internet's technical infrastructure self-censor their Internet-mediated communication.

Although technology has become more important as a condition for the effective enjoyment of communicative freedom, fundamental rights doctrine has a hard time adequately conceptualizing the constraints and opportunities of materialities (for a discussion, see *The End(s)* and Cohen 2017b). The current discussion about the relationship between law and technology is unsatisfactory not only in legal doctrine but also in the relevant branches of the social sciences. Legal practitioners tend to treat technologies as a black box when analyzing cases or designing solution strategies. Accordingly, they are blind with regard to technologies as constraints and opportunities for effective fundamental rights enjoyment. Scholars of science and technology studies (STS) in turn have provided sophisticated analyses on the relationship between the material and the social. Meanwhile they have mostly been treating law and regulation as a closed book rather than considering their built-in dynamics, which is unsatisfactory as well.

Adopting a legal sociology perspective, this chapter seeks to take the debate about law and technology further and situate AI-driven technologies in a framework of affordance theory and fundamental rights. In a first step it will argue for a conceptualization of affordances in the light of Bryan Pfaffenberger's (1992) technological drama before asking whether such a theoretical perspective can also be employed to analyze AI. The current debate about AI creates an image of AI technology as something impenetrable. The chapter argues that this is mostly ideology and that normative expectations regarding the functionality of AI technologies can emerge from civil society to some extent. Finally, a sociological systems theory inspired perspective of fundamental rights is introduced, understanding such rights *sociologically* as those institutions of society where normative expectations about the protection of individual and social autonomies are bundled.

THE PROMISE OF AFFORDANCE THEORY

The Concept of Affordance

Over the last couple of years the notion of 'affordance' has increasingly been used in law, society and technology scholarship to conceptualize the constraints or opportunities for social action that are built into a technology. The notion was originally coined by the perceptual psychologist James Gibson in 1979 (see Gibson 1979 and Hutchby 2001, 447). For Gibson, animals are equipped to perceive information in their environment selectively, in function of the information's relevance for the animal's survival. Within this scheme, the environment's affordances (opportunities or invitations) are considered to be functionally relevant information for the living system (see Lievrouw 2014, 48). Ten years later the concept was appropriated and popularized by Donald Norman, a designer (see Norman 1988, Lievrouw 2014, 48). According to Norman (1988, 8), the term 'affordance' refers to the design aspects of an object, 'primarily those fundamental properties that determine just how the thing could possibly be used'. While Norman was mostly interested in a user's perception of the technological design, for Gibson it was the specific environment that made certain things possible or impossible for a living system. In the *The End(s)* (at 169–70), Mireille Hildebrandt used the term 'affordance' in the sense of Gibson to underpin her pluralistic understanding of information and communication infrastructures. Like Gibson, who emphasized the relative independence of an environment's affordances from a living system's perception thereof, Hildebrandt (*The End(s)*, 170) underscored that it is more important what a technology affords than what is perceived by an agent.

Hildebrandt originally applied the term 'affordance' to technologies, emphasizing the relative and relational aspect in a technology's design and subsequent uptake (*The End(s)*, 169–71). In response to some of *The End(s)* reviewers who had criticized the absence of a comprehensive theory of affordance in the book, Hildebrandt recently extended the concept beyond material technologies to include also 'affordances of the law' (Hildebrandt 2017). What at first sight may appear as a sensible approximation to Julie Cohen's (2017b) understanding of fundamental rights as affordances has a considerable downside, in my view. The downside is that 'affordance' thus lost its edge for conceptualizing the relationship between the social and the material in the design and reception of a digital technology. If not only a material object but also a discourse or social system can have its affordances, the concept tends to become watered down. In the following I would thus like to redefine the concept of 'affordance' with a focus on the *possibilities and constraints of a technology*. Informed by Pfaffenberger's 'technological drama', the process through which affordances come into a technology will be reconstructed as a dialogue between a 'design constituency' and an 'impact constituency' in which a technology's materiality and sociality are co-determined (Pfaffenberger 1992, 283 and 296).

In his 1990 book *Technology and the Lifeworld*, Don Ihde conceptualized technology as 'multistable', arguing that what a technology is depends on how it is socially embedded (Ihde 1990, 144, see also *The End(s)*, 171). Basing his view on a similar understanding of technology and applying it to the concept of affordance, Pfaffenberger argued two years later that a technology's affordances are 'inherently multiple' (Pfaffenberger 1992, 284). According to Pfaffenberger there is always flexibility – not only in the design of a technology but also in its uptake. The flexibility in the design of a technology results from design constituencies being able to choose the politics/values that a certain technology embodies when it is created. But there is also flexibility in the way the impact constituency can interpret a technology.

An Internet-related example that supports this flexibility thesis is the hashtag. The hashtag was suggested by Twitter's impact constituency in 2007 as a means of structuring discourse on the microblogging platform (see Leavitt 2014, 137). In a tweet from 23 August 2007, Chris Messina asked the Twitter community, '[H]ow do you feel about using # (pound) for groups. As in #barcamp [msg]?' (Messina 2007a). This was the birth of the hashtag on Twitter, the 'hash' being the # sign and the 'tag' a specific keyword such as 'netneutrality'. While the hashtag sign had been used before, inter alia as annotation referring to channels of Internet Relay Chat (IRC) (see Gannes 2010), the innovative element of Messina's contribution was to convince the Twitter community of its usefulness as a means of indexing microblogs and grouping conversations (see Halavais 2014, 36). Adding the hashtag #netneutrality to a tweet allows the marking and contextualizing of communication through metadata that relates the post to a new or ongoing Twitter discussion about net neutrality (see Bruns and Burgess 2011). Messina (2007b) described the advantage of the hashtag as representing 'a solid convention for coordinating ad-hoc groupings and giving people a way to organize their communications in a way that the tool (Twitter) does not currently afford'. The hashtag's innovation consisted in the possibility of structuring a conversation on Twitter without the need to follow a particular twitterer. This is an example of user innovation that greatly improved Twitter's significance for public communication and which was later officially incorporated into the platform's architecture by Twitter Inc. (see Bruns and Burgess 2011, 2). It demonstrates how an impact constituency may be able to respond to a technology's affordances. Although things have prescriptive capacities (see Latour 1992, 232–40) enlisting users into a certain role, they do not have innate regulatory aims. Rather than having built-in agency (or politics) (see Winner 1980), there is plasticity in the design of material things (Pinch and Bijker 1987). But how exactly should we envisage the process through which affordances come into a technology?

How do Affordances Come Into a Technology?

A persuasive answer to that question is given by Pfaffenberger's theory of the technological drama, re-constructing the process through which affordances come into a technology as a 'discourse of technological "statements" and "counterstatements"' (Pfaffenberger 1992, 285). Pfaffenberger's theory explains how the social and the material interact when technologies are designed and received by different constituencies. The drama reconstructs the design and uptake of an artefact as recursive interactions between different constituencies in which the materiality and sociality of a technology are co-determined. According to Pfaffenberger, 'the reciprocal construction of political aims and artifacts' is 'coupled with the deliberate fabrication of controlled social contexts' (1992, 291). As ideal-types, three processes or acts can be distinguished in a technological drama, including technological regularization, technological adjustment and technological reconstitution.

The drama starts with technological regularization – that is, the creation of a technological artefact by the design constituency. The newly designed artefact has no meaning until it is interpreted by the design constituency in a discursive process. At this stage, meaning is implanted into the artefact in such a way that some of its technical features embody a political aim (Pfaffenberger 1992, 291). This is the process that Pfaffenberger describes as the establishment of a cultural mythos – that is, a dominant view in society about what a certain technology is and what it can do. Through the establishment of the mythos, the design constituency tries to define alternative interpretations away (1992, 295). Irrespective of the design constituency's efforts to take 'logonomic control' (1992, 296) of the artefact's social context, ambiguities will always subsist.

Remaining ambiguities can be exploited by the impact constituency in the second act of 'technological adjustment'. At this stage the impact constituency constructs alternative interpretations and tries to establish a 'counter mythos' of what the technology is or can do. The call to use the hashtag on Twitter for the purpose of discourse structuring is an example illustrating a process of technological adjustment. While such a process does not involve a change in the technology, the ensuing stage of technological reconstitution consists of a material redesign of the technology through the impact constituency.

Regarding reconstitution, the drama's third act, an example is the emergence of technology allowing users to block advertisements on the websites they visit (The Economist 2015). Ad-blocking technology was created as a 'counterartefact' (Pfaffenberger 1992, 304) with the purpose of technically reconstituting the functionality of behaviour-tracking cookies. According to Helen Nissenbaum (2011, 1382), the advertising industry's lobbying backed the introduction of the so-called 'third-party' cookie by decision RFC 2965 of the Internet Engineering Task Force in 1997. The 'third-party' cookie turned out to be particularly invasive on people's privacy as it allows websites to follow people even when they visit new websites. Ad-blocking technology can be seen as a technical answer to 'third-party' cookies. While Adblock Plus, a creation of Eyeo, an Internet company, is the most widely used ad-blocker, many other companies are also producing such software. The meaning and value of the counterartefact, however, does not come from such companies but from those who are negatively affected by the original technology – in the case of ad-blocking, the myriad users who feel annoyed by intrusive online advertisements.

Pfaffenberger postulates that the fabrication of a counterartefact can sometimes shift from technological reconstitution to regularization, the first act of a new technological drama. Evidence for the truth of this thesis is again the ad-blocking case. As ad-blocking makes online publishers lose money, several such companies, including Axel Springer, Spiegel online and Süddeutsche Zeitung sued Eyeo in the German courts.[5] In what can be seen as a (new) act of technological adjustment, Eyeo then offered a compromise, authorizing net publishers who were willing to pay Eyeo six per cent of their revenues, to integrate a tag on their websites that let selected ads show up (Neue Zürcher Zeitung 2016). Hence the technology changed from blocking any advertising to selecting ads that – for whatever reason – were not considered as bad. Eyeo for their part were busy explaining this move through the creation of a counter myth of their software, arguing on their website that:

> [W]e have learned that most users wouldn't mind seeing better, more informative ads. In fact, the majority of people we've talked to are keenly aware that advertising plays a pivotal role in keeping content online free. Trouble is, most Internet ads are still low on quality and high on annoyance, and the two sides – users and advertisers – rarely come together. That's where we come in. We find ourselves uniquely positioned to broker a compromise that makes the Internet better for all parties. We aim to make the entire ecosystem more sustainable by encouraging true innovation and non-intrusive ad standards, on the one end, and a better user experience on the other.[6]

The counter mythos that Eyeo was suggesting focuses on a trade-off between information and annoyance. The success of this suggestion is, however, doubtful as it is easy to see that Eyeo is a company that wants to make money, and the introduction of whitelists is essential to secure their business model. It is no surprise therefore that the drama continues and the suggested mythos is rejected by websites that are not willing to pay a fee. While some of these websites have developed software that blocks users who block their ads, others ask their audience to voluntarily accept ads as a contribution to high-quality news reporting (The Economist 2015).

For Pfaffenberger (1992, 308) 'the drama can drop out of the technology'. This would be a stage of 'designification' which can be reached when, because of unforeseen technological or social reasons, the recursively intertwined dynamics come to an end. For Nissenbaum (2011, 1379) this would be a dangerous stage because people would then be 'inclined to accept that technology is neutral' and 'forget that there are values or politics involved in technology at all'.

In sum, Pfaffenberger's theory paves the way to a conceptualization of affordances as being co-determined in recursive practices of material design and social interpretation (for a similar view, see Lievrouw 2014, 48). The question addressed in the next section is whether affordance theory can also be applied to analyze the co-determination of AI technologies. The success of such an endeavour seems unlikely as AI is generally viewed to be impenetrable.

AI AND AFFORDANCE THEORY

What is AI?

These days everybody is talking about AI and we are in the midst of AI hype. An article in Forbes even declared 2017 the year of AI (Forbes 2017). But what is AI? According to the OECD (2017, 295), there is no universally accepted definition of AI. Yarden Katz, a Harvard neuroscientist and AI philosopher, argues that AI is a messy concept, standing for a 'confused mix of terms – such as "big data", "machine learning" or "deep learning" – whose common denominator is the use of expensive computing power to analyse massive centralised data' (Katz 2017).

While the hype is recent, the term AI is more than 60 years old (Calo 2017, 401). It was coined in 1955 in a research project that a group of four young mathematicians and computer scientists, including John McCarthy, Marvin Minsky, Nathaniel Rochester and Claude Shannon, proposed for the 1956 summer workshop at Dartmouth College (McCarthy et al. 2006). According to the workshop mission statement the term AI referred to computers fulfilling certain tasks that normally only humans could do and the hypothesis was that 'every aspect of learning or any other feature of intelligence can in principle be so precisely described that a machine can be made to simulate it' (2006, 12).

In early euphoria some AI enthusiasts predicted that in no more than a generation machines would be as intelligent as human beings. In a 1970 interview Marvin Minsky told *Life* magazine

> In from three to eight years we will have a machine with the general intelligence of an average human being. I mean a machine that will be able to read Shakespeare, grease a car, play office politics, tell a joke, have a fight. At that point the machine will begin to educate itself with fantastic speed. In a few months it will be at genius level and a few months after that its powers will be incalculable. (Darrach 1970, 58D)

These lofty predictions turned out to be wrong and instead of AI flourishing, what followed were many years of what became known as the 'AI winter' (BBC iWonder n.d.).

It is only recently that AI has attracted increasing media attention. For the OECD (2017, 296) the publicity is mainly due to breakthroughs in machine learning, which are enabled by the 'availability of big data and cloud computing'. Katz (2017, 3) relates the hype to a 're-branding' of the 'somewhat nebulous' meaning of AI. He has reconstructed how the approaches to the meaning of AI changed from 'symbolic and logic based' perspectives in the 1970s to placing neural networks and statistical tools in the foreground in the 1980s. 'It seems', Katz observes, 'that the term "AI" can be made to fit nearly any cutting-edge computation offered by computer scientists'. This claim is confirmed by the current association of AI with the latest breakthroughs in the realm of machine learning and big data. For Katz, AI's conceptual malleability is a key consideration explaining how the concept's meteoric rise from 'zero to hero' was possible, establishing it as the epitome of the next technological revolution. Another important consideration relates to business interests of the major platforms, including Google, Apple, Facebook and Amazon, which are the driving forces behind the media attention on AI. Google, Facebook, Amazon, Microsoft and IBM have engaged in a partnership on AI (The Guardian 2016). Katz (2017, 13) maintains that the current AI hype has actually been manufactured by the giant platform firms and that the rejuvenation of the AI brand is closely linked to profit motives of 'surveillance capitalism'. According to Shoshana Zuboff, 'surveillance capitalism' is 'a new form of information capitalism aiming to predict and modify human behaviour as a means to produce revenue and market control' (Zuboff 2015).

Ideology of AI Supremacy[7]

The claim that the current AI hype has been manufactured should be read together with recent critique by Katz and others that the talk about AI supremacy is mostly ideology. Arguably, the platform corporations want to make us believe that machine intelligence is outperforming human intelligence. Such claims, Katz contends, are based on a narrowly empiricist epistemology that ignores the historical context of human life (Katz 2017, 8). Katz criticizes the tech industry for creating a myth about AI technology as something impenetrable and inevitable. Referring to Karl Marx's concept of 'commodity fetishism', Jack Balkin makes a similar point (Balkin 2017, 1225). In 'Capital' Marx coined the term 'commodity fetishism' to criticize people treating commodities as if they had inert value whereas in reality the commodity's value is a social construct (Marx 1989, 185–98). According to Balkin, AI fetishism serves the purpose of producing effects making society believe that AI technologies substitute for human beings (Balkin 2017, 1224).[8]

Using the word 'mystic' to describe the commodity's fetish character, Marx (1989, 85) alluded to a religious charging of material objects. Today, a religious transfiguration of AI can be observed, for example, in Anthony Levandowski's 'Way of the Future', a new religion of artificial intelligence, whose activities focus on 'the realization, acceptance, and worship of a Godhead based on Artificial Intelligence (AI) developed through computer hardware and software' (see Harris 2017).

The AI myth is so strong that nobody dares to question it. What is more, the hype has eclipsed critical evaluation within science. As an explanation, Katz refers to the fact that the big tech companies are hiring the most influential AI scientists and are thus preventing independent research on the subject (Katz 2017, 4). A more critical view on AI, however, would show its limitations. While a combination of machine learning and big data supposedly allows AI to identify patterns in large data sets (OECD 2017, 296), Katz, for example, has denounced the shortcomings of image recognition algorithms producing large numbers of absurd mismatches between images and verbal descriptions of these images (Katz 2017, 9). Others have pointed to a deep gap between what is marketed and what is possible, for example in the identification of criminals at a football stadium (Wales Online 2018) or the performance of a deep learning based system playing Atari (Lake et al. 2017, Lapuschkin et al. 2019), or have ridiculed an AI program that was trained on articles from The Economist's science and technology section to produce a piece of its own (The Economist 2017).

In 2016, AlphaGo, one of Google's AI-based computer programs, managed to win against Lee Sedol, the world's top Go player (Kasparov 2017, 75). Is this the ultimate proof of AI supremacy? Rolf Pfeifer, a leading robotics scholar at the University of Zurich, explains that computers such as AlphaGo may outperform humans in very narrow and specific tasks whereas human intelligence can only be understood in relation to an individual's (natural, physical and social) environment. Human beings are constantly acting and every action stimulates a large number of sensors. This is completely different from feeding an algorithm with data. AlphaGo, for example, does not even know that it is playing Go (Tages Anzeiger 2017; see Esposito 2017, 261).

The second point in Katz's critique of AI ideology refers to the mystification of AI indecipherability. AI indecipherability or impenetrability is the impression that platform firms create when they talk about algorithms that are arguably so complex that they are not even understood by the programmers themselves (see Weinberger 2018). Katz warns that the blanket acceptance of indecipherability is a gift to systems of power: 'If AI systems outperform us (and hence must be used), yet are indecipherable, then who can be held accountable?' (Katz 2017, 16). When it is believed that computers are more intelligent than humans, this implies either that we cannot do anything or that the technology itself (or the firm controlling it) will resolve the problem.

AI and Societal Response

The critical voices of Katz, Balkin, and others counteract the building of an ideology of AI supremacy. AI supremacy is an ideology wanting to make us believe that AI technology is a substitute for human beings since it is more effective and faster than humans and outstrips human decision-makers. Balkin calls this the 'substitution effect' of AI (Balkin 2017, 1224). According to Balkin, the substitution effect includes the treatment of AI technology as if it were alive (2017, 1224). As an effect of this substitution the responsibility for social costs of AI is shifted to the technology rather than to those who design and operate it. Balkin argues that this does not make sense from a governance perspective. In order to protect the public interest, we do not need laws for AI (algorithms or robots, for example) but we do need laws for those who design, implement and use the technology (2017, 1226).

From the perspective of affordance theory and the technological drama, these critical writings can be interpreted as challenges to the mythos that the AI design constituency is striving for. They remind us that there is flexibility not only in the design of AI technology but also in its reception. The affordances of AI are shaped by the institutional logic in which these technologies 'are designed, implemented, and used' (Zuboff 2015, 85). The critical voices contribute to technological adjustment and confront attempts of the big platform firms to impose their view on society and establish a cultural mythos about AI technology. Balkin's contribution is notable as it claims that law and regulation – rather than playing no part in the technological drama – can contribute to hammer out an AI mythos that would be promoting the public interest. For Balkin, a way to achieve that would be to impose certain public interest duties on operators of AI technology to make sure that they do not 'pollute', that is, 'unjustifiably externalize the costs of algorithmic decision-making onto others' (Balkin 2017, 1238).

The potential of the societal response to AI technology is not limited to the act of 'technological adjustment' and can extend to 'technological reconstitution'. An example to mention here is Gobo, a technology developed by the MIT Media Lab.[9] Gobo lets you decide which of your Twitter or Facebook posts are prioritized or minimized (see Talbot 2017). Gobo retrieves posts from people that a user follows on Twitter and Facebook and analyses them by employing simple machine-learning based filters. Two sliders are available to the user to filter out unwanted posts from her feed or filter in posts that she probably does not read every day. For example, posts can be filtered out that contain rude, viral or advertising information. In the same way she would also be able, for example, to filter out all posts from men and display a 'women only' news feed. The second slider, called 'politics', instead of filtering out allows filtering in of posts from media outlets that the user, because of her profile, would normally not see (Zuckerman 2017).

Gobo can be conceived as a technological response to online content personalization on Twitter and Facebook as it involves a change in the operation of personalization algorithms. It can be associated with the act of reconstitution because it affects the technology's material design. While Gobo is still strongly invested in the existing infrastructure of the platforms, a more radical tool to mention would be Diaspora, a social network developed by four students at NYU in 2010 (Huffington Post 2010).[10] Diaspora allows secure sharing of information between friends by storing the data on decentralized servers (rather than on centralized ones as in the case of Facebook, for example). A further example of AI reconstitution would be de-identification software, which has been developed by Privacy Analytics, a small Israeli start-up.[11] The software can be employed by webpages to slightly distort images of people's faces so that they cannot be identified by facial recognition algorithms. These examples of AI reconstitution show the creative potential of hacking. According to Zuboff (2015, 85) '[h]acking intends to liberate affordances from the institutional logics in which they are frozen and redistribute them in alternative configurations for new purposes'.

The examples of Gobo, Diaspora and de-identification software show that a social response to AI technology is possible in principle and that it is possible not only as technological adjustment but also as technological reconstitution. As *The End(s)* rightly emphasizes, the problem is that many affordances of 'pre-emptive computing' (which would be a synonym for AI as I have been using the term so far) are hidden (*The End(s)*, 170). Hildebrandt distinguishes between material settings at the level of hardware and software, which determine the technology's potential uptake, while its functionalities are shaped in its actual uptake. With regard to AI, one therefore needs to caution that the extent to which affordances can be reconstituted depends on the question of whether the technology's potential uptake can also become the subject of a process of co-determination in which impact constituencies can play a role despite asymmetries of power and knowledge. While this is a question that goes beyond the scope of this chapter, in the next section I ask more generally how one should understand – from a legal sociology perspective – the relationship between the emergence of social expectations about a technology's affordances and fundamental rights. The analytic framework underlying this reflection is provided by Niklas Luhmann's theory of social systems.

AFFORDANCES AND FUNDAMENTAL RIGHTS

From a systems theory perspective, the first step in shedding light on the relationship between affordances and fundamental rights is to recall that the *function* of the law (as a system of society) is to generalize and stabilize normative expectations. Normative expectations are those expectations in society which are not changed when they are disappointed. Normative expectations are distinct from cognitive expectations which are adapted if the expectation is not fulfilled. To perform its function, the legal system selects those expectations within society that are normative ones and makes sure that they apply society-wide (generalization) and become fixed (stabilization).

Normative expectations are not limited to the behaviour of human actors or social systems but include affordances of technology. When people interact with technology they themselves develop cognitive and normative expectations about the technology. As we have seen above, this also applies broadly to AI technologies as their affordances are generally co-determined in recursive practices of material design and social interpretation. Accordingly, the social response to material design is an expression of cognitive or normative expectations. If such expectations are normative they imply that a certain interpretation of a technology's functioning would be considered as a must.

As mentioned before, the problem is that some of the affordances of AI technologies are hidden (*The End(s)*, 170). A question for further research therefore is whether existing socio-legal theories about the constitutionalization of normative expectations can be extended to AI and smart technologies. A perspective that I recommend as a basis for further work is Gunther Teubner's theory of societal constitutionalism (Teubner 2012). Building on that theory, I have argued in earlier work for the example of Net Neutrality that normative expectations about the design of the Internet emerge from the middle of society before they are eventually juridified and, if specific conditions are met, may become constitutionalized as a fundamental right (Graber 2017). As Net Neutrality also covers highly complex affordances of the Internet that a non-expert user cannot perceive, an extension of that theoretical approach to pre-emptive computing does not seem to be a priori excluded.

According to Teubner (2012, 103–4), normative expectations are likely to emerge from a specific sub-system of society. Which is the sub-system of society where normative expectations about AI technologies are likely to emerge? In my above-mentioned research I have argued that normative expectations about Net Neutrality emerge from the economic sub-system of society. Considering the huge economic interests of giant platform companies that are involved in the development of AI technologies, my guess is that normative expectations regarding AI technology will arise from the economic system.

Teubner (2012, 88–96) argues that the economic system is internally differentiated into an organized professional sphere (corporations and other formal organizations) and a spontaneous sphere (consumer organizations and other civil society segments). Both spheres are driving the evolutionary process in the economic system but their mutual interplay is a democratic challenge (Teubner 2012, 90). A problem from a social policy perspective is that the organized sphere does not receive direct input from the spontaneous sphere (Teubner 2012, 91–2). Accordingly, social pressure often seems to be the only way to irritate the organized sphere and trigger internal structural adaptation. Regarding AI and smart technologies, a considerable problem here is the above-mentioned asymmetry of power and knowledge that exists between those who design and operate the technology (the design constituency – particularly the corporations that are able to hire the most brilliant and most expensive software developers) and those heterogeneous segments of civil society that are in one way or another affected by the technology (the impact constituency). Corporations have an advantage in this situation as their knowledge about the effects of the technologies allows them to anticipate consumer reactions and always be one step ahead of everybody else.

Juridification is the second stage within Teubner's theory of social constitutionalism (Teubner 2012, 104). Juridification means that normative expectations are brought into the form of a legal norm in a social process that is structured by a distinct legal authority. As a consequence of being reformulated in the language of the law by a court or similar legal authority they will be contrafactually stabilized and become part of the legal system. At the stage of juridification, socially harmful ways of how a technology can be interpreted may be defined away, or the creation of an environment may be supported that is more hospitable towards other technologies which have the same effect but better balance the interests of all parties (for a similar suggestion, see Nissenbaum 2011). Finally, a constitutionalization of normative expectations in the form of a fundamental right (as institution of the law) would require a reflexive process where the juridified norms would be observed by means of a binary code constitutional/non-constitutional (Teubner 2012, 110–11). As we can learn from the ongoing debate about Net Neutrality, a constitutionalization process is likely to take decades just for the second stage (juridification) to be accomplished (Graber 2017). The third stage (constitutionalization in a narrow sense) would require, in theory, the participation of a 'constitutional court' (at national, supra-national or international level) recognizing a (formal) fundamental rights protection of certain individual or social autonomies with regard to the implications of AI technologies.[12] At the moment there is no empirical evidence that refers to the dynamics of juridification or constitutionalization of AI technology; as the technology and its applications are still very new this is no surprise.

What is the part of government regulation in all this? My thesis is that social policy and regulation can contribute to providing for discourse conditions that are favourable for society's autonomous production of normative expectations regarding AI technologies. The problem of hidden affordances of AI technologies has already been mentioned. A further challenge is that the generation of normative expectations about pre-emptive technologies needs time. AI and smart applications thereof are relatively new and most people lack practical experience of interaction with these technologies. Hence, they will not have settled expectations about what these technologies are and what they do. Considering these difficulties I would like to conclude with the following recommendations:

1) The debate about AI in society should be as inclusive as possible. AI should not be developed in geographically or sectorally siloed environments, and a top-down approach to drafting 'AI ethics guidelines' would not be sufficient (European Commission 2018, 4 and 14–17).
2) Financial support of *independent* scientific research about the social implications of AI technology is crucial; furthermore intermediaries

(such as quality mass media, expert bloggers, specialized websites etc.) are needed who can 'translate' expert knowledge about the social implications of 'pre-emptive computing' into a 'language' that non-expert users will also understand.
3) There is a challenge also for the education system; it is important that young people at all levels of education get an understanding of the new technologies and their impact on human life (European Commission 2018, 13). This includes legal education (Susskind 2017), where interdisciplinary approaches to law, technology, philosophy and ethics should feature in programmes and courses.
4) We need to examine how access to data could be diversified so that AI can contribute to the public good (European Commission 2018, 11).

NOTES

1. Parts of section 2 are an update from a version already published as Christoph B. Graber, 'Freedom and Affordances of the Net'. *Washington University Jurisprudence Review* 10, 221–56. I would like to thank Hoda Heidari, Yarden Katz, Dana Mareckova and Loredana Martignetti for comments. Special thanks are owed to the anonymous reviewer and the book editors.
2. For their self-reproduction, given historical societies have depended on specific information and communication technologies. See *The End(s)*, chap. 8.
3. Although Google, Apple, Yahoo, Microsoft, Facebook and AOL denied having given NSA consumer data for surveillance purposes, Rajesh De, the NSA general counsel, testified in a hearing of the Privacy and Civil Liberties Oversight Board (an independent agency within the US Government) on 19 March 2014 that 'all communications content and associated metadata harvested by the NSA under a 2008 surveillance law occurred with the knowledge of the companies – both for the internet collection program known as Prism and for the so-called "upstream" collection of communications moving across the internet'. *The Guardian*, 19 March 2014.
4. The seminal text on the chilling effect doctrine in US First Amendment adjudication is still Schauer (1978). See also Kendrick (2013). For a landmark decision of the European Court of Human Rights on the subject see *Magyar Jeti Zrt v. Hungary*, Application No. 11257/16, 4 December 2018, para 83.
5. See, for example, German Supreme Court (Bundesgerichtshof), Case No. I ZR 154/16, 19 April 2018.
6. See Eyeo: Our Mission, available online at <https://eyeo.com/>.
7. While the focus is on myth creation about AI and its critique, this section does not intend to deny that there are many useful applications of AI (for example in the realm of medicine or for the prediction of natural disasters etc.).
8. Sharon and Zandbergen (2016) use the term 'data fetishism'.
9. See MIT Media Lab, Project Gobo, at <www.media.mit.edu/projects/gobo/overview/>.
10. I am grateful to Yarden Katz for pointing this out.
11. See Privacy Analytics' webpage at <https://privacy-analytics.com/software/>.
12. To avoid misunderstanding, I would like to stress that the spontaneous processes of constitutionalization will not replace the formal ones. Rather than mutually exclusive, the relationship between the spontaneous and formal processes of constitutionalization should be viewed as mutually stimulating. For details see Graber (2017, 548–53).

REFERENCES

Balkin, J. 2017. 'The Three Laws of Robotics in the Age of Big Data'. *Ohio State Law Journal* 78, 1217–41

BBC iWonder. n.d. *AI: 15 Key Moments in the Story of Artificial Intelligence.* <www.bbc.co.uk/timelines/zq376fr>

Bruns, A. and J. E. Burgess. 2011. 'The Use of Twitter Hashtags in the Formation of Ad Hoc Publics'. *Proceeedings of the 6th European Consortium for Political Research (ECPR), General Conference.* University of Reykjavik, 24–27 August 2011. <http://eprints.qut.edu.au/46515>

Calo, R. 2017. 'Artificial Intelligence Policy: A Primer and Roadmap'. *UC Davis Law Review* 51, 399–435

Cavender, B. 2017. 'The Personalization Puzzle'. *Washington University Jurisprudence Review* 10 (1), 97–121

Cohen, J. E. 2017a. 'Law for the Platform Economy'. *UC Davis Law Review* 51, 133–204

Cohen, J. E. 2017b. 'Affording Fundamental Rights: A Provocation Inspired by Mireille Hildebrandt'. *Critical Analysis of Law* 4 (1), 78–90

Council of Europe. 2018. 'Recommendation CM/Rec(2018)2 of the Committee of Ministers to Member States on the Roles and Responsibilities of Internet Intermediaries'. 7 March 2018

Darrach, B. 1970. 'Meet Shaky, the First Electronic Person – The Fearsome Reality of a Machine with a Mind of its Own'. *Life*, 20 November 1970

The Economist. 2015. 'Online Advertising: Block Shock: Internet Users are Increasingly Blocking Ads, Including on Their Mobiles'. *The Economist,* 6 June 2015. <www.economist.com/news/business/21653644-internet-users-are-increasingly-blocking-ads-including-their-mobiles-block-shock>

The Economist. 2017. 'From our AI Correspondent. Computer Says. . .'. *The Economist*, 23 December 2017

The Economist. 2018. 'Taming the Titans. Google, Facebook and Amazon are Increasingly Dominant. How Should They Be Controlled?' *The Economist*, 20 January 2018

Esposito, E. 2017. 'Artificial Communication?: The Production of Contingency by Algorithms'. *Zeitschrift für Soziologie* 46 (4), 249–65

European Commission. 2018. 'Communication from the Commission to the European Parliament, the European Council, the Council, the European Economic and Social Committee and the Committee of Regions, Artificial Intelligence for Europe, COM (2018) 237 final'. 25 April 2018

Eyeo. n.d. *Our Mission.* <https://eyeo.com/>

Forbes. 2017. 'Why 2017 is the Year of Artificial Intelligence'. *Forbes*, 27 February 2017. <https://www.forbes.com/sites/forbestechcouncil/2017/02/27/why-2017-is-the-year-of-artificial-intelligence/#25d709ba57a1>

Fortune. 2017. 'Why Google and Facebook Prove the Digital Ad Market is a Duopoly'. *Fortune*, 28 July 2017. <http://fortune.com/2017/07/28/google-facebook-digital-advertising/>

Gannes, L. 2010. 'The Short and Illustrious History of Twitter #Hashtags'. 30 April 2010. Accessed 22 January 2018. <https://gigaom.com/2010/04/30/the-short-and-illustrious-history-of-twitter-hashtags/>

Gibson, J. J. 1979. *The Ecological Approach to Visual Perception.* Boston, MA: Houghton Mifflin

Graber, C. B. 2017. 'Bottom-up Constitutionalism: The Case of Net Neutrality'. *Transnational Legal Theory* 7 (04), 524–52

Graber, C. B. 2018. 'Freedom and Affordances of the Net'. *Washington University Jurisprudence Review* 10, 221–56

Greenwald, G. 2014. *No Place to Hide: Edward Snowden, the NSA, and the U.S. Surveillance State.* New York, NY: Metropolitan Books/Henry Holt

The Guardian. 2014. 'US Tech Giants Knew of NSA Data Collection, Agency's Top Lawyer Insists'. *The Guardian*, 19 March 2014

The Guardian. 2016. '"Partnership on AI" Formed by Google, Facebook, Amazon, IBM and Microsoft'. *The Guardian*, 28 September 2016. <www.theguardian.com/technology/2016/sep/28/google-facebook-amazon-ibm-microsoft-partnership-on-ai-tech-firms>

Halavais, A. 2014. 'Structure on Twitter: Social and Technical'. In *Twitter and Society*, edited by Katrin Weller, Axel Bruns, Jean Burgess, Merja Mahrt and Cornelius Puschmann, 29–42. New York, NY: Peter Lang

Harris, M. 2017. 'Inside the First Church of Artificial Intelligence'. *Wired*, 15 November 2017. <www.wired.com/story/anthony-levandowski-artificial-intelligence-religion/>

Hildebrandt, M. 2015. *Smart Technologies and the End(s) of Law: Novel Entanglements of Law and Technology.* Cheltenham, UK; Northampton, MA: Edward Elgar

Hildebrandt, M. 2017. 'Law as an Affordance: The Devil is in the Vanishing Point(s)'. *Critical Analysis of Law* 4 (1), 116–28

Huffington Post. 2010. 'Diaspora: NYU Students Develop Privacy-Based Social Network'. *Huffington Post*, 6 December 2010. <www.huffingtonpost.com/2010/05/11/diaspora-nyu-students-dev_n_571632.html>

Hutchby, I. 2001. 'Technologies, Texts and Affordances'. *Sociology* 35, 441–56

Ihde, D. 1990. *Technology and the Lifeworld: From Garden to Earth.* Bloomington, IN: Indiana University Press

International Panel on Social Progress. 2016. 'Chapter 13 – Media and Communications'. 20 August 2016

Kasparov, G. 2017. *Deep Thinking: Where Machine Intelligence Ends and Human Creativity Begins.* New York, NY: Public Affairs

Katz, Y. 2017. *Manufacturing an Artificial Intelligence Revolution.* 27 November 2017. <https://ssrn.com/abstract=3078224>

Kendrick, L. 2013. 'Speech, Intent, and the Chilling Effect'. *William & Mary Law Review* 54 (5), 1633–91

Lake, B., T. D. Ullman, J. B. Tenenbaum and S. J. Gershman. 2017. 'Building Machines that Learn and Think Like People'. *Behavioral and Brain Sciences* 40, 1–72

Lapuschkin, S., S. Wäldchen, A. Binder, G. Montavon, W. Samek and K.-R. Müller. 2019. 'Unmasking Clever Hans Predictors and Assessing What Machines Really Learn'. *Nature Communications* 10, 1096

Latour, B. 1992. 'Where are the Missing Masses? The Sociology of a Few Mundane Artefacts'. In *Shaping Technology/Building Society: Studies in Sociotechnical Change*, edited by Wiebe E. Bijker and John Law, 225–58. Cambridge, MA: MIT Press

Leavitt, A. 2014. 'From #FollowFriday to YOLO: Exploring the Cultural Salience of Twitter Memes'. In *Twitter and Society*, edited by Katrin Weller, Axel Bruns, Jean Burgess, Merja Mahrt, and Cornelius Puschmann, 137–54. New York, NY: Peter Lang

Lievrouw, L. A. 2014. 'The Materiality of Mediated Knowledge and Expression'. In *Media Technologies: Essays on Communication, Materiality, and Society*, edited by Tarleton Gillespie, Pablo J. Boczkowski and Kirsten A. Foot, 21–51. Cambridge, MA: MIT Press

Marx, K. 1989. *Das Kapital: Kritik der politischen Ökonomie*. Vol. 1. Berlin: Dietz. (English translation: Karl Marx. 2011. *Capital: A Critique of Political Economy*. Translated by Samuel Moore and Edward Aveling. Mineola, NY: Dover Publications)

Mayer-Schönberger, V. and K. Cukier. 2013. *Big Data: A Revolution That Will Transform How We Live, Work and Think*. London: Murray

McCarthy, J., M. Minsky, N. Rochester and C. Shannon. 2006. 'A Proposal for the Dartmouth Summer Research Project on Artificial Intelligence, August 31, 1955'. *AI Magazine* 27 (4), 12–14

Messina, C. 2007a. '(@chrismessina) Twitter'. 23 August 2007. <https://twitter.com/chrismessina/status/223115412> Accessed 22 January 2018

Messina, C. 2007b. 'Twitter Hashtags for Emergency Coordination and Disaster Relief'. 22 October 2007. Accessed 22 January 2018. <https://factoryjoe/2007/10/22/twitter-hastags-for-emergency-coordination-and-disaster relief/>

MIT Media Lab. n.d. *Project Gobo*. <https://www.media.mit.edu/projects/gobo/overview/>

Neue Zürcher Zeitung. 2016. '"Adblock-Plus"-Macher reichen Medienhäusern die Hand'. *Neue Zürcher Zeitung*, 14 September 2016

Nissenbaum, H. 2011. 'From Preemption to Circumvention: If Technology Regulates, Why Do We Need Regulation (and Vice Versa)?'. *Berkeley Technology Law Journal* 26, 1367–86

Norman, D. A. 1988. *The Psychology of Everyday Things*. New York, NY: Basic Books

OECD Publishing. 2017. 'OECD Digital Economy Outlook 2017'. <http://dx.doi.org/10.1787/9789264276284-en>

Pariser, E. 2011. *The Filter Bubble: What the Internet is Hiding from You*. New York, NY: Penguin Press

Pasquale, F. 2016. 'Platform Neutrality: Enhancing Freedom of Expression in Spheres of Private Power'. *Theoretical Inquiries in Law* 17, 487–513

Penney, J. W. 2016. 'Chilling Effects: Online Surveillance and Wikipedia Use'. *Berkeley Technology Law Journal* 31 (1), 118–82

Pfaffenberger, B. 1992. 'Technological Dramas'. *Science, Technology and Human Values* 17 (3), 282–312

Pinch, T. J. and W. E. Bijker. 1987. 'The Social Construction of Facts and Artifacts: Or How the Sociology of Science and the Sociology of Technology Might Benefit Each Other'. In *The Social Construction of Technological Systems*, edited by Wiebe E. Bijker, Thomas P. Hughes, and Trevor J. Pinch, 17–50. Cambridge, MA: MIT Press

Privacy Analytics. n.d. <https://privacy-analytics.com/software/>

Schauer, F. F. 1978. 'Fear, Risk and the First Amendment: Unraveling the Chilling Effect'. *Boston University Law Review* 58, 685–732

Sharon, T. and D. Zandbergen. 2016. 'From Data Fetishism to Quantifying

Selves: Self-Tracking Practices and the Other Values of Data'. *New Media and Society* 19 (11), 1695–709

Sunstein, C. R. 2017. *#Republic: Divided Democracy in the Age of Social Media.* Princeton, NJ: Princeton University Press

Susskind, R. 2017. *Tomorrow's Lawyers: An Introduction to Your Future.* 2nd edition. Oxford: Oxford University Press

Tages Anzeiger. 2017. '*Das ist immer noch ein Hype'*. 8 January 2017. <www.tagesanzeiger.ch/wissen/technik/das-ist-immer-noch-ein-hype/story/20650392>

Talbot, D. 2017. 'The Robots are Coming'. *Boston Magazine,* 12 November 2017. <www.bostonmagazine.com/news/2017/11/12/ai-research-boston/>

Teubner, G. 2012. *Constitutional Fragments: Societal Constitutionalism and Globalization.* Translated by Gareth Norbury. Oxford: Oxford University Press

Wales Online. 2018. 'Facial Recognition Wrongly Identified 2,000 People as Possible Criminals When Champions League Final Came to Cardiff'. *Wales Online*, 5 May 2018. <www.walesonline.co.uk/news/wales-news/facial-recognition-wrongly-identified-2000-14619145>

Weinberger, D. 2018. 'Don't Make AI Artificially Stupid in the Name of Transparency'. *Wired*, 28 January 2018. <www.wired.com/story/dont-make-ai-artificially-stupid-in-the-name-of-transparency/>

Winner, L. 1980. 'Do Artifacts Have Politics?'. *Daedalus* 109, 121–36

Zuboff, S. 2015. 'Big Other: Surveillance Capitalism and the Prospects of an Information Civilization'. *Journal of Information Technology* 30 (1), 75–89

Zuckerman, E. 2017. *Who Filters Your News? Why We Built gobo.social.* <https://medium.com/mit-media-lab/who-filters-your-news-why-we-built-gobo-social-bfa6748b5944>

12. Throttling machine learning
Paul Ohm

INTRODUCTION

As machines gain the capability to make important decisions about the lives of human beings, scholars and other commentators have highlighted the threats this development poses to important human values such as fairness, due process and equality. The great weight of this work has focused on characterizing the nature of the looming problem – ranging from theoretical ruminations on the essence of decision-making, to more applied inquiries into specific problems or risks that rise in particular contexts such as hiring, autonomous vehicles, medicine or criminal justice.

My immediate contribution to this debate shifts the focus from problems to possible solutions. I introduce a category of novel tools we might use to try to fend off some of the most significant disruptions caused by machine learning decision-making. Once we have concluded that a machine poses a potential threat to fairness, due process, equality or some other human value, what can we do about it?

One answer is to slow things down, to put measures in place that stand in the way of the development and adoption of machine learning systems that threaten important human values. Several scholars have proposed the use of friction or forced inefficiency as a bulwark for important human values. This chapter embraces these calls, and explores how we might measure, monitor and regulate these approaches.

I offer a category of tools I refer to as 'throttling metrics'. These are quantitative measurements of some aspect of a machine learning system. They serve as rules-of-thumb and as progress indicators during the construction and deployment of machine learning systems. They amount to a much more direct intervention than calls by others for increased transparency, accountability or interpretability.

I focus on two metrics. The first, described in Part II, is the ratio that compares the performance of an artificial intelligence system to the human decision-maker who today serves the same purpose. Too often we implicitly (or sometimes explicitly) set the target of this metric at the value of one, at simple equivalence. Any AI that performs 'as well as' a human is ready to be deployed. Instead, we would often be better off setting this metric at a higher value, requiring an artificial intelligence to be two or three or even 50 times better than a human before it should be deployed. The specific appropriate value for this metric will depend on a host of contextual factors. But we should shake our tendency to assume that this metric should equal one.

The second metric, discussed in Part III, measures the incompleteness of the data used to train a machine learning system. The rise of so-called 'big data' has spurred the recent rush of activity and attention being paid to decades-old machine learning algorithms. Thanks to massive data-collection technologies such as the internet and the smartphone, machine learning experts have been given access to more information about human behaviour than ever before. In this environment, anything that forces a researcher to analyze less than the maximum amount of available data, for example a privacy rule allowing an individual to opt-out of the research, has begun to be characterized as deviant or anti-science. I argue instead that we should sometimes consider the forced contraction of training datasets as a second metric, something we should protect and preserve rather than try to argue out of existence.

MACHINE LEARNING AND ITS DISCONTENTS

Before introducing and defending the metrics, let us review some of the concerns that have been raised about the rise of machine learning decision-making.

Concerns about Machine Learning

A large and rapidly growing body of literature from many different disciplines has raised concerns about the machine-learning models that can make important decisions involving human affairs. These concerns can be categorized generally as concerns about transparency, accuracy, bias, fairness and manipulation.

Many worry about the opacity of machine learning systems, which operates on many different levels and stems from many root causes (Pasquale 2015). Machine learning techniques are arcane, requiring expertise in both computer programming/science and statistics (Barocas and Selbst 2016). Machine learning systems are built not only from human-readable source code, but also from massive datasets that change over time. Designers of machine learning models often use legal restrictions such as trade secrecy law to deny access to the internals of the system (Wexler 2018).

Others worry simply that these models will fail to make accurate sense of the world. For a decision of classification (e.g. this person will re-offend, this person will not), models might generate false positives or false negatives (Angwin, Larson, Mattu and Kirchner 2016).

Many worry about biased machine learning outcomes (Barocas and Selbst 2016). These worries involve two connotations of the word bias, both a systematic tendency to be incorrect in a particular direction; or the more legalistic word meaning a tendency to treat particular groups of people with shared traits or circumstances worse than others. Particularly for the second type of concern, many worry that ceding authority to a machine will heighten or exacerbate pre-existing biases and divisions in society.

Both versions of bias connect to broader concerns about machines making decisions unfairly. What is meant exactly by the word unfair has proven to be quite complicated and even controversial. One scholar has catalogued at least 21 different meanings of the word in debates about machine learning (Narayanan 2018).

Finally, scholars are worried about the tendency to build 'intelligent' systems that manipulate human beings (Susser, Roessler and Nissenbaum 2018). Some have focused on this primarily in the commercial sphere, noting how online advertising models have preyed upon vulnerable populations (Calo 2014). Others worry about manipulation through a much broader lens, worrying about how complex machine intelligence is stripping us of our humanity or warping our society (Frischmann and Selinger 2018).

Proposed Solutions

In contrast to the varied approaches that have been given to characterizing the problems with machine learning and automated decision-making, far less attention has been given to solutions to fix some of these problems.

I am not limiting this chapter to legal solutions alone. The solutions I am interested in operate as well at the level of discourse and rhetoric as they do at the level of statutes and regulations. The question I am asking is, what can any person or institution do to address concerns about machine learning? The best way to attack these problems might be to impose social pressure on companies commercializing machine learning tools; influence what is taught to machine learning students; or enshrine a principle in a new law. This chapter will not focus on the differences of these three modes of reform. Instead, it will focus on solutions that might operate in all of these institutional modes. This is a discussion about what we ought to change, not how best to try to effect that change.

The problem with most of the work that has come before is that they seem to start from a position of resignation to the continued spread of machine learning decision-making. Rather than try to resist this march of innovation and progress – better to try to stop the tides – many have advocated for greater methods of transparency and accountability (Pasquale 2015). This work has suggested mandating government or public access to the source code or the training data used to develop a machine learning system.

More recently, this work has shifted from transparency to interpretability (Selbst and Barocas 2019). Recognizing how difficult it can be to impose meaningful transparency in such a complex system, this work has considered requiring a more limited explanation of what mattered to machine. This seems to contemplate a narrative or other explanation a human observer can access to try to make sense of why the machine has made the choice it has made.

Bolder commentators have proposed steps to at least slow the tide. Cathy O'Neil has argued that we are simply not prepared to use automated systems to determine which public school teachers to fire, at least not at the scale with which such systems are being deployed today (O'Neil 2016).

Semantic Discontinuity, Agonistic Machine Learning and Desirable Inefficiency

The idea of throttling metrics builds primarily on related work that fall under the labels semantic discontinuity and agonistic machine learning, which dovetails with work I have done on desirable inefficiency.

Julie Cohen introduced semantic discontinuity as 'gaps and inconsistencies within systems of meaning and to a resulting interstitial complexity that leaves room for the play of everyday practice' (Cohen 2012). Brett Frischmann and Evan Selinger apply semantic discontinuity to smart systems driven by machine learning and other forms of artificial intelligence. They call for 'gaps and seams between smart techno-social systems' and the intentional engineering of 'transaction costs and inefficiencies to support human flourishing' (Frischmann and Selinger 2018).

Agonistic machine learning comes from the work of Mireille Hildebrandt (2019). Spurred by the argument that human beings should not be reduced to 'computable' lives, agonistic machine learning 'demand[s] that companies or governments that base decisions on machine learning must explore and enable alternative ways of datafying and modeling the same event, person, or action' (Hildebrandt 2019, 106).

In other work, I have similarly considered the need to design intentional inefficiencies into complex technology. My work, with Jonathan Frankle, focuses on how designers themselves have begun to use inefficiency as a tool for introducing human values into design. The creators of the IEX stock exchange force all trades to take a round-trip through 38-miles of fibre optic cable, introducing just enough delay to thwart particular forms of 'unfair' high-frequency trading. The bitcoin blockchain protocol requires bitcoin miners to race to solve small cryptography puzzles as a way to enforce a policy of 'one CPU, one vote', supporting the conditions for consensus to emerge (Ohm and Frankle 2018). This style of systems design gives concrete form to the 'transaction costs and inefficiencies' called for by Frischmann and Selinger, which in turn try to operationalize Cohen's semantic discontinuity.

The metrics I offer in this chapter continue to extend the project. These metrics are quantitative measures we can use to impose desirable inefficiency, semantic discontinuity and agonistic machine learning on a broad swath of machine learning decision-making technology in order to preserve important human values.

MACHINE VERSUS HUMAN PERFORMANCE

How much better must a machine be at making decisions than a human before we replace the human with the software? This question plays a background but important role in every debate about the rise of machine learning decision-making, yet it is rarely given sufficient isolated attention.

Let's call this first throttling metric the *machine-to-human performance ratio* or MHPR. It compares how well a machine system performs at a given task, using some measurable metric, compared to the performance of an average human at the same task. A value of half signifies that the machine is only half as effective (according to that metric) as the human. A value of two means the machine is twice as effective as the human. The question is replacement: at what MHPR should we consider replacing a human decision-maker with a machine?

The Default Assumption: Equivalence

Artificial intelligence systems can already defeat the world's best humans at games like chess, Go and Jeopardy (Jennings 2016). Studies indicate that machine learning models already outperform humans at diagnosing cancers (Liu et al. 2017). With even more complex and abstract questions, such as predicting the outcome of Supreme Court cases (Guimerà and

Sales-Pardo 2011), or whether a pedestrian is hiding a weapon (Goel et al. 2017), computers might be better than trained human experts performing the same task.

In popular debate, there seems to be a persistent yet implicit assumption that the goal in the competition of human versus machine is mere equivalence. So long as humans continue to perform better than the insurgent machines, we still must rely on the people. But as soon as the machines are 'as good as' the people, we ought to begin a serious discussion about replacement.

Consider autonomous driving. In March 2018, a video was posted to social media that by now has been viewed hundreds of thousands of times (Levin 2018). It's a pair of videos spliced together, the first a dash cam video shot from an autonomous vehicle being tested by Uber, the second the view of the human 'safety driver' of the same vehicle, recorded at the same time. The contents of the video are disturbing, because they depict the final moments of a human life, the 49-year-old woman struck and killed by the Uber car while walking her bicycle across a two-lane road in Tempe, Arizona, on 18 March 2018.

Every time the video is posted to social media, it elicits in the accompanying comments an impromptu debate about whether robots are ready to take over from human drivers. Some commenters will insist that there is no way any human driver would have reacted quickly enough to avoid the collision. Others will respond with as much certitude that any human driver could have avoided the crash. Jurors in the former group will note the poor lighting conditions; those in the latter will count the six seconds from the time the first pixels comprising the cyclist come into view before the collision.

What nobody in these debates points out or calls into question is the fact that both sides implicitly assume that robot-human equivalence is the metric for analyzing the situation. All sides presume that the debate will be won or lost by determining whether a hypothetical human operator could have avoided the collision. As soon as robot drivers are 'as good as' human drivers, we should start taking humans away from behind the wheel.

Adding Context to Our Balancing is Not Enough

Experts are more nuanced about when machines will become capable of replacing humans, but many are likely to argue that the correct ratio of expertise will vary on the context. At least for those willing to embrace the utilitarian calculus, experts will engage in a balance between the costs and benefits of the machine intelligence, and use this weighing to decide when it might be justified to replace a human with a machine.

If the decision is one that can save lives or ease human suffering, we might be inclined toward deciding that mere equivalence is good enough. The use of machine learning in medicine is a prime example. As soon as the machine radiologist is better than its human counterpart at accurately diagnosing a cancer from an x-ray, we should begin replacing the human (Froomkin, Kerr and Pineau 2018).

In the opposite extreme, when the stakes seem exceedingly low, we might not care enough to demand more than equivalence. In many industrial contexts not directly implicating human safety, as soon as an artificial intelligence is as good as a human, there will be economic pressure toward replacement. We might not object if a corporation wants to replace warehouse workers with robots as soon as the robots were 'as reliable as' the humans (this is of course putting to the side important considerations about the disruption to the human workforce).

Like lay commenters, experts seem to assume that the neutral starting point for the analysis is that robots might replace humans as soon as they match human capability. Context considerations such as the prospect of saving human lives might drive this baseline down while considerations such as potential invidious bias might drive this baseline up, but these experts almost always start from equivalence.

The Argument for Equivalence

It makes sense that for most commentators, the baseline assumption is equivalence. After all, from a strictly utilitarian point of view, the notion of 'as good as' is fundamental: on the graph tracing the line of increasing machine performance, 'as good as' is the point of inflection at which the machine flips from being 'worse' to being 'better'. And 'better' means more efficient, or fewer lives lost, or cheaper, or fewer errors.

Fixating on equivalence seems to reflect a perfectly natural utilitarian response. If we were talking about selecting between two human workers, two college applicants or two athletes, after all, 'as good as' would loom large in our considerations.

The argument for equivalence is especially strong when we are talking about saving human lives or easing human suffering. If an autonomous car might be trained to have fewer accidents, we would feel a significant moral pull to begin pulling humans out of drivers' seats. Waiting for an MHPR of two or three (or higher) would be decreeing death sentences for the people who would otherwise not been involved in an accident.

These arguments are compelling and natural, but they should not so often prevail. We should recalibrate our expectations, setting MHPR at a larger value than one, at least as a baseline assumption. Let us turn to the reasons why.

The Arguments for an MHPR Greater than One

At the very least, we should be conscious of our tendency to assume the baseline of equivalence as the standard MHPR for replacing human decision-making. But in many contexts, we need more than awareness; we need to set the MHPR at a value higher than one. There are many reasons to support this recalibration of our expectations.

PICKING DIFFERENT WINNERS AND LOSERS

Even if a human and a robot perform a task with exactly the same accuracy rate, the errors they generate will not be identical. The two will generate different false positives and false negatives, meaning they will select different winners and losers. The errors differ as a result of the very different processes that machines and humans use for making decisions. There are many salient examples of the ahuman errors that machine learning systems make, from IBM's Watson selecting 'Toronto' as a final Jeopardy answer in the category 'U.S. Cities' (Castillo 2011), or the research that tricked a Google image recognition system to mis-identify a 3D-printed turtle as a rifle (LabSix 2017).

Because machine intelligence will always select different winners and losers, substituting a machine for a human will generate a distributional effect, leading to entirely different sets of people unjustly denied a benefit, wrongly suspected of a crime, or errantly subjected to a medical treatment. Every replacement of a human with a computer thus creates a redistribution of benefit and burden.

Such a redistribution might itself be illegal, if it shifts the burden to a racial minority or to women, for example (Kim 2017). Even if not illegal, it might represent poor policy, for example if it shifts a burden from wealthier to poorer people, exacerbating inequality.

But even putting aside clearly undesirable redistributions like these, the losers of machine decision-making have grounds to object to the way they've been treated. But-for the switch from a human to a machine, they will argue, they would have (or might have) been deemed a winner rather than a loser. Especially if the accuracy rate of the machine is the same as, or only marginally better, than the human who has been replaced, the shift to the machine has caused individual harm without a corresponding benefit to the accuracy of the system. We ought to treat concerns like these with respect, putting a thumb on the side of the scale opposing replacing human decision-makers.

THE ILLUSION OF OBJECTIVITY

Another reason to set the target MHPR greater than one is as an act of epistemological humility. Both the numerator and the denominator of the ratio calculation measures some objectively defined baseline. In criminal justice contexts, this might be the percent of arrestees predicted not to re-offend who go on to commit another crime (i.e. false negatives); in autonomous driving contexts, it might be the number of car accidents per mile of travel; and in medicine it might be the number of benign tumours misidentified as malignant (i.e. false positives).

Epistemological humility is required with measures like these for many reasons. First, we can only 'manage what we measure', meaning we focus on the easily quantified over what we truly care about. For example, many studies of poverty focus on measurements of wealth when this might be a proxy for values we care more about but do not know how to measure such as happiness or human flourishing.

This critique resonates once again with the work of Cohen and Hildebrandt, who both argue about the tendency to use data-driven analysis to justify building systems that intrude on our self-development. Hildebrandt, in particular, worries about our tendency to reduce human life events to data, confusing the representation (data about people) with what is represented (human lives) (Hildebrandt 2019).

Second, even if we can measure the value we care about, we might disagree fundamentally about which measure of accuracy matters most. For example, although we might agree that what ought to be measured in the pre-conviction recidivism context is the probability of the commission of another crime, there are many ways to use that measurement. I might care that African-American arrestees who are predicted to re-offend commit no other crime at a higher rate than white arrestees predicted to re-offend (in other words, comparing false positives). Instead, I might care that African-American arrestees are twice as likely to be mistakenly placed in the re-offend category than white arrestees (in other words, comparing false positives to the total population of arrestees) (Kleinberg et al. 2017, Chouldechova 2016, Corbett-Davies et al. 2017).

Mandating a metric, a thumb on the side of keeping a human-in-the-loop, preserves some humility about the objectivity of the decision-making enterprise. We should constantly be skeptical of the seeming mathematical clarity of a single, measurable quantity. Once we defer decision-making to a machine, it will become tempting to forget the limits of what we can measure and know and instead mistakenly to assume that the value we have selected is meaningful and correct.

MHPR AS A SAFETY FACTOR

Returning to our initial analogy, setting the MHPR target greater than one operates as a safety factor. A safety factor accounts for uncertainty and risk. Although engineers trust in the correctness of the calculations they have developed over time, they understand that there are always factors they cannot or have not accounted for. Perhaps the wind gusts in a particular span will interact with a particular building material in a way that has not been observed before. Safety factors account also for the unpredictable and less understood effects of time and aging on materials.

Safety factors might also be seen as a measure of the immaturity of a particular area of knowledge or science. The less a particular technique, approach or calculation has been tested, the larger the safety factor, to account for what is left unknown. A bridge built using a new material, or in a part of the world where this kind of construction is rare, might necessitate a relatively large safety factor, but when the tenth or one hundredth bridge is built of that material or in that part of the world, perhaps the safety factor can be reduced.

A PROGRESS BAR FOR DISRUPTION

Finally, a throttling metric gives humans a measurable indicator for a coming disruption. Consider it a progress bar for human-to-machine disruption. If the metric being measured is objectively defined, and if the calculations of progress are shared publicly, then outside observers will have an early warning about the looming removal of humans and the resulting disruptions to the workforce, legal system or the economy.

Where Should We Set the Metric?

It is probably quite enough to advocate that there ought to be a metric, but it would be a fool's errand to try to assign a specific value for the metric for general purposes, detached from specific inquiry. Everything is context in this complex age, most would conclude, so we should leave it to subject-matter experts in areas sliced finely to determine whether the correct metric in a context ought to be 2X, 3X, 10X or 100X.

Not disagreeing with any of this, I think it yet is useful to offer a specific value, as ill-suited as it is for one-size-fits-all use, for a few reasons. First, we already have a built-in bias for equivalence, for a value of one, so we might offer a new, higher value as a counterpoint. Of course, whatever baseline we set will need be adjusted – up or down – based on contextual factors in specific cases, but we have to start somewhere.

Second, the baseline value we are trying to replace is deeply embedded. The simplicity, intuitiveness and salience of the number 'one' puts down deep tendrils that we need to work hard at to uproot, so ending this section without an equally concrete counter-proposal would not do enough to advance the argument. Third, an essential premise of semantic discontinuity is that we ought to draw clear, bright lines delineating gaps without falling prey to the argument for scientific precision (Cohen 2012). Delaying the selection of a replacement for one to another day feeds the tendency to believe that we can draw precise and narrow gaps that weave and bend throughout competing interests. That approach leads to an intricate maze of tiny separations, not the bright gaps of semantic discontinuity.

Finally, the assumption of equivalence is itself built on underappreciated arbitrariness, the arbitrariness of the performance metric we've decided to use. If my proposed replacement is attacked as arbitrary, it at least invites the person making the argument to reflect on why we've concluded that one isn't also arbitrary.

Having liberated myself from a scientifically-defined proposal, let's turn (arbitrarily) to fiction. Douglas Adams' *The Hitchhiker's Guide to the Galaxy*, describes Deep Thought, a planet-sized computer with artificial intelligence, which takes 7.5 million years to calculate the answer to 'Life, the Universe, and Everything', which it solemnly announces to be '42'. The characters in the book (and countless, nerdy fans of the book over the decades) never learned the question to which 42 provides an answer (Adams 1979). I'm ready to do so now. The question Deep Thought was answering is: how much better must an artificial intelligence be before we allow it to replace the work of human beings? It's appropriate that a machine that possessed an intelligence so many times more powerful than a human thought that this was the question being asked.

To allow a tiny bit of context to seep into this exercise, I offer three different targets based on Deep Thought's calculation. Because a multiplier of 42 seems unacceptably high, let's use logarithms. For ordinary decision-making contexts, we ought to require performance from an AI that is at least $\log(42)$, or approximately 1.6, times better than the average human at the same task. For decisions that implicate sensitive human interests, the kind of interests that speak to freedom of thought or expression for example, we should require $\log(42^2)$ or 3.25 times better performance.

Facebook's algorithm for removing suspected pornography or Google's algorithm for removing copyrighted music from YouTube would fall into this category. Finally, for calculations that potentially involve life and death or human liberty, we should dispense with the logarithm and require 42 times better performance. Any algorithm used for prison sentencing or the capability of an autonomous car should fall into this category.

Once again, rail all you want at the seeming arbitrariness of 42. But as you do so, reflect on why it is significantly more arbitrary than the equivalence it is meant to displace.

THE VIRTUE OF LESS DATA

The second throttling metric measures the amount of data used to train a machine learning system. Let's call it the *completeness quotient* or CQ of a dataset. It compares the amount of data in the dataset to the unattainable 'full' dataset in the entire population being measured. So a value of 0.9 would mean that the dataset contains 90 per cent of the information available in the entire population of possible data.

The CQ might measure completeness along several different dimensions. For a given, set number of data fields (columns) in a dataset, the CQ might measure the number of data records (rows) in the dataset versus the size of the total population. That is the definition we primarily have in mind. But the CQ might also represent the number of columns in the dataset versus the number of other data fields knowable about these data records. Or it might measure the full quantity of information (columns times rows) versus the full population of information available.

In all except the most trivial of contexts, the goal of a complete dataset is an unattainable target. The limitations of data gathering tools and the variability and subjectivity of human lives ensure that not even the most diligent and careful researcher could ever hope to approach completeness. Yet part of the allure of big data is the potential it provides to nudge us closer to the complete. Social scientists salivate at the prospect of massive databases full of indicators of human psychology and behaviour available for analysis at scale. The march toward completeness drives down statistical uncertainty and improves the power of the correlations that are discovered.

Tantalized by the drive toward completeness, people attack barriers to data collection or distribution as perverse and unnatural, characterizing them as constraints that stand in the way of knowledge creation and science.

For example, the idea that individuals should be allowed, under data protection or privacy law, to choose to 'opt out' their personal information from a dataset useful for research strikes some as antithetical to science and to knowledge. An opt-out is seen as a hostility to the development of knowledge and the beneficial policies that flow from knowledge.

The rhetoric these critics of opt-out solutions deploy mislead. They suggest that now that we live in a world where massive datasets of evidence of human behaviour are within grasp, the alternative of small sample data is nothing but garbage science.

The conventional approach to respond to arguments like these is to highlight the dignity and autonomy interests of the person requesting the opt-out. I take a different approach: the reduction of scientific certainty that results from being forced to evaluate an incomplete dataset is another metric we should sometimes fight to preserve.

Most importantly, datasets shrunken by those opting out can still be the basis for robust and verifiable science. To classify statistics based on small data as garbage science is intentionally to obfuscate the state of scientific knowledge. Statistics derived from small or sample data can still be useful. From the birth of their field, statisticians have dealt with samples, and they have developed numerous strategies and methods for producing statistics with validity even if they are infected by bias and uncertainty.

Of course, the gold standard for this kind of work requires a random sampling. Any other mechanism for culling a sample from a population is fraught with selection bias. Back to privacy law, the cohort of a population who choose to opt-out are of course not randomly selected. They share at least one trait – the willingness to bear the cost and overcome the barriers to opting out – that doubtless correlate with many other traits that will skew the results, and not in easily predictable ways. A dataset assembled by researchers who choose to respect opt-out choices will probably lead to less scientific certainty than one built by researchers who ignore opt-out choices, which might lead to worse risk analysis, worse efficient allocation of resources, more uncertainty and worse policy.

But 'worse' isn't 'useless'. We should use the techniques that have been developed to address systemic biases in statistical methods to both account for and correct for the statistical uncertainty, risk, inefficiency, and reduced utility of analyzing data rendered incomplete by an opt-out.

In addition, just as the MHPR allows us to deal with epistemic humility, so too does forcing researchers to live with a CQ much smaller than one. In reality, of course, all datasets are incomplete. Data collection is messy, complex and fraught with error. It is important to remember that we are never talking about a difference between 'all the data' and 'some of the data', but instead we are focused on relative quantities of incompleteness (Hildebrandt 2019). A researcher who thinks that she has 'all the data' might never confront the reality that her dataset is always missing something important, but the researcher forced to live with a lower CQ cannot avoid confronting that fact.

The uncertainty imposed by a low CQ gives breathing room for thinking about other approaches. We tend to allow the clarity of a single number or elegant model to swamp other approaches to analyzing a question. We can offset this tendency to glorify the quantitative by giving us reason to doubt the number or model. This will spur us to study the question in other ways, putting pressure on interdisciplinarity and methodological diversity.

There are other salutary reasons to preserve (or at least not fret about) low CQ datasets. The data scientist who finds holes in the data because of opt-out has a strong incentive to try to find the people in the data to ask them to reverse their opt-out choice. Data scientists can try to explain the compelling benefits of the research more clearly to the reluctant hold-outs. They can promise to limit unwelcome data reuse or repurpose by contract as consideration for participation. Most importantly, they are forced to think of the rows in their data as real, breathing human beings who deserve to be consulted about the work, rather than impersonal fields of data to be crunched.

A low CQ also protects semantic discontinuity. The uncertainty inherent in the statistics generated give space for individuals and institutions to move freely within the world engineered by the statistics.

Finally, a low CQ addresses the problem of data reuse. Today, massive databases that are closer to 'complete' because data subjects are not given the ability to opt-out can be reused for purposes beyond the reason the information was gathered. This results in analysis creep. In contrast, the statistical uncertainty imposed by an incomplete dataset will only be compounded when combined with other datasets that are incomplete in different ways. The power of statistical analysis will decrease with each new recombination.

A small dataset is thus subject to a lovely property of decay with time. It instantiates the fair information practice of use limitation inside its columns and rows. Two datasets individually might pose a particular threat to privacy or liberty or autonomy, but combined, the threat is worse. By forcing each dataset to have a low CQ, we face the threat of combination with this new principle of data decay. Rather than becoming more powerful and controlling over time, data instead becomes more enfeebled and begins to wither over time.

CONCLUSION

What the two throttling metrics, MHPR and CQ, have in common is a recognition of the intrinsic one-way nature of human innovation. Our species builds better tools and then replaces them with even better tools. Progress moves only in one direction, and you cannot turn back once a choice has been made. Given this ancient dynamic, and given what is at stake if we embrace machine learning decision-making before we have worked out all of the implications for humanity, the two metrics I have proposed will act like a brake, slowing down our inexorable march, to give us time to understand what we are doing.

Setting the threshold for decision-making accuracy before human replacement at higher than one doesn't halt progress for eternity; it simply slows things down enough for us better to test the effects of the replacement and to prepare for the negative impacts. Allowing for datasets that are full of small holes introduces the salutary notion of decay into our systems, and forces researchers to replenish and refresh the data they analyze.

If we are to tame the power of machine learning, to bend the rate of its development curve to something that is more consistent with the rule of law, we need to think beyond accountability, transparency and explainability (*The End(s)*). This chapter has offered two proposals for doing so, two throttling metrics, and doubtless there are others. This offers a template for a new, more aggressive, more meaningful form of prescription for offsetting the disruptive rise of machine decision-making. I hope it will inspire others to suggest other proposals along these same lines.

REFERENCES

Adams, D. 1979. *The Hitchhiker's Guide to the Galaxy.* London: Pan Books
Angwin, J., J. Larson, S. Mattu and L. Kirchner. 2016. 'Machine Bias'. *ProPublica*, May 23, 2016, <www.propublica.org/article/machine-bias-risk-assessments-in-criminal-sentencing>
Barocas, S. and A. Selbst. 2016. 'Big Data's Disparate Impact'. *California Law Review* 104, 671–732
Calo, R. 2014. 'Digital Market Manipulation'. *George Washington Law Review* 82, 995
Castillo, M. 2011. 'Why did Watson Think Toronto is a U.S. City on "Jeopardy!"?' *Time*, Feb. 16, 2011, <http://techland.time.com/2011/02/16/why-did-watson-think-toronto-is-a-u-s-city-on-jeopardy/>
Chouldechova, A. 2016. 'Fair Prediction with Disparate Impact: A Study of Bias in Recidivism Prediction Instruments'. *FATML* 2016, <https://arxiv.org/abs/1610.07524>
Cohen, J. 2012. *Configuring the Networked Self: Law, Code, and the Play of Everyday Practice.* New Haven, CT: Yale University Press
Corbett-Davies, S. et al. 2017. 'Algorithmic Decision Making and the Cost of Fairness'. *KDD'17*, <https://arxiv.org/abs/1701.08230>
Frischmann, B. and E. Selinger. 2018. *Re-Engineering Humanity.* Cambridge: Cambridge University Press

Froomkin, A. M., I. Kerr and J. Pineau. 2018. 'When AIs Outperform Doctors'. working paper (We Robot 2018 Conference Draft) (on file with author)

Goel, S. et al. 2017. 'Combatting Police Discrimination in the Age of Big Data'. *New Criminal Law Review* 20, 181–232

Guimerà, R. and M. Sales-Pardo. 2011. 'Justice Blocks and Predictability of U.S. Supreme Court Votes'. *PLoS ONE* 6(11), e27188. <https://doi.org/10.1371/journal.pone.0027188>

Hildebrandt, M. 2019. 'Privacy as Protection of the Incomputable Self: From Agnostic to Agonistic Machine Learning'. *Theoretical Inquiries in Law* 20(1), 83–120

Hildebrandt, M. 2015. *Smart Technologies and the End(s) of Law: Novel Entanglements of Law and Technology.* Cheltenham, Edward Elgar Publishing

Jennings, K., 'The Go Champion, the Grandmaster, and Me'. *Slate*, 15 March 2016, <www.slate.com/articles/technology/technology/2016/03/google_s_alphago_defeated_go_champion_lee_sedol_ken_jennings_explains_what.html>

Kim, P. 2017. 'Data-Driven Discrimination at Work'. *William and Mary Law Review* 48, 857–936

Kleinberg, J. et al. 2017. 'Inherent Trade-Offs in the Fair Determination of Risk Scores'. *Proceedings of Innovations in Theoretical Computer Science*, <https://arxiv.org/abs/1609.05807>

LabSix, 2017. 'Fooling Neural Networks in the Physical World with 3D Adversarial Objects', 31 Oct. 2017, <www.labsix.org/physical-objects-that-fool-neural-nets/>

Levin, S. 2018. 'Video Released of Uber Self-Driving Crash that Killed Woman in Arizona'. *The Guardian*, 21 March 2018, <www.theguardian.com/technology/2018/mar/22/video-released-of-uber-self-driving-crash-that-killed-woman-in-arizona>

Liu, Y., K. Gadepalli, M. Norouzi, G. E. Dahl, T. Kohlberger, A. Boyko, S. Venugopalan, et al. 2017. 'Detecting Cancer Metastases on Gigapixel Pathology Images'. ArXiv:1703.02442 [Cs], March. <http://arxiv.org/abs/1703.02442>

Narayanan, A. 2018. '21 Fairness Definitions and their Politics'. Posted 1 March 2018. <www.youtube.com/watch?v=jIXIuYdnyyk>

O'Neil, C. 2016. *Weapons of Math Destruction.* New York, NY: Crown

Ohm, P. and J. Frankle 2018. 'Desirable Inefficiency'. *Florida Law Review* 70, 777–838

Pasquale, F. 2015. *The Black Box Society.* Cambridge, MA: Harvard University Press

Selbst, A. and S. Barocas. 2019. 'The Intuitive Appeal of Explainable Machines'. *Fordham Law Review* available at <https://papers.ssrn.com/sol3/papers.cfm?abstract_id=3126971>

Susser, D., B. Roessler and H. Nissenbaum. 2018. 'Online Manipulation: Hidden Influences in a Digital World' <http://dx.doi.org/10.2139/ssrn.3306006>

Wexler, R. 2018. 'Life, Liberty, and Trade Secrets: Intellectual Property in the Criminal Justice System'. *Stanford Law Review* 70, 1343–430

13. In the hall of masks: Contrasting modes of personification*
Niels van Dijk

INTRODUCTION: A NEW ENTRY

There is talk of a possible new person in town, a new actor on stage. The press is buzzing, eager as always to get first sensational coverage. The critics are scandalized, by such a provocative introduction (Open letter 2018, Bryson et al. 2017, Teubner 2018). Of course, some visionaries can claim that they had long foreseen that this would happen (Solum 1992).[1] And business is already assessing the risks and the opportunities this event could bring along. What is all this fuss about? . . . We are here speaking about the *electronic person*. The notion has been proposed by the European Parliament (EP) in a legislative recommendation. It is a 'specific legal status' to be granted to robots. This would create the possibility to attribute liability directly to the robot for damages caused by its 'autonomous decisions', instead of attributing these to the robot's producers or owners. The Parliament's initiative does not come in isolation. In October 2017 Saudi Arabia became the first country in the world to grant citizenship to a robot called 'Sophia'.[2] Although it is unclear what the consequences will be, this event by itself put robotic persons firmly in the public spotlight.

The proposal of personhood for robots moves this idea from science fiction to potential legislative reality. The development of robots has historically been closely tied up with mythological and science fiction visions on building autonomous machines. Predominantly these visions served as a mirror for humans to understand themselves through artificial recreation, but recently they are increasingly directed towards the enhancement of humans and the societies we live in. These imaginaries have also taken hold of the Parliament's proposal, testified in its remarkable opening full of references to science fiction and the potential of artificial intelligence to address societal challenges.[3] Key developments that spurred electronic personhood are the promises of smart, data-driven techniques in the fields of machine learning and data mining. According to the EP, these have resulted in robots acquiring 'the ability to learn from experience and take independent decisions' (EP 2017, 6). Robots are expected to exhibit increasingly autonomous reasoning and behaviour free from human control and will thus become less and less predictable. This has led to the attribution of 'reasoning' and 'perception' capabilities to robots, which makes them 'similar to agents that interact with their environment and are able to alter it' (ibid).[4] The more autonomous robots will become, the less they can be considered as mere tools in the hand of humans, and the more they obtain *active digital agency*. In this context, issues of responsibility and liability for behaviour and possible damages resulting from the behaviour would become pertinent.

'Personhood' is an elusive concept. It is at once very familiar as a frequent ingredient of everyday speech, but at the same time ephemeral when one is prompted to explain what it means. The Parliament's proposal provides an occasion to reflect upon this notion. The purpose is not to start a philosophical discussion about the *singular nature* of personhood, or, strongly related, about the concept of *natural persons*.[5] Instead, we will be dealing with the concept of persons as a *multiplicity of doubles* for human individuals or for other entities. These doubles are deployed according to a variety of modalities, such as art, law, politics, statistical science and machine learning, mainly as distinct ways to *represent* subjects. We will thus encounter: 1) dramatic persons, 2) legal persons, 3) public persons, 4) average persons, 5) profile persons and 6) (active and passive) digital persons. This will turn this text into a gallery of portraits, an exhibition of masks, or a kind of 'Hall of Faces' as presented in the popular HBO television series *Game of Thrones*. This Hall is hung with many kinds of faces ready to be worn as masks for assuming different characters and to which new entries are sometimes added.[6]

The exposition in this chapter will be chronological, showing how a certain mode of personification has historically developed out of, or in reaction to its predecessor. A profile of personhood will be drawn up for each of the types of persons mentioned, to explore the diverse ways in which this concept has both been given conceptual meaning, but also visual sense. This set-up is not primarily meant for a recognition of patterns of similarity, but rather to see what makes them drift apart. The juxtaposition of profiles allows us to put them in contrast, to get insights into how their representative attributes and functions are differentiated.

This can in turn be used for better situating the new entry of the electronic person within the hall of other masks. We could briefly state upfront that the electronic person is a legal mask (*juristic person*) for an *active digital person* that is physically embodied (robot), and whose smartness in dealing with its social environment is based on machine learning techniques that render both digital group portraits (*profile persons*) and digital individual portraits (*passive digital persons*) of humans. To this we can add that this legal status is proposed by the European legislator (*public person*),[7] these active digital persons currently still have their main existence as protagonist actors in the narratives of science fiction (*dramatic persons*), and these machine learning techniques evolved from populational statistics rendering *average persons*.

PERSONA: A MASK ON STAGE

> [W]hat can be so unreal as poetry, the theatre or stage-plays? And yet, in that sort of things, I myself have often been a spectator when the actor-man's eyes seemed to me to be blazing behind his mask, as he spoke those solemn lines.
> (Cicero 1967, XLVI)

The etymology of the term 'person' goes back to the Latin term *persona* and has roots in theatre roots. It meant a mask such as the wooden or clay ones that actors used to wear in Roman theatrical plays (Figure 13.1) and which visually indicated which roles they were taking on, together with the rest of their costume or 'disguise'. It is related to the term *per-sonare*, which means 'to sound through' where the mask becomes something that is spoken through and which allows one individual (the masked actor) to *impersonate* another individual, to play their role or *character* and to speak and act in their name. This theatrical technique makes it possible to detach

Figure 13.1 Roman Masks, Comic and Tragic. Author of Image unknown, taken from: Parton 1877

the human subject from the person.⁸ It also has a strong visual component in that the mask allows this individual to be seen as another person. It shares this visual connotation with the term representation (*representaere*) that is crucially related to that of the *persona*. Representation in its most literal meaning, refers to making something or someone present again, either through images and objects, and later through other persons.

This theatrical mechanism was available as a cultural resource and could be mobilized metaphorically for understanding other phenomena. This especially happened in the writings of Cicero who uses the notion of persona to understand the idea of representation both in a legal and a political context. He uses it in this first sense when the lawyer speaks for a client in a trial in court, bearing his person as an actor (Cicero 1967, XLVI–XLVII). Cicero also uses it in a political sense, when a magistrate acts or speaks in the name of the city or public community. In this sense it is the duty of a magistrate 'to bear the person of the city' (*personam civitatis*) by upholding its dignity, keeping the laws, and dispensing rights (Cicero 1928, XXXIV). In this case the magistrate acts for the people and hereby stands in their place. We will hereafter turn to these two senses.

JURISTIC PERSONS: FICTIONS WITH EFFECTS

> The subterfuge of personification traditionally served . . . to institute a point of imputation for rights and obligations . . . The subject is double: he is himself more the function that the law assigns him, and it is precisely to the extent that a subject is invested with this function that he is called 'person'.
> (Thomas 1998, 98)

> [A] person is defined as the holder of rights and obligations, whereby as a holder not only a human being can function, but also . . . other entities.
> (Kelsen 2002, 171–2)

The concept of the juristic person shares in the theatrical meaning as a legal mask, which allows an individual to become an actor in the legal world (in the sense of being capable of acting and being acted upon). It sets up a double for an individual subject, distinguishing the human being of flesh and blood from the juristic person. These two levels need to be kept apart. Many confusions about the concept have arisen because of the tendency to take this juristic person in a symbolic sense and turn it into a being with certain essential physical or biological attributes, like possessing a will, a consciousness, or even life. As Smith argued, 'a more difficult task than to define the concept [of the legal person] itself is to explain this persistent tendency to make it mysterious' (Smith 1928, 284).⁹ This is the

Figure 13.2   Erbore African Man. Image by YellowMonster, adapted by Victor Bornia

result of reading qualities of human beings into the legal person. Against this it has been argued that in law, 'personification', the act of qualifying someone or something as a person, is often used for the exact opposite purpose: *denaturalization*. It is used to abstract from the concrete physical or biological details of the concrete individual, or even to introduce presumptions against what is taken as the natural order, to obtain certain desired results.[10]

In Medieval times, jurists called these constructions 'chimera', because they could also allow entities into being that were not considered to exist in nature: such as corporations, cities and states. Such entities have a fictive mode of existence in law. We should be clear here in what we mean by this. The juristic person, it has often been noted, is a legal artifact (Dewey 1925–6, Smith 1928, Kelsen 2002, Thomas 1998, Despret and Gutwirth 2009). It institutes a 'point of imputation' for legal relations, a foothold within the legal system for attributing certain rights and obligations to someone (Thomas 1998, 93–4). This pointillist mask, not unlike African or Balinese variants (Figure 13.2), hereby allows an entity to become actor in the ritual of legal processes and to perform legal actions.[11] Fiction here however operates in a different register from the theatrical universe, where a successful play manages to shift us out from the theatre setting and transpose us into the narrative world acted out on stage, and to take this world of disguises for real for the duration of the play (suspension of disbelief). Legal fictions, to the contrary, are constructions always intended to shift attention back to the real world. There they become reattached and reassigned to the acts of the individuals who are represented in the legal narrative (in theatrical terms this would be akin to a structural break down of the 'fourth wall' separating actors and audience). This reattachment always entails concrete consequences, such as being attributed rights or obligations.[12] A masked performance with performative effects.

This is a first indication that the legal persona is more complex than the dramaturgic metaphor suggests. There is however more added complexity to this notion, since in law the relation between the human individual and the legal mask runs more out of sync. This pertains both to the numerical relation between persona and the individuals that bear it (the mutual *divisibility* of personhood) and to the kind of entities that can be attributed personhood (the *subject* behind the persona). First, in law the relation between individual and person is divisible. The same individual can assume two or more personae, whereas two or more different individuals can assume one single persona.[13] This is due to the concept of legal person as a point of imputation for legal rights and obligations, which makes the persona concept dependent on these types of legal relations in which the entity becomes implied. These legal relations are not all the same kind and can vary in intensity. Second, although human beings are the prototypical bearers of juristic persona, this is not a necessity. There are many present and historical examples of differences between the kinds of rights and obligations pertaining to human beings. Some humans only enjoy(ed) limited sets of these like non-citizens, children, criminals, or in past times, slaves, ethnic minorities and women. Moreover, there are non-human entities that have be granted juristic personhood, ranging from objects,[14] plants and animals,[15] or even (parts of) entire ecosystems.[16] In past times or in other countries these can also include Gods or spirits. The proposal of electronic personhood for robots also fits in this line, primarily as a new type of legal mask for a novel non-human entity.

Since such non-human entities cannot by themselves engage in legal acts (e.g. signing a contract) or claim their rights in a court of law, the constructions of juristic persons become practically enabled by the mechanism of representation. Representation makes this non-human entity – the represented abstract person – capable of acting through somebody else – the representative (such as a lawyer or another type of agent) who is authorized to act in its name. This is also the case with what is the most emblematic case of juristic persons, namely that of legal personhood for corporations. Here the law recognizes a form of limited personhood for corporations as an association of humans. This concept allows a group of people to act and be treated as a single entity, which can be attributed certain rights, protections, privileges, responsibilities and liabilities. It thus gives a composite of different people one face in law.[17]

PUBLIC PERSONS: UNIFYING A MULTITUDE

> A multitude of men, are made one person, when they are by one man, or one person, represented; so that it be done with the consent of every one of that multitude in particular. (Hobbes 1998, 109)

In the Middle Ages, lawyers started to first use the word representation for the personification of collective life. In contrast to canonical literature at the time, in which representation was taken as a mystical union or symbolical embodiment of Christ or the Christian community, the jurists took this persona in a fictive sense. A collective of human beings is here not a juxtaposition of concrete individuals but is itself taken as an autonomous entity. This is not a real ontological one, but a person that exists only through representation (*persona non verà sed repraesentata*) (Pitkin 1967). Through this fiction of representation these people can come to be seen as a person. This visual aspect was more than a metaphor. As we remarked before, it was an important aspect in the concepts of 'representation' and of the 'person' (Gamboni 2005).

These concepts eventually also became applied to public life and public communities by political writers, especially in the seventeenth century in England. Arguably one of the most known instances is in the work of Thomas Hobbes through his person-based model for the state. His Leviathan is one of the first theories of the state and of political representation, and the concept of the person plays a crucial role (Pitkin 1967).[18] According to his argument, humans in their natural condition live together as enemies with continuous fights amongst them. They manage to pull themselves out of this state of war by mutually *consenting* through the mechanism of a social contract to erect the common power of the sovereign. Before this contract, the social body is thus 'dissociate', consisting out of a 'disunited multitude' of people, who 'are not one person' (Hobbes 1998, XVIII). The public thus does not pre-exist as a coherent community. It is only through the mechanism of the social contract that this multitude of people is *unified* into one public person: that of the State (or *civitas*). The one that bears this public person is the sovereign. Hobbes builds this aspect of his theory on models of personhood and representation that we have discussed before (going back to Cicero's theatrical discussion of the mask). He defines a person as 'he, whose words or actions are considered, either as his own, or as representing the words or actions of another man, or of any other thing to whom they are attributed, whether truly or by fiction' (Hobbes 1998, XVI). To this more theatrical sense, he adds a legally inspired model of authorization by which one person or group of persons (the authors) give another person (the actor) the right of performing

In the hall of masks 237

Figure 13.3   Frontispiece to Leviathan, taken from Hobbes (1998)

an action in their name, thus acting by authority and becoming their representer.

This personification of the state is also clearly represented in the famous frontispiece to Hobbes' Leviathan (Figure 13.3). This image is what is called a *composite picture*, in the tradition of Arcimboldo. We can see a multitude of single individuals that become unified in the torso and arms of the main character, who carries the sword and crown of ultimate power. This composite image thus literally depicts the unification of the composite body politic in a single sovereign person.[19] This artistic genre has remained a popular mode of visual representation, first in court art and later in caricature, throughout modern political history, all the way up to present-day software mosaics of political figures created out of assembled individual photographs.[20]

AVERAGE PERSONS: STATISTICAL REALITIES

> One may ask if there exists, in a people, un homme type, a man who represents this people by height, and in relation to which all the other men of the same nation must be considered as offering a deviation that are more or less large. (Quetelet 1844, cited in Hacking 1990, 105)

From the eighteenth century onwards, there is an evolution from a governmental regime focused on the legally influenced kind of sovereignty that Hobbes emphasized, to a regime focused on governmental techniques around the notion of the *population*. Through the rise of the science of statistics in the service of State administration, the population started to appear as 'a new subject', with its own regularities and problems (Foucault 1994). This new type of statistical expertise could be mobilized for a new mode of governing populations.

The application of statistics to the behaviour of citizens eventually spurned a quest for the *social laws* that govern people, just as physical laws govern natural phenomena. An important name in this development is Quetelet (1842), who observed that large quantities of data about human attributes (such as height, weight and strength) had a certain pattern in distribution that allowed one to calculate the *mean* and thus the deviation from this mean. The statistical techniques he used were developed to measure phenomena like coin tosses or stars, where such distributions of instances and the mean were thought to have objective features. In applying these techniques to biological and social phenomena, he turned populational means into real qualities as well. We should see his introduction of the term *'average man'*, say someone who has married 0.73 times and has 1.8 children, in this light (ibid). He conceived of these, obviously not as the quality of a real person, but as the *real quality* of a certain population (Hacking 1990, ch. 13).

This development was strengthened by the work of Galton on physical characteristics of humans. Quetelet still resorted to probabilistic realities to repair for our ignorance of all the small causes behind these phenomena. Galton turned these normal distributions of human traits into an autonomous statistical law that no longer needed to resort to these underlying causes. Furthermore, he observed that many of the human traits that were statistically described before were not independent of each other but were in fact mutually hereditary related: they were correlated. Galton turned these correlations into the same kind of populational realities as Quetelet had done for averages.[21]

Galton's work was closely linked to his anthropometric studies in measuring physical human traits in many individuals. An important goal was to find the physiognomy of a certain race, by identifying certain (character) *types of humans* from their outer appearance. Galton reacted against the dominant physiognomic method of making images of individuals that are judged representative of a prevalent type. Instead, he invented the new technique of *composite photography* (Figure 13.4), consisting in superimposing several images of different people through successive exposures on the same sensitive photographic plate. In this

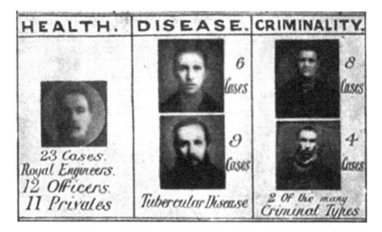

Figure 13.4   Specimens of Composite Portraiture [fragment], taken from Galton 1907

way, one could generate one single composite image by combining the portraits of many individuals.[22] When these images were taken from a certain 'class' or community of people (based on attributes like race, occupation, criminal record, illness or family statuses), they could thus form a certain 'type' of person for that class, such as the 'criminal type', a sick type and a healthy type. These pictures were meant to show the physical and mental traits common to that type. In this way, Galton thus constructed a visual instantiation of average persons as the statistical realities of certain populational classes, instead of having to choose a representative image. This "pictorial statistics" also constitutes a distinct way of constructing a composite person.

The goal of this exercise was not only to obtain knowledge, but also to control and improve populations.[23] The face and qualities of the healthy type, constructed out of the pictures of army officers and privates, could for instance be taken as a 'central type' in relation to which others were deviations and thus 'probably gives a clue to the direction in which the stock of the English race might most easily be improved' (Galton 1907, 10). The criminal type on the other hand might show a certain hereditary direction in which a population might be deteriorating from this central type and which needed to be restrained. This formed the basis for eugenic *policies* for populational control and improvement.

PROFILE PERSONS: MACHINE-GENERATED 'GROUP' PORTRAITS

> In the case of group profiling . . . the data subject may be the result of profiling, not necessarily pre-existing as a group. (Hildebrandt and Gutwirth 2008, 19)

The second half of the twentieth century saw the rise of the fields of artificial intelligence, machine learning and data mining. Especially machine learning and data mining share much of their methodology with statistics, but also exhibit some notable differences. They are sometimes considered more of an art than a science (Von Luxburg et al. 2012). The goal is not to test hypotheses against data, but rather to let the algorithm create the appropriate profile or hypothesis that provides the most reliable predictions given a certain data set. In this sense, these practices have a rather constructive and pragmatic ring to them (De Vries 2006).[24]

When machine learning or profiling processes are applied to people, we can describe the result – the profile – as a correlation between data that can be used to represent or identify a human subject as a member of a classifying group or category. Profiling techniques generate *correlations* between data, which constitute a certain category (such as 'all people with attributes, x, y, z'). This is called a group profile, which can be of an existing group of people who form a *community*, or of a non-existent *virtual grouping* of people (Hildebrandt and Gutwirth 2008, 18). Such correlations can be used for identifying someone, or for assessing the risks or opportunities someone poses. In this sense, they render a 'knowledge that is defined by its effects', which can subsequently be acted upon in a decision-making process (e.g. offering or withholding a service) (ibid). Moreover, these profiling techniques are also crucial in enabling smart digital agents or robots to interact with their human environments, a capability put centre stage in the discussion about electronic personhood.

One of the distinguishing aspects about machine learning and data mining is that computer programs can learn from experience without explicit programming, but rather by only receiving an indirect set of instructions on how to recognize similarity. This is called 'unsupervised learning', where the desired outcome is not known in advance. The algorithm is unleashed on unlabelled data sets and goes in search of patterns between these data, based on what it takes as similar. It goes through the data sets in several iterations until it reaches a certain optimum. In this way it arrives at certain data 'clusters' that each have their own mean or 'centroid' within the data that it groups together (De Vries 2006, 390–2).

In the hall of masks 241

Figure 13.5   The optimal stimulus according to numerical constraint optimization. Machine-generated image, taken from Le et al. (2012)

One field of application is in image recognition, where an algorithm clusters together the images in which it detects similarities. Researchers from Google have built a neural network algorithm that can detect certain shapes using a set of images that have not been labelled for their content (Le et al. 2012). These algorithms could successfully detect visual patterns for human faces. Interesting are the visualization techniques for verifying the results. One of these seems to provide the *mean* of this data cluster, showing the pattern of the average human face the algorithm has learnt (Figure 13.5). This ghostly facial archetype shows a remarkable resemblance to the *composite portraits* encountered in the work of Galton.

A further step is taken in recent experiments with 'generative adversarial networks' (GANs), applied to facial generation. GANs are also neural network algorithms consisting of two competing networks. The first is a generator that creates a set of target candidates such as images, based on a training set. The second is a discriminator that evaluates these candidates. Here the goal is not to 'discover' a 'human face' pattern in a data set, but to generate new human faces.[25] Based on a training set with images of real celebrities, researchers have used these GANs to create photos of non-existent celebrities, which the discriminator could no longer validate as fake after many iterations (Figure 13.6) (Karras et al. 2018). This constitutes an interesting variation of Galton's composite portraiture of *human types*, in this case the healthy ideal type. Here the photos are however not blurred ghostly average persons, but ones that look like real individuals. It holds a curious middle between a digital portrait of an individual and of a group and constitutes an interesting visualization of the relation between the two within profiling processes.

Figure 13.6 Progressive Growing of GANs for Improved Quality, Stability, and Variation. Machine-generated image, taken from Karras et al. (2018)

DIGITAL PERSONS: DIVIDUAL DATA PORTRAITS AND SMART AGENTS

> [I]t is ever more possible to create an electronic collage that covers much of a person's life – a life captured in records, a digital person composed in the collective computer networks of the world. (Solove 2004, 1)

Profiles can constitute one kind of digital representation of an individual (as member of a correlated group). Together with other data sources about that individual these can constitute what has been called someone's 'digital persona'. These other sources include not just data actively created by the subject him or herself (service data and disclosed data), but also information about a subject provided by others (incidental data), data tracked by a site on the subject's online habits and behaviour (behavioural data), and, as we just mentioned, data algorithmically inferred from these former data sources through profiling (derived data).[26]

The term digital persona was coined by Clarke (1996) who emphasized that this model is 'intended for use as a *proxy* for the individual'. This highlights the operational aspects of digital personae. They are a model of an individual that is used for a certain purpose in a specific context (often *service provision*). There, the person function as a digital 'mask', which allows the individual to act and be acted upon in the digital world. These

In the hall of masks 243

data making up the digital person can be pervasive and cover large parts of our lives, but also have limitations in the way they capture us (Solove 2004, 49).[27]

The digital person has strong representative aspects that show its link to a real-world subject, which it renders 'identifiable', either directly or indirectly. We can here loosely borrow the term '*data subject*' from European data protection law as the one to whom the data relates.[28] The digital person however provides a very dispersed and fragmented representation of this subject based on distributed, partial data sets from very different sources (Figure 13.7), rather than providing a holistic reach. Deleuze has introduced the term '*dividual*' to indicate how information technologies have allowed an endless divisibility of people in different data representations that become separated from us (Deleuze 1992). Such technologies also make it possible to recombine these and other data sources in order

Figure 13.7   Frontispiece to Digital Personae and Profiles in Law (Roosendaal 2013), image by Tobias Groenland, taken from www.tobiasgroenland.nl

to create a digital person, as what we could call a *'recombinant identity'*.[29] Recombinations can happen in various ways based on criteria set by those who have access and control over this information (Williams 2005). Such *'data controllers'* are often large ICT organizations and so such criteria are often market-based.[30]

It has been said that the digital persona is 'an image of an individual, albeit in the form of an entire data set' (Roosendaal 2013, 243). The digital persona of an individual constitutes his or her *digital portrait*, or rather a series of dividual and recombinant data portraits (depending on the context and purpose).[31] A 'group profile' in this sense constitutes a digital 'group portrait'. Interestingly, when Clarke introduced the concept of the digital persona in 1993, he made an explicit difference between passive persons and active persons. The passive person is the data representation of individuals that form their digital mask, which allows them to digitally act or to be acted upon. The *active digital person* however goes beyond data alone, when it becomes a kind of representative for the individual. This is based on a different concept of representation, not of a digital portrait depicting the individual (representing through image and likeness), but a *digital agent* acting on behalf of the individual (representing through authorization), e.g. the negotiation and execution of contracts by software agents in the name of their principal. Clarke even included the possibility that this active digital person may at one point in time become an independent agent capable of autonomous behaviour and thus decreasingly controllable by humans (Clarke 1996).[32] In this scenario representativeness becomes blurred and the question to whom such actions can be attributed becomes pertinent. This brings us back to our starting point: the introduction of *electronic personhood* as a special *legal* status for robots or smart *digital agents*.[33]

FINDINGS: DRAWING CONTRASTS

The potential entry of electronic persons in the Hall of Faces sparked an exploration of a variety of profiles of personhood. In this text we have set up a space, in which these profiles have been juxtaposed and related, to put them into contrast and see whether we can 'find' differentiating patterns between salient attributes. The attributes of the personae chosen here are answers to the following questions: what is it (visually)? Who represents? Who is represented? What is their representative relation? How and through which means? What does this allow? We can put the results in the following ordering:

{person}	{visualization}, {representer}, {represented}, {relation}, {means}, {affordance}
1. Dramatic Persons	(mask), (actor), (character), (impersonation), (staging), (suspending disbelief)
2. Juristic Persons	(pointillist mask), (agent, lawyer), (divisible subject), (legal representation), (legal fiction), (imputation of rights & obligations)
3. Public Persons	(composite figure), (sovereign), (public [community]), (public representation), (social contract: unification by assent), (public action)
4. Average Persons	(composite portrait), (statistician), (population), (socio-physical realization as human type), (mean & correlation), (knowledge for policy)
5. Profile Persons	(composite portrait), (machine), (community or virtual group), (inductive aggregation), (mean & correlation), (knowledge for service)
6. Digital Persons	(dividual data portrait), (data controller [& data subject]), (data subject), (identifiability), (multiple: disclosure, tracking, profiling), (proxy for service)

This comparison of profiles does not provide a full-fledged taxonomy with mutually exclusive categories. As has been shown, these types of persons often have many overlapping aspects and they historically evolved from one another. This list is rather an experimental heuristic for mutually differentiating modes of personification and for situating new candidates.

We can highlight a few interrelated contrasts between these profiles of personhood. First, whereas the public person and the average person both share their composite nature, there is an important contrast regarding the *means of composition*, relating to the notion of assent. The public person of the Leviathan is composed through the unification of a multitude of people through the consent of each of them in a social contract, by which the sovereign comes to represent this assembled public community and was authorized to perform public actions. The average person of statistics to the contrary becomes assembled based on statistical grouping, either of the population as a whole, or of the people making up a certain community or a class. Such communities 'were united by fate, not choice' (Gamboni 2005, 182), when ordered along a mean. The visualizations make this apparent. In the composite image of

Leviathan all the people that compose the political body of the public person remain individualized, their wills juxtaposed. In the composite portraits by Galton, but also by Google, the separate individuals become superimposed and lose their individuality, only to (e-)merge in the new reality of the average person as a certain ghostly human (arche-)type, either of an existing community or of a virtual new grouping. The digital person is again quite different, moving back to the level of the individual. It is the result of another 'personalization' process premised on division and recombination of data representations (recombinant identity) from a multiplicity of data sources, thus creating a dispersed data portrait of the subject. Divisibility here hinges on criteria of identifiability of the subject and in relation to questions of service provision. This contrasts with the juristic person in which divisibility also played a prominent role. In law however, divisibility always hinges on a legal entity or relation (e.g. a promise, a patrimony) and always in relation to a certain set of rights and obligations.

Second, we have seen that the persona is often an action point, whether it is legal, average, digital or political. There are however significant differences relating to whom the actors bearing the mask are (the *representers*), and what they can and will do based on these representations (the *affordances*). In the case of the production of average human types, this statistical knowledge could be used to set out the normative coordinates for new 'public goods' (e.g. based on the socio-biological 'healthy' type) and 'public bads' (e.g. the 'criminal' type). This could form the basis for making general governmental policies aimed at controlling and improving the population and its relevant classes of people. Similarly, the profiled human types 'mined' by algorithmic techniques also constitute productive information. The clustering together of people is here even more virtualized, not necessarily given by pre-established criteria, but rather by data correlations as a web of links in a hyperspace of attributes. The data controller can utilize the resulting 'interested' or 'interesting' types, or, to the contrary, 'risky' types, for (often private) decision-making processes whether to grant a certain service or not. These inferences allow a degree of '*personalization*' of services, which was unattainable merely based on populational statistics. This term well describes the productive aspect of these socio-technical machinations: the production of a (digital) person through the modality of recombinant identity, to act upon the subject by proxy. There is an important contrast here with the juristic mask. A juristic mask is worn during a legal process often by a lawyer who has the duty to legally represent the subject ('client') and act in their interest, with the goal of letting certain rights be imputed and actions assigned to them. The digital mask, to the contrary, is often operated by the data controller, who uses it not so much on the (data) subject's behalf, but based rather on their own organizational, often market-based interests, to act upon this subject.[34]

Lastly, we can focus on the *representative relation*. We have seen that Quetelet and Galton conceived of the notions of the 'average man' and the 'correlation' between physical and mental human traits as statistical realities, i.e. they were real socio-biological qualities of populations that could be acted upon in policy-making. Composite photography even provided a means for a visual instantiation of these real average persons or human types. This contrasts with the notion of the juristic person as a double for the individual. These two layers needed to be strictly kept apart to avoid confusion. No human social or biological qualities of humans should be attributed to the juristic person. The juristic person can produce its effects as a denaturalizing device when human nature is kept at bay, and a fictive point can be set up in legal space that could function as a foothold for attributing rights and duties. It is an empty legal form, the most anonymous of masks, which can be distributed to everyone in the multitude (or even to such a multitude itself) precisely because it abstracts from traits that make each specific.

Historical innovations in personifications, like those in the thirteenth century when the concept of the juristic person became applied to communities, addressed the economic and political problematizations of the time. These newly created figures did not respond to a concern to conceive of these new persons as something ontological (Thomas 1998, 94). Personification rather functions as one specific type of legal operation to achieve certain results, namely by imputing rights and obligations (rather than protect something by qualifying it as an inviolable thing for instance) and should always be compared to alternative possible legal operations that might be deployed to address the issue at stake.

This message is significant to retain when we judge the entry of the electronic person in the Hall of Faces as a new type of legal mask for a physically embodied digital agent. It is important not to be carried away by the imaginary, symbolic discourses on artificial agency and the smart traits they would possess. These are fuelled by the take-up of science fiction, speculative A.I. philosophy and overambitious (funding) promises of roboticists,[35] themselves sometimes staged to suspend the disbelief of an increasingly wary public. Legal masks however, are non-dramatic fictions with important (financial) effects. Keeping the symbolic and legal level apart allows us to study the problem constellations around robotics and its economic and political dimensions, which are related to setting up the European digital single market, fuelling a promising economic sector, using robots to address societal problems like ageing populations, and avoiding stifling of innovation due to uncertainty about a possible accumulations of liability claims. The machine-centric narrative that has managed to captivate the legislative imagination of some representatives of our European public person, should not divert attention from how the introduction of a new type of person can upset the relations between already existing persons,[36] especially when it could affect the imputation of fundamental rights to people, or the equilibration of power relations in society more broadly.

NOTES

* This chapter builds on a previous published work: van Dijk, N., *Profiles of Personhood. On Arts of Representing Subjects.* In: E. Bayamlioglu, L. Jansen, I. Baraliuc and M. Hildebrandt (eds). Being Profiled. Cogitas ergo Sum, Amsterdam University Press, 2018, 122–129.
1. See Koops et al. (2010) for an overview of the debate on personhood for artificial agents.
2. <www.arabnews.com/node/1183166/saudi-arabia>.
3. See Rommetveit et al. (2019) for a description of the processes that lead up to the term's proposal.
4. On the notion of smart data-driven agency and its legal consequences, see Hildebrandt (2015).
5. I elsewhere explored this philosophical conception of personhood and the challenges posed by 'intelligent' profiling technologies (Van Dijk 2010).
6. This metaphor serves as a reminder that such a textual hyperspace that allows for juxtaposition, comparison and correlation analysis harbors a forceful decontextualization.
7. This is of course a sweeping simplification. In this chapter, I however wish to steer clear from questions about (Hobbesian) sovereignty of the European Union as a political entity, or the power of the Parliament in the EU.
8. One actor could be wearing different masks and assume different roles, whereas different actors could be wearing the same mask impersonating the same character.
9. The legal subject should not be confused with the primary autonomous subject of philosophy. Dewey argues for a 'legal agnosticism' implying that 'even if there is be such an ulterior subject per se, it is of no concern of law, since courts can do their work without respect to its nature, much less having to settle it' (Dewey 1926, 660).
10. As an example, we can take the relation between human biological reproduction and adoption in Roman law. Adoption law introduces presumptions and inversions of kinship lineages resulting from biological reproduction (Thomas 1998, 106).
11. On the characteristic pointillist operations of law, see Van Dijk (2017).
12. On this notion of legal fiction see Thomas (1995) and on its difference with common fiction, see Latour (2010), Van Dijk (2017).
13. An example of the first would be a slave commonly owned by two masters making a promise, which splits him in two representative persons. An example of the second would be a father and son constituting the same person regarding a certain heritage (*patrimoine*). See Thomas (1998).
14. Smith (1928) mentions ships or Hindu idols.
15. Teubner (2006) mentions many historical examples of animals directly put on trial, addressing them as legal actors.
16. Legal personhood for nature has been recognised to different degrees in Ecuador, Bolivia and Colombia. Article 10 of Ecuador's constitution stipulates that 'Nature shall be the subject of those rights that the Constitution recognizes for it'. Environmental features that have received personhood in several countries include rivers and national parks.

17. This original meaning of mask is still evidenced in the legal operation of 'veil-piercing' of corporations, which allows to 'lift' the legal disguise to get at the real people behind whose interests are at stake. See Bryson et al. (2017).
18. See a nuance in Skinner (2005).
19. Political representation has become less monolithic since Hobbes, with its definitive and unconditional moment of transferring power through the social contract. The political body (*res publica*) needs to be constantly re-composed (Latour 2010, 269–70). For an interesting visual account, see Gamboni (2005).
20. Arcimboldo provided the most influential model of composite pictures through double mimesis. Gamboni describes several other historical examples ranging from Hobbes, up to software mosaics of political figures created from individual photographs (Gamboni 2005).
21. This is Hacking's claim (Hacking 1990, chapter 21).
22. '[T]he photographic process of which I there spoke enables us to obtain with mechanical precision a generalised picture; one that represents no man in particular, but portrays an imaginary figure possessing the average features of any given group of men' (Galton 1907, 221–2).
23. What Foucault (1994) has called bio-politics.
24. See also Rouvroy and Berns (2013) about the difference between classical statistics and machine learning, allowing for algorithmic governmentality.
25. This is the inverse of the goal in classic machine learning to classify different data based on similarity. Here one often begins with random noise and creates a target candidate, such as an image.
26. See Schneier (2010) on this data taxonomy.
27. 'A digital persona is a digital representation of a real-world individual, which can be connected to this real-world individual and includes a sufficient amount of (relevant) data to serve, within the context and for the purpose of its use, as a proxy for the individual' (Roosendaal 2013, 41).
28. Article 4.1 GDPR. On the applicability to digital persons, see (Roosendaal 2013).
29. Recombinant DNA is based on biotechnologies that bring together genetic material from various sources (e.g. from different individuals or even species), resulting in the creation of new, otherwise non-existent DNA sequences.
30. Article 4.7 GDPR.
31. On the applicability of portrait law or personality rights to digital persona, see Van Dijk et al. (2016), Roosendaal (2013).
32. Hildebrandt (2015) describes an evolution of different degrees of smartness for such electronic agents.
33. Teubner (2018) introduces the term 'digital personhood' as a partial legal status for such autonomous software agents, in response to the EP's proposal.
34. This contrast has been well elucidated by Kerr (2013).
35. Interestingly, 156 AI and robotics experts have claimed that the creation of electronic personhood for 'autonomous', 'unpredictable' and 'self-learning' robots is 'based on an overvaluation of the actual capabilities of even the most advanced robots, a superficial understanding of unpredictability and self-learning capacities and, a robot perception distorted by Science-Fiction and a few recent sensational press announcements' (Open Letter 2017).
  For a description of this process, see Rommetveit et al. (2019).
36. Bryson et al. (2017) mention two kinds of abuse of the rights of humans and legal persons: 1) exploiting robots to insulate oneself from liability and 2) robots unaccountably violating the rights of humans.

REFERENCES

156 Experts. 2018. Open Letter to the European Commission. Artificial Intelligence and Robotics

Bryson, J., M. E. Diamantis and T. D. Grant. 2017. 'Of, for, and by the People: The Legal Lacuna of Synthetic Persons'. *Artificial Intelligence and Law* 25:3, 273–291

Cicero. 1928. *De Officiis*. London: Woods & Soni

Cicero. 1967. *De Oratore*. London: W. Heinemann

Clarke, R. 1996. 'The Digital Persona and its Application to Data Surveillance'. *Information Society* 10(2), 77–92

Deleuze, G. 1992. 'Postscript on the Societies of Control'. October 59, 3–7

Despret, V. and S. Gutwirth. 2009. 'L'affaire Harry'. *Terrain* 52, 142–51

De Vries, K. 2016. *Machine Learning/Informational Fundamental Rights*. PhD Thesis. VUB. Brussels

Dewey, J. 1925–6. 'The Historic Background of Corporate Legal Personality'. *Yale Law Journal* 35, 655–73

European Parliament. 2017. Report with recommendations to the Commission on Civil Law Rules on Robotics, 2015/2103(INL). Brussels

Foucault, M. 1994. *Dits et Écrits 1954–1988*. Paris: Gallimard

Galton, F. 1907. *Inquiries into Human Faculty and its Developments*. London: J.M. Dent and Sons (Everyman)

Gamboni, D. 2005. 'Composing the Body Politic. Composite Images and Political Representation, 1651–2004'. In *Making Things Public*. Edited by Latour, B and P. Weibel. Cambridge, MA: MIT Press

Hacking, I. 1990. *The Taming of Chance*. Cambridge: University Press

Hildebrandt, M. and S. Gutwirth. 2008. *Profiling the European Citizen*. Dordrecht: Springer

Hildebrandt, M. 2015. *Smart Technologies and the End(s) of Law*. Cheltenham: Edward Elgar

Hobbes, T. 1998. *Leviathan*. Oxford: University Press

Karras, T., T. Aila, et al. 2018. 'Progressive Growing of GANs for Improved Quality, Stability, and Variation'. Conference paper at ICLR 2018

Kelsen, H. 2002. *Pure theory of Law*. Clark, NJ: Lawbook Exchange

Kerr, I. 2013. 'Prediction, Pre-emption, Presumption: The Path of Law After the Computational Turn'. *Privacy, Due Process and the Computational Turn*. Edited by Hildebrandt, M., K. de Vries. London: Routledge

Koops, B. J., M. Hildebrandt and D.-O. Jaquet-Chiffelle. 2010. 'Bridging the Accountability Gap: Rights for New Entities in the Information Society?'. *Minnesota Journal of Law, Science & Technology* 11(2), 497–561

Latour, B. 2010. *The Making of Law*. Cambridge: Polity

Le Q. V., M. A. Ranzato, et al. 2012. 'Building High-Level Features Using Large Scale Unsupervised Learning'. Proceedings of 29th International Conference on Machine Learning, Edinburgh

Von Luxburg, U., R. C. Williamson and I. Guyon. 2012. 'Clustering: Science or Art?' JMLR: Workshop and Conference Proceedings 27, 65–79

Parton, J. 1877. *Caricature and Other Comic Art*. New York, NY: Harper

Pitkin, H. F. 1967. *The Concept of Representation*. Berkeley, CA: University of California Press

Quetelet, L. A. J. 1842. *A Treatise on Man and the Development of his Faculties.* Edinburgh: W&R Chambers

Rommetveit, K., N. van Dijk and K. Gunnarsdóttir. 2019. 'Make Way for the Robots! Human- and Machine-Centricity in Constituting a European Public-Private Partnership'. *Minerva.*, doi: https://doi.org/10/1007/s11024-019-09386-1

Roosendaal, A. 2013. *Digital Personae and Profiles in Law.* Oisterwijk: Wolf Legal Publishers

Rouvroy, A. and T. Berns, 2013. 'Algorithmic Governmentality and Prospects of Emancipation'. *Réseaux* 1(177), 163–96

Schneier, B. 2010. 'A Taxonomy of Social Networking Data'. *IEEE Security and Privacy* 8(88)

Skinner, Q. 2005. 'Hobbes on Representation'. *European Journal of Philosophy* 13(2), 155–184

Smith, B. 1928. 'Legal Personality'. *Yale Law Journal* 37(3), 283–99

Solove, D. J. 2004. *The Digital Person.* New York, NY: University Press

Solum, L. B. 1992. 'Legal Personhood for Artificial Intelligences'. *North Carolina Law Review* 70, 1231–87

Teubner, G. 2006. 'Rights of Non-humans? Electronic Agents and Animals as New Actors in Politics and Law'. *Journal of Law & Society* 33(4), 497–521

Teubner, G. 2018. 'Digital Personhood? The Status of Autonomous Software Agents in Private Law'. *Ancilla Juris* 35–78

Thomas, Y. 1995. 'Fictio Legis. L'Empire de la Fiction Romaine et ses Limites Medievales'. *Droits* 21, 17–73

Thomas, Y. 1998. 'Le sujet de droit, la personne et la nature'. *Le débat* 100, 85–107

Van Dijk, N. 2010. 'Property, Privacy & Personhood in a World of Ambient Intelligence'. *Ethics and Information Technology* 12(1), 57–69

Van Dijk, N. 2017. *Grounds of the Immaterial.* Cheltenham: Edward Elgar

Van Dijk, N., K. de Vries, et al. 2016. Copyrights and Rights in Digital Persona on Online Social Networks, D.3.12. USEMP Project. FP 7, <https://www.usemp.eu/wp-content/uploads/2017/05/usemp_deliverable_d3.12.pdf>

Williams, R. W. 2005. 'Politics and Self in the Age of Digital Re(pro)ducibility'. *Fast Capitalism* 1(1)

RESPONSE

14. Life and the law in the era of machine agency
Mireille Hildebrandt[1]

INTRODUCTION

This volume contains a wealth of new and old ideas on the cusp of law and life in the era of data-driven environments. The chapters present myriad configurations of the interaction between human agency and the 'agency' of pre-emptive computing systems that inform, shape and tweak our everyday world. Warnings are given, fingers are raised, in-depth analyses presented, and complex though lucid argumentations developed in the domains of legal and political theory, human-computer-interaction, computer science, policy science, ethics and philosophy of technology. The chapters are more or less inspired by some of the arguments put forward in *The End(s)*, prompting a response on my side, that will start with the ends (goals) advocated by many of the authors, followed by a discussion of the new beginnings this will require. For ease of reading I have refrained from adding all the references that are relevant, as most of them can be found in the relevant chapters of this volume and in *The End(s)* itself, though I do refer to some recent work.

Whereas I often speak of data-driven agency, in this final chapter I refer to machine agency, to make sure that we remain aware that such agency is generated by machines, thus also distancing myself from those who believe human beings are nothing but machines.

THE ENDS: SEAMFUL ENVIRONMENTS ENDOWED WITH 'APPARENCY' AND PRAGMATIC TRANSPARENCY

In 1984 the Japanese computer scientist Ken Sakamura developed the notion of 'computing everywhere' – long before Mark Weiser dreamt up the idea of 'ubiquitous computing'. As discussed in *The End(s)* (at 108): 'Though Weiser is forever credited as the "father" of ubiquitous computing, it seems that Sakamura was already on track with his own project of calm, invisible, hidden, pervasive, everyday, sentient, amorphous computing'. Sakamura's and Weiser's notions of ubiquitous computing heralded the idea of a seamless and surreptitious world where 'the environment itself is the interface', hiding the computational backend of an environment that is forever guessing our next move, pre-empting our needs and desires as a tireless butler in the service of our humanity. This prescient *Umwelt* is what the *Onlife Manifesto* coined an onli*fe* world, a term that refers to the curious responsiveness of an environment that fuses online and offline interventions, turning human inhabitants into data engines as well as guinea pigs for large scale behavioural experimentation.

Throughout this volume, authors have highlighted the poor assumptions and disruptive implications of seamless and surreptitious environments, capable of nudging us into e.g. viewing extreme content online, into following 'influencers' on twitter, into voting behaviours, and into e.g. sharing our preferences via 'like' buttons, our emotions via 'emoticons' and a host of biometric behaviours via a plethora of health apps. Julie Cohen (this volume) highlights the fact that this environment intervenes as if it were a limbic system similar to the human neural networks 'that play vital roles in a number of precognitive functions, including emotion, motivation, and habit-formation'. She argues that such subliminal influencing tricks people into 'consumptive self expression' as if this were equivalent with human freedom, and points to a paradoxical employment of addiction research that, combined with psychometrics, aims to enable microtargeting and ad-driven content optimisation, presenting marketing as a behavioural science.

In *The End(s)* I have developed the notion of a digital unconscious, demonstrating by way of both narrative and analysis how the invisibility and performance of such a pre-emptive environment affords a corruption of human agency. Neither Cohen nor I endorse naïve understandings of human agency, but both Cohen and I warn against the attempt to subvert our capability to reflect on how we navigate our world. Human agency begins where we engage in critical reflection, aided by the grammatical first person perspective that springs from being addressed as a grammatical second person. This is why machine behaviour differs from human interaction; though computational systems can easily develop n-order perspectives on their own system, they do not experience their *Umwelt* from the perspective of an 'I' in the sense that humans do.

Dumouchel highlights the fact that the computational backend of our brave new world is not merely a matter of cognition and perception, but moreover a matter of intervention and pre-emption. AI is no longer an attempt to automate the application of preconceived knowledge (as good old-fashioned AI or GOFAI) but an attempt to automate the learning process based on pattern detection in massive amounts of dynamically updated training data (as with AI the modern approach or AIMA). As with any learning process, machines learn best when confronted with the implications of their interventions, resulting in the social domain becoming one huge resource for experimentation; an unlimited living lab to test the latest combination of machine learning and nudge theory. This clarifies that while training on real life settings, machine learning alters the world it models, creating feedback loops that cannot be undone, making it increasingly difficult to imagine alternative ways to navigate the shared space of human society.

Between the lines I hear Dumouchel casting doubt on the methodological integrity of machine learning in the social domain, in opposition to its use in the natural and life sciences. I must admit that since writing *The End(s)* five years ago, I have become appalled by the pseudo-science that is being sold as viable data-driven intelligence, and I am now convinced that whereas *human bias* is often a sign of our 'ecological rationality' (Gigerenzer 2018), the *machine bias* that is generated in data-driven learning can easily spiral out of control, notably when working with behavioural data (Desjardins 2018). On top of that, the use of data-driven interventions based on psychometrics are perhaps even more questionable, due to the 'scientific varnish' that hides its questionable assumptions about human interaction (Rogers 2018, Stark 2018). Finally, advances in adversarial machine learning demonstrate how easily supposedly highly accurate deep learning systems can be side-tracked into nonsensical decisions (e.g. Finlayson et al. 2018). Put in another way, the narrative that kicks off *The End(s)* requires some serious pruning – which makes the questions it raises even more salient and pertinent (since there is no sign that big players in the social domain have an interest in erring on the side of caution).

Dumouchel's analysis strikes a note with both schraefel et al.'s move from semantic to pragmatic transparency and Delacroix and Veale's call for actionable counter profiling. All three chapters highlight that transparency in an era where machines combine cognition with action requires more than a rebalancing of epistemic knowledge asymmetries, calling for ways to reclaim control over the consequences of one's actions. As explained in *The End(s)*, perception is shaped by action. This is how Gibson explains his concept of an affordance, marking the relational nature of both an agent and their environment. The mutually constitutive nature of action and perception is also a core finding in phenomenology, cybernetics and in robotics; agency emerges where the agent is triggered to perceive the actionable environment based on continuous feedback loops.

Perception, in that sense, is anticipation. It is both agent-dependent and environment-dependent. This is why semantic transparency is indeed not enough where machines are acting upon their anticipation of our behaviours (machines cannot read our behaviour as action, their perspective remains external and unconcerned, though there is nothing neutral about such 'unconcern'). Counter profiling, therefore, cannot be restricted to propositional statements about the persuasive interventions of the limbic system; it must instead generate an intuitive heuristics to turn the tables on unwarranted manipulation.

One way to generate such intuitive heuristics is schraefel et al.'s proposal to reconfigure the affordances of what I would term onli*fe* environments, turning away from seamless to seamful interaction with the world we inhabit. Instead of smooth and convenient interfaces, they foresee software layers that interrupt users, making apparent what would otherwise remain hidden, calling out the limbic system instead of employing it to nudge users into meaningless consent. This 'apparency' should afford the shift they promote from semantic to pragmatic transparency, reinstating consent as an act that has both meaning and consequences, thus reenabling the human capability to act instead of merely to behave.

Ohm similarly advocates a seamful environment, introducing two 'throttling' metrics that should slow down the uptake of scarcely tested machine learning technologies. Whereas schraefel et al. seem to focus all their efforts on the need to reenable meaningful consent, suggesting that users are willing to engage in persistent and enduring negotiations while navigating their everyday lives, Ohm's 'throttling' metrics aim to slow down the introduction of algorithmic environments. Instead of disturbing the functioning of such environments, these metrics entail a precautionary approach that may prevent the roll-out of questionable decision-systems. It is better to stop halfway than to persevere in error. This relates back to Delacroix and Veale where they argue that the point is not to enable consumers in making the right choice, but to get our fingers behind who and what is framing the choice architecture. Ohm, Delacroix and Veale as well as schraefel et al. all highlight the importance of the design of our onli*fe* world. In that sense they all argue for a sustained interaction between what Graber (this volume) calls the 'design constituency' and the 'impact constituency' whenever new technologies are introduced. This rings bells with a notion I recently developed, advocating a shift from agnostic to agonistic machine learning (Hildebrandt 2019), ensuring that the design of our onli*fe* environment is not taken for granted as neutral while instigating an agonistic dialog on the potential impact with those who will suffer the consequences.

The idea of a 'design constituency' interacting with an 'impact constituency' also aligns with the idea of a choice architecture, a notion I hijacked from nudge theory's behaviourist's vocabulary. A choice architecture determines what *types* of choices we get to make. Do we get to choose between 37 sorts of wine, or do we also get to choose between wine, juices and waters? Or, should our choice be situated at the level of choosing between options that contribute to sustainable development and those that do not? Might a democracy decide to restrict choice to sustainable options per se? Our onli*fe* surroundings may provide us with a host of choices, but these choices have been prefabricated in ways that may filter what matters, and prime us for behaviours that are profitable or desirable for those who run the backend systems. As De Vries notes, thanks to big data and AI, tech platforms and others do not merely manipulate existing preferences but frame and subliminally constitute publics. By mapping our choice architectures, data-driven environments are optimized to nourish our sense of autonomy by nudging us into experiencing e.g. consumptive self-expression as a superior type of freedom (Cohen, this volume), meanwhile coaxing us into the direction of ever more lucrative behaviour (which most often concerns behaviour that leaves a data trail to be used for further nudgings).

NEW BEGINNINGS: INNOVATION AND CONSERVATION

So, if the end (the goal) of designing our onli*fe* world is a seamful ICI that offers a pragmatic transparency that enhances human agency rather than diminishing it, where should we begin? And who is we: the developers, the industry, academia, activists, public administration, the legislature, the courts, or those who suffer the consequences? Or all of us? This brings me to the issues of innovation, conservatism, technological determinism and the viability of democracy and the Rule of Law in times of machine agency.

Delacroix and Veale advocate 'unexpectancy' and serendipity to counter increased dependence on algorithmic systems that depend on probability and plausibility. They seem to intuit that technological determinism is not so much a belief, but an attempt to design compliance into an architecture. This presents an interesting counter narrative for 'innovation' that is often taken for granted as beneficial for society, based on the idea that the best way to predict the future is to create it. In alignment with the seamfulness advocated by schraefel et al., designing for 'unexpectancy' disrupts the desire to freeze the future by ever more refined feedback loops between predictions and pre-emptions. Machine agency may surprise us, if we find ways to incorporate seams and gaps into the fabric of data-driven textures, steering free from the wish to hold sway over a shared future that features repetition instead of imagination. Though I do not believe that technological determinism is true, we may fear that it becomes true. To resist overdetermination by machine agency we need to find the right combination of technological innovation (seeking intended consequences) and design for 'unexpectancy' in ways that enhances our human agency, including our capability to resist and contest algorithmic decision making.

There is a very interesting dissenting voice in this volume, defending a choice architecture that primes us for a sense of social justice. Stevens reads the opening narrative of *The End(s)* in a far more open and constructive way than most of my readers. I deeply appreciate his argumentation, because the scenarios I framed actually aimed to open the stage for a serious discussion on the extent to which data-driven pre-emption is problematic and where it may in point of fact contribute to the good life without jeopardizing what Ess calls *phronesis* or practical wisdom. Stevens is concerned with social justice, which usually translates into distributive justice, diversity and non-discrimination. Following a Rawlsian analysis, he believes that whereas the preconceived and engineered choice architecture of our onli*fe* environment should not interfere with our own version of the good life, there are good arguments to interfere with the development of a sense of social justice. He advocates such nudging if people would otherwise sustain an unacceptable sense of justice, for instance treating certain people as if they are inferior, based on ethnicity or other grounds. Stevens believes that if education has failed to prime people for a sense of social justice, the digital unconscious may be employed by a government to make up for that.

Stevens' concern with deliberate harm to others, as a topical example of displaying an unacceptable sense of justice, touches upon Delacroix and Veale's fundamental commitment to equality. Delacroix and Veale, however, emphasize the fact that subliminal profiling enables those without a sense of social justice to invisibly transform the construction of human identities. They are concerned with the diminishment of human agency that is achieved by subliminal influencing, comparing it to the 'social cruelty' of, for instance, genocide. Though one may be shocked by the comparison of genocide with subliminal influencing, the point is not to get carried away by the analogy. In both cases, one could argue, human beings are treated as mere instruments to achieve the goals of others, disrespecting the dignity of the human person. And in both cases, the main concern of Delacroix and Veale is the flagrant inequality of treating some of us with such disrespect, whereas others enjoy human freedom and autonomy (freedom as a privilege instead of a right). Perhaps they suspect that treating a group of people as if their agency does not matter is a first step on the road from invisible manipulation to physical abuse, which may end in annihilation. Which is, evidently, not to say that subliminal influencing is equivalent with genocide.

Pitting Delacroix and Veale against Stevens seems to bring out the difference between procedural and substantive justice. Whereas Delacroix and Veale argue that we may not treat people as manipulable pawns, Stevens finds that we may do just that if it contributes to them developing a sense of justice. Though all agree on the value of social justice, Delacroix and Veale situate that value in the construction of an individual's identity, which includes their sense of justice. Stevens clearly believes that society cannot afford a constituency that is not properly primed for this sense of justice and though he prefers education to the digital unconscious, he cannot reject the latter when push comes to shove.

My take here is that thinking in terms of priming and nudging implies a utilitarian, behaviourist approach that seems to be at odds with Rawls' deontological perspective. Though human learning has aspects of priming, notably in education and other institutional contexts, a designed choice architecture will only achieve a sense of justice if it triggers a habit of reflection and self-reflection. Habit, however, is not mere regularity or meaningless custom, but a deeply normative dimension of human society (see e.g. 3.3 in *The End(s)*); practical wisdom cannot be imposed, it must be developed as all habits must. That is, a designed environment should not impose a specific sense of justice by tweaking the environment in such a way that wrong choices cannot be made. Instead, it should invite a concern for justice by engineering the ICI such that people are forced to develop the kind of practical knowledge that is constitutive of our moral judgement.

In his discussion of the Aristotelian notion of *phronesis*, or practical wisdom, Ess suggests that the development of practical wisdom aligns with my focus on interpretation as core to law and the Rule of Law. I could not agree more. With great acuity, Ess emphasizes the difference between calculation and judgement, highlighting that human judgement is embodied, historical and otherwise situated and connected with the mutual double anticipation that creates the shared world (*Welt*) beyond our immediate environment (*Umwelt*). He also connects practical wisdom and judgement to Plato's original notion of *cybernetes* (pilot, steersman), which may be closer to *knowing how* (tacit knowledge) than to computational renderings of *knowing that* (explicit knowledge), and closer to art than to science. This implies an entirely different understanding of cybernetics than the control perspective that informs the regulatory paradigm in some parts of legal theory, depicting cybernetics in terms of standard setting, monitoring and behaviour modification. Under the regulatory paradigm, law is regulation, which in turn is framed as an attempt to influence people to achieve compliance with a standard (a regulation), based on recurrent monitoring. Here we are back with Stevens. *The End(s)*, on the contrary, sees law as a relational architecture that aims for legal certainty, purposiveness and justice, based on a system of checks and balances that roots legitimate mutual expectations. In that view law and the Rule of Law address individuals as agents capable of giving reasons for their actions, not as objects to be influenced into whatever a government believes is best. In the same vein *The End(s)* grounds the legitimate mutual expectations generated by legal norms in the fact that in a democracy the addressor and the addressee of these norms coincide, by way of representation, deliberation and participation (Hildebrandt and Gutwirth 2007).

Above, I advocated an onli*fe* world that integrates intuitive heuristics for counter profiling. If that is what Stevens is after, I fully agree. I would not qualify this as paternalism, because it aims to liberate people from deliberate attempts to lure them into habits that are profitable in whatever sense for those who paid for the system. Note that whichever environment, whether or not designed, whether or not intended, has specific affordances. It is up to us, as a political and legal community, to develop and sustain environments that respect and nourish human agency. The Rule of Law aims to do just that, as it institutes a system of checks and balances that protects people against their government, due to the internal division of sovereignty into a legislature, public administration and an independent judiciary; it thus binds the state to the mast (to its own laws) while waxing its ears (making sure the judiciary has the final word on the interpretation of these laws), such that it cannot succumb to the lure of nudging its constituency into docility (on the mast and the wax, see *The End(s)*, 199, 206, 220, 222).

In the era of machine agency we need to reinvent this system of checks and balances, and it must be inscribed into the operations of our new, digital unconscious. Conservation here, requires a specific type of innovation. This is what I have termed 'legal protection by design', which includes ensuring both the vertical and the horizontal effect of human rights, preventing both government agencies and big economic players from violating privacy, non-discrimination, due process, the presumption of innocence and freedom of expression. To some extent, legal protection by design should develop in compliance with the General Data Protection Regulation, that instigates seamful personal data processing systems, pragmatic transparency and a precautionary approach towards the risk that personal data processing operations and automated decisions present to fundamental rights and freedoms. But legal protection by design should move beyond data protection by design, it should become a default check for the introduction of all new technologies, assessing whether, and if so to what extent, their large-scale employment diminishes the substance of fundamental rights, or rules out resistance and contestation.

If that makes me a conservative in the sense that I aim to preserve the substance of fundamental values on which we agreed as democratic polities, then be it so. I cannot but agree with the conservatism of O'Hara and Garnett, where they argue with Burke for a state that protects against mob rule, with Tocqueville against the egalitarian atomism of public management, and with Oakeshott, defending the unpredictable nature of human conduct against the lure of a digital unconscious built on manipulative atomisms. The same goes for De Vries, who engages Montesquieu's analysis of the *nature* and the *principle* of democracy, vouching for a relational rather than a minimalist understanding of democracy – which rings many bells with my own analyses on democratic theory and the Rule of Law. For instance, De Vries' reference to Whitehead's *fallacy of mistaken concreteness* is an excellent reminder of the dangers of Schmitt's later work on 'concrete order thinking' (Hildebrandt 2015). And obviously, the idea of agonistic machine learning is directly related to Dewey's constitution of concerned publics (Hildebrandt and Gutwirth 2007), which could be further developed by integrating Graber's excellent employment of Pfaffenberger's interaction between the 'design constituency' and the 'impact constituency'.

In the final chapter of this part, Van Dijk moves back to the idea of human and machine agency, confronting the question of whether some machine agents should obtain the status of electronic persons. This is a political question about a legal qualification, because only the legislator can decide to attribute such personhood to non-human agents. Van Dijk offers the reader an interesting extension of Facebook, namely a 'Hall of Faces'. Though tweaked from the *Game of Thrones*, this Hall holds promise in ways that differ from facial recognition in either the infamous online social network or the morbid scalps of a twenty-first century soap opera.[2] Whereas Facebook follows a 'real name' policy, it clearly invites its users to construct a very specific type of mask, consisting of portrayals of a 'likeable' self. One's Facebook self, therefore, is indeed a mask (as one of my daughters said many years ago: 'Facebook is reputation management; cumbersome and rather boring'). On the other hand, I would argue that the facial skin that hangs to dry in *Game of Thrones*' Hall of Faces may resemble a mask, but is no such thing. A mask hides a living person by offering them an artificial face that enables them to play a specific role. The scalps do no such thing. The term 'persona' derives from the theatrical masks of antiquity, enabling to play one's role in a theatre play. The legal 'persona' similarly concerns the role one plays in law, not the person of flesh and blood, who remains hidden behind their legal subjectivity. The legal 'persona' enables us to act in law, while shielding the embodied human self from overexposure. This nicely presents the double instrumentality of legal subjectivity, which (1) enables us to act in law, and (2) protects our incomputable self from being overdetermined by legal qualification. We need a similar double instrumentality for our computational doubles (avatars), enabling us to act in the onli*fe* world, while protecting our incomputable self from overdetermination by data-driven applications (Hildebrandt 2019).

Van Dijk's 'Hall of Faces' was triggered by a proposal from the European Parliament (EP) to create of a new type of legal personhood for smart systems. The EP indeed invited the European legislature to consider the creation of e-persons for smart systems, but as part of a Recommendation that mostly concerned an upgrade of private law liability in the case that AI contraptions cause harm. As I have argued elsewhere, I believe that next to a fundamental right to data protection we need to reinvent competition law to reign in big tech (Hildebrandt 2018a) and create strict liability for harm caused (e.g. Koops, Hildebrandt and Jacquet-Chiffelle 2010), complemented with a requirement to preregister the machine learning research design whenever a machine learning application is put on the EU internal market (Hildebrandt 2018b). Whether legal personhood for autonomous systems would provide further benefit is – as Van Dijk rightly explains – as yet unclear. An environment that is saturated with interacting machines that feed on our behavioural data can only be safe, fair and conducive to human agency if those who profit from their employment can be held to account. They should not be given the chance to hide behind the façade of a new legal person. Not because autonomous systems are not 'real' persons but because we should not allow those who put such systems on the market to shift the risk of harm that is caused to others, thus giving them a free hand to take more risk instead of less. Obviously, we need a precautionary approach to data-driven machine agency, and a proper understanding of where it can do great things and where not.

In other words, we can engage in legal innovation by inventing legal personhood for electronic persons, as long as we preserve the equal respect and concern that legal systems owe each individual human person.

FINALS: FACING DATA-DRIVEN MACHINE AGENCY

In his magnificent double history of *Face and mask*, Hans Belting (2017, 6) tells us that 'In this book the face is the cynosure of all images, which are always subject to time and thus break down and lose the competition with the living face when confronted with the impossibility of representing it accurately'. As San Francisco, where I am finalising this chapter, is on the verge of banning the use of facial image recognition technologies by local police, the confrontation between human and machine agency is taken to a new level. The famed techniques of 'deep learning' (DL) that were once expected to result in general artificial intelligence (GAI), have made major leaps in terms of image and speech recognition. That is why this ban has been proposed. But it turns out that the accuracy of DL collapses with minor tweaks of their objects (based on adversarial machine learning, see e.g. Liang 2018). This kind of machine agency does not recognize faces as we do, and functions best when trained against its own kind, given a set of rules that define a closed game (as demonstrated by DeepMinds' AlphaZero, Wu 2018). This exemplifies the gap between subject and image, face and portrait, presence and representation, self and me; it also shows us the gap between a pixelated capture of a living face and its ephemeral embodied object.

Though I still believe we should learn to take the intentional stance towards data-driven machine agency (*The End(s)*, 6.5.1 and endnote 69), I would now emphasize a better understanding of how that agency differs from our own, of the limits of computer science and machine learning and of how we can learn to respect those limits without suggesting that we should reject either computer science or data-driven agency.

NOTES

1. With credits to Aniek Den Teuling for helping to prepare this chapter and the introductory chapter; her 'reading' of the chapters of this volume further clarified what makes this a salient volume; and many thanks to my co-editor for his critically constructive commentaries.
2. See the *Game of Thrones wiki* entry on 'Hall of Faces': <https://gameofthrones.fandom.com/wiki/Hall_of_Faces>.

REFERENCES

Belting, H. 2017. *Face and Mask: A Double History*. Translated by Thomas S. Hansen and Abby J. Hansen. Princeton, NJ: Princeton University Press

Desjardins, J. 2018. 'Here are 15 Common Data Fallacies to Avoid', *Visual Capitalist*, April 3, <https://www.visualcapitalist.com/here-are-15-common-data-fallacies-to-avoid/>

Finlayson, S. G., H. Won Chung, I. S. Kohane and A. L. Beam. 2018. 'Adversarial

Attacks Against Medical Deep Learning Systems'. *ArXiv:1804.05296* [*Cs, Stat*], April. <http://arxiv.org/abs/1804.05296>

Gigerenzer, G. 2018. 'The Bias Bias in Behavioral Economics'. *Review of Behavioral Economics* 5 (3–4), 303–36, <https://doi.org/10.1561/105.00000092>

Hildebrandt, M. and S. Gutwirth. 2007. '(Re)Presentation, PTA Citizens' Juries and the Jury Trial'. *Utrecht Law Review* 3 (1), <http://www.utrechtlawreview.org/>

Hildebrandt, M. 2015. 'Radbruch's Rechtsstaat and Schmitt's Legal Order: Legalism, Legality, and the Institution of Law'. *Critical Analysis of Law* 2 (1) <http://cal.library.utoronto.ca/index.php/cal/article/view/22514>

Hildebrandt, M. 2018a. 'Primitives of Legal Protection in the Era of Big Tech Platforms'. *Georgetown Law and Technology Review* 2(2), 252–73

Hildebrandt, M. 2018b. 'Preregisration of Machine Learning Research Design. Against P-Hacking'. In *BEING PROFILED:COGITAS ERGO SUM*. Amsterdam: Amsterdam University Press

Hilderbrandt, M. 2019. 'Privacy as Protection of the Incomputable Self: From Agnostic to Agonistic Machine Learning'. *Theoretical Inquiries in Law* 20 (1), <http://www7.tau.ac.il/ojs/index.php/til/article/view/1622>

Koops, B. J., M. Hildebrandt and David-Olivier Jacquet-Chiffelle. 2010. 'Bridging the Accountability Gap: Rights for New Entities in the Information Society?' *Minnesota Journal of Law Science & Technology* 11 (2), 497–561

Liang, James. 2018. 'Breaking Machine Learning With Adversarial Examples'. *Towards Data Science*. 10 November 2018. <https://towardsdatascience.com/breaking-machine-learning-with-adversarial-examples-a3ddc5c75ea4>

Rogers, A. 2018. 'The Cambridge Analytica Data Apocalypse Was Predicted in 2007'. *Wired*, 25 March 2018. <https://www.wired.com/story/the-cambridge-analytica-data-apocalypse-was-predicted-in-2007/>

Stark, L. 2018. 'Algorithmic Psychometrics and the Scalable Subject'. *Social Studies of Science* 48 (2), 204–31. <https://doi.org/10.1177/0306312718772094>

Wu, Katherine J. 2018. 'Google's New AI Is a Master of Games, but How Does It Compare to the Human Mind?' Smithsonian. 10 December 2018. <https://www.smithsonianmag.com/innovation/google-ai-deepminds-alphazero-games-chess-and-go-180970981/>

Index

accountability
   algorithmic accountability 81, 204, 262
   data collection, design options for accountability 107–8
   personhood *see* personhood
   of platform operators *see* fundamental rights, accountability of platform operators
   see also transparency
actor-network theory (Latour) 143
Adams, Douglas 224–5
advertising 19
   ad-blocking technologies 199–201
   behavioural microtargeting *see* behavioural microtargeting
   gamification of commercial surveillance 64–7
   online tracking by advertisers 25, 69, 103–4, 107, 200
   on social media 68
      political advertising *see* social media, political discourse on
affective computing 6, 84, 85–8
affordances
   concept 196–8, 255
   and fundamental rights 206–9
   of law 26–9, 32, 120, 129, 197, 255–6
   of technology
      AI and affordance theory 201–6
      Pfaffenberger's 'technological drama' 10–11, 196, 197–201, 256, 261
      technological design use 5, 105–6, 197
agency
   affordances of law, agent-dependent nature of 26–7, 28–9, 255–6
   consent to data collection *see* data collection, consent mechanisms
   data-driven *see* data-driven agency
   data transformed into information and knowledge by 26
   definition 1, 128
   and individuality 17, 187
   liberty *see* liberty
   personhood *see* personhood
   relational autonomy (Hildebrandt) 118, 120
   self-definition *see* subjectivity
   value of 161–2
   trade-off with well-being 156–7, 160–67
agent-dependent nature of affordances of law 26–7, 28–9, 255–6
agonistic machine learning 217, 222, 256, 261
AI *see* artificial intelligence (AI)
algorithms
   accountability for 81, 204, 262
   algorithmic government 30, 140–41, 153, 156–7, 171–2, 246
   algorithmic intermediation *see* platform-based massively-intermediated environments
   characteristics 55
   decision-making by *see* decisions guided by technology
   master algorithm notion 45, 47, 50
   see also artificial intelligence (AI); machine learning (ML)
AlphaGo 203–4
Amazon 69, 86, 87, 202
Andrejevic, Mark 60
anticipatory digital decision-making *see* pre-emptive computing
apparency 5–6, 104–5, 112–15, 256
Apple 113, 195–6, 202
Arendt, Hannah 36, 37–8, 86, 88, 92, 94, 124

Aristotle *see phronēsis*
artificial cognitive systems 53, 54, 55, 56
artificial intelligence (AI)
　affective computing (emotional AI) 6, 84, 85–8
　AI fetishism 203
　algorithms for *see* algorithms
　concept 201–2
　ML for *see* machine learning (ML)
　robots *see* robots
　smart technologies *see* Internet of Things (IoT), smart technologies
　societal responses to
　　normative expectations 206–9
　　technological reconstitution 204–6
　supremacy over human intelligence claims about 202–4
　　machine-to-human performance ratio >1 proposal 218–25
　　transparency concerns *see* decisions guided by technology, transparency concerns
autocratic rule 144, 146, 147, 151, 182–3
automated decision-making *see* decisions guided by technology
autonomic machine learning 158, 159
autonomous vehicles 219, 220
autonomy *see* agency
average persons 237–9, 245–6, 247

Balkin, Jack 203, 204–5
Ball, Kirstie 68
Barlow, John Perry 120, 131, 135, 154
Beer, Dave 48
behavioural microtargeting 19, 67–8, 254
　political decision-making influenced by 135, 136–8, 140, 149
　techniques of 69–70
　unpredictability of 30, 31–2, 68
　see also advertising; decisions guided by technology
behaviourism, data 86
Belting, Hans 262–3
Berry, David 131
Bertolotti, Tommaso 27

bias
　human bias 56, 72–3
　machine bias 49–50, 52, 56, 216, 222–3, 255
big data
　bullshit problem 24
　characteristics 46, 48–50, 57
　data behaviourism 86
　distributed big data space 18–19, 30–31
　Hildebrandt on 119
　machine learning, proposed use of less data 225–7
　and science 4, 46–9
　　bias concerns 49–50, 52, 56, 216, 222–3, 255
　　'data speaks for itself' claim 49, 50–51, 53–4, 56
　　natural sciences use 51–2
　　value of using less data 225–7
bioinfomaticians 51, 57
black box technologies 4, 5, 10, 12–13, 196
body politic metaphor 139, 146, 151, 237
bots and botnets 23, 31, 139–40, 149, 179
Brexit referendum (2016) 36, 73, 136–8
Brighouse, Harry 170
Brownsword, Roger 21, 22
bullshit 23–5
Burke, Edmund 27–8, 34–7, 176, 177–81, 190
Burrell, Jenna 55

Cambridge Analytica 80, 136
Canali, Stefano 46
Carlyle, Thomas 137
cascades of information 71–2, 73
Cascone, Kim 131
causality 4, 49
Chalmers, Matthew 105
change principle 35
　change *versus* preservation 37–40
'chaotic pluralism' online 135, 141, 179, 180–81
chilling effect doctrine 195–6
choice *see* agency
choice architecture 18, 256–7

Cicero 232, 233
citizens
  body politic metaphor 139, 146, 151, 237
  dual capacity of 148, 165
  duties of 171, 188, 189
  electoral decisions by *see* elections
  liberty of (Montesquieu) 152
  plurality of *see* plurality/pluralism
  reasonable disagreement among 165, 169–70, 172
  as 'the public' 151
  well-being of *see* well-being
  see also community
Citron, Danielle 73
Clarke, Roger 242, 244
clickbait 70
Clinton, Hillary 8, 73, 136
coercion 163
cognitive computing 47, 54–6
Cohen, Julie E. 5, 69, 217, 218, 222
Coke, Sir Edward 129
common law, digital 23, 29, 33
community
  crowd-based judgements 71–2
  disintermediated community (de Tocqueville) 181–5
  embodiment of 131
  group profiling of communities 240, 245–6
  Hobbes on 236
  see also citizens
completeness quotient 225–7
  see also machine learning (ML), 'throttling' metrics (proposed)
compliance by design 21–2, 33
composite pictures/photography 237–9, 241, 245–7, 249
conception of the good (Rawls) 165
consciousness 19, 128, 233
  digital unconscious 19, 29–32, 61, 70, 74, 254
consent to data collection *see* data collection, consent mechanisms
conservatism 9–10, 22, 34–7, 175–6, 190–91, 261
  change *versus* preservation 37–40
  modern conservatism (Oakeshott's agonistic pluralism) 10, 185–6, 187–9, 190–91

Hildebrandt's views compared 37–40, 185, 186–7, 188, 189
  traditional (Burkean) conservatism 34–7, 176, 177–81, 190
  weak social ties, de Tocqueville's warning against 181–5
constitutional democracies 82, 117, 118, 120, 194
  societal constitutionalism (Teubner) 207–8
consumptive self-expression 67, 254, 257
content optimization 67, 70, 254
contestability requirement of digital technologies 21–2, 32, 80–81, 84–5, 119–20, 127, 184–5
contextual integrity 23, 118, 177
control *see* agency
'controlled' ambiguity 126
cookies 25, 103, 105, 107, 110–11, 199–200
correlations, data processed 4, 24, 46, 49, 50–51
  behavioural microtargeting *see* behavioural microtargeting
  profiling by means of 240, 246, 247
counter-profiling 6, 82–3, 255–6, 260
credit scoring 62, 64
crowd-based judgements 71–2
Cukier, Kenneth 46, 49
cybernetics 124, 259

data
  big data *see* big data
  bullshit 23–5
  information and knowledge distinguished 25–6
data behaviourism 86
data collection
  consent mechanisms 255–6
    apparency, design options for 104–7, 112–15, 256
    controllability and accountability, design options for 107–8
    current mechanisms, transparency concerns 102–4
    negotiation of terms 109–10
    for smart devices 101–2, 110–15
    timing of consent provision 103, 108–9

gamification for 64–7
by tracking online activity 25, 69, 103–4, 107
data controllers 34, 95, 244
data-driven agency
  bullshit problem 24
  conservative critiques of *see* conservatism
  decision-making *see* decisions guided by technology
  definition 1–2
  digital unconscious 19, 29–32, 61, 70, 74, 254
  happiness promise of 13
  knowledge and science, relationship with 45–6
    big data and science *see* big data, and science
    'knowing' associated with doing 53–6
  liberal critiques of 176
  'mindless' nature of 19, 20, 61
  ML *see* machine learning (ML)
  theoretical initiatives 2–3
  trade-off with well-being 156–7, 160–67
  see also agency
data protection under EU law *see* General Data Protection Regulation 2016 (GDPR)
data science *see* big data, and science
data trust proposal 34
de-identification software 205–6
de Tocqueville, Alexis 176, 181–5, 190
debate between the editors (Hildebrandt and O'Hara)
  on affordances of law 26–9, 32
  on conservatism, plurality and natality 34–40
  on data, knowledge and information 23–6
  on digital unconscious phenomenon 29–32
  on legal protection by design (LPbD) 20–23, 27, 29, 33–4
  on mode of existence of modern positive law 32–4
  on privacy in digital modernity/ onli*fe* world 16–20

see also *Smart Technologies and the End(s) of Law* (Hildebrandt, 2015)
decisions guided by technology
  behavioural microtargeting *see* behavioural microtargeting
  choice architecture 18, 256–7
  credit scoring 62, 64
  ML for decision-making *see* machine learning (ML)
  political decision-making *see* democracy, potential threats to
  pre-emptive decision-making *see* pre-emptive computing
  profiling *see* profiling
  recommender systems 19, 62–3, 89–90, 91–2, 95
  social security decisions 2
  transparency concerns 215–16
    counter-profiling 6, 82–3, 255–6, 260
    'epistemic impenetrability' *see* epistemology, 'epistemic impenetrability' of AI
    information asymmetry 186–7
    transparency rights 30, 80–81, 88
  see also data-driven agency
deep learning (DL) 4, 5, 203, 255, 263
Deleuze, Gilles 243, 244
democracy
  constitutional democracies 82, 117, 118, 120, 194
    societal constitutionalism (Teubner) 207–8
  democratic legitimacy 137, 142, 150, 170
  elections *see* elections
  government *see* government
  laws, acceptability requirement 164–7, 169
  minimalist conception of 8, 138–41
    critiqued 141–4, 261
  as modernity ideal 17
  plurality/pluralism *see* plurality/ pluralism
  potential threats to
    algorithmic government 30, 140–41, 153, 156–7, 171–2, 246

behavioural microtargeting 135, 136–8, 140, 149
digital technology generally 8–9, 149–54, 166, 195
extremism 71–2, 73–4
fake news 8, 19, 23, 31, 73, 140, 149, 179–80
populism and autocracy 137–8, 181
utilitarian concerns 18, 22, 118–19
weak social ties 182–3
reasonable disagreement among citizens 165, 169–70, 172
relationist conception 144–9
resilience of 137, 140
'soft' despotism, de Tocqueville's warning against 182–3
see also politics; rule of law
denaturalization 234, 247
Dennett, Daniel 19
deontology 118, 120, 259
design constituency (Pfaffenberger) 10–11, 197–8, 199, 207, 256, 261
design options for 'seamfulness'
affordances 5, 105–6, 197
consent to data collection *see* data collection, consent mechanisms
fostering self-definition 88–95
LbD (legal by design) 21–2, 33
LPbD *see* legal protection by design (LPbD)
ML 'throttling metrics' *see* machine learning (ML), 'throttling' metrics (proposed)
unexpectedness/serendipity by design 91–3, 95, 257–8
desirable inefficiency (Ohm and Frankle) 11, 217, 218
despotism 144, 146, 147, 151, 182–3
Dewey, John 8, 27, 147–9, 151, 152, 153, 248, 261
Diaspora (social media site) 205–6
digital modernity 17–18, 176, 185–6, 190
digital persons 242–4, 245
digital unconscious 19, 29–32, 61, 70, 74, 254
disgust 161, 166

Disraeli, Benjamin 178
distributed big data space 18–19, 30–31
Diver, Laurence 26–7
'dividuals' (digital persons) 243, 244, 245
divisibility of personhood 235, 244, 246
Dix, Alan 93
DL (deep learning) 4, 5, 203, 255, 263
Domingos, Pedro 45, 53–4
double mutual anticipation 19–20
dramatic persons 232–3, 234, 245
Dreyfus, Hubert 124, 129
Dworkin, Ronald 39, 170

e-commerce
advertising *see* advertising
gamification of commercial surveillance 64–7
recommender systems 19, 62–3, 89–90, 91–2, 95
weak social ties of 182
eBay 63, 182
education 146, 147, 209
for a sense of justice 9, 167–8, 170, 171, 258, 259
elections 139–40, 142
electoral law 144, 147, 149, 150, 153–4
electoral systems 149, 150, 153, 154
fake news in campaigns 73, 149
UK Brexit referendum (2016) 36, 73, 136–8
US Presidential election (2016) 8, 73, 136–8
see also democracy
electronic persons 230–32, 235, 244, 247–8, 249, 261–2
Elster, Jon 163
embodiment
embodied tacit knowledge 117–18, 124–5
faces *see* faces
platforms as 'limbic system' 4–5, 7, 9–10, 61, 254
technological embodiment of law 20, 26–7

emotions
    affective computing (emotional AI)
        6, 84, 85–8
    detected by technology 85–8
    disgust 161, 166
    empathy 122, 128
    ethical decision-making, role in
        126–8, 159–60, 166–7
    happiness *see* happiness
    love 127–8
    manipulated by technology
        Facebook's newsfeed
            manipulation experiment
            (2014) 29, 33–4, 69, 92
        platforms as 'limbic system' 4–5,
            7, 9–10, 61, 254
        'Toma' *see* personal digital
            assistants (PDAs), 'Toma'
            (Hildebrandt)
    see also subjectivity
empiricism 46–7
End(s) see *Smart Technologies and
    the End(s) of Law* (Hildebrandt,
    2015)
Enlightenment 17, 122, 123, 125,
    127
epistemology
    algorithms as epistemic objects 55
    conservatism as epistemological
        position 35
    'epistemic impenetrability' of AI
        54–5
    efforts to redress 81, 82, 83, 94,
        255
    epistemological humility, need
        for 222
    human judgement *see* judgement,
        human judgement
equality *see* justice
ethics
    deontology 118, 120, 259
    ethical decision-making
        emotions, role in 126–8, 159–60,
            166–7
        guided by 'Toma' *see* personal
            digital assistants (PDAs),
            'Toma' (Hildebrandt)
    justice *see* justice
    utilitarianism 18, 22, 118–19,
        219–20, 259

virtue ethics 121–5
    Hildebrandt on 125–30
EU law
    data protection *see* General Data
        Protection Regulation 2016
        (GDPR)
    electronic personhood, legislative
        recommendation 230–32, 248,
        262
eudaimonia (contentment) 122–3
evolution 53–4
explanation facilities in machine
    learning systems 82–3
explicit knowledge 259
extremism 71–2, 73–4
Eyeo (ad-blocking software) 200–201

Facebook 63, 69, 90, 184, 202
    accountability of *see* fundamental
        rights, accountability of
        platform operators
    Beacon service 65
    behavioural microtargeting by 70
    Cambridge Analytica data breach
        scandal 80, 136
    'Like' button 66
    newsfeed manipulation experiment
        (2014) 29, 33–4, 69, 92
    persecution of Rohingya people of
        Myanmar on 179
    self-presentation on 261
    user surveillance by 195–6, 209
    see also platform-based massively-
        intermediated environments;
        social media
faces
    facial generation technology 241–2
    facial recognition technology 52–3,
        54, 205–6, 241, 261, 263
    masks 232–3, 234, 261
fake news 8, 19, 23, 31, 73, 140, 149,
    179–80
fallacy of misplaced concreteness
    (Whitehead) 141–4, 261
feelings *see* emotions
feminist philosophy and ethics 118,
    122, 123, 131
flourishing 122–3, 222
FourSquare (social networking
    application) 65, 66

framing 13, 18, 60, 80, 158
Frankfurt, Harry 23-4, 25, 128
Frankle, Jonathan 11, 218
freedom *see* liberty
friendship 18, 50, 71, 122-3, 125, 127-8, 148, 163
Frischmann, Brett 217, 218
fundamental rights
  accountability of platform operators 194-5
  affordances and fundamental rights 206-9
  materiality of technology, effect of 195-6, 197
  discriminatory machine learning 221, 222
  privacy *see* privacy
  protection by design *see* legal protection by design (LPbD)
  transparency rights 30, 80-81, 88

Galton, Francis 238-9, 246, 247, 249
Game of Thrones 231, 261
gamification of commercial surveillance 64-7
Gandy, Oscar 13
GANs (generative adversarial networks) 241-2
General Data Protection Regulation 2016 (GDPR) 101, 102, 108, 136, 190, 260
  consent to online tracking 107
  'profiling' definition 95
  right to be forgotten 137, 184
  'super-complaint' mechanism 82
generative adversarial networks (GANs) 241-2
Gibson, James 5, 10, 26, 27, 197, 255
Gilligan, Carol 123
Gobo (social media filtering system) 205-6
Google 69, 137, 184, 202
  accountability of *see* fundamental rights, accountability of platform operators
  AlphaGo 203-4
  behavioural microtargeting by 70
  facial recognition technology 241
  user surveillance by 195-6, 209
  YouTube 19, 64, 70, 225

see also platform-based massively-intermediated environments
government
  algorithmic government 30, 140-41, 153, 156-7, 171-2, 246
  definition 138, 141-2
  Dewey's relationist account 147-9, 151
  establishment and maintenance of 145-6, 154
  internet surveillance for security purposes 118, 178, 187-9, 195-6, 209
  moderate governments 146-7, 151
  nature and principle of 8, 144
  types 144
Groupon (social shopping site) 65
Gutwirth, Serge 240

habit-formation 61, 92, 95, 254, 259
hacking 205
Halford, Susan 36
'Hall of Faces' *(Game of Thrones)* 231, 261
happiness
  as promise of technology 13
  state-induced, de Tocqueville's negative vision 183-4
  technologically-induced 29-30, 222
  see also well-being
hashtags on Twitter 198, 199
Hastings, Warren 177-8
hate speech 73, 179
HCI *see* human-computer interaction (HCI)
Hegel, G.W.F. 28, 36
Hildebrandt, Mireille 27
  on agonistic machine learning 217, 222, 256, 261
  on agonistic pluralism of Oakeshott 37-40, 185, 186-7, 188, 189
  debate with O'Hara *see* debate between the editors (Hildebrandt and O'Hara)
  End(s) see *Smart Technologies and the End(s) of Law* (Hildebrandt, 2015)
  Profiling the European Citizen (2008, with Gutwirth) 240

Hirschmann, A.O. 22
Hobbes, Thomas
  on democracy 141, 142, 152–3
  Leviathan frontispiece 139, 147, 237, 245–6
  state concept 138–9, 179, 236–7
human-computer interaction (HCI) 5
  affordances *see* affordances, of technology
  design options for *see* design options for 'seamfulness'
  PDAs *see* personal digital assistants (PDAs)
  user interfaces 30–31
human rights *see* fundamental rights
humanity
  agency *see* agency
  bodies *see* embodiment
  consciousness *see* consciousness
  faces *see* faces
  judgement *see* judgement, human judgement
  personhood *see* personhood
  subjectivity *see* subjectivity
Hume, David 12–13
Humphreys, Paul 54
Huxley, Aldous 13, 119, 187

ICE (Information and Computing Ethics) 122, 123, 130
identity formation 81, 90, 118, 125, 128, 259
  design options fostering 88–95
  self-presentation online 62–4, 261
  see also agency; subjectivity
ideology of AI supremacy 202–4
Ihde, Don 10, 26, 40, 117, 197–8
impact constituency (Pfaffenberger) 10–11, 197–8, 199, 207, 256, 261
individuality/individualism 17, 18, 150, 180, 187–8, 190
information 25, 26
  cascades of 71–2, 73
Information and Computing Ethics (ICE) 122, 123, 130
innovation 22, 36, 38–9
intentional stance 19, 263
interactive machine learning 93
interfaces, user 30–31

intermediation, algorithmic *see* platform-based massively-intermediated environments
Internet of Things (IoT)
  predicted expansion of 101
  seamlessness ideal *see* seamless *versus* 'seamful' interactions in digital world
  smart technologies 19
  autonomous vehicles 219, 220
  central heating systems 2
  consent to data collection by 101–2, 110–15
  fitness trackers 65, 66, 113
  PDAs *see* personal digital assistants (PDAs)
  social security systems 2
  traffic signs 4
  and subjectivity *see* subjectivity, smart technologies affecting
interpretation, law as 32, 129, 188, 259
intimacy 17, 122–3, 125, 127–8, 182

Japanese notion of relational self (*wakimae*) 118, 128
Jensen, Klaus Bruhn 120
judgement
  guided by technology *see* decisions guided by technology
  human judgement
    Arendt on 88, 92, 94, 124
    bias affecting 56, 72–3
    crowd-based 71–2
    emotions, role in *see* emotions
    'judgement of law' (Coke) 129
    phronēsis (practical wisdom/reflective judgement) 7, 122, 123–5, 126, 128, 129, 258, 259
    reasonable disagreement 165, 169–70, 172
  pre-emptive computing *see* pre-emptive computing
junk data (bullshit) 23–5
juristic persons 233–5, 245, 246–7, 261–2
justice
  and constitutional democracy 118
  egalitarian justice, de Tocqueville's negative vision 183–4

Rawls on 170, 171
'sense' of 165, 167–8
   technologically induced 9, 157, 168–72, 258–60

Kang, Byungkyu 89
Kant, Immanuel 29
Katz, Yarden 201, 202–3, 204
Kelleher, John D. 50
Kelsen, Hans 233
knowledge 25–6
   data-driven agency, relationship with 45–6
      big data and science *see* big data, and science
      'knowing' associated with doing 53–6
   explicit knowledge 259
   knowledge principle 35, 36
   tacit knowledge 117–18, 124–5

Latour, Bruno 8, 143
law
   acceptability requirement 164–7, 169
   affordances of 26–8, 32, 120, 129, 197, 255–6
   code-driven regulation *versus* law 20, 33, 40, 151–2, 153
   justice *see* justice
   Montesquieu's conception of 144–7, 152
   rule of law *see* rule of law
   and technology 10, 32–3, 196
   text-driven nature 20–21, 27, 28, 32–3, 119–21, 129
Lebenswelt 36, 39, 40
legal by design (LbD) 21–2, 33
legal fictions 234–5, 248
legal persons 233–5, 245, 246–7, 261–2
legal protection by design (LPbD) 121, 260–61
   affordances by design 27, 29
   characteristics 21, 23
   definition 20
   feasibility questioned 22–3, 33–4, 39–40
   legal by design (LbD) distinguished 21–2
   techno-regulation distinguished 21

legal sociology 196, 206
legal technology 20, 21
legibility 30, 36
legitimacy, democratic 137, 142, 150, 170
Lessig, Lawrence 184
Levandowski, Anthony 203
Leviathan frontispiece 139, 147, 237, 245–6
   see also Hobbes, Thomas
liberty 37
   liberté (Wiener) 123, 127
   Montesquieu on 152
   Oakeshott on 186
limbic system, platform environments as 4–5, 7, 9–10, 61, 254
Lindgren, Simon 131
literacy-print (Medium Theory) 120
Locke, John 17
love 127–8
Lowrie, Ian 55
LPbD *see* legal protection by design (LPbD)
Luhmann, Niklas 10, 206

machine agency 253, 257–8, 260–61, 263
   see also data-driven agency
machine learning (ML) 2, 254–5
   autonomic ML 158, 159
   cognitive computing 47, 54–6
   concerns about 215–16
      bias 49–50, 52, 56, 216, 222–3, 255
      proposed solutions 216–17
      transparency *see* decisions guided by technology, transparency concerns
   deep learning (DL) 4, 5, 203, 255, 263
   explanation facilities in ML systems 82–3
   interactive ML 93
   'learning'/'knowing' associated with doing 53–6
   profiling *see* profiling
   'throttling' metrics (proposed) 11, 214–15, 217–18, 227–8, 256
      completeness quotient (use of less data) 225–7

machine-to-human performance
    ratio >1 218–25
see also artificial intelligence (AI)
Magnani, Lorenzo 27
manipulation of emotions *see*
    emotions, manipulated by
    technology
Margetts, Helen 180–81
marketing *see* advertising
Marx, Karl 203
masks 232–3, 234, 261
Massumi, Brian 131
master algorithm notion 45, 47, 50
Mayer-Schönberger, Viktor 46, 49
McLuhan, Marshall 119, 120
McQuillan, Dan 47, 55
Mead, G.H. 81
mean (average) persons 237–9, 245–6, 247
media regulation 179
Medium Theory 119–21, 131
Messina, Chris 198
Microsoft 195–6, 202
microtargeting *see* behavioural
    microtargeting
Mill, John Stuart 179, 188
mindless distributed agency 19, 20, 61
Minsky, Marvin 202
ML *see* machine learning (ML)
mode of existence of modern positive
    law 32–4
modelling data (scientific technique)
    54–5, 80, 82–3, 102, 112–14,
    215–16, 227
modernity 17–18, 178, 185, 190
Montaigne, Michel de 35
Montesquieu 8, 144–7, 149, 152, 153,
    154, 261
morality *see* ethics
multitude *see* plurality/pluralism,
    multitude
mutual double anticipation 19–20

natality 37–8
natural selection 54
negotiation online
    consent mechanisms for *see* data
        collection, consent mechanisms
        lacking 109–10
Net neutrality 207, 208

news services
    biases amplified by 72–3
    'clickbait' headlines 70
    fake news on 8, 19, 23, 31, 73, 140,
        149, 179–80
    Slashdot 63
Nissenbaum, Helen 23, 118, 177, 200,
    201, 208
non-humans, legal personality of 235
Norman, Donald 5, 197
normative expectations about AI
    206–9
Nozick, Robert 169–70
nudge theory 18, 30, 31, 67, 189, 256–7

Oakeshott, Michael 10, 185–191
Obama, Barack 136
O'Brien, Flann 160
obscurity 17, 20–21
O'Hara, Kieron 177, 189
    debate with Hildebrandt *see*
        debate between the editors
        (Hildebrandt and O'Hara)
Ohm, Paul 11, 218
O'Neil, Cathy 217
Ong, Walter 119, 120
onli*fe* world 3, 40, 254
    online/offline binary rejected 131
    privacy in 18–20
    'seamful' interactions in 5–6, 12,
        254, 256
    design options for 'seamfulness'
        see design options for
        'seamfulness'
online campaigns 71, 135, 136
    see also elections
online content
    optimization 5, 61, 64–5, 67–8, 70,
        83–5, 88, 94–5, 157
    personalization 62, 90, 94, 194–5,
        205, 246
ontology 12, 47–8
    relationist ontology of the internet
        143
opacity of digital decision-making *see*
    decisions guided by technology,
    transparency concerns
optimization of online content 5, 61,
    64–5, 67–8, 70, 83–5, 88, 94–5, 157
Orwell, George 119

Paine, Thomas 178, 180
Pasquale, Frank 13
PDAs *see* personal digital assistants (PDAs)
Pearl, Judea 51
personal data collection *see* data collection
personal digital assistants (PDAs)
  Alexa and Echo (Amazon) 86, 87
  'Toma' (Hildebrandt) 100, 156
    manipulation of human user (Diana) by 158–61
    objections to 161–7
    defence of 9, 167–72, 258–60
personalization of online content 62, 90, 94, 194–5, 205, 246
personhood 11–12, 231–2
  average persons 237–9, 245–6, 247
  digital persons 242–4, 245
  divisibility of 235, 244, 246
  dramatic persons 232–3, 234, 245
  electronic persons 230–32, 235, 244, 247–8, 249, 261–2
  faces *see* faces
  juristic persons 233–5, 245, 246–7, 261–2
  person types compared 244–8
  profile persons (machine-generated 'group' portraits) 240–42, 245, 246
  public persons 236–7, 245
  see also accountability; agency; subjectivity
persuasion 163
Pfaffenberger, Bryan 10–11, 196, 197–201, 261
Pfeifer, Rolf 203–4
Phillips, Whitney 73
phronēsis (practical wisdom/reflective judgement) 7, 122, 123–5, 126, 128, 129, 258, 259
Picard, Rosalind 85
platform-based massively-intermediated environments 34, 60–61
  accountability of *see* fundamental rights, accountability of platform operators
  behavioural microtargeting in *see* behavioural microtargeting

collective unreason amplified by 70–74
gamification of commercial surveillance in 64–7
as 'limbic system' 4–5, 7, 9–10, 61, 254
online content
  optimization 5, 61, 64–5, 67–8, 70, 83–5, 88, 94–5, 157
  personalization 62, 90, 94, 194–5, 205, 246
reputational capital on 62–4, 261
social media *see* social media
see also Facebook; Google
Plato 124
Plessner, Helmuth 81
plurality/pluralism
  body politic metaphor 139, 146, 151, 237
  'chaotic pluralism' online 135, 141, 179, 180–81
  multitude
    Burke on 180
    de Tocqueville on 10, 183–4
    Hobbes on 236, 237, 245–6
  Oakeshott's agonistic pluralism 10, 185–6, 187–9, 190–91
    Hildebrandt's views compared 37–40, 185, 186–7, 188, 189
  see also conservatism; democracy
Podesta, John 73
politics
  algorithms to replace 30, 140–41, 153
  political conservatism 35–6, 175
  political liberty *see* liberty; social contract theory
  social media discourse *see* social media, political discourse on
  see also democracy; government
Popper, Karl 138, 141, 152
population *see* community
portraiture
  composite pictures/photography 237–9, 241, 245–7, 249
  digital portraits 12, 231–2, 242–4
  group portraits 12, 231–2, 240–42
  see also personhood
post-digital era 7, 130–32

Postman, Neil 119
power
  agency *see* agency
  delegated to platforms 151–3, 194
  democracy, implications for *see* democracy, potential threats to
  government power *see* government
practical wisdom *(phronēsis)* 7, 122, 123–5, 126, 128, 129, 258, 259
pragmatic transparency 5–6, 105, 106, 114
pre-emptive computing 6, 21, 121, 186, 206, 254
  PDAs *see* personal digital assistants (PDAs)
  profiling for *see* profiling
  recommender systems 19, 62–3, 89–90, 91–2, 95
  subjunctive digital world 18, 19, 20, 38
precautionary approach 16, 39, 256, 260, 262
preferences
  inferred by smart technologies 19, 69, 85, 91–2
  shaped by smart technologies *see* decisions guided by technology
  see also profiling; subjectivity
preservation *versus* change 37–40
privacy
  consent to data collection *see* data collection, consent mechanisms
  as 'contextual integrity' (Nissenbaum) 23, 118, 177
  in digital modernity/onli*fe* world 16–20
  GDPR *see* General Data Protection Regulation 2016 (GDPR)
  intimacy 17, 122–3, 125, 127–8, 182
  as modernity ideal 17
  in pre-modern world 16–17, 20
  privacy policies on websites 24, 102–4
  research use of personal data, opt-out decisions 225–6, 227
  right to be forgotten (EU law) 137, 184

profiling 80–81
  counter-profiling 6, 82–3, 255–6, 260
  data collection for *see* data collection
  design options fostering self-definition 88–95
  digital 'readings' of persons
  contestability requirement 21–2, 32, 80–81, 84–5, 119–20, 127, 184–5
  resistibility requirement 7, 21–2, 84–5, 127, 206
  information asymmetry of 186–7
  policy-making on basis of 246
  profile persons (machine-generated 'group' portraits) 240–42, 245, 246
  recommender systems 19, 62–3, 89–90, 91–2, 95
  for security purposes 118, 178, 187–9, 195–6, 209
  as social cruelty 6, 83–5, 258–9
  see also subjectivity
public persons 236–7, 245
public/public interest concept (Dewey) 147–9, 151, 153

Quantified Self movement 66, 90
Quetelet, Adolphe 237–8, 247

Rawls, John 9, 165, 168, 169, 170, 171, 259
Raz, Joseph 163, 170–71
reading brain (Wolf) 38–9, 130
'readings' of persons, digital *see* subjectivity, digital 'readings' of persons
reasonable disagreement among citizens 165, 169–70, 172
recombinant identities 244, 246
recommender systems 19, 62–3, 89–90, 91–2, 95
reductionism 47
reflexivity *see* subjectivity
regulation *see* law
relationism
  online 143
  relational autonomy (Hildebrandt) 118, 120

relationist conception of democracy 144–9
relativisation 72–3
representation of persons *see* personhood
reputational capital online 62–4, 261
resistibility requirement of digital technologies 7, 21–2, 84–5, 127, 206
respect for other persons 6, 39, 94, 119–20, 128, 160, 165–6
right to be forgotten (EU law) 137, 184
robots
   humans replaceable by, debate on 218–25
   personhood of 230–32, 235, 244, 247–8, 249, 261–2
   sexbots 127–8
   see also artificial intelligence (AI)
Roosendaal, Arnold 243, 244, 249
Rosanvallon, Pierre 137–8, 139, 142, 150
Rousseau, Jean-Jacques 164–5
Rouvroy, Antoinette 86
Ruddick, Sara 127
rule of law 32, 39, 118–19, 132, 260
   Burke's view of 177
   digital technologies
      contestability requirement 21–2, 32, 80–81, 84–5, 119–20, 127, 184–5
      resistibility requirement 7, 21–2, 84–5, 127, 206
      as rule of law threat 121
   justice *see* justice
   print technology, dependency on 119–21, 137
   social contract theory *see* social contract theory
   see also democracy
Runciman, David 137

Sakamura, Ken 253–4
Sangiovanni, Andrea 83
Schmitt, Carl 40, 261
Schumpeter, Joseph 138, 141, 152
science and big data *see* big data, and science
science fiction 230, 232, 247
Scott, James C. 17, 29

seamless *versus* seamful interactions in digital world 5–6, 12, 254, 256
   design options for 'seamfulness' *see* design options for 'seamfulness'
search engine optimization 64
secondary orality (Medium Theory) 120
seduction 163
self-definition *see* identity formation; subjectivity
self-determination *see* agency
Selinger, Evan 217, 218
semantic discontinuity 217, 218, 224
semantic transparency 5, 105, 106, 107, 114, 256
serendipity by design 91–2, 95, 257–8
sexbots 127–8
Sittlichkeit (Hegel) 28, 36
Slashdot (social news website) 63
Sloterdijk, Peter 141
smart digital agents 244
smart technologies *see* Internet of Things (IoT), smart technologies
Smart Technologies and the End(s) of Law (Hildebrandt, 2015) 1, 2
   on big data 119
   on democracy threats 183
   on digital unconscious phenomenon 61, 254
   on legal protection by design (LPbD) 20, 21–2
   on plurality 37, 185
   post-digital era, *End(s)* contextualized in 7, 130–32
   on profiling and counter-profiling 6, 81–3, 85, 186–7, 189, 260
   reviews of 3
   on rule of law *see* rule of law
   theoretical framework of
      ethical concerns 118–19, 121–2, 125–30
      Medium Theory 119–21, 131
      phenomenological foundations 117–18, 125–6
   on 'Toma' *see* personal digital assistants (PDAs), 'Toma' (Hildebrandt)
   vocabulary of 18–19
   see also debate between the editors (Hildebrandt and O'Hara)

Smith, Bryant 233
Snowden, Edward 178, 195
social contract theory 17
   Burke's critique 27–8
   Hobbes's account *see* Hobbes, Thomas
   Rawls's account 9, 165
   Rousseau's account 164–5
social justice *see* justice
social machines 34
social media
   advertising on 68
   Diaspora 205–6
   Facebook *see* Facebook
   Gobo (social media filtering system) 205–6
   political discourse on 8, 31, 150–51
      collective narratives and action promoted 70–74
      fake news 8, 19, 23, 31, 73, 140, 149, 179–80
      transparent social media strategies, call for 153–4
   self-presentation on 63–4, 261
   Slashdot 63
   Twitter *see* Twitter
   weak social ties on 182
   YouTube 19, 64, 70
social networking platforms *see* platform-based massively-intermediated environments
societal constitutionalism (Teubner) 207–8
societas (state as civil association) 10, 187, 188
Solove, Daniel J. 242
sovereignty
   Hobbes on 139, 142, 147, 236–7, 238
   Montesquieu on 144, 149
Sparrow, Robert 164
state concept
   body politic metaphor 139, 146, 151, 237
   democratic state (Dewey) 147–9, 151
   of Hobbes 138–9, 179, 236–7
   societas (state as civil association) 10, 187, 188
   therapeutic state (Oakeshott) 189, 190

universitas (state as monolithic entity) 10, 188, 189, 191
   see also social contract theory
statistics 49, 226–7
   average persons 237–9, 245–6, 247
   big data *see* big data
Stiegler, Bernard 131
Stone, Allucquere Roseanne 131
subjectivity 19–20
   digital 'readings' of persons
      contestability requirement 21–2, 32, 80–81, 84–5, 119–20, 127, 184–5
      resistibility requirement 7, 21–2, 84–5, 127, 206
   digital unconscious 19, 29–32, 61, 70, 74, 254
   emotions *see* emotions
   personhood *see* personhood
   phronēsis (practical wisdom/reflective judgement) *see phronēsis*
   profiling as cruelty against 6, 83–5, 258–9
   Quantified Self movement 66, 90
   self-presentation online 62–4, 261
   smart technologies affecting
      design options fostering self-definition 88–95
      emotions detected 85–8
      emotions manipulated *see* personal digital assistants (PDAs), 'Toma' (Hildebrandt)
      personal preferences inferred 19, 69, 85, 91–2
   wakimae (Japanese notion of relational self) 118, 128
   see also agency
subjunctive digital world 18, 19, 20, 38
Sunstein, Cass 195
surprise by design 91–3, 95, 257–8
surveillance
   gamification of 64–7
   for security purposes 118, 178, 187–9, 195–6, 209
   'surveillance capitalism' (Zuboff) 136–7, 151, 183, 184
   tracking online activity 25, 69, 103–4, 107, 200

Swift, Jonathan 179
'systematic' ambiguity 126
systems theory (Luhmann) 10, 206

tacit knowledge 117–18, 124–5
techno-regulation 21
'technological drama' of Pfaffenberger 10–11, 196, 197–201, 256, 261
  see also affordances, of technology
technological imaginaries 36–7
Teubner, Gunther 10, 207–8, 248
text-driven law 20–21, 27, 28, 32–3, 119–21, 129
therapeutic state (Oakeshott) 189, 190
Thomas, Yan 233
thriving 122–3, 222
Tierney, Brendon 50
Tintarev, Nava 90
Tocqueville, Alexis de 176, 181–5, 190
'Toma' *see* personal digital assistants (PDAs), 'Toma' (Hildebrandt)
tracking online activity 25, 69, 103–4, 107
transparency
  apparency (precursor of transparency) 5–6, 104–5, 112–15, 256
  consent to data collection *see* data collection, consent mechanisms
  counter-profiling 6, 82–3, 255–6, 260
  digital decision-making *see* decisions guided by technology, transparency concerns
  information asymmetry of data profiling 186–7
  political discourse on social media, call for transparent strategies 153–4
  pragmatic transparency 5–6, 105, 106, 114
  semantic transparency 5, 105, 106, 107, 114, 256
  transparency rights 30, 80–81, 88
  see also accountability; democracy
trolls 135, 136, 139–40
Trump, Donald 24, 175, 181
  Presidential election campaign (2016) 8, 73, 136–8
Turkle, Sherry 128
Turow, Joseph 69

Twitter 8, 66, 89–90, 182
  behavioural microtargeting by 70
  hashtag use 198, 199
  retweeted falsehoods 179
  Twitter bots (fake news generators) 23, 31, 179
  user surveillance by 195–6
  see also social media

ubiquitous computing 253–4
UK Brexit referendum (2016) 36, 73, 136–8
Umwelt (phenomenology) 117–18, 254, 259
unexpectedness by design 91–3, 95, 257–8
universitas (state as monolithic entity) 10, 188, 189, 191
US Presidential election (2016) 8, 73, 136–8
User Experience research *see* human-computer interaction (HCI)
user interfaces 30–31
utilitarianism 18, 22, 118–19, 219–20, 259

Vallor, Shannon 123, 127
Vassileva, Julita 89
virtual assistants *see* personal digital assistants (PDAs)
virtue ethics 7, 121–5, 222
  Hildebrandt on 125–30
visualization techniques for facial recognition 241, 246
vulnerability of citizens online 61, 63–4, 83–5, 216

wakimae (Japanese notion of relational self) 118, 128
Waldron, Jeremy 37
Webster, Andrew 89
Weiser, Mark 253–4
Weizenbaum, Joseph 124
well-being
  eudaimonia (contentment) 122–3
  happiness *see* happiness
  technologically induced, trade-off with agency 156–7, 160–67
  therapeutic state (Oakeshott) 189, 190

Welt (phenomenology) 117–18, 125–6, 259
Whitehead, Alfred North 141, 261
Whitson, Jennifer 67
Wiener, Norbert 123, 124, 127
Wolf, Maryanne 38, 130
Wood, David Murakami 68
Wu, Xiaolin 52–3, 54

YouTube 19, 64, 70, 225

Zhang, Xi 52–3, 54
Zittrain, Jonathan 184
'zombie lovers' (sexbots) 127–8
Zuboff, Shoshana 136–7, 140, 151–2, 183, 205